THE POLITICS OF JUDICIAL INTERPRETATION

RECONSTRUCTING AMERICA SERIES
Paul A. Cimbala, *series editor*

The Politics
of Judicial
Interpretation:

*The Federal Courts,
Department of Justice, and
Civil Rights, 1866–1876*

Robert J. Kaczorowski

FORDHAM UNIVERSITY PRESS
NEW YORK 2005

Reconstructing America Series, No. 9
ISSN 1523-4606

Library of Congress Cataloging-in-Publication Data

Kackorowski, Robert J.
    The politics of judicial interpretation: the federal courts, Department of Justice and civil rights, 1866–1876 / Robert J Kaczorowski.
    p. cm.—(Reconstructing America (Series): no. 9)
    Originally published: Dobbs Ferry, N. Y.: Oceana Publications, 1985.
    Includes bibliographical references and index.
    ISBN 0–8232–2382–5 (pbk.)

    1. African Americans—Civil rights—History—19th century. 2. Judicial review—United States—History—19th century. 3. Political questions and judicial power—United States—History—19th century. 4. Reconstruction (U.S history, 1865–1877) I. Title. II. Series.

    KF4757. K33 2005
    342. 7308' 73—dc22

                    2005000446

Printed in the United States of America
08 07 06 05   5 4 3 2 1

First Oceana Publications edition, 1985

First Fordham University Press edition, 2005

To Jane, Tom, and Paul

Contents

Acknowledgments

Over the years of researching and writing this book I have become indebted to many people. I would like to acknowledge their contributions and express my deep gratitude to them. The cheerful and skillful assistance of the staffs of the libraries and archives in which I worked lightened the solitary burden of historical research. I wish to thank the staffs of the National Archives, Library of Congress, Chicago Historical Society, The Filson Club, Maryland Historical Society, Maine Historical Society, New Jersey Historical Society, Historical Society of Pennsylvania, Rutherford B. Hayes Library, Burton Collection of the Detroit Public Library, New York Public Library, Columbia University Library, William R. Perkins Library of Duke University, Houghton Library of Harvard University, University of Iowa Library, University of Minnesota Libraries, Southern Collection of the University of North Carolina, and Alderman Library of the University of Virginia. Grants from the National Endowment for the Humanities, the Wagner College Faculty Research Fund, the Putnam D. McMillan Fund, and the University of Minnesota enabled me to work in these libraries and archives, and I am grateful for their support.

Several people directly and indirectly helped me bring this work to completion. Debbie Moritz edited the manuscript for publication. Dorothy Blumenthal skillfully proofed it with typical thoroughness. To her and her family I am especially grateful. Three individuals deserve special recognition for the professional expertise, emotional support, and personal friendship they have given to me. Paul L. Murphy's standards of excellence and humanitarianism continue to influence my work as a scholar and teacher though many years have passed since I was one of his graduate students. My Wagner College colleague and close friend George D. Rappaport was an extremely valuable critic and constant source of encouragement and support. William E. Nelson has earned lasting gratitude and friendship for the countless contributions he has made to my professional growth. His close reading of this manuscript and insightful comments substantially improved it. I also have benefited from the helpful comments of

Herman Belz, LaWanda Cox, George M. Dennison, Kermit Hall, Stanley N. Katz, and A. Keir Nash.

I am most grateful to Jane, Tom, and Paul for their love and encouragement, which nourished and consoled me through many lonely hours of this work.

Abbreviations

Department of Justice Records:

S.C.F.   "Source Chronological File" File of letters received by the Attorney General. 1790–1870 identified as Attorney General's Papers; 1870–1884 known specifically as Source Chronological File.

M699   Letters Sent by Department of Justice: General and Miscellaneous, 1818–1904 (91 volumes on 81 rolls of microfilm).

M701   Letters Sent by the Department of Justice: Instructions to U.S. Attorneys and Marshals, 1867–1904 (231 volumes on 212 rolls of microfilm).

M702   Letters Sent by the Department of Justice to Executive Officers and to Members of Congress, 1871–1904 (94 volumes on 91 rolls of microfilm).

M703   Letters Sent by the Department of Justice to Judges and Clerks, 1874–1904 (34 volumes on 34 rolls of microfilm).

Records of the Bureau of Refugees, Freedmen, and Abandoned Lands:

BRFAL   Bureau of Refugees, Freedmen, and Abandoned Lands.

M742   Selected Series of Records Issued by the Commissioner of the Bureau of Refugees, Freedmen, and Abandoned Lands, 1865–1872 (7 volumes on 7 rolls of microfilm).

M752   Register and Letters Received by the Commissioner of the Bureau of Refugees, Freedmen, and Abandoned Lands, 1865–1872 (33 volumes on 74 rolls of microfilm).

M798   Records of the Assistant Commissioner for the State of Georgia, Bureau of Refugees, Freedmen, and Abandoned Lands, 1865–1869 (34 volumes on 36 rolls of microfilm).

*Introduction to the
Fordham University Press
Edition*

Thinking about why any one should be interested in reading this reissue of a book published twenty years ago brings to mind George Santayana's admonition: "Those who cannot remember the past are condemned to repeat it." This book is being republished at a time that bears a striking resemblance to the nation's political and constitutional history at the turn of the twentieth century. The events of the last third of the twentieth century in many ways repeated the history of the last third of the nineteenth century. The nation's commitment to constitutional freedoms and equality generated by the Civil War climaxed during Reconstruction, but it gradually diminished from the 1870s into the twentieth century. This commitment surged again a century after the Civil War, in the middle of the twentieth century, peaking during the 1960s to the early 1970s. But this resurgence ended in a gradual decline that began in the 1970s and continues to the present. Contemporary values and constitutional principles of individual liberty and equality were created from the bloody experience of the Civil War, and the legal doctrines and legal processes devised to implement these principles originated in the gory aftermath of the Civil War. This introduction to the new edition will briefly recount this history as context for the contents of this book.[1]

The primary result of the Civil War era was the abolition of slavery and the admission of former slaves to full and equal citizenship. At the height of Reconstruction, Congress proposed and secured the ratification of three constitutional amendments and several statutes to implement them. The framers of this legislative program of rights guarantees believed that the first of these amendments, the Thirteenth Amendment, secured individual liberty for all Americans. The framers of the Fourteenth Amendment defined this individual liberty more precisely as the status and rights of United States citizenship. They believed citizenship rights included the generic rights to life, liberty, and property, and rights incident thereto, such as rights guaranteed in the Bill of Rights, and that these constitutional guarantees delegated to Congress plenary power to secure and enforce them. The Fourteenth Amendment also guaranteed to each inhabitant of the United States due process of law and the equal protection of the law to ensure their personal safety and personal freedom. The third amendment, the Fifteenth Amendment, secured to black American citizens the equal right to vote free from racial discrimination. Congressional Republicans enacted civil rights acts in 1866, 1870, 1871, and 1875 to make the guarantees of these amendments practical realities.[2]

This book shows that, despite the opposition of President Andrew Johnson, the Freedmen's Bureau and the United States military in the former slave states made significant efforts to enforce the Civil Rights Act of 1866. Remarkably, the United States attorney and federal district court in Kentucky exercised jurisdiction the Act conferred upon them to dispense criminal justice in cases arising under state law because Kentucky rules of evidence prohibited blacks from testifying in cases in which whites were parties. Consequently, black victims of crimes committed by whites could not bring these criminals to justice in state court. The federal court therefore supplanted state courts and enforced state criminal law in these cases.[3]

With the election of Ulysses S. Grant to the presidency in 1868, the executive branch of the federal government put its full weight behind the enforcement of the Reconstruction Amendments and implementing statutes. Grant appointed Amos T. Akerman as attorney general to head the newly created Department of Justice, and he appointed Benjamin H. Bristow as the department's first solicitor general. Bristow was the federal attorney who brought criminal defendants to justice in Kentucky.

Threats to constitutional freedom and racial equality became extreme during President Grant's first administration. The Ku Klux Klan and similar organizations embarked on a reign of terror to keep southern blacks under white control and to eliminate the Republican Party from southern politics. As I note in this book, the Klan was a paramilitary wing of the Conservative Democratic Party of the South, and it was actually fighting a guerilla war as a continuation of the Civil War. The threat to the nation presented by KKK. terrorists during Reconstruction was as dangerous as the threat posed by al Qaeda terrorists today. But, unlike today, Congress and the president during Reconstruction chose to combat terrorism through federal criminal process, observing rules of due process and fairness without sacrificing civil liberties.[4]

Congress utilized its delegated powers under the Reconstruction Amendments to enforce the rights they secured when it enacted the Enforcement Act of 1870 and the Ku Klux Klan Act of 1871. These statutes greatly expanded the federal system of civil and criminal justice. This book recounts that the Grant administration's enforcement of constitutional rights reached its high point during Akerman's tenure as attorney general. Federal legal officers reported that, under his enforcement policies, they were effectively destroying the Ku Klux Klan through the criminal prosecutions brought under the recently enacted federal enforcement statutes.[5]

One of this book's major conclusions is that all three branches of the federal government cooperated with one another in enforcing the constitutional rights of all Americans through the early 1870s. This intergovernmental harmony and cooperation enabled Justice Department lawyers to curtail the violence and terrorism that motivated the federal government to act, and to destroy the Ku Klux Klan, which was responsible for the mayhem that pervaded many of the former Confederate states. This book shows that, at this very moment of success, President Grant decided to cut back on his administration's efforts to enforce constitutional rights.

Despite this early success, the federal effort to prevent racial violence and discrimination ultimately failed. This failure is attributable, in part, to Congress's and the president's unwillingness to put the nation on a war footing to combat the racial and political insurrection with which the Klan confronted the nation. Admittedly, the decision to fight guerrilla warriors through criminal process may have been misconceived. Legal process is probably the wrong way to combat rebellion and insurrection under any circumstances. This means that Congress and the president's methods to secure constitutional rights from Ku Klux Klan terrorism may have been doomed to failure, especially since they were unwilling to commit the extraordinary human and financial resources the effort required. Nevertheless, the Reconstruction Amendments conferred on Congress plenary power to enforce and protect the rights they secured, and the statutes Congress enacted to enforce the Reconstruction Amendments were sufficient to remedy violations of the constitutional rights they protected. This book concludes that any failure to redress constitutional rights violations during Reconstruction cannot be attributed to inadequate legal authority. Although some scholars disagree, this critical conclusion has never been successfully challenged.[6]

George H. Williams replaced Akerman as attorney general in early 1872 and continued Akerman's enforcement policies through the presidential election of 1872. As this book shows, southern conservatives met with Williams in September 1872 to ask that President Grant curtail his administration's vigorous enforcement policy. Williams informed them that the president would consider cutting back if the terrorist organizations disbanded and southern violence ceased. Southern conservatives responded by helping to make the election of 1872 the most peaceful election since before the Civil War. The Grant administration reciprocated by curtailing federal prosecutions and eventually abandoning them during the spring and summer of 1873. These changes in enforcement policy were motivated by a variety of political considerations, also discussed in this book.

Coincidentally, as the president was cutting back on constitutional rights enforcement, the United States Supreme Court issued its first interpretations of the Reconstruction Amendments and the statutes Congress had enacted to enforce them. The Court interpreted Congress's power to enforce the rights these amendments secured more narrowly than had lower federal court judges. The president's decision to withdraw from constitutional rights enforcement, combined with the Supreme Court's decisions regarding the scope of the federal government's power to enforce the rights secured by the Reconstruction Amendments, began a decline in federal rights enforcement that continued into the next century.

The Supreme Court issued the first of these decisions in April 1873. In the *Slaughter-House Cases*, New Orleans butchers asked the Court to interpret broadly the Fourteenth Amendment's guarantee of the privileges and immunities of United States citizenship and to strike down a Louisiana statute they claimed infringed their right to engage in their trade. In a 5–4 decision, the Court rejected the butchers' claim and interpreted the Fourteenth Amendment narrowly, declaring that the right to pursue a lawful calling, along with other fundamental rights, was a right secured to individuals by virtue of their state citizenship and, consequently, was within the exclusive jurisdiction of the states.[7]

This book explains that the impact of the *Slaughter-House* decision on Congress's power to enforce civil rights did not become apparent until the Grant administration attempted to bring to justice the perpetrators of the bloodiest racial massacre in Louisiana history. Known as the Grant Parish massacre, some 60 blacks were killed and their bodies mutilated in a struggle for control of local political offices, which Democratic Conservatives viewed as a test of white supremacy. Attorneys for the white defendants successfully challenged the constitutionality of these prosecutions and the federal court's jurisdiction to try them. Extending the reasoning of the *Slaughter-House* decision to crimes of racial violence, the Court in *United States v. Cruikshank* held that Congress's power to enforce the Fourteenth Amendment was limited to violations of individuals' constitutional rights attributable to the actions of the states. Congress's enforcement powers did not extend directly to the actions of private individuals.[8]

The Court continued to interpret the Fourteenth Amendment in ways that were hostile to civil rights enforcement. In the *Civil Rights Cases* decided in 1883, it declared unconstitutional provisions of the Civil Rights Act of 1875. Congress enacted the 1875 Act to enforce the Fourteenth Amendment's guarantee of equal protection of the law by outlawing racial discrimination in places of public accommodations, such as hotels, restaurants, theaters, railroads, etc. The Court extended its ruling in *Cruikshank*, explaining that the federal statute acted directly on private proprietors of these business, which exceeded Congress's Fourteenth Amendment enforcement powers.[9]

Although the overall effect of the Court's interpretations of the Fourteenth Amendment was to sharply constrict constitutional guarantees of civil rights, the Court's interpretations of the Constitution's guarantees of voting rights, especially the Fifteenth Amendment, preserved sufficient constitutional authority to protect the voting rights of United States citizens to the end of the nineteenth century. Presidents Hayes, Garfield, Arthur, and Harrison attempted in different ways to build a political base in the South, but they all realized that free and honest elections and federal protection of voting rights in the South were essential to this goal. All of these presidents supported the federal government's enforcement of federal election statutes. Federal circuit and district court judges uniformly upheld the constitutionality of these statutes after Reconstruction ended in 1877, and the legal and administrative structure for voting rights enforcement remained largely intact through the end of the nineteenth century. However, the federal government's commitment to enforcing citizens' voting rights was problematic through the last third of the nineteenth century.[10]

Like the Fourteenth Amendment, the Fifteenth Amendment prohibits the states, as well as the federal government, from infringing upon the right of United States citizens to vote on the basis of race, color, or previous condition of servitude. The Supreme Court held that it clearly authorized Congress to enforce these prohibitions. However, the Court also declared that the Fifteenth Amendment conferred the right to vote free from denials or infringements motivated by racial animus. Consequently, this amendment empowered Congress to protect the voting rights of all qualified voters in state and local elections against private individuals who infringed upon their right to vote because of racial animus. The Court also held that Congress enjoyed the power to protect the right to vote in federal elections against any violations. It was not until the turn of the twentieth century that the Supreme Court, in a reversal of its prior decisions, held that Congress's enforcement powers under the Fifteenth Amendment were limited to state action, like its powers under the Fourteenth Amendment. The Court also rejected its earlier rulings that Congress could enforce voting rights against the actions of state officials who violated Fifteenth Amendment rights whether they acted in conformity with state law or in violation of state law.[11]

It was during the closing decades of the nineteenth century that white supremacy and black subordination hardened into a legal system known as Jim Crow. Segregation was not inevitable; it, too, was a matter of choice, according to C. Vann Woodward, the foremost authority on the subject. The Supreme Court had held that the Fourteenth Amendment prohibited states from denying or infringing upon the right of every person to the equal protection of the law because of racial discrimination. But, just before the turn of the twentieth century, the Court held that states may require the proprietors of hotels, theaters, and rail-roads—as well as local school districts—to discriminate on the basis of race, so long as they provided separate but equal accommodations for blacks and whites. The Court thus put the authority of the Constitution at the service of white supremacists and declared that the United States Constitution permitted the states to require racial segregation by law. The Court gave legal force to racial bigotry.[12]

By the beginning of the twentieth century, the federal government had all but abandoned the Reconstruction policies of enforcing civil and political rights and racial equality. The nation's political system of constitutional law sunk to a nadir in these areas. Southern blacks were reduced to a state of peonage analogous to slavery. They were disenfranchised, and their subordination was enforced through lynching and other forms of racial violence. The cumulative effect of the Supreme Court's interpretations of the Reconstruction Amendments and the policy deci-sions made by political leaders contributed to making black Americans second-class citizens. No one decision was responsible for this result. The steps leading to the degradation of black Americans occurred over several decades. The Court explained its decisions as attempts to restore a states' rights–centered federalism and to protect states' rights against a misconceived centralization of power in the federal government. Political leaders sought to build political power, promote eco-nomic development, and restore peace and social stability. The ultimate degrada-tion of black Americans may not have been foreseen.[13]

This low-water mark sprouted organizations such as the National Association for the Advancement of Colored People, the Urban League, and the American Civil Liberties Union, which adopted litigation strategies to combat legal and political oppression. Over the decades of the first half of the twentieth century, they were increasingly successful in extending constitutional freedom and in enforcing the equality portion of "separate but equal." Then, in 1954, the United States Supreme Court, speaking through Chief Justice Earl Warren, announced that the principle of racial segregation in public schools was unconstitutional.[14]

The civil rights movement exploded during the 1950s and 1960s, bringing down Jim Crow and opening new opportunities for black Americans. The rise of civil rights organizations such as the Congress of Racial Equality, the Southern Christian Leadership Conference, and the Student Nonviolent Coordinating Committee, and civil rights leaders such as Martin Luther King, Jr., Ralph Abernathy, and Fred Shuttlesworth, supplemented the litigation strategy of the NAACP with direct political action to press demands.[15]

The federal government eventually put its weight behind eliminating Jim Crow and combating racial bigotry. Though reluctant at first to alienate the southern wing of the Democratic Party, President John F. Kennedy ultimately committed the moral authority of the presidency to end racial discrimination, announcing to the nation in a presidential address that racial segregation and the racial prejudice which motivated it were immoral. He used the powers of his office to promote racial equality in voting, in public schools, in employment, in public facilities, in housing, and in the practices and policies of the federal government. Shortly before his death, Kennedy initiated the impetus behind civil rights legislation that was enacted after his assassination. Kennedy's successor, President Lyndon B. Johnson, committed the presidency even more completely and vigorously than did Kennedy to combating racial prejudice and securing racial equality, getting Kennedy's programs adopted, and going beyond them. Nevertheless, both presidents intervened to combat anti–civil rights violence only reluctantly, and only when the failure of local authorities to suppress white terrorists forced them to act.[16]

In other respects, President Johnson demonstrated his commitment to civil rights, declaring, "I'm going to be the President who finishes what Lincoln began." Like Congress in the 1860s and 1870s, Congress in the 1960s enacted three statutes that outlawed segregation and authorized the Department of Justice to enforce racial equality in virtually all aspects of American life. The Civil Rights Act of 1964 outlawed racial discrimination in public accommodations and employment. Significantly, it empowered the attorney general to initiate civil suits to desegregate public schools and allowed the Departments of Health, Education, and Welfare (HEW) to withhold federal education funds from school districts that failed to desegregate. The enforcement of these provisions by the Department of Justice and HEW, rather than the Supreme Court's decision in *Brown v. Board of Education*, accounted for the sharp increase of black children attending desegregated schools in the South—from 1.18 percent in 1964 to about 90 percent in 1973. The Voting Rights Act of 1965 prohibited racial discrimination in voting rights and quickly opened the political process to southern blacks. It contributed to a sharp increase in voter registration and voting in the South, which increased the number of black officeholders from a few hundred in 1965 to 6,000 in 1989. The Open Housing Act of 1968 outlawed racial discrimination in the rental and sale of housing.[17]

The United States Supreme Court upheld the constitutionality of the 1964 Civil Rights Act, the 1965 Voting Rights Act, and the 1968 Open Housing Act. The 1960s, like the 1860s, was a period in which the president, Congress, and the federal judiciary expanded constitutional and statutory protections of Americans' civil and political rights and racial equality. This period understandably became known as the Second Reconstruction. But there was a switch in the parties supporting and opposing federal guarantees of civil rights. Democratic presidents and Democrat-controlled Congresses in the 1960s were supporters of civil rights and racial equality, and their efforts to achieve racial equality cost the Democratic Party the "Solid South;" southern white voters began to flee the Democratic Party for the Republican Party in 1964, and they have contributed to the election of Republican presidents in 8 of the 11 presidential elections from Richard M. Nixon in 1968 to George W. Bush in 2004.[18]

The turning point in federal civil rights enforcement occurred when Richard Nixon ran for the presidency in 1968. He developed his "Southern Strategy" during his 1968 election campaign, which he devised to take advantage of the southern white backlash to civil rights reform and liberal Supreme Court decisions on race and civil liberties. George Wallace contributed to the anti–civil rights politics that were an increasing reaction to the liberal reforms of the 1960s. Wallace was an outspoken segregationist who, as governor of Alabama, stood in the doorway of the University of Alabama, blocking the path of students led by Deputy Attorney General Nicholas deB. Katzenbach and a team of federal marshals to integrate the university. Nixon and Wallace won a combined 57 percent of the popular vote against Hubert Humphrey, a longtime and unswerving fighter for racial equality and other liberal causes. As president, Nixon changed White House policy, endeavoring to curry favor among southern and northern blue-collar and white-collar workers, ethnics, and Catholics who became disaffected with the liberal policies of the Democratic Party on civil rights and civil liberties. Although the president quietly contributed to continued desegregation of southern public schools and advanced equal rights in other areas, Justice Department lawyers opposed the integration of public schools in legal arguments presented to federal courts. Nixon ultimately came out publicly against busing to achieve desegregated public schools, and he supported Republican efforts in Congress to prohibit busing to achieve desegregation.[19]

President Nixon began a reversal of President Johnson's policies of vigorous civil rights enforcement that his Republican successors broadened and accelerated.

Presidents Ronald Reagan and George H. W. Bush retarded federal enforcement efforts in the areas of school desegregation, affirmative action, equal employment opportunities, fair housing, and voting rights, they claimed, for many of the same reasons that nineteenth-century political leaders curtailed civil rights enforcement: to preserve states' rights and state autonomy; to stop what they considered to be an inordinate centralization of power in the federal government and to return that power to the states; to curtail what they considered inordinate federal spending and to reduce the size of a bloated federal government; and to eliminate policies, judicial decisions, and enforcement of statutory provisions they believed actually violated the constitutional principles of equal rights.[20]

Republican presidents from Richard Nixon to George H. W. Bush were also successful in appointing judges to the United States Supreme Court who reflected their conservative views. The Supreme Court under Earl Warren strove to enforce constitutional rights, expanding the body of constitutional rights enforceable in the federal courts, broadening federal protection available to racial minorities, and increasing the number of groups entitled to protected status. The Court's liberal orientation began to change when President Nixon appointed Warren Burger to succeed Earl Warren as Chief Justice in 1969. He also appointed Harry Blackmun and the very conservative William Rehnquist with the intention of shifting the Court in a more conservative direction. In a series of decisions, the Burger Court complemented President Nixon's policies regarding school desegregation by limiting the power of federal courts to order affirmative action to desegregate public schools. Federal courts were constitutionally empowered to issue such orders only in cases involving school districts which officially discriminated on the basis of race. Limiting federal relief to *de jure* segregation, thus excluding *de facto* segregation, the Court eliminated the legal authority of the federal government to desegregate public schools that were the result of segregated housing. This doctrine insulated many segregated school districts in the North from federal desegregation orders, and it produced the ironic consequence that public schools in the South were desegregated while those in the North largely remained segregated. Moreover, many segregated school districts that were desegregated under federal court orders became segregated again because of white flight.[21]

Presidents Ronald Reagan and George H. W. Bush extended the conservative path of the Supreme Court by appointing to the Court additional conservative justices, namely, Sandra Day O'Connor, Anthony Kennedy, Antonin Scalia, and Clarence Thomas. President Reagan appointed Justice Rehnquist to succeed Warren Burger as Chief Justice when Burger retired in 1986. The five-justice majority of the Rehnquist Court adopted legal doctrines that limit the constitutionality of state and federal affirmative action programs to instances of proven racial discrimination, and these doctrines allow racial preferences only if race-neutral strategies have failed to remedy the effects of discriminatory actions. The Rehnquist court also diminished the scope of civil rights statutes enacted by the Reconstruction Congresses, and it curtailed the power of Congress to enforce the rights secured by the Fourteenth Amendment and to remedy their violation, which its framers intended to give to Congress.[22]

Looking back at the history of racial decline in the late nineteenth century, one cannot identify a single action or moment in which blacks were degraded to second-class citizenship and quasi-slavery. Rather, this degradation occurred gradually in a series of small steps. The cumulative effect of these actions, however, was to generate deep racism and to place the federal and state governments in support of racism. One of the lessons of this book is that it shows how actions of the Grant administration and decisions of the Supreme Court after the Civil War contributed to the degradation of black Americans, even though these actions were not taken for that purpose. In retrospect, the decision of President Grant to curtail federal civil rights enforcement in order to restore peace in the South looks like a sellout of southern blacks. The Supreme Court's decision in the *Slaughter-House Cases,* which held that the Fourteenth Amendment did not protect the fundamental rights of white butchers in order to preserve the states' police powers, actually proclaimed that the Fourteenth Amendment was adopted to protect black Americans from racial subjugation. Few recognized at the time that it set out a constitutional doctrine that would render the federal government incapable of protecting blacks from white violence and racial degradation. It is important for us today to be cognizant of the history recounted in this book because it can sharpen our awareness that governmental policies and Supreme Court decisions in the present and recent past may be contributing to another downward trend in the fortunes of black Americans.

Introduction to the Oceana
Publications Edition

American leaders of the 1860s and the 1870s greatly relied upon law and legal institutions to solve some of the nation's most important political problems. Indeed, the history of the Civil War and Reconstruction is distinguished by the way in which politics affected the development of law, and the way in which law, in turn, influenced the contours of American politics.

The most urgent political issues leading to the Civil War involved the definition of American federalism and the division of legal authority between the national and state governments over the status of slaves. The North went to war in 1861 to establish as political reality the legal doctrine that the Union is perpetual and indestructible. The emancipation of slaves became a Union objective two years later. The Union's victories secured the nation against secession and emancipated the Southern slaves. These military victories, however, once again confronted the nation with the political questions that had led to the Civil War: which government, national or state, possessed primary legal authority to determine the status and enforce the rights of the citizens and inhabitants of the United States.

The Union's military victory seemed to resolve this question in favor of the national government. In the years following the Civil War, however, Southerners continued to resist national authority and emancipation. With the support of local and state governments, they opposed political groups and economically intimidated and physically assaulted individuals associated with the Union's Civil War objectives. The Southern defiance forced Congress to amend the Constitution and enact statutes to protect fundamental rights in order to implement the Union's Civil War objectives.

The adoption of the Thirteenth, Fourteenth, and Fifteenth Amendments and the various civil rights statutes was predicated on the primacy of national authority over the rights of citizens. These amendments and statutes gave federal officers and federal courts criminal jurisdiction over civil rights cases. This jurisdiction, previously held under state authority by state officers, was a novel one for the federal judiciary. Federal jurisdiction over criminal violations of citizens' civil rights required judicial acceptance of legal theories that affirmed the primacy of national authority to enforce and protect fundamental rights. Congress's civil rights legislation thus encompassed revolutionary constitutional and legal theories and revolutionary changes in federal functions.

The nation's judicial and legal officers played a far more important role in shaping the political and constitutional history of Reconstruction than historians and legal scholars have realized. Almost without exception, federal judges affirmed the primacy of the national government's authority over the rights of American citizens. Armed with judicially sanctioned constitutional authority to prosecute civil rights violators, the Department of Justice and federal courts became extensively involved in the administration of criminal justice after 1870.

The federal administration of criminal justice was inherently political. As this study will show, the enforcement of civil rights required that the federal courts affirm constitutional theories and apply substantive law over which political parties were divided. Moreover, the federal prosecutions were invariably brought against groups associated with the Democratic Conservative Party for crimes committed against individuals connected with the Republican Party.

Republicans' support of a nationalistic federal protection of civil rights extended their Civil War commitment to national supremacy and emancipation. Democratic Conservative opposition to federal enforcement of civil rights represented a parallel evolution of the Confederate commitment to states rights and slavery. In enforcing civil rights, therefore, the federal courts preserved the Republican Party's Civil War aims and advanced the Party's interests during Reconstruction.

The efforts of federal judges and Justice Department officers ultimately failed to bring about lasting peace in the South. In retrospect, Congress seems astonishingly presumptuous in expecting the federal courts successfully to eliminate and punish Southern lawlessness of a magnitude that prostrated local law enforcers. Yet, the success with which the federal courts initially met this challenge is equally astonishing. Federal prosecutions succeeded, where local law enforcement failed, in destroying organized terrorist groups and in bringing to the South a period of relative peace.

Federal success depended, however, on the commitment of the national government to enforce civil rights statutes, and that commitment was short lived. In 1873, President Grant ordered the Department of Justice to stop bringing prosecutions against Southern lawbreakers, and he pardoned those who earlier had been convicted and incarcerated by the federal courts. As Southern United States attorneys and marshals had predicted, the president's clemency invited a revival of large-scale violence by the fall of 1874. When the attorney general ordered a resumption of federal prosecution of civil rights violators, he discovered that the federal courts no longer recognized federal jurisdiction over the administration of criminal justice. He thereupon ordered legal officers to discontinue their efforts to enforce civil rights until the Supreme Court clarified the government's authority.

The United States Supreme Court's 1873 decision in the *Slaughterhouse Cases* was responsible for the shift by the federal courts after 1873. This decision took much of the Civil War victory away from the Union nationalists and transferred it to Southern states' rights proponents by declaring that primary authority over the status and rights of citizens is a part of state power, not national power. The Court expanded this states rights ruling two years later in *United States v. Cruikshank,* by eliminating much of the national government's legal authority to secure the civil rights, personal safety, and property of American citizens.

The elimination of national jurisdiction over civil rights relegated Southern blacks and white Republicans to the protection of local law and law enforcement agencies. These agencies were unable or unwilling to redress civil rights violations. The result was the virtual re-enslavement of Southern blacks and the eventual destruction of the Republican Party in the South. The supremacy of national authority and black emancipation were replaced by states' rights and black peonage.

This study is a history of an ignored aspect of the Civil War and Reconstruction era. It analyzes the legal theory of national authority over citizens and citizens' rights expressed in the rulings of federal judges that interpreted the Reconstruction Amendments while enforcing federal civil rights legislation. It recounts the efforts of federal judges and legal officers to protect American citizens in the South and to punish civil rights violators, and it describes the difficulties confronted by legal and judicial officers who were involved in the federal administration of criminal justice. It concludes with an explanation of the Supreme Court's rejection of the primacy of national authority to protect civil rights—a rejection that prevented the federal courts from enforcing and protecting the civil rights of American citizens for almost 100 years.

The study concludes that the Civil War and Reconstruction had a far more revolutionary impact on American constitutionalism than scholars have appreciated. This revolution was achieved by federal judges and attorneys who used federal authority to combat politically and racially motivated terrorism in the South. The revolution was short lived. But, its brevity was due to conscious choices made by the president and the Supreme Court to withdraw and curtail federal authority to secure civil rights. The choices were made at the very moment when federal officers believed they were winning their struggle against Southern terrorism. One wonders what the political and racial history of the United States might have been if the president and the Supreme Court had made other choices.

1   Judicial Interpretations of National Civil Rights Enforcement Authority, 1866–1873

Between the years 1866 and 1873, a legal theory of national civil rights enforcement authority emerged in the courts of the United States that manifested a revolutionary impact of the Civil War upon the constitutional and legal structure of American federalism. The constitutional grounding of this theory was the Thirteenth and Fourteenth Amendments; its first expression was the product of judicial interpretations of the Civil Rights Act of 1866, of the concept of United States citizenship, and of the national government's authority to fix the status and to secure the fundamental rights of American citizens.

The legal theory of national civil rights enforcement authority affirmed by judges may be succinctly stated. Judges defined United States citizenship under the Thirteenth and Fourteenth Amendments as the status of freemen. They equated the rights of United States citizenship to the natural rights of freemen. Judges reasoned that, since natural rights were now secured by the United States Constitution to United States citizens as such, Congress possessed plenary authority to protect these rights in whatever manner it deemed appropriate, consistent with the Constitution. The Constitution therefore authorized Congress to confer upon the federal courts primary jurisdiction directly to enforce these fundamental rights and directly to punish their violation. In short, the legal theory of national civil rights enforcement authority under the Thirteenth and Fourteenth Amendments posited a virtually unlimited national authority over civil rights.

The primacy of national civil rights enforcement authority was a revolutionary legal theory because the states had traditionally determined the status and rights of individuals and provided for their security. For example, Southern states before the Civil War legally sanctioned slavery and defined in law the status of Afro-American slaves as chattel, virtually without any rights recognizable in law. Northern as well as Southern states relegated free blacks to a second-class citizenship by legally withholding from them some of the basic rights that state statutes extended to white citizens as "inalienable rights" of freemen. At the same time the states functioned as the traditional guardians of life, liberty, and property. This guardianship was exercised through state institutions, statutes, and judicial decisions that served to punish crimes and resolve civil disputes that involved the basic rights of citizens.

Although the states functioned as the primary guarantors of the fundamental rights of citizens, they did so without a settled legal theory that authorized their exercise of this power. Legal theories of citizenship and the primacy of state as opposed to national authority over the status and fundamental rights of citizens were still disputed at the outbreak of the Civil War. Legal theorists agreed that citizenship conferred on individuals a right to the governmental protection of a broad range of rights and privileges. However, individuals were citizens of both the nation and a state. National and state citizenship were considered to be different aspects of the same status. Therefore, both the national and the state governments theoretically possessed the constitutional authority and obligation to enforce and protect the fundamental rights of citizenship.[1]

Ambiguities in legal theory became urgent political questions as disagreements over the power to determine the status and rights of slaves, fugitive slaves, and free blacks increasingly divided North and South. The conflict over slavery forced the nation to resolve the ambiguities of the past and to determine where primary authority over the status and rights of individuals was located, in the nation or in the states. The resolution of this question was a corollary of the more fundamental constitutional issue that was central to the Civil War, namely, whether ultimate sovereignty was constitutionally delegated to the national or to the state governments. This constitutional conflict between national supremacy and union on the one side and state sovereignty and secession on the other side determined whether the United States was a sovereign political community that transcended state boundaries or a federation of sovereign and independent states. The determination of this question also resolved the issue of where primary authority over the status and rights of citizens was located, for sovereignty of necessity encompasses such primary authority.

The North and national sovereignty prevailed on the battlefields. The Northern Republican–controlled Reconstruction Congresses expressed this nationalist military victory in constitutional amendments and statutes that attempted to resolve the antebellum ambiguities concerning citizenship by defining the status and some of the rights that individuals enjoyed as citizens of the United States. Congress's formulation of American citizenship and its determination of the status and rights of American citizens manifested its assertion of primary authority over citizenship. The nationalization of citizenship expressed in law the military determination of the United States as a sovereign political community that transcends state boundaries.[2]

Congress understood the primacy of national citizenship to be a consequence of the supremacy of national sovereignty. National authority over citizenship was primary because national rather than state citizenship now determined the status and rights of individuals as citizens. Since this status and its attendant rights were conferred upon individuals by the Constitution and laws of the United States, Congress was authorized to secure these rights in any manner that it deemed appropriate, consistent with the Constitution. The scope of this authority was potentially destructive of American federalism. If Congress chose, it could legislate criminal and civil codes that displaced those of the states. Furthermore, Congress could confer upon the federal courts jurisdiction over ordinary crimes and civil disputes that supplanted the jurisdiction of state courts. In short, the supremacy of national sovereignty so centralized power in the national government that the states as separate and autonomous political entities could have been destroyed.

Congress chose not to destroy the states as separate political entities. Indeed, Congress wanted to preserve the states and expected them to continue their traditional functions. Congress therefore articulated a theory of national citizenship and federally enforceable rights that assumed concurrent responsibility and authority between the nation and the states to enforce and protect the civil rights of Americans. Federalism was preserved. But, it was a new federalism that required the courts of the United States to redefine the lines of jurisdiction between national and state authority under the post–Civil War constitutional amendments and civil rights acts.

The analysis of judicial opinions that follows examines how federal judges redefined and applied national jurisdiction over citizenship and citizens' rights under the Reconstruction Amendments and civil rights statutes. The issues that this analysis addresses include judicial interpretations of the rights that the congressional framers of the amendments and statutes intended to secure; it explores the judicial understanding of the procedures Congress provided in statutes for the enforcement of citizens' civil rights. It also presents the legal theory of citizenship and civil rights enforcement that judges derived from the Thirteenth and Fourteenth Amendments and the statutes enacted by Congress to enforce them. It was this theory that provided judges with the legal basis for asserting primary authority over the fundamental rights of citizenship.

Congress involved the United States government in the judicial enforcement of civil rights when it enacted the Civil Rights Act of 1866. This statute was a legislative precursor of the Fourteenth Amendment, for it defined United States citizenship and enumerated some of the civil rights that the courts of the United

States were to secure. The rights to testify, to sue and be sued, to enter into legally enforceable contracts, to own and dispose of property, and to the equal protection of personal rights under law were among the rights that Congress specifically enumerated as nationally enforceable rights under the act. The Civil Rights Act declared that the infringement of these rights under color of law or custom was a federal crime. However, the law not only authorized the federal courts to punish and redress these wrongs, but it also provided for the removal of state court proceedings to the federal courts where a party claimed that he was not able to protect or enforce his rights in the state court. In such cases, the Civil Rights Act provided that the federal courts sit as courts of original criminal or civil jurisdiction and try the cases.[3]

The legal theory that affirmed the primacy of national civil rights enforcement authority was initially expressed judicially in cases that challenged the constitutionality of the Civil Rights Act of 1866. Congress had enacted the Civil Rights Act to implement the Thirteenth Amendment, which, on its face, merely abolished slavery. In explaining how an amendment that abolished slavery could provide constitutional authority for a statute that secured civil rights, judges resurrected the theory of natural rights asserted before the Civil War by radical abolitionists to insist that slavery was illegal and coupled it with the nationalist tradition of constitutional interpretation that attributed broad powers to the national government.[4]

All federal and most state appellate judges who considered challenges to the Civil Rights Act upheld its constitutionality under the Thirteenth Amendment. They explicitly or implicitly interpreted the Thirteenth Amendment as conferring upon Congress primary authority over citizens' civil rights. Citing Supreme Court decisions, such as *McCulloch v. Maryland,* that expressed the nationalist tradition of constitutional interpretation, they asserted that the recognition of rights by the United States Constitution confers upon Congress the requisite power to secure those rights. They found a constitutional guarantee of civil rights in the Thirteenth Amendment by broadly interpreting it as accomplishing more than the abrogation of chattel slavery. In abolishing slavery, the amendment provided the more significant constitutional guarantee of personal liberty. They reasoned that in recognizing the personal right to liberty, the Thirteenth Amendment conferred upon Congress the requisite power to secure personal liberty and all of the rights that are incidents of personal liberty. In other words, the Thirteenth Amendment was understood as conferring upon all Americans the status of "freemen." Citing such legal authorities as Blackstone, Kent, and Story, judges who espoused this view equated the status of "freeman" with the status of "citizen." Consequently, in making all Americans "freemen," the Thirteenth Amendment conferred citizenship upon them. The Thirteenth Amendment thereby authorized Congress to secure the civil rights of "freemen" as federally enforceable rights of United States citizenship. This legal theory was a direct outgrowth of antebellum radical abolitionist natural rights theory. A certain propriety, therefore, accompanied its incorporation into the Constitution of the United States through judicial interpretations of the Thirteenth Amendment. However, judges who embraced this revolutionary interpretation of national civil rights enforcement authority under the Thirteenth Amendment in upholding the constitutionality of the Civil Rights Act declared that they were merely implementing the intent and understanding of the statute's congressional framers.[5]

Judges expressed the belief that the Reconstruction Amendments and the Civil Rights Act were intended to establish the primacy of national citizenship and national authority over the rights of citizens. Supreme Court Justice Noah H. Swayne acknowledged this change wrought by the Thirteenth Amendment as circuit justice for Kentucky. In the first reported interpretation of the Civil Rights Act by a federal judge, he observed that the states had "always claimed and exercised the exclusive right to fix the status of all persons living in their jurisdiction." However, the Thirteenth Amendment, he declared, "reversed and annulled the original policy of the Constitution." Not only did it prohibit the states from deciding whether slavery should or should not exist, but it also conferred upon the national government the power to fix the status of persons within the United States. For Swayne, it was the Thirteenth Amendment, and not the Civil Rights Act, that conferred citizenship on the former slave by making him a "freeman." Insofar as the act confers citizenship, Swayne concluded, it is "unnecessary and...inoperative."[6]

States' rights-oriented judges resisted this revolutionary impact of the Thirteenth Amendment and Civil Rights Act by sometimes invoking an alternative legal tradition that was central to the states' rights view of American federalism. This tradition characterized the authority of the national government as limited to those powers that are explicitly delegated to it by, or are necessarily implied in, the Constitution of the United States. The Supreme Court's decision in *Barron v. The Mayor and City Council of Baltimore* was compatible with this view, for it held that the negatively worded provisions of the Bill of Rights were limitations upon the exercise of the nation's governmental powers and not delegations of legislative authority to the national government to secure fundamental rights. States' rights-oriented judges argued by extension that the original

Constitution left the governing power over fundamental rights to the states, and, applying a literalist interpretation to the Thirteenth Amendment, they declared that it merely abolished slavery.[7]

Unlike the Bill of Rights, this amendment contains an express delegation of legislative authority to enforce it. However, states' rights-oriented judges circumvented a potentially broad application of the Thirteenth Amendment with their narrow interpretation of its scope. In other words, they interpreted the Thirteenth Amendment as authorizing Congress merely to prohibit the reestablishment of chattel slavery, not as an expansive authorization to secure personal liberty. They thereby continued to assert the primacy of state authority over citizenship and citizens' rights.

However, even states' rights-oriented judges who held that the act was unconstitutional acknowledged the natural rights and nationalist interpretation of the Thirteenth Amendment as the congressional understanding of national civil rights enforcement power. They conceded that the legislative supporters of the Civil Rights Act considered the Thirteenth Amendment to be a constitutional guarantee of the civil rights of citizens that authorized Congress to enforce and protect these rights. Legislative intent notwithstanding, these judges warned that if the act was constitutional and "this be the correct theory, and if the Thirteenth Amendment embraces so wide a scope as this, it results of necessity that Congress has supreme authority over all our civil rights...." Recognizing the revolutionary implications of the nationalist legal theory of civil rights enforcement, they feared that the national government would supplant the states' authority over state citizens and usurp the most important function of local government—securing the lives and property of their citizens. They felt it incumbent upon themselves to declare the Civil Rights Act unconstitutional and to repudiate the nationalist legal theory upon which it was based to preserve a states' rights-centered federal constitutionalism.[8]

For example, the Kentucky High Court of Error and Appeals in 1867 reversed a lower court conviction of a white man for grand larceny. The conviction was based on the testimony of a black witness that was admitted at trial under the Civil Rights Act. The Kentucky Court reversed the conviction, affirmed the Kentucky statute prohibiting the testimony of the black witness, and struck down the act as an unconstitutional invasion of the sovereign power of the state to confer and secure the rights of its citizens. However, such explicit judicial rulings upholding the primacy of state authority over citizens' rights were rare.[9]

State judges who disapproved of the Civil Rights Act were reluctant directly to challenge the legal theory on which it was based. They instead sought to preserve state control over citizens' rights with oblique challenges to the Civil Rights Act that sidestepped the question of the primacy of Congress's authority over citizens' rights. For example, in an 1867 case involving the admissibility of Negro testimony contrary to state law, the Delaware Court of General Sessions characterized the right to testify as a state rule of judicial procedure instead of a civil right of citizenship. The court declared the Civil Rights Act unconstitutional "so far as it attempts directly, to regulate the proceedings in the State Courts. . . ." This retreat to the narrow ground of state authority over rules of civil and criminal procedure in state courts as a bar to the Civil Rights Act suggests how authoritative among even unsympathetic judges was the legal theory that sustained the Civil Rights Act of 1866. The Maryland Court of Appeals disagreed with the policy contained in the act, but it nevertheless upheld it because of the supremacy of federal law. Decisions adverse to the constitutionality of the Civil Rights Act under the Thirteenth Amendment were exceptional, and the primacy of congressional authority to secure the civil rights of citizens was generally established throughout the courts of the United States by 1869.[10]

Regardless of whether judges approved or disapproved of the Civil Rights Act, they shared a common understanding of its intended objectives and scope. Judges expressed the belief that the act's congressional supporters intended to confer upon the federal courts complete authority directly and effectively to secure civil rights as federally enforceable rights of American citizenship. Indeed, some state judges who declared the Civil Rights Act unconstitutional did so, in part, precisely because they understood this to be its intended purpose. What judges understood to be the specific rights Congress intended to secure will be discussed below. The important point here is that judges uniformly understood that the Civil Rights Act of 1866 expressed a legal theory that assumed that Congress and the federal courts possessed primary authority to protect civil rights because these rights were recognized and secured by the United States Constitution as rights of American citizenship.[11]

The specific rights secured by the Civil Rights Act were more problematical than the enumeration of rights in the act would have suggested. The natural rights theory by which judges interpreted the Thirteenth Amendment and American citizenship accounts for this uncertainty. If, as judges ruled, the rights of American citizenship consisted of the natural rights of freemen, that is, the rights to life, liberty, and property and rights incidental thereto, then the specific rights of American citizenship enforceable in the federal courts transcended the specific rights enumerated in the Civil Rights Act. Thus, black Americans invoked the Civil Rights Act to challenge their exclusion from public facilities, and they were often successful. The United States District Court at Mobile, Alabama, for example, ruled in the summer of 1867 that the right to ride on a privately operated city railroad car was a personal right secured by the Civil Rights Act of 1866. It ordered the president of the Davis Avenue Railroad Company to stand trial under section 2 of the act for refusing access to a black passenger. In some cases, money damages were awarded to black plaintiffs, while, in others, proprietors were fined who excluded black patrons from their establishments or common carriers. Blacks were also admitted to juries under the Civil Rights Act even though access to juries was not expressly guaranteed. Of course, judges did not always agree that access to public accommodations constituted a natural right of American citizenship. Nor did the enforcement of the right of blacks to public accommodations necessarily result in integrated facilities. Separate but equal was usually regarded by the courts as consistent with the ideal of equal rights. However, judicial applications of national civil rights enforcement power to these areas manifested judges' understanding of the scope of national civil rights enforcement authority as including an undefined and indefinitely broad body of natural rights as rights of American citizenship.[12]

The exercise of national civil rights enforcement power within a continuing American federal constitutional structure raises the additional question of how judges interpreted the civil rights jurisdiction conferred upon the federal courts by the Civil Rights Act of 1866. Judges believed that Congress intended that American citizens, white as well as black, be allowed to employ federal legal and judicial process when they were unable to protect or enforce their rights in the state courts. They therefore interpreted the Civil Rights Act as conferring upon the federal courts concurrent jurisdiction over civil rights. Judges rejected attempts of defense attorneys to read into the Civil Rights Act an interpretation that limited its application to cases in which rights were infringed by some form of racially discriminatory state action. Federal jurisdiction was applied whether or not state discrimination was involved; federal courts sat as courts of primary jurisdiction and tried cases that ordinarily would have been heard only in state courts; federal courts tried cases whether the parties were state officials or private individuals.

Justice Swayne's 1867 circuit court opinion is illustrative. The case involved a federal prosecution of the crimes of burglary and robbery. Three white defendants were convicted in the United States District Court at Louisville of robbing the home of a black family living in Nelson County, Kentucky. The case was tried in the federal court because the United States attorney, Benjamin H. Bristow, had reason to believe that the criminals would not have been brought to justice if the crime had been left to local law enforcement agencies. The obvious reason is that the state laws of evidence prohibited blacks from testifying in cases in which whites were parties. The legal inability of blacks to testify against whites permitted whites to terrorize and otherwise commit crimes against blacks with impunity, because blacks were often the only witnesses to the crimes. The federal court therefore assumed primary criminal jurisdiction under section 3 of the 1866 Civil Rights Act as soon as the crime was reported, before the local authorities had an opportunity to act.[13]

The defense demurred to the prosecution on several grounds. In addition to challenging the constitutionality of the Civil Rights Act, defense counsel narrowly interpreted the law as merely securing an equality in the rights enumerated in its first section and, then, only against discriminatory state action. Observing that the indictment did not aver a denial of equal rights and that discriminatory state action was not present since the local courts had not been given the opportunity to try the case, counsel insisted that the indictment was defective and the federal court lacked jurisdiction in the case. The government's case was presented by United States Attorney Bristow who simply argued for jurisdiction on the grounds that the victims of the crime were unable to enforce in the state courts a right secured to them by the Constitution and laws of the United States.[14]

In a subtly reasoned opinion, Justice Swayne upheld the constitutionality of the Civil Rights Act and federal jurisdiction. To sustain jurisdiction, he had to reject the defense's interpretation of the Civil Rights Act, for the court only would have been authorized to set aside the discriminatory state statute under that interpretation. The federal court would not have been able to try the defendants for crimes against the substantive civil rights of citizens. Furthermore, the basis of federal jurisdiction would have had to be the discriminatory state statute, but Bristow had not argued state discrimination as the basis for federal jurisdiction. Therefore, Justice Swayne upheld these prosecutions on the grounds that citizens were denied substantive rights secured to them by the Thirteenth Amendment and the Civil Rights Act. It was the infringement of nationally secured rights, not discriminatory state action or inaction, that conferred jurisdiction upon the federal courts under the Civil Rights Act.[15]

Judges sometimes explicitly stated that Congress intended the Civil Rights Act to secure the civil rights of black citizens against the racial prejudices that frequently prevented them from enjoying their rights. In an 1866 charge to the Federal Grand Jury at Huntsville, Alabama, United States District Judge Richard Busteed expressed this view and added that the statute was to be applied against "any person, official or non-official, legislator, Governor, magistrate, or citizen . . ." who acted under law or custom. The United States District Judge for Mississippi, Robert A. Hill, charged the Grand Jury at Jackson in July 1871 to enforce the Civil Rights Act in a similar way even though he observed that the state legislature had "wisely repealed all laws in conflict . . ." with its provisions. The Texas Supreme Court in 1873 agreed that the Civil Rights Act secured civil rights even in the absence of discriminatory state statutes, for "[a]ny other construction . . ." the court declared, "would render the whole act almost entirely useless for any good purpose whatever." Even the United States Supreme Court thought this was the obvious interpretation of the law in 1872:

> It is also well known that in many quarters, prejudices existed against the colored race, which naturally affected the administration of justice in the state courts, and operated harshly when one of that race was a party accused. These were evils, doubtless, which the Act of Congress had in view, and which it intended to remove. And so far as it reaches, it extends to both races the same rights, and the same means of vindicating them.

With very few exceptions, federal and state appellate courts either expressly applied federal protection against private infringements of citizens' rights, or they rejected attempts to impose state action limitations upon national civil rights enforcement power.[16]

Although these rulings prescribed a uniformity in the rights of citizens, they also allowed for variations among the states in the conditions under which these rights were to be exercised so long as the variations were reasonable. For example, they permitted the states to vary the enjoyment of civil rights according to age, sex, mental capacity, and alienage, since such discriminations were considered reasonable and even necessary. This interpretation of the Civil Rights Act maintained the concurrence in national and state authority over civil rights. Consequently, private law, such as property law, contract law, torts, etc., remained under state jurisdiction even though natural rights were nationalized. The same was true of criminal law.[17]

However, judges interpreted the Civil Rights Act as additionally securing the right to nondiscriminatory state law and administration of state law. The act explicitly secures to citizens the same rights as are enjoyed by whites. Judges interpreted this clause to mean that all citizens were to enjoy civil rights under the same conditions established by state law for their most favored citizens, whites. Thus, Justice Swayne found that the Kentucky rules of evidence violated the Civil Rights Act because they prohibited blacks from enjoying "the same right to testify 'as is enjoyed by white citizens,'" because blacks could not testify under the same conditions as whites. The California Supreme Court explained the broader implications of this clause in 1869:

> If in a given State the title to real property of any character may be conveyed by writing not under seal, then all citizens, of every race and color, may convey property of that character in the same mode.... And so of statutes regulating the competency of witnesses.

Nevertheless, that California might allow such a conveyance did not bind another state to make such allowance. While the right to convey property was secured to all citizens under national law, the conditions under which that right, and other civil rights, was to be enjoyed continued to be prescribed by the states so long as the states did not illegally discriminate or until Congress exercised that power.[18]

The Civil Rights Act contained a feature that could potentially limit its seemingly indefinite reach. The weakness was recognized by United States Attorney Bristow when he was preparing his argument in the *Rhodes* case. Bristow observed that the third section gives to the federal courts jurisdiction over "all causes, civil and criminal, affecting persons who are denied or cannot enforce in the courts...the rights secured to them by the first section of this act. . . ." The essential question raised in cases involving crimes committed by white defendants against black victims was whether a criminal prosecution was "a cause affecting" the victims of the crime. Judicial precedent appeared to be against federal jurisdiction, for the United States Supreme Court had ruled years earlier in *United States v. Ortega* that a criminal prosecution was a "case" that affected only the defendant and the state against whose laws the crime was committed. The victim of the crime was not a party to the case. Bristow wrote to the law's author, Senator Lyman Trumbull, and expressed grave concern that a ruling based on *Ortega* would preclude federal prosecutions of white defendants for crimes committed against black victims, such as the prosecution in the *Rhodes* case. The source of Bristow's concern was his reluctance

> to rely on state authorities to furnish protection to the colored race. To deliver these people over to the State Courts *now* would be equivalent to a national decree authorizing a general destruction of the race.

He asked the senator for corrective legislation that would "furnish the colored people of Ky. complete & ample protection from outrage & oppression." In the meantime, Judge Ballard wrote to Chief Justice Salmon P. Chase requesting that Justice Noah H. Swayne preside over the constitutional challenge to the Civil Rights Act that was brought before Ballard's court.[19]

Justice Swayne adroitly resolved the problem in favor of federal jurisdiction. He distinguished between the wording of the statute and the Supreme Court's ruling in *Ortega* by defining "case" and "cause" differently. A "case," he said, was a specific legal action in which, if it is a criminal prosecution, the only parties affected are the defendant and the state. A "cause," on the other hand, was "the origin or foundation of a thing, as of a suit or action; a ground of action." The *Ortega* decision did not apply to the Civil Rights Act because the act referred to causes of civil actions and criminal prosecutions, not to the specific cases themselves. Swayne concluded that the victims of a crime were parties affected by the prosecution within the meaning of the Civil Rights Act, and the federal courts could assume primary criminal jurisdiction in the prosecution of crimes when the state courts failed to bring defendants to justice.[20]

The circumstances of the *Rhodes* opinion gave it a much greater significance than it enjoys as the first reported federal judicial interpretation of the scope and constitutionality of the Civil Rights Act of 1866. It appears to have been the result of a cooperative effort among the United States attorney, the United States district judge, justices of the United States Supreme Court, and the legislative author of the statute. Their purpose was to assure a federal judicial interpretation of the law that was not only consistent with the intent of its legislative framers, but also broad enough to authorize the federal judiciary to replace selectively local law enforcement agencies in the administration of justice. The magnitude of this expansion of national power ensured a continuing challenge by anti-civil rights forces until the issue was finally resolved by the Supreme Court of the United States. How the Supreme Court responded to this challenge will be discussed in Chapter 7.

Not surprisingly, judicial interpretations of the Fourteenth Amendment and the civil rights statutes enacted to enforce it expressed a similar legal theory of national civil rights enforcement authority. This similarity is not surprising because judges understood the Fourteenth Amendment as virtually identical in meaning, scope, and objectives to the Civil Rights Act of 1866, and they understood the Enforcement Acts of 1870 and 1871, statutes enacted to implement the Fourteenth Amendment, as extensions of the Civil Rights Act of 1866. In short, judges understood section 1 of the Fourteenth Amendment as the product of its legislative framers' efforts to clarify and incorporate more explicitly into the

United States Constitution the legal theory that provided the constitutional authorization for the Civil Rights Act of 1866.

The first section of the Fourteenth Amendment contains four clauses. The first clause explicitly constitutionalizes the meaning that most judges attributed to the Thirteenth Amendment as it relates to citizenship. It fixes the status of all persons born or naturalized in the United States and subject to its jurisdiction as citizens of the nation and of the states in which they reside. The language of the next three clauses constitutes a threefold prohibition on the exercise of state powers. The states are prohibited from enacting or enforcing any law that abridges the "privileges or immunities" of United States citizens; from depriving any person, citizen or not, of life, liberty, or property without due process of law; and from denying any person the equal protection of the law.

Judicial examinations of the Fourteenth Amendment addressed the following questions. What is the impact of the amendment upon the primacy of national or state authority over citizens' rights? What rights constitute the privileges and immunities of United States citizenship? What are the rights of state citizenship? What authority does the Fourteenth Amendment confer upon Congress to secure and enforce citizens' rights?

Federal judges addressed these questions relating to the Fourteenth Amendment as they considered the scope and constitutionality of the Enforcement Acts of 1870 and 1871. The act of May 31, 1870, was primarily aimed at securing the Fifteenth Amendment right of citizens to vote free from racially discriminatory interference by the state or private individuals and groups. It was secondarily intended to protect against racially and politically motivated interference by disguised or conspiratorial groups with any right, privilege, or immunity secured by the Constitution and laws of the United States. Federal courts were given exclusive jurisdiction to try these offenses. The Ku Klux Klan Act of April 20, 1871, was a more elaborate legislative attempt to ensure against violations of nationally enforceable political and civil rights of American citizens by conspiratorial terrorist groups such as the Klan. It defined as federal crimes activities in which the Klan was engaged to prevent citizens from exercising their civil rights. It also empowered the president to declare martial law and suspend habeas corpus under certain conditions.[21]

National civil rights enforcement authority under the Fourteenth Amendment and Enforcement Acts was most seriously challenged in those Southern federal judicial districts in which the Klan was most active. Alabama was one such district, and a case that was prosecuted in the United States Circuit Court at Mobile is illustrative of the legal reasoning judges employed in seeking answers to the difficult and novel questions raised in this new area of federal law.

About one year after his appointment to the newly created Circuit Court for Alabama, future Supreme Court Justice William B. Woods was confronted with the prosecution of a group of Ku Klux under the Enforcement Act of 1870. A federal grand jury at Mobile found that, during the fall 1870 election campaign, the suspects raided a political meeting of Republicans at Eutaw, Greene County, Alabama out of political and racial animosity. Two persons were killed and over fifty others wounded during the melee. As a result of the grand jury's findings, the defendants were indicted and charged with conspiring to injure, oppress, threaten, and intimidate the victims with the intent and for the purpose of depriving them of their rights of freedom of speech and of assembly.[22]

The defense demurred on grounds that forced Judge Woods to resolve two of the constitutional questions with which the federal courts were confronted in Enforcement Acts cases. These questions were whether First Amendment guarantees had been transformed by the Fourteenth Amendment into federally enforceable rights of American citizenship, and whether crimes committed by private individuals that infringed these rights were punishable in the federal courts.

The political as well as legal consequences of these issues may have been too grave for Judge Woods to resolve on his own, because he turned to Circuit Justice Joseph P. Bradley for help. Justice Bradley's elevation to the Supreme Court of the United States was even more recent than Woods's appointment to the circuit court. Bradley nevertheless accepted the challenge. His comments suggest that this was the first occasion in which he gave serious thought to the application of the Fourteenth Amendment to private infringements of civil rights, for he initially missed the point of Judge Woods's inquiry. His comments betray a lack of familiarity with the legal nuances of the challenge to national civil rights enforcement authority. His discussion is also noteworthy for the absence of any references to the legislative history of the Fourteenth Amendment. Justice Bradley instead analyzed the amendment purely on the basis of his own ideas concerning citizenship and the constitutional principles expressed in the language of the Fourteenth Amendment. His unfamiliarity with the amendment's legislative history is not surprising for a New Jersey corporate attorney who eschewed politics.

Justice Bradley's legal analysis of national civil rights enforcement authority under the Fourteenth Amendment represented a curious blend of conflicting legal traditions. He unequivocally asserted that "[t]he right of the people to assemble together and discuss political questions...is one of the most sacred rights of citizenship. . . ." However, he also viewed these First Amendment guarantees as prohibitions against the national government, and he applied them to the states in his interpretation of the negatively worded Fourteenth Amendment. He concluded that these fundamental rights were federally enforceable rights of citizenship "and cannot be abridged by any state."[23]

Judge Woods quickly pointed out that the issue before him dealt specifically with violations of First Amendment guarantees committed by private individuals without any state involvement. He reminded Justice Bradley that he had to decide whether "the breaking up of a peaceable political meeting, by riot and murder, when committed simply for that purpose . . ." was a felony against the First Amendment punishable in a court of the United States. He pressed the question of whether that offense was punishable in the federal courts in view of the wording of the First Amendment.

Until the adoption of the Fourteenth Amendment, Justice Bradley responded, such an offense was not punishable in a federal court. However, the Fourteenth Amendment authorized Congress to protect the fundamental rights of citizenship against state action and state inaction. This apparent state action interpretation notwithstanding, Bradley believed that the amendment's scope authorized civil rights enforcement legislation that punished private as well as state infringements of citizens' rights. He reasoned that,

> as it would be unseemly for Congress to interfere with state enactments, and as it cannot compel the actions of state officials, the only appropriate legislation it can make is that which will operate directly on offenders and offences and protect the rights which the Amendment secures.

Justice Bradley's explanation of why Congress could directly punish private offenders despite the Fourteenth Amendment's language assumed the nationalist tradition of constitutional interpretation that holds that a right that is recognized or secured by the Constitution of the United States confers upon Congress the authority to protect it. He therefore concluded that "[t]he extent to which Congress shall exercise this power must depend on its discretion in view of the circumstances of each case." He relied upon this legal tradition in suggesting to Judge Woods a defense against anticipated objections to this national interference with the local administration of criminal justice. He stated emphatically: "it must be remembered that it is for the purpose of protecting federal rights; and these must be protected whether it interferes with domestic laws or domestic administration of laws."[24]

Reassured by the approving comments and legal analysis of Justice Bradley, Judge Woods rejected the demurrer. He upheld the constitutionality of the Enforcement Act of 1870 and the criminal indictments brought under it against private individuals for infringing the victims' First Amendment rights to freedom of speech and assembly. His opinion closely followed the reasoning of Justice Bradley. Indeed, portions of it were verbatim copies of Justice Bradley's letter.[25]

However, Judge Woods made explicit certain conclusions and theories concerning federal citizenship that Justice Bradley had only implied or assumed. For example, Judge Woods stated that the Fourteenth Amendment revolutionized citizenship by making United States citizenship "independent of citizenship in a state, and citizenship in a state is [now] a result of citizenship in the United States." Judge Woods underscored this expression of the primacy of national over state citizenship by asserting that American citizens are, "without reference to state constitutions or laws, entitled to all the privileges and immunities secured by the Constitution of the United States to citizens thereof." As Justice Swayne had concluded in his examination of the Thirteenth Amendment, Judge Woods forecast that the status and rights of citizens would henceforth be fixed by national law.[26]

Judge Woods also employed natural rights theory and judicial precedent in equating the privileges and immunities secured by the Fourteenth Amendment to the natural rights of free men. "Privileges and immunities" is a legal term of art whose meaning had been explored by Supreme Court Justice Bushrod Washington in his 1823 Circuit Court opinion in *Corfield v. Coryell*. Judge Woods quoted from Justice Washington's opinion as authority for his conclusion that the "privileges and immunities" of American citizens are the natural rights of freemen. He asserted that these natural rights include Bill of Rights guarantees. Although these guarantees were regarded as mere limitations upon Congress before the Civil War, Judge Woods observed, the Fourteenth Amendment "introduced great changes" in American constitutionalism. By virtue of the Fourteenth Amendment,

> the right of freedom of speech, and the other rights enumerated in the first eight articles of amendment to the Constitution of the United States, are the privileges and immunities of citizens of the United States, ...they are secured by the Constitution, ...Congress has the power to protect them by appropriate legislation.

Federal and state appellate judges generally held that the citizenship and privileges and immunities clauses of the Fourteenth Amendment incorporated natural rights, including Bill of Rights guarantees, as nationally enforceable rights of the newly defined American citizenship; they also held that these rights were to be recognized and secured throughout the nation under national and state law. With judges interpreting the nationally enforceable rights of citizenship in such generic terms, the specific rights that were thought to be enforceable under national law were indefinite in scope. The task of specifying these rights was to be performed by the courts on a case by case basis as the United States Supreme Court ruled in 1855.[27]

One of the rights of national citizenship under the Fourteenth Amendment is the right to become a citizen of the state of one's residence. National and state citizenship were considered to be two dimensions of the same status. Judges therefore spoke of national law conferring citizenship, not national as distinguished from state citizenship. The distinction between national and state citizenship that the Supreme Court found so profoundly important in 1873 was apparently considered insignificant by lower federal court and state appellate court judges, because they virtually ignored it.[28]

However, judges did recognize that individuals enjoyed certain rights as citizens of a particular state. But, these state-conferred rights were not among the natural rights of citizenship; rather, they were regarded as special privileges that the states might choose to extend to or withhold from their respective citizens. Because they were not natural rights, citizens could not claim them by virtue of their humanity or status as freemen or national citizenship. For example, a United States citizen residing in a particular state could not demand a public school education if the state did not extend that privilege to its citizens, because a public education was not considered to be an incidental right of life, liberty, or property. Conversely, a citizen could demand the right to testify in the courts precisely because judges considered that right to be essential to life, liberty, and property. The right to testify was to be enjoyed in every state and territory because it was a nationally enforceable right of citizenship. Similarly, any other right deemed to be essential to life, liberty, or property would be an incident of these natural rights and, therefore, a right of United States citizenship that was enforceable by Congress and the federal courts throughout the entire nation. It was because the rights peculiar to state citizenship were privileges rather than the natural rights inherent in freemen that allowed states the discretion of extending them to, or withholding them from, their own citizens or citizens of other states.[29]

The rights that judges regarded as state conferred rather than natural rights of citizenship often related to important areas of social interaction and political power. In addition to public education, judges asserted that suffrage, office holding, and marriage were rights or privileges that the states could confer or withhold. Still, rulings relating to these privileges were not uniform. Although judges generally recognized a distinction between civil rights and political rights, some judges included political rights among the fundamental rights of citizenship secured by the Thirteenth and Fourteenth Amendments and the Civil Rights Act of 1866. Interracial marriage was another controversial legal issue because of state antimiscegenation laws. Marriage could be viewed as a contract secured by the first section of the Civil Rights Act and the Fourteenth Amendment as a natural right of citizenship; or, it could be regarded as a domestic institution that was completely within the authority of the states' police power. Most judges accepted the second interpretation of marriage and allowed the states the freedom to prohibit interracial marriage. Courts were virtually unanimous over the status of public education as a state-conferred privilege.[30]

Even though judges identified certain rights as state conferred, they conceded to the national government certain powers to enforce them. A citizen could not demand that his state extend to him rights that were not essential to life, liberty, or property. But, if the state did extend such rights to its citizens, then all citizens of the state could demand that the state secure those rights in a racially impartial manner. The right to racially impartial state law and administration of state law was recognized as a right of United States citizenship under the Fourteenth Amendment. The constitutional authority of the national government to secure an equality in state-conferred rights stemmed from the nature of the newly defined federal citizenship. Since citizenship in the United States also conferred citizenship in the state of one's residence, then national citizenship also conferred a right to the rights encompassed within state citizenship. However, the reader should remember that equal rights in the nineteenth century permitted segregation. This concept of equal rights still allowed the states to maintain schools on a segregated basis so long as they provided schools for blacks. If they did not, however, courts held that black children must be admitted to schools established for white children. Similarly, antimiscegenation laws were upheld so long as they applied equally to both races. The right to an equality in state-conferred rights was understood within the context of separate but equal.[31]

Despite its language, state action limitations were not attributed to the Fourteenth Amendment's scope in securing rights of national citizenship. Judges implied or explicitly employed the natural rights and nationalist legal traditions in interpreting the negative prohibitions of the Fourteenth Amendment as positive guarantees of fundamental rights as they did in interpreting the negatively worded Thirteenth Amendment as a positive guarantee of personal liberty. Indeed, these traditions were applied by judges in interpreting all three Civil War Amendments as delegations of legislative authority to protect the rights of freedom, citizenship, and political participation. The legal reasoning that transformed these negative prohibitions into positive guarantees of rights and corresponding delegations of legislative authority was succinctly expressed by the United States district judge for Delaware, Edward Bradford, in an 1873 case involving the infringement of black voting rights by local registrars of election. He said that

> it is difficult to conceive of the constitutional prohibition on the states and general government, from denying or abridging a constitutional right, without at the same time conceding the grant of the right; for such prohibition or denial appears to be an absurdity if the grant be not admitted, for otherwise there would be no subject matter for the denial or prohibition to work upon.

In a separate opinion in the same case, Supreme Court Justice William Strong, as Circuit Justice, agreed that "[t]he prohibition is itself an acknowledgement of the right," and he added that the Civil War Amendments were "manifestly intended to secure the rights guaranteed by them…. Not only were the rights given…but power was expressly conferred upon Congress to enforce the articles conferring the right." These amendments therefore contained a double authorization of legislative power: the recognition of the rights which, under the broad nationalist legal tradition, conferred legislative authority upon Congress to secure the rights, and a separate enforcement section that expressly conferred that authority upon Congress.[32]

Federal and state appellate court decisions prior to 1873 generally acknowledged that a revolution in federal citizenship had been wrought by the Thirteenth and Fourteenth Amendments and the statutes enacted to enforce them. These decisions held that the Reconstruction Amendments conferred upon the national government primary authority over the enforcement and protection of citizens' civil rights. They defined the nationally enforceable rights of American citizens as the natural rights of freemen that included Bill of Rights guarantees. Because these rights were understood in such generic terms, the specific rights of United States citizenship were indefinite in scope. Nevertheless, the Thirteenth and Fourteenth Amendments were interpreted by judges as conferring upon Congress the necessary authority to secure the rights to life, liberty, and property and the rights incidental thereto because these rights were recognized and secured by the Constitution of the United States to American citizens. Judges understood Congress's legislative authority to secure citizens' rights as virtually limitless, and they held that the civil rights laws Congress enacted to punish infringements of these rights were constitutionally authorized. Indeed, it was the virtual limitlessness of congressional authority that confronted federal judges with troublesome questions of jurisdiction as they struggled to define national judicial criminal jurisdiction without displacing state jurisdiction over ordinary crimes. This doctrinal problem of jurisdiction will be discussed in Chapter 6. Nonetheless, it is no small irony that jurisdictional problems that troubled federal judges in their efforts to secure and protect civil rights stemmed from an abundance, rather than a paucity, of national civil rights enforcement authority under the Thirteenth and Fourteenth Amendments. Elaborating the theory of national civil rights enforcement authority sufficient to secure civil rights was relatively easy. The actual judicial administration of justice proved more difficult.

2 The Freedmen's Bureau and Civil Rights Enforcement, 1866–1868

The first systematic effort of the United States government to secure the civil rights of American citizens was entrusted to the United States Army and the Bureau of Refugees, Freedmen, and Abandoned Lands, otherwise known as the Freedmen's Bureau. Established in 1865, the Bureau was the first federal social welfare agency. As Southern whites' resistance to black freedom and equality took increasingly violent and criminal forms, and as the administration of justice, criminal as well as civil, was withheld from blacks by the Southern states, the Bureau's responsibilities increased. First by Bureau circulars and general orders, and then by direct congressional legislation, Bureau agents and army personnel were authorized to secure the personal safety and civil liberty of blacks.

Historians have concluded that the efforts of Bureau agents to protect and enforce freedmen's rights were insufficient and ineffective. Explanations of this ineffectiveness have emphasized various inadequacies and weaknesses within the administration of the Bureau and the practical context in which it functioned. The analysis that follows parallels and is partially based upon these earlier studies.[1]

This analysis, however, sharply differs from others in at least one important respect. It concludes that Bureau agents possessed and exercised sufficient civil legal authority to secure the civil rights and personal safety of the freedmen of the South. Bureau ineffectiveness, therefore, was not attributable to the insufficiency of national civil rights law. Rather, that inadequacy was due primarily to the virtually insurmountable practical obstacles to civil rights enforcement that confronted Bureau agents. Bureau failure, then, was due to an insufficiency of political power and failure of will, not to an insufficiency of civil legal authority.

The political and institutional context of Bureau activities reveals the hopeless conditions that impeded, if not precluded, effective civil rights enforcement. A discussion of this context is a prerequisite to an underriding of the ways in which Bureau officers understood the scope of their legal authority to enforce civil rights, because it largely explains why they failed to secure civil rights even though they possessed sufficient legal authority to do so.

Bureau agents operated as law enforcers within a milieu that was generally characterized by a disregard for law and order. When combined with deep-seated hatred toward blacks and their white Unionist allies, this lawlessness erupted into violent assaults upon both groups. Bands of terrorists freely roamed the Southern countryside preying upon blacks and their white defenders. These "regulators" presaged the Ku Klux Klan by committing their outrages in disguises and at night, which made identification difficult, if not impossible. The bulk of these crimes were committed in the most remote areas of the Southern states, where Bureau and military authorities were unable to reach them. When crimes were within geographic reach and suspects were identified, arrests were attempted under the greatest personal danger to the arresting officers. The outlaws frequently outnumbered them and violently resisted. Arrests often required the assistance of the United States Army. Military forces, however, were numerically insufficient to render adequate assistance. The ineffectiveness of federal agencies in maintaining law and order increased disrespect for federal authority and encouraged additional lawlessness. Even the black and white Unionist victims of terrorism sometimes withheld their support from federal authorities out of fear and hopelessness. It is not surprising, therefore, that the freedmen reported so few of the crimes committed against them.[2]

Community attitudes toward the Bureau and national authority further hampered agents' efforts to protect civil rights. Law enforcement depends upon the cooperation and support of the community, and when that support is lacking, law enforcement is impossible, except through authoritarian methods. Not only did the Bureau lack community support and cooperation, but it was also faced with the defiant resistance and active opposition of the white-dominated communities in which it operated. The actions of local authorities often reflected the lawless and defiant spirit of their communities. Local peace officers usually failed to bring terrorists to justice, either because of fear for their personal safety or because of their support for the terrorists. Sheriffs refused to arrest suspects, judges refused to try defendants, and juries refused to convict them.[3]

Local judges subverted justice and assisted the lawless in other ways. They refused to admit the testimony of black witnesses that was essential to indictments and convictions. They declared the Civil Rights Act unconstitutional, or they simply ignored it. Prosecutions were sometimes brought against terrorists in the local courts to prevent federal prosecutions. However, the terrorists were not charged with the felonies they had allegedly committed. Rather, they were charged with misdemeanors carrying nominal penalties. Their cases were called for trial without adequate notice to the victims, who were prevented thereby from giving testimony and presenting witnesses against their attackers. Federal authorities effectively were prevented from bringing subsequent prosecutions against the defendants because of the legal difficulties presented by the Fifth Amendment's guarantee against double jeopardy. They were also handicapped by the political considerations of appearing arbitrary and vengeful in "persecuting" people who had already been given "justice" in the local courts. Moreover, local authorities sometimes used state law directly against federal officers by bringing charges and supporting civil suits against officers who attempted to make arrests. Arresting officers found themselves charged with false arrest, assault, assault with intent to kill, and other crimes because of the force they were sometimes required to use in making arrests. Local authorities virtually legitimated lawlessness by participating in it and insulating it from punishment in federal tribunals.[4]

State legislatures also contributed to the defiance of federal authority. They appropriated funds to pay the legal expenses of local judges who were prosecuted in federal courts for violations of the Civil Rights Act. Most of the prosecutions were brought against these judges for refusing to admit the testimony of blacks in cases involving whites. However, judges were also prosecuted for imposing unequal punishments upon black defendants. Lawmakers sometimes legislated to impede local judges who were conscientious in securing the rights of blacks. The Maryland legislature, for example, went so far as to curtail the power of the Baltimore Criminal Court because Judge Hugh Lennox Bond effectively protected the civil rights of black apprentices from their former masters.[5]

With the freedmen and white Unionists forced to seek refuge under national authority, civil rights violators found refuge under state authority. In this clash of national authority and civil rights protection with states' rights and white supremacy, the latter held every advantage. The obstacles to effective civil rights enforcement appeared to be so insurmountable that some Bureau agents despaired of achieving even the semblance of civil rights protection. General W. P. Carlin, Bureau commander in Tennessee, expressed the view of many other agents when he informed General O. O. Howard, commissioner of the Freedmen's Bureau, that only the exercise of "arbitrary power" could protect the freedmen. Knowing that such power was not forthcoming, many agents bowed to what they believed was inevitable and tried to minimize or eliminate confrontations with local authorities and their communities by acceding to the wishes of the dominant white conservatives and landholders at the expense of the freedmen.

Indeed, Bureau agents were often recruited from local magistrates who shared interests and prejudices in common with the white supremacists. Political, economic, and social self-interests, in addition to other practical obstacles to civil rights protection, reinforced racism and prompted many Bureau agents to cater to locally dominant white racists rather than to serve the needs of blacks.[6]

Administration politics presented additional obstacles to effective civil rights enforcement. The military character of the Bureau's legal authority and institutional structure helps to explain how the president impeded its effectiveness. The Freedmen's Bureau and the United States Army derived their authority to secure civil rights primarily from the war powers and the Freedmen's Bureau Act of July 1866. They were also ordered to enforce the Civil Rights Act of 1866, but under military authority. To implement these provisions, agents were instructed to arrest persons who were charged with offenses against citizens "in cases where the civil authorities have failed, neglected, or are unable to arrest and bring such parties to trial, . . ." and to hold them for trial. Bureau agents were to refer cases involving blacks either to Bureau courts, military tribunals, or federal civil courts, depending upon the seriousness of the crime, when blacks were unable to receive justice in the local courts of the state. When agents were confident that the local courts were willing to dispense impartial justice, they were to return the administration of justice to them. In this event, agents were to continue to protect the interests of the freedmen in the local courts by representing them as counsel.[7]

Bureau agents functioned without the support of their president, Andrew Johnson. Indeed, President Johnson undermined the jurisdiction and authority of the military tribunals and Bureau courts with his peace proclamations of 1866. Since these courts functioned under the war powers, the president rendered doubtful the constitutionality of military and Bureau jurisdiction over civilian criminal and civil cases when he proclaimed that peace was established, the rebellion was ended, and the rebellious states were restored to the Union. Furthermore, President Johnson stridently expressed his opposition to the trial of civilians by military tribunals and ordered Bureau officers to return the administration of justice to local authorities as quickly as possible.[8]

The Supreme Court of the United States added to the confusion about Bureau legal authority in November 1866 when it announced its decision in the *Milligan* case. This decision prohibited the trial of civilians by military tribunals in areas where civil government was functioning. Although General Howard believed that the Supreme Court justices did not intend this ruling to apply to the operations of Bureau courts in the South, President Johnson used the ruling as justification for ordering the cessation of agents' efforts to secure equal justice in those tribunals even when local courts failed to do so. General Howard sought to bring a test case before the Supreme Court to settle the issue of Bureau court jurisdiction, but President Johnson deterred him by ordering military personnel to stop trying civilians and to free prisoners. Because the use of military institutions to dispose of civilian cases was antithetical to American civil liberties sensibilities and, apparently, to a ruling of the Supreme Court, the president's opposition to civil rights enforcement took on an air of legitimacy. Federal officers who sought to use the military and Bureau courts to enforce civil rights were vulnerable to charges of despotic militarism as well as to presidential censure. With the president openly opposed to and actively impeding the Bureau's and the military's efforts to protect the rights of the freedmen, the effectiveness of these agencies to protect blacks' civil rights was never fully realized.[9]

State legislatures added to the pressures to restore local civil government. Legislatures, with varying alacrity, repealed many of the racially discriminatory statutes. These statutes had provided the best legal and political evidence that blacks could not receive equal justice in state courts and that the active participation of Bureau tribunals in the administration of justice was required to protect blacks. The repeal of these statutes created the appearance that Southern statutes were providing equal justice in form, while the states continued to deny equal justice in substance. The enactment of impartial statutes gave the harried and unsympathetic Bureau and military officials a justification for returning jurisdiction to local civil authorities. At the same time, the statutes compounded the difficulties confronting conscientious federal officials who sought to go beyond form and secure the substance of justice for the freedmen. Although the mere existence of impartial laws did not guarantee impartial justice, so long as they did exist, Bureau agents were hard put to prove injustice in a court of law and in the court of public opinion, especially when such efforts were opposed by President Johnson. With the legal authority of Bureau courts and military tribunals over civilians in serious doubt because of their military character, with the federal courts practicably inaccessible, with administration pressures pushing toward a full restoration of local civil authority, Bureau agents were compelled to use local courts to secure justice for the freedmen however imperfect that justice proved to be.[10]

The repeal of discriminatory statutes also created a false optimism among Bureau agents regarding the evolution of racial harmony in the South. Burdened by a self-defeating and undesirable mission, some officers seized upon the enactment of impartial laws as evidence of a growing disposition of Southern whites to recognize and respect the rights of blacks. Finding other signs of greater racial harmony that enabled them to equate impartial laws with impartial justice, they began to make optimistic reports about relations between blacks and whites in the South. Some officials reported that the higher state courts and courts located in larger cities and near military posts were already dispensing impartial justice. They also observed that the quality of justice varied within states according to the proclivities of individual magistrates. In their opinion, the disposition of individual judges more than the content of the law determined the quality of justice dispensed to blacks. In light of the evidence they saw of the increasing legal and judicial recognition of freedmen's rights, many Bureau agents concluded that, because of their efforts, Southerners were beginning to accept and respect the rights and safety of the freedmen.[11]

However, just as the quality of local justice meted out to blacks varied, Bureau agents' efforts to secure justice to blacks were uneven. Confusion in the Freedmen's Bureau's policies also caused inconsistency in the efforts of agents to secure equal justice. The president and the commissioner disagreed over the substance of these policies. General Howard wanted Bureau agents and tribunals to continue to exercise unsparingly federal authority to enforce freedmen's civil rights. However, President Johnson opposed Howard's policy objectives and insisted that Bureau tribunals lacked authority over civilians. The president also considered the Bureau's civil rights activities to be unnecessary and demanded the expeditious restoration of local government. General Howard capitulated to his commander-in-chief, and he reluctantly encouraged his assistant commissioners to restore local civil authority even though this policy left the freedmen unable to protect their rights. Pressured by the president, General Howard instructed agents to avoid actions that might unnecessarily arouse opposition to the national government and the Bureau and to disband Bureau courts if state agencies indicated they would recognize freedmen's rights. General Howard specified that local government was to be restored when state legislatures replaced racially discriminatory statutes with impartial ones. The repeal of the black codes, the legislative recognition of freedmen's rights, and the enforcement of equal rights in some of the state courts gave many agents an irresistible rationalization and justification for the restoration of local civil authority.[12]

However, General Howard's instructions also gave each agent the discretion of assessing the quality of justice available to the freedmen in the local courts. Field officers, therefore, possessed the authority to restore local government or to continue using federal military and, where United States district courts were available, federal civil tribunals to try cases involving the freedmen. Some officers followed the letter of Bureau policy and restored civil authority as soon as state legislatures enacted impartial laws. Others followed the spirit of Bureau policy and continued to exercise military authority because citizens could not receive justice in local courts despite the impartial laws. For the same reason, others reasserted military jurisdiction after they had restored local civil authority. These circumstances suggest that agents who refused to restore local government despite these inducements to do so were either unusually vindictive or unusually committed to securing freedmen's rights.[13]

The ability of federal officers to remove cases to the federal courts was severely hindered by administration policy and political pressures to restore local authority and end federal interference in local affairs rather than by inadequate legal authority. General Howard identified the difficulty when he complained that federal courts could not assert their jurisdiction under the Civil Rights Act over state prosecutions unless the state court denied some right secured by the act. He observed that "[i]t is difficult to prove actual 'deprivation' of justice in such manner as to 'remove the cause' to the U.S. District or Circuit Court." Even federal judges who wanted to secure justice for the freedmen, he continued, "can do nothing under the Civil Rights Act until the local Courts shall have been tested."[14]

General Howard's lament appears to support scholars who argue that the act's restricted application to discriminatory state action hampered federal efforts to secure civil rights under the Civil Rights Act of 1866. Further investigation and analysis suggests that such a conclusion is not supported. First, the cases to which General Howard refers were initiated by local authorities. They necessarily involved state actions brought against private citizens in the state courts. Section 3 of the Civil Rights Act authorizes the removal of a state court trial to a federal court if the state court failed to enforce, or if it infringed, the rights of one of the parties. Given the hostile political climate, it is understandable that a federal judge would require a petitioner to show that he could not enforce his rights in the state court before he would authorize the defendant to remove his case to the federal court. But this is a problem of judicial administration rather than one of jurisdiction. Moreover, the scope of the entire Civil Rights Act of 1866 should not be measured by this section of the act that authorizes the removal of state trials to the federal courts. Federal jurisdiction over these cases is distinct from federal jurisdiction over cases *initiated* by federal authorities in the federal courts under federal law.[15]

A search of General Howard's correspondence failed to yield any letters from judges who felt legally compelled to force citizens to exhaust state remedies before federal courts could assume jurisdiction under the removal section of the

Civil Rights Act of 1866. Certainly, General Howard had no statutory basis for his comment concerning the need to test the state courts before the federal courts could act. The Civil Rights Act imposes no such limitation. In fact, the statute was interpreted as authorizing the interruption of a state trial on the motion of the defendant who claimed that he could not enforce his rights in the state court. The judge advocate general of the army, Joseph Holt, informed General Howard of this interpretation in an official opinion in which Holt declared that a state judge who refused to allow such a case to be removed to a federal court was subject to federal prosecution. Clearly, a defendant was not required to exhaust state remedies or to test the other state courts before his case could be removed to a federal court. Significantly, Holt's interpretation of the Civil Rights Act was in reference to a case involving a *white person* who claimed that he could not receive a fair trial in the state court because of *political* prejudice.[16]

Federal prosecutions could also be initiated without first testing the local courts. General Jeff Davis, for example, reached an agreement with the United States district judge for Kentucky, Bland Ballard, under which Davis was to arrest all persons who mistreated or committed outrages against blacks in Kentucky and to turn them over to the federal court for prosecution. Judge Ballard and General Davis anticipated that state authorities would fail to enforce state law to punish crimes committed against blacks and that the state courts would refuse to admit the testimony of blacks. Out of this arrangement emerged the first reported federal case to uphold the constitutionality of the Civil Rights Act and of the federal prosecutions of white citizens for crimes against black citizens. Throughout the Southern states federal authorities who attempted to enforce the Civil Rights Act typically did not wait for the state courts to act, nor did they exhaust the state courts before bringing cases into the federal courts and other federal tribunals. On the contrary, they took immediate action. Not only were the local courts not tested, they were not even tried.[17]

The only letters that tended to support General Howard's complaint concerning the difficulty of removing state cases to the federal courts were dated after he made his complaint to Secretary Stanton. These letters are noteworthy because they are unique. Major William L. Vanderlip reported from Maryland in March 1867 that the Civil Rights Act failed to protect blacks from assaults and other outrages "by [not] providing for the punishment of the White man who commits outrages." Nor did the act protect freedmen from white employers who refused to pay them, he complained. The major did observe that the act "applied a remedy in such cases," but he added that the remedy "seems to be beyond the reach of the freedman." A suit in the state court was always decided against the freedman, but he could not bring his case into the federal court "without such expense as he is unable to meet." In civil cases, then, the expense of litigation rather than the inadequacy of legal authority prevented blacks from securing remedies offered under the Civil Rights Act.[18]

Major Vanderlip also suggested that criminal cases could be better handled "if the Civil Rights Act conferred on the District Courts *concurrent jurisdiction* with the State Courts over persons accused of outraging free people." Freedmen then could bring their cases into the federal court "in the first instance." He evidently was not aware of Bureau activities in Kentucky, nor did he seem to understand the statute. The Civil Rights Act did confer expressly at least concurrent jurisdiction, as Justice Swayne ruled in *United States v. Rhodes,* especially in a state such as Maryland where state statutes excluded the testimony of blacks in state courts. Even when the state legislature repealed the discriminatory statutes, local ordinances continued to discriminate. Consequently, the Civil Rights Act would have authorized the federal courts to assume primary jurisdiction in these cases even under a state action interpretation of the act that limited its application to states that retained discriminatory state statutes.[19]

Colonel James V. Bamford also protested that he lacked adequate authority to enforce civil rights in North Carolina. He reported that the military could not make arrests "until the entire routine of *civil remedies* have been exhausted in vain." (Emphasis added.) Because the federal courts were not established in North Carolina until June 1867, some three months after his letter was written, his remark was directed at his inability to exercise military jurisdiction in those cases, not to the inadequacy of federal civil authority. The Freedmen's Bureau courts and military tribunals had assumed jurisdiction over cases where blacks failed to receive justice in the local courts, even after discriminatory statutes were repealed by the North Carolina legislature in July 1866. Colonel Bamford's problem was created by President Johnson's proclamation ordering the restoration of civil authority when discriminatory state statutes were replaced by nondiscriminatory laws. Consequently, the colonel's comments did not relate to federal civil authority to protect civil rights; rather, they referred to inadequate military jurisdiction under the president's policy of reconstruction.[20]

General Howard did receive one letter that might have prompted the complaint he made to Secretary Stanton. However, the letter related to military prosecutions of Memphis police officers growing out of the Memphis Riots of 1866. In this letter, General Clinton B. Fisk vaguely referred to opinions of federal law enforcement officers that the Civil Rights Act was of no use in this situation. The general indicated, however, that federal prosecutions were not brought against the rioters because of political considerations rather than inadequacies in the provisions of the Civil Rights Act. Federal prosecutions against public officials, as well as private citizens, were authorized by Tennessee Bureau officers in 1867. Further, the assistant commissioner for Tennessee in 1867, General W. P. Carlin, authorized the removal of cases to federal courts when the local courts failed to dispense impartial justice. Both of these facts support the conclusion that political considerations and practical difficulties were the primary reasons that federal prosecutions were not brought against the Memphis rioters in 1866.[21]

Evidence from other states also supports the conclusion that political considerations rather than the inadequacy of legal authority prevented more effective civil rights enforcement by the Freedmen's Bureau and the military. General Charles Griffin reported from Texas that the state's statutes were discriminatory, oppressive, and tyrannical in their effect and in their enforcement, but they did not discriminate on their face. Therefore, he concluded: "I have not felt at liberty to disregard them." That the general's remark was directed to constraints of policy rather than to limitations of legal authority is evidenced by the actions of Bureau agents in Texas who continued to assume jurisdiction in cases where individuals were unable to receive justice in the local courts. Furthermore, the United States attorney in Texas did not find racially impartial state statutes to be an obstacle to enforcing civil rights under the Civil Rights Act in the federal courts. General Griffin's comment more likely expressed his reluctance to clash with local authorities. Because of the administration's demand for the restoration of, and cooperation with, local authorities, Bureau agents acted circumspectly even when state laws, such as the black codes, discriminated on their face. Both President Johnson's insistence upon the rapid restoration of local government and the Bureau's consequent policy of cooperation with local authorities in looking after freedmen's interests within local institutions help to explain why more civil rights cases were not brought into federal military tribunals and district courts.[22]

Agents' decisions to prosecute actions under the Civil Rights Act do not appear to have been based on the presence or absence of discriminatory state action. Federal officers failed to prosecute when discriminatory state action was present; they brought prosecutions when discriminatory state action was not present.

This evidence suggests the need for an alternative explanation of General Howard's lament. If General Howard's complaint was not an expression of the constitutional and legal inadequacy of the removal power under the Civil Rights Act of 1866, it was probably directed at the political and practical difficulties encountered by federal legal officers in transferring the jurisdiction and the functions of the state courts to the federal courts. The political upheaval must have been great at both the local and national levels. Both a dislike of the racial and political interests served by federal courts and a desire to preserve local autonomy aroused local opposition to federal involvement in the administration of justice. Moreover, federal efforts to secure civil rights undermined cooperative relationships Bureau agents had been directed to establish with local authorities. At the national level, the federal enforcement of civil rights contravened the policies and political interests of the Johnson administration. These circumstances explain why federal judges who might have wanted to secure justice for the freedmen were constrained to wait until the local courts were tested before asserting their jurisdiction even if they felt no legal or constitutional restrictions on their authority to do so.

Although they often felt impeded by Bureau policy, Bureau agents interpreted their legal authority under the Civil Rights Act as sufficient to secure freedmen's rights. One of the primary objectives of the Bureau was to achieve a uniform and impartial administration of justice in the state courts. Impartial laws were essential to this objective, but more important was the impartial administration of the laws by local officials. To achieve this goal, Bureau officers arrested and prosecuted judges and her state officers who refused or neglected "to perform any official act required by law, whereby due and rightful protection to person and property shall have been denied." State judges were prosecuted for declaring the Civil Rights Act unconstitutional, for enforcing discriminatory state laws, for imposing unequal punishments upon blacks, and for refusing to admit the testimony of blacks in their courts whether their refusal was authorized by, or was in violation of, state law. Other state officials were prosecuted for failing to make arrests on complaints filed by blacks and unpopular whites, for infringing the rights of blacks to carry firearms and to be protected against unreasonable searches and seizures, for participating in outrages committed against blacks, and for prosecuting white Unionists on trumped-up charges for political reasons. Local officials were prosecuted under the Civil Rights Act for generally victimizing blacks and white Unionists and for failing to provide them with the equal protection of the law and equal justice under law. Since Bureau agents understood the Civil Rights Act as primarily intended to secure the civil rights of citizens, they brought charges against local officers who infringed such rights of citizenship as the rights to bear arms, to be free from unreasonable searches and seizures, to testify in the courts, and to the full and equal benefit of the laws for the protection of person and property. And, agents brought charges against local officials whether the victim was black or white.[23]

Bureau agents did not stop at prosecuting state officials who violated civil rights in their official capacities. They also prosecuted private individuals. Where the state law enforcement machinery failed to mete out justice, Bureau agents and tribunals assumed primary jurisdiction and law enforcement functions such as investigating alleged crime, making arrests, trying and, upon conviction, sentencing criminals. Crimes that were prosecuted by Bureau agents ranged from murder, manslaughter, and assault to theft and involuntary servitude. Federal authorities also assumed primary jurisdiction in civil cases under similar circumstances. Cases were tried in Bureau courts or military tribunals, or, when they were available, cases were turned over to United States commissioners and the United States district courts. Where federal courts were unavailable and Bureau officers felt that Bureau courts and military tribunals were unauthorized to try civilians, they held the prisoners until a local court was prepared to try them. Bureau officers felt that they were authorized to take these actions whether the laws of the state discriminated or were impartial. Their criterion was the necessity for federal action created by the failure of the local authorities to bring offenders to justice. When the impartial administration of justice could not be achieved under local law, federal officers supplanted the local authorities and performed this governmental function.[24]

Federal officers also assumed jurisdiction in state prosecutions of blacks and whites who could not receive a fair trial in the local courts. In these cases, the exercise of federal jurisdiction was more difficult because the state judge might refuse to allow the case to be removed to a federal court. Furthermore, to justify the removal of a state prosecution to a federal court that would then sit as the criminal court of primary jurisdiction, the defendant had to show that he could not enforce some right or receive impartial justice in the state court. Or, if the trial had been completed and the defendant had been convicted, he had to show that he had not received a fair trial. Such a showing was very difficult in the absence of some obvious evidence, such as a discriminatory law or a determination of the jury that was grossly contrary to the evidence presented in the trial. Here again, the personal proclivities of Bureau agents were important. Some of them asserted federal jurisdiction when merely aware of local prejudice and its impediment to a fair trial. Others were loathe to interfere with the local courts and were content to settle for as fair a trial as was possible, even if they believed the trial was unfair.[25]

Although Bureau officers were hampered by the inadequacy of military jurisdiction over civilian crimes and by the form and rules of judicial procedure, they rarely complained of inadequate constitutional authority under the Civil Rights Act. A few cases will illustrate this point and the confluence of political, policy, and legal factors in hampering the power of the federal government to enforce civil rights.

Early in 1867, President Johnson reported to Congress three violations of the Civil Rights Act of 1866. He made this report pursuant to a unanimously adopted Senate resolution that requested that the president report to the Senate all violations of the Civil Rights Act that came to his knowledge. He was also instructed to report the actions he had taken to enforce the law and to punish the offenders. This unusual act of bipartisan cooperation suggests that both Democrats and Republicans believed that their political self-interests could be furthered thereby.[26]

Not surprisingly, only Secretary of War Edwin M. Stanton, the sole member of President Johnson's cabinet who supported civil rights enforcement, reported violations of the Civil Rights Act despite the fact that Attorney General Henry Stanbery was well aware of others. According to the Secretary of the Navy, Gideon Welles, Generals Grant and Howard submitted to Secretary Stanton a report listing 440 violations. The conservative Welles considered these reported violations "an omnigatherum of newspaper gossip, rumors of negro murders, neighborhood strifes and troubles…vague, indefinite party scandal which General Howard and his agents had picked up…." He recorded that some cabinet members were surprised by the report, but they rejected it as irrelevant. Secretary of the Interior, Orville Browning, identified the partisan potential of the report when he accused General Howard and his agents, whom he called "radical partizans," of compiling exaggerations as "a mean, malicious" attempt to force the president

> to send out to the country, endorsed by him as facts, these prejudiced and in many instances false, and in almost all exaggerated statements, or place himself, by refusing to send them to Congress, in a position where they could falsifly [sic] but plausibly charge him with the suppression of facts.

His own partisan sensitivities prompted the president to pare down the number of violations to three. The message President Johnson wished to convey in reporting so few civil rights violations was that local authorities in the South were adequately securing freedmen's rights and that the federal presence there was unnecessary.[27]

All three cases reported by the president represented attempts by federal officers to enforce the personal rights of United States citizens. Two of the three cases involved federal review of state courts, and the other involved the intervention of federal authority into the state's pretrial law enforcement process.

They are useful, therefore, as case studies showing the manner in which federal officers interpreted the Civil Rights Act of 1866 shortly after it was enacted.

The first case involved the vagrancy conviction in Georgia of William Fincher, a freedman who was then serving as vice president of the Pike County Equal Rights Association. The United States attorney at Savannah, Henry S. Fitch, reported to Attorney General Stanbery that Fincher had been unjustly convicted by a biased jury, presumably because of his political activism in furthering the rights of blacks and because of his suspected adultery. However, Fitch could find no remedy under state law because Fincher's attorney, Freedmen's Bureau agent W. T. C. Brannon, had failed to file a bill of exceptions within the prescribed time limit of thirty days. Fitch could not remove Fincher's case to a federal court under the Civil Rights Act of 1866 because he could not show that Fincher had not received impartial justice in the local court. He reported that "there is nothing in Fincher's case, according to the present laws of Georgia, rendering it an exception either in the mode of procedure or the punishment inflicted." If the evidence demonstrated that Fincher was guilty as charged and the punishment imposed was prescribed by law, how could Fitch argue that Fincher was denied any rights or that he suffered prejudicial treatment in the state court, particularly since his trial lawyer had not alleged any violations of Fincher's rights during the trial?[28]

Fitch proposed an alternative legal strategy to get Fincher's case into the federal court. He suggested challenging the constitutionality of the Georgia vagrancy statute as a violation of the Thirteenth Amendment and the Civil Rights Act of 1866. This strategy was first recommended to Fitch by United States District Judge John Erskine who described the vagrancy law as "barbarous," "cruel and illegal, and a palpable renewal of human slavery in its most revolting and degrading form." Although Fitch expressed a willingness to challenge the Georgia statute, he declined to do so without specific instructions from the president or the attorney general. Those instructions were never sent.[29]

Fincher's case shows the unwillingness of the federal attorney to use federal law to remedy the injustice a freedman apparently had suffered. Politics seem to explain Fitch's reluctance to use federal law to correct a state injustice, since this action would have furthered the interests of the Republican Party. Fitch was a conservative supporter of President Johnson who actually used the powers of his office to prosecute local Radical Republican officeholders for political reasons. He had also embarrassed General Howard by informing the administration of the general's desire to get a test case before the United States Supreme Court to legitimate the powers of Bureau courts in the South contrary to the president's policy. Fitch was one of the very few federal legal officers who discouraged Bureau agents from using the Civil Rights Act to punish crimes against blacks because, he said, the act would not sustain such legal action. This could explain why Fincher's defense counsel failed to remove the case to a federal court for trial on the grounds that Fincher could not receive impartial justice in the Pike County Court. Given Fitch's politics, his refusal to try cases in the federal courts appears to be the result of political machinations more than the inadequacy of the Civil Rights Act.[30]

In contrast to the Fincher case, the Freedmen's Bureau and military in Texas found no impediments to assuming jurisdiction in the case of Dick Perkins. Perkins was a former slave living near Courtney, Grimes County, Texas. He had been shot by his former master in a fight over whether he was to return to his master's employ. Perkins, who also had a gun, shot at his attacker in self-defense after he had been wounded. The local sheriff subsequently arrested Perkins without a warrant and confined him in irons in the Anderson, Grimes County jail for six weeks without medical attention. Perkins eventually escaped with the help of a United States soldier who also had been confined in the jail, and he was taken to the Freedmen's Bureau hospital in Houston. While Perkins was recuperating in the hospital, the city marshal arrested him with the intention of placing him in the custody of his former master, the man who had shot him. However, the subassistant commissioner, Colonel J. C. DeGress, removed Perkins from the custody of the city marshal and held him for trial.

Colonel DeGress believed he had authority to hold Perkins and to remove his case for trial in the United States District Court under the Civil Rights Act. The colonel believed that the defendant would not receive impartial justice or the protection of the laws in the county court. The fact that the local authorities had imprisoned Perkins without medical attention and had intended to return him to the custody of his assailant supported this conclusion. Colonel DeGress did not doubt that the federal court had jurisdiction in this case, and the United States attorney agreed.[31]

The third reported violation of the Civil Rights Act concerned the murder of a freedman, one William Medley, by a prominent white physician of Rockbridge County, Virginia, Dr. James L. Watson. Dr. Watson apparently acted because he believed that Medley had insulted his wife and daughter. Confessing that he had shot Medley, Dr. Watson turned himself over to the local authorities. However, the Lexington Examining Court, by a 3 to 2 margin, refused to indict him. According to General J. M. Schofield, the assistant commissioner of the Freedmen's Bureau in Virginia, the evidence presented to the examining court was sufficient for an indictment for murder, and the general believed that Dr. Watson should have been held over for trial. He also believed that the failure to try Dr. Watson for murder would encourage whites to feel immune from prosecution, which would gravely threaten the personal safety of blacks in the state. The danger and injustice to which blacks in Virginia were already subjected, General Schofield reported, were "not so much on account of any inequality in the laws, nor yet from undue severity of the courts, but from individual violence and wrong." The Medley murder, therefore, was an assault upon the rights and personal security of all blacks living in Virginia. Consequently, General Schofield ordered the arrest of Dr. Watson for trial by a military commission. He claimed authority to try a civilian for murder under section 14 of the Freedmen's Bureau Act of 1866 and General Order No. 44, which was issued to enforce the Civil Rights Act of 1866.[32]

Dr. Watson was arrested on December 4, 1866, and was brought to Richmond to stand trial for the murder of William Medley. General Schofield chose to try Dr. Watson by military commission instead of in the federal district court because he wanted to test the authority of military commissions to try crimes involving blacks when local authorities failed to bring the defendants to justice. The general felt a test case was needed because of the confusion caused by the president's peace proclamations issued earlier that year. General Howard was delighted with this opportunity to clarify the scope of military authority in the area of civil rights enforcement. However, President Johnson intervened and dissolved the military tribunal. He justified his action by citing the opinion of Attorney General Stanbery that the Supreme Court's *Milligan* decision prevented the trial of civilians by military tribunals where the civil government was functioning. Dr. Watson was released, and the case to test the authority of military tribunals to try civilians in the South dissolved. The American repugnance toward trying civilians in military tribunals conveniently provided the president with a plausible, if not wholly justifiable, excuse for impeding civil rights enforcement by undermining military authority.[33]

Far from complaining of inadequate constitutional authority under the Civil Rights Act, Bureau officers expressed the belief that blacks would enjoy full security in their civil rights if the act were enforced as it was intended. Indeed, federal officers reported that, where the Civil Rights Act was enforced, blacks were treated much more equitably in the local courts and by private citizens. General Howard himself suggested that constitutional authority was adequate to secure civil rights if only it could be used. The ineffectiveness of the Freedmen's Bureau and the military in protecting civil rights was not the result of inadequate civil legal authority to enforce civil rights. Rather, it was the result of a number of factors including: the confusion over military authority and policy caused by conflicting orders issued by the president and the commissioner of the Freedmen's Bureau; political pressures to restore local authority as soon as possible; the insufficient numbers of federal legal officers, troops, and courts; the immense distances that had to be covered; the enormous number of crimes that had to be prosecuted; the inefficiency of the case method of dispensing justice; the personal opposition of many of the Bureau agents to protecting civil rights; the ubiquitous resistance of Southern whites to federal law; and the deeply felt Southern defiance of, and hatred for, federal authority.[34]

The efforts of the military and the Freedmen's Bureau to secure civil rights were as short lived as they were circumscribed. The use of Freedmen's Bureau tribunals rapidly declined through 1867, and they ceased to function by the end of 1868 when statutory authority for most Bureau activities expired. The process of restoring the former Confederate states to the Union was completed in most of those states by 1868, and in all of them by 1870. With the restoration of civil government, civil and criminal judicial process became the sole means of redressing civil rights violations.

| 3 | The Politics of Civil Rights Enforcement in the Federal Courts, 1866–1873 |

G iven the expansive definitions of federal power they had formulated, the federal courts were relatively inactive in enforcing the Civil Rights Act of 1866 during the last years of the 1860s. Since the conditions for which the Civil Rights Act was enacted existed in many parts of the former Confederacy, opportunities abounded in the South for the federal courts to enforce civil rights. In some places, statutes that discriminated against blacks were enforced by local judges in defiance of the Civil Rights Act. In other areas, statutes were impartial on their face, but local judges and juries acted in such a prejudicial manner that blacks and unpopular whites could not receive justice. Although the freedmen and white Unionists could not expect to receive justice or judicial enforcement of their civil rights in state courts, relatively little was done to bring their cases into the federal courts[1]

Several reasons explain the relative inactivity of the federal judiciary in protecting civil rights in the years immediately following the Civil War. Perhaps the most important reason was the Johnson administration's opposition to federal enforcement of civil rights. Racism, although important, was not the sole factor in the administration's aversion to the federal government's involvement in the protection of civil rights. The administration's political philosophy and political affiliations were equally decisive. Its commitment to states' rights and a Democratic Conservative political coalition rendered the federal enforcement of the civil rights of Southern blacks and Republicans at the expense of the local authority of Southern Democrats antithetical to its political interests and political values. These values and interests reinforced racial antagonisms.[2]

The Johnson administration's opposition to federal enforcement of civil rights must have discouraged even those federal officers who took seriously their responsibility for executing the congressional mandate to secure civil rights. The posture taken by the attorney general in his correspondence with United States attorneys and United States marshals inhibited their active involvement in civil rights issues. Cautious legal officers who requested instructions from the attorney general concerning civil rights enforcement policy received no clarification. The attorney general consistently refused to instruct subordinate legal officers as to their responsibilities under the Civil Rights Act or to answer their questions concerning the meaning and scope of federal civil rights enforcement authority, "believing that to be entirely a judicial question." Federal officers were left to act on their own, but, in light of the president's known opposition to civil rights enforcement, politics and self-interest were powerful inducements toward inaction.[3]

The administration's opposition to the exercise of national power and the enforcement of national laws extended beyond the Civil Rights Act. The attorney general refused to give instructions and interpretations of federal laws generally. He withheld his encouragement and support, as well as his cooperation, from federal legal officers. The president's opposition to federal law enforcement was more than passive. He appointed legal officers who shared his opposition to national authority and nullified the efforts of conscientious legal officers by pardoning prisoners who had been convicted of violating federal laws. The United States district judge for Kentucky, Bland Ballard, expressed the frustration produced by such policies when he complained that under President Johnson many

> [r]evenue officers were either corrupt or had no sympathy with the Government, and the veriest criminals had only to ask pardon to obtain it. I sometimes feel that all my labors were vain, that it was no use to hold court at all. I was often engaged a week or more in the trial of some swindler who was pardoned in less than a week from the conviction and sentence.[4]

The judicial business of the federal courts mushroomed after the Civil War. This uncontrolled increase in federal case loads added to the pressures to curtail national law enforcement. Legal and judicial officers complained that the business of the attorney general's office and the federal courts had expanded beyond the capacities of these agencies. They attributed increases in the federal legal and judicial work load to the accretion of powers, jurisdiction, and functions of the national government during the Civil War era. United States District Judge Robert A. Hill of Mississippi, for example, observed that "the consequences of the War have greatly increased the business in the U.S. docket." Further, he complained that the disorganization of the state courts induced all litigants who could to transfer their cases into the federal courts. Inadequate staffing forced the attorney general to hire special counsel to assist United States attorneys in the federal courts. The creation of the Department of Justice in 1870 was an attempt to meet the workload crisis and to eliminate the need to hire special counsel. However, appropriations to finance the operations of legal officers and the courts did not match the expanding workload. The creation of the Department of Justice in 1870 and the United States circuit courts in 1869 suggests that congressional Republicans were aware of the need to improve the administration of federal law enforcement. But inadequate financing of these operations shows that Republicans in Congress were reluctant nationalizers of the federal courts and were unwilling to dispense completely with traditional arrangements to achieve a fuller implementation of their policies. The attorney general thus struggled with penurious Congresses to increase appropriations to enable the federal courts to exercise the expanded authority Congress conferred on them while he exerted pressure upon legal and judicial officers to curtail expenses.[5]

Other kinds of practical difficulties impeded the enforcement of civil rights. Judge Hill reported that he was aware of many violations of the Civil Rights Act, but only a very few cases had been brought before the United States grand jury. He explained that the violations occurred in areas of the state that were too remote from the places in which he held court to bring witnesses to testify. The physical remoteness of federal courts meant that parties had to travel long distances requiring extended absences from home and work. The expense and inconvenience were prohibitive, especially to indigent blacks. Furthermore, federal courts were slowly reestablished after the Civil War in many areas, or, if established, they were severely handicapped by the absence of judges, United States attorneys, marshals, and deputy marshals. Where the courts were functioning, they met infrequently and for intervals that were too brief to provide the kind of continual availability required of courts of primary jurisdiction.[6]

The implementation of federal law has been difficult throughout our history. During the 1960s, for example, Democratic administrations were committed to civil rights enforcement; they enjoyed substantial budgets and relatively abundant federal law enforcement officers. Yet they were unable to achieve more than a mediocre record of civil rights enforcement. Federal officers in the 1860s enjoyed none of these advantages. Moreover, local resistance to federal enforcement of civil rights was even more virulent in the 1860s than in the 1960s. Local opposition complemented the policies and political interests of Andrew Johnson's administration. Considerations of personal safety and political self-interest precluded federal legal officers from seizing the initiative to enforce the Civil Rights Act specifically and prompted them to be less than energetic in asserting federal authority generally. It was safer to do nothing than to risk disapproval from an administration that was hostile to the exercise of national power to secure the civil rights of blacks at the expense of state prerogatives and white supremacy. The posture of the president, combined with the practical obstacles encountered in civil rights enforcement, prevented even well-intentioned federal judicial officers from offering effective protection. At the same time, these factors created an aura of legitimacy around the attitudes and inactivity of federal officials who were unsympathetic or opposed to civil rights enforcement. It is not surprising that so little effort was exerted by federal legal officers to enforce civil rights during the 1860s.[7]

The efforts of federal legal officers in Kentucky are striking exceptions to the lethargic civil rights enforcement under the Johnson administration. The Civil Rights Act was enforced more vigorously there than in any other state. The reason lies largely in the moral and political commitments of the federal legal officers in the state. The United States attorney was Benjamin H. Bristow, a native Kentuckian who opposed secession and strongly supported the Union cause during the Civil War. He had been appointed to his position by an old family friend, James Speed, Lincoln's attorney general. After he resigned as attorney general, Speed returned to his native state and assisted Bristow in civil rights cases in the federal courts and served as legal advisor and legal counsel for the Freedmen's Bureau in Kentucky. Bristow's political circle included the federal district judge, Bland Ballard, and the federal legal officers in Kentucky who, as Republicans, were committed to the enforcement of the civil rights of blacks.[8]

But, even here, the debilitating influence of the Johnson administration was evident. The enforcement of civil rights was cautious, halting, and inadequate under Attorney General Stanbery. When the Civil Rights Act was enacted by Congress, United States Attorney Bristow instructed federal officers to assume primary criminal jurisdiction only after blacks were denied justice in the state courts. When the constitutionality of the Civil Rights Act was challenged in the courts, Bristow halted prosecutions and refused to accept additional ones. However, when the law's constitutionality was upheld by the United States Circuit Court for Kentucky in 1867, Bristow's enforcement policy changed. He instructed Freedmen's Bureau officers to transfer all cases involving blacks to the federal courts whenever the blacks' personal and pecuniary interest would be served thereby. Still, civil rights enforcement in Kentucky continued to be cautious until Ulysses S. Grant was elected to the presidency. During the Grant administration the effectiveness of civil rights enforcement improved, apparently because of the cooperation that local federal legal officers received from Grant's attorney general, E. Rockwood Hoar.[9]

Even with a sympathetic presidential administration, civil rights enforcement in Kentucky continued to be hampered by limited human and financial resources. Bristow estimated that the workload of his office and of the federal courts in Kentucky increased threefold after 1866 because of revenue and civil rights cases. Bristow's successor as United States attorney, G. C. Wharton, also complained of the burdensome workload, which he attributed primarily to these kinds of cases. This prompted Wharton, along with Judge Ballard, to express the hope in 1870 that they would soon be relieved of the onerous job of trying criminal cases involving blacks. Their earlier commitment to civil rights enforcement had waned, since they were prepared to return such criminal cases to the state courts as soon as the legislature extended to blacks the right to testify in cases involving whites. They apparently were satisfied that the recognition of this right would result in impartial justice. Their specious conclusion that statutory recognition of the right to testify ensured impartial justice for blacks is a measure of how oppressive civil rights enforcement had become.[10]

As national civil rights enforcement under the Civil Rights Act of 1866 was winding down in Kentucky, federal courts in other areas of the South were becoming preoccupied with civil rights protection under the Enforcement Acts of 1870 and 1871. The catalyst to this change in judicial enforcement of civil rights was the increasingly virulent Southern resistance to Reconstruction as Republicans captured control of Southern state governments after 1867. White supremacist groups such as the Ku Klux Klan emerged as terrorist wings of the Democratic Conservative parties of the South. Their political purpose was to unseat Republican officeholders and to disenfranchise Southern blacks. The paramilitary structure of the Ku Klux Klan and other terrorist groups made their intimidation of black and white Republicans more systematic and effective.

The federal effort to destroy terrorism triggered the most extensive involvement of the national government in the administration of criminal justice up to that time. Congress enacted the Enforcement Acts of 1870 and 1871 to supplement the Civil Rights Act of 1866 by defining as federal crimes certain offenses against the persons and property of citizens. The Enforcement Acts represented a more elaborate and explicit expansion of the federal criminal code than the Civil Rights Act of 1866. They consequently required greater participation of the federal government in the administration of justice than did the Civil Rights Act of 1866. The assumption of this function by the national government produced such a fundamental and profound reordering of the constitutional structure of the federal Union that it eventually spawned a judicial reaction that virtually eliminated the national protection of civil rights for almost a century.

The reign of terror inaugurated by the Ku Klux Klan and other terrorist groups has been well documented. The story need not be repeated here except as it affected criminal law enforcement. Terrorism became a concern of the federal government because local law enforcement agencies and officers were utterly unable or unwilling to deal with it. Whole sections of Southern states experienced breakdowns in law and order. Their populations were subjected to the mercy of organized bands of criminals who attacked them with impunity. While whipping was the most common form of violence, shooting, beating, murder, rape, and various forms of torture were not infrequent. Further, these criminals destroyed property and stole weapons. Economic intimidation and social ostracism were also included in the arsenal of the Ku Klux Klan.[11]

The brutality and savagery of these crimes made them distinctive. United States circuit judge Hugh L. Bond was appalled when he learned that a North Carolina woman was dragged from her cabin, beaten, and then "her hair burned off her privates." Aghast at other crimes that came before him in his court, Judge Bond was moved by the facts of one case to declare: "I never saw a worse, more outrageous and unprovoked assault with intent to kill a man who was absolutely unknown to most of his would be murderers than this." Fearful of being too explicit in a letter, he wrote his wife Anna from South Carolina in the fall of 1871:

I never believed such a state of things existed in the U.S. I will tell you all when I come home what I am afraid to pour out on paper—I do not believe that any province in China has less to do with Christian civilization than many parts of this state.

He made the impossible resolve of never returning. Attorney General Amos T. Akerman, himself a Southerner from Georgia, sadly wrote that the Ku Klux Klan

has revealed a perversion of moral sentiment among the Southern whites which bodes ill to that part of the country for this generation. Without a thorough moral renovation, society there for many years will be—I can hardly bring myself to say savage, but certainly very far from Christian.

In his opinion, the Klan was "the most atrocious organization that the civilized part of the world has ever known."[12]

Southern terrorism was distinctive for a far more important reason than its savagery. With membership rolls numbering into the hundreds in some counties,

the Klan effectively paralyzed local government agencies and officers. Many public officers were members of the Klan and participated in their crimes.
Consequently, though hundreds of crimes were committed, local officers moved
against very few. Even when they wanted to bring the criminals to justice, local
officers were too frightened and/or unable to do so. In York County, South
Carolina, for example, some 1,500 to 2,000 suspects were said to have fled military arrest while hundreds of others were actually arrested by federal authorities. Local officials and agencies were overwhelmed by the magnitude of such
criminality.[13]

Equally significant was the Ku Klux Klan's militaristic organization. Federal
officials emphasized that it was organized, armed, uniformed, and drilled, and
they came to regard the Klan as a paramilitary operation fighting a rear-guard
action in continuation of the Civil War. The United States attorney for Alabama,
John A. Minnis, explicitly attributed Klan activities to "the old disunion secession doctrine that led the South into her troubles." Attorney General Akerman
concluded from his experience in Georgia and reports from the field that "these
combinations amount to war, and cannot be crushed on any other theory." Judge
Bond reached the same conclusion and more explicitly asserted that martial law
was the only effective way to combat the Klan.[14]

Even Southern sympathizers perceived the South as engaged in war with the
national government, but they placed the onus on the national government. The
Charleston *Daily Courier,* for example, said in an editorial that the Civil War was
being perpetuated by the continuing federal military presence in the South, by
the suspension of civil law, and by the imposition of martial law. The editor
viewed blacks as members of the federal war machine against which Southerners
were forced to defend themselves. Aimed at overthrowing Republican-controlled
state governments in the South and preventing the realization of equal rights for
blacks, the Klan and similar organizations essentially were in armed rebellion
against the United States.[15]

In light of these assertions by Southerners, it is curious that Northern
Republicans did not perceive Klan terrorism as a revival of the South's rebellion
against the United States. Indeed, they were not even sure that reports of Klan
violence were anything more than Southern Republican political propaganda.
Northerners apparently longed too much for an end to the political and racial
problems of Reconstruction to admit that the preservation of the North's Civil
War victory would require their continued determination to use military
authority against recalcitrant Southerners. The lack of official authorization and
support of state governments for the Klan's guerrilla-type violence distinguished

it from the Confederate war effort and contributed to Northern Republican blindness to its paramilitary and insurrectionary nature.

Southern conservative newspapers also played a role in blunting the Northern awareness of the nature of Southern violence. They denied the very existence of the Klan and Klan terrorism and attributed reports of violence to scheming Republicans out for political advantage. Undeniable instances of violence were attributed to the victims or explained away as isolated incidents. It was easy for the increasingly disinterested Republicans of the North to discount reports of Southern violence and turn their attention to other interests. Furthermore, Democratic Conservatives attributed Southern disorders to federal interference in local affairs, providing Northern Republicans with a rationalization to justify an end to Reconstruction. They could facilely persuade themselves that the elimination of federal intrusions into Southern affairs would bring about the peace they desired.

Congress attempted to put down this armed insurrection in the South through the federal judicial process. The nearest it came to providing the kind of martial response called for by federal officials, however, was a statutory provision authorizing the president to suspend the writ of habeas corpus in areas where armed bands overthrew local government or where local officials were unable or unwilling to maintain law and order because of terrorist activities. As a result, Congress was confronted by a problem that had arisen during its consideration of the Civil Rights Act of 1866 and had troubled federal judicial officers trying to enforce the act. Legislation aimed at Klan activity inescapably thrust the federal courts into the administration of criminal justice on a massive scale. Congress somehow had to authorize the federal courts to punish offenses against personal rights without at the same time supplanting local criminal jurisdiction over ordinary crimes. Congress resolved this dilemma by defining as federal crimes offenses that were peculiar to the Klan and similar organizations. Thus, offenses that were committed for the purpose of depriving citizens of their political or civil rights or because of racism or political prejudice or because of the victim's previous condition of servitude were made crimes against the United States. Offenses that were committed by armed combinations of men, or in disguise and at night, or conspiracies to deprive citizens of their rights for the motives just mentioned were also made crimes against the United States. However, Congress continued to give state criminal codes an important role in federal law enforcement. Punishments were not specified for these crimes. Rather, they were to be commensurate to the penalties prescribed by state laws for the actions committed. Congress thus sought to authorize the federal courts to punish crimes, such as murder, by broadly defining them as violations of federally enforceable civil rights in order to avoid the accusation that the federal courts were unconstitutionally supplanting state courts in punishing offenses against the criminal laws of the states.[16]

The legal reasoning expressed in the congressional debates leading to the adoption of the Ku Klux Klan Act of 1871 paralleled the judicial understanding of the authority of the federal government to enforce civil rights up to that time. Congressional proponents of the Klan Act argued that the natural rights of citizenship, including the Bill of Rights guarantees, were federally enforceable rights of United States citizens. They invoked the broad nationalist legal tradition of constitutional interpretation and insisted that Congress possessed the authority to protect these rights in whatever manner it deemed appropriate. On the other hand, opponents of the Klan Act applied the narrower states' rights legal tradition and denied that Congress could protect personal rights, because that authority was among the exclusive powers of the states. Opponents perceived civil rights proponents as legislating to secure Bill of Rights guarantees, because they relied on the Supreme Court's ruling in *Barron v. Baltimore* to insist that the Bill of Rights was not a delegation of legislative authority but a prohibition against congressional authority.[17]

Although Congress exercised far-reaching powers to put down the Ku Klux Klan, federal legal officers who bore the responsibility of enforcing the civil rights laws of 1870 and 1871 soon discovered that dealing with armed insurrection through ordinary criminal process was far more difficult than anyone realized. Some of the difficulties were the same as those experienced by federal officials connected with the Freedmen's Bureau. These obstacles became more acute in the 1870s, and new ones were added.

The first problem with which federal attorneys, marshals, and commissioners were confronted was securing complaints and evidence for the purpose of indicting suspects. Victims were "often ignorant, poor and timid," and possessed "neither the knowledge, the means, nor the courage to bring the case to the notice of the proper officers." The vast size of judicial districts and the enormous numbers of individuals implicated in the crimes overwhelmed the sparse number of legal officers. Forced to travel hundreds of miles to the scene of a crime and to spend weeks to work up a case, they had to neglect other official business to conclude their investigations. Although federal courts convened more regularly in the 1870s than immediately after the Civil War, they still met infrequently for short periods and at few locations. It was difficult to get witnesses to leave their homes to travel the great distances to the federal court. Even willing witnesses and victims could ill afford the journey or the time away from their work. To try the tremendous number of crimes and cases would have required months before continual sitting judges instead of the days available before the sporadic terms of the federal courts. Both time and space, therefore, were impediments to civil rights protection and invitations to civil rights violations.[18]

Further complicating the investigations was the lack of cooperation within the communities in which the crimes occurred. Indeed, members of the communities did what they could to impede federal officers. Alerted to the approach of arresting officers, suspects were able to organize a forceful resistance or to flee. Some suspects left their homes permanently and resettled in distant places. Those who remained and resisted arrest usually outnumbered the federal authorities, who were forced to rely on the military to make arrests. When arresting officers responded to violent resistance with force, they were indicted in local courts for crimes that ranged from assault to murder. In making their arrests, federal authorities first had to find their suspects and then avoid being assaulted and even murdered, and, if they survived the arrest, they had to avoid being arrested and jailed by local authorities. Complainants and witnesses were subjected to the same intimidation. Violent retaliations usually met those who brought complaints to federal authorities or who supported complaints with evidence. The violent confrontation between the forces of nationalism and states' rights was thus expanded into the local and federal courts. The danger these local prosecutions posed to the successful federal enforcement of civil rights alarmed federal legal officers. United States attorney for Virginia, H. H. Wells, declared that "if such a practice is continued or becomes general, the criminal laws of the United States cannot be enforced." The attorney general instructed him to challenge the constitutionality of these local prosecutions all the way up to the United States Supreme Court if necessary.[19]

As a community rallied to assist suspects in avoiding arrest, it helped defendants who were brought to trial. Mention has already been made of the actions state legislatures took to defend state officers in federal prosecutions of civil rights violations. In various Southern states, collections were taken up for the defense of private individuals in the federal courts. The moneys were spent to hire the best attorneys to defend "'our boys' that have been kidnapped by the Yankees...." "Money seems like water for 'our boys,'" wrote a United States marshal from Mississippi, and he added that Mississippians "will go to any extreme to get them clear." These fund-raising campaigns were led by some of the South's leading citizens. For example, Wade Hampton headed one such campaign that raised $10,000 to employ former Attorney General Henry Stanbery and Senator

Reverdy Johnson to defend Klansmen in the federal court at Columbia, South Carolina, and to challenge the constitutionality of the Enforcement Acts up to the Supreme Court of the United States. The amount raised was larger than the annual salary of the federal judges before whom the cases were argued and many times the salary of the United States attorney. Furthermore, leading members of the bar frequently donated their services. Since many Southern lawyers opposed federal civil rights enforcement, defendants were usually represented by the best legal talent in their states.[20]

Often times defendants themselves were leading citizens of an area who enjoyed the advantages of wealth, political influence, and social prominence. They were able to use their influence against federal prosecuting attorneys who were, after all, political appointees removable at the discretion of the president. Prosecutions in North Carolina, for example, were reportedly postponed at the instigation of the governor, and, when the trials finally resulted in convictions, additional pressures were put on the court to give suspended sentences. The district judge and the United States attorney, however, were able to resist such pressures because the attorney general supported their efforts to punish Ku Klux terrorists.[21]

While the defense enjoyed a surfeit of talent, the United States attorneys suffered from inadequate assistance and exhaustion. They often worked seven days and nights per week to prepare Enforcement Acts cases. Days were spent examining witnesses while nights were used in recording the days' testimony. By day they appeared before grand juries to present cases for indictment, and their evenings were spent preparing evidence and formulating strategy for the trials themselves. While defense counsel were relatively free to plan their cases, United States attorneys were "harassed and annoyed" by demands to draw bills and complaints in other areas of federal law. During prosecutions at one term of court, United States attorneys had to be preparing cases for trial at the next term. Because of the technical complexities posed by the language of the Enforcement Acts, United States attorneys were sometimes required to assist federal commissioners frame arrest warrants and conduct preliminary hearings.[22]

The nature of the offenses defined by the acts further handicapped United States attorneys. Committed late at night under the cover of disguises, these crimes were the work of men who were sworn to secrecy and refused to implicate their coconspirators. Consequently, the evidence in these cases required "laborious arrangement and preparation," United States Attorney E. P. Jacobsen informed Attorney General Akerman, because "[i]t is almost wholly circumstantial and of such a nice character that if it does not receive the closest attention, the Government cannot expect to succeed in the prosecution." Furthermore, the need to prove an intent to deprive the victims of these crimes of some constitutional right, Jacobsen noted, required "the examination of many witnesses, which will have to be repeated in most of the cases." He concluded that the "preparation of these cases will require great and attentive care, and, in view of the wealth and influence opposed to the Government, they are in themselves more than one counsel can attend to."[23]

The expansion of the workload in the federal courts continued unabated into the 1870s and added to the judicial strain. Attorney General James Speed complained in 1866 that recent "legislation superinduced by the altered conditions and new relation of the nation has developed into such massive proportion…," that it would be difficult to conduct the business and interests confided to his office "without sinking under them." Speed's complaint was echoed by Attorney General Akerman in 1871 when he confided to a friend: "I am on the rack from morning till night, and frequently far into the night, and yet, with all that, I can hardly keep down this pile of business." Akerman explained that the state courts "are not as trusted [by all litigants] as formerly," and litigants who could used the federal courts. He also noted that new legislation had greatly expanded the number of criminal cases the federal courts heard. The Enforcement Acts and the revenue laws accounted for most of this accretion in the criminal docket.[24]

By 1871, the situation in some districts was desperate. Jacobson, the United States attorney for the Southern District of Mississippi, traveled to the Northern District to assist the United States attorney there, G. Wiley Wells, because Enforcement Acts cases threatened to overwhelm Wells. Jacobson volunteered his services. A few months later Jacobson was in danger of being overwhelmed himself, and he informed the attorney general that he simply could not "physically perform the necessary labor." Conditions in Tennessee were no less dismal, for the United States attorney at Nashville, R. McPhail Smith, informed United States Circuit Judge Halmer H. Emmons:

I fear that it will not be in my power to get up for you anything like the preparation you will desire. I have no means of assembling my witnesses & conferring with them prior to the trial of cases. We have usually relied, in criminal cases at least, upon eliciting from witnesses, whose testimony obtained the indictment before the grand jury, the details of the case for the first time when upon the stand.

He did not even have an assistant who could take notes during the grand jury hearing. Instead, "the prosecuting officer 'goes in' pell mell & takes the chances." It is not surprising that other federal officials sought his removal for "inefficiency, want of zeal, or...the unsatisfactory results here...." However, Judge Emmons defended him to the attorney general and attributed Smith's unsatisfactory performance to the conditions under which he labored:

> I am only surprised at the progress he has made in securing testimony, scattered as it is over the district, in so many of the hundreds of cases under his charge. As a matter of course, he cannot unaided prepare as they should be any considerable number of them upon the facts, and have one moment left for legal examination.

Other United States attorneys were equally harried.[25]

The plight of legal officers engaged in civil rights prosecutions during Reconstruction was somewhat analogous to that of the present legal staff of the Federal Trade Commission, which has been trying to bring antitrust suits against some of the large oil conglomerates. Although the legal issues in civil rights cases were not as complex, nor the legal procedure as vexatiously consuming as the antitrust cases, nineteenth-century legal officers were similarly opposed by better-paid and better-staffed lawyers who were able to raise fine points of law that challenged the skills and exhausted the time and energy of government counsel. Like present-day government attorneys, they were at a decided disadvantage to opposition counsel, and this disadvantage adversely affected their performance.[26]

The situation was no better for federal judges. They, like federal attorneys, lacked adequate assistance. Not only did they struggle with insufficient clerical help, but also they sometimes did not have a legal library or copies of federal statutes. Under such conditions backlogs developed that, over time, became exceedingly burdensome. When he assumed his judicial duties in Memphis, Tennessee, in November 1871, Judge Emmons found some three to four hundred cases on the docket, some of which were described as "long standing and ... of the highest national as well as local importance." The equity docket for the district had not been called for five years, "and such has been the pressure upon the District Judge that the administration of Federal law has been practically suspended." "It is no proper designation of this condition of things to say it is unfortunate," the judge concluded, "it is simply disgraceful." The condition of the federal courts in Tennessee may have been extreme, but federal judges generally were burdened by a lack of resources, expanding workloads, and backlogged dockets.[27]

The racial and class character of the Enforcement Acts prosecutions not only presented difficulties to the government, but it also called into question the very legitimacy of the federal courts in the South. Defendants were always white and frequently men of wealth and influence; victims were usually black. Racism and class bias worked against the credibility of government witnesses. Even when juries were willing to convict, federal attorneys were hard pressed to persuade juries to accept the testimony of persons regarded as inferior against that of highly respected leaders of the community.[28]

The legitimacy and credibility of these prosecutions were severely undermined by their unavoidably partisan nature. The Ku Klux Klan was an instrument of the Democratic Party that was dedicated to the destruction of the Republican Party in the South. Consequently, defendants in these trials were invariably Democrats while the government's witnesses were almost always Republicans. Without these prosecutions, federal officers observed, the Republican Party could not survive, and individual Republicans could not enjoy such fundamental rights as freedom of speech and assembly, the right to vote for the candidates of their choice, of life itself. United States District Judge Richard Busteed went so far as to boast, albeit with apparent exaggeration, that without his judicial assistance the Republican Party would have disappeared from Alabama. When the federal courts implemented the Enforcement Acts they almost always acted against Democratic Conservatives and in the interest of Republicans. The federal judiciary quickly assumed the appearance, if not the reality, of being an instrument of the Republican Party.[29]

For Republicans, the survival of their fundamental liberties depended upon the success of Enforcement Acts prosecutions. For Democrats, local self-determination and white supremacy required their cessation. The national government's administration of criminal justice represented to Democratic Conservatives and white supremacists an intrusion into local democratic government tantamount to a revolution in the federal structure of the Union that ensured the destruction of individual liberty. The national government's intervention with military force and suspension of habeas corpus gave credence to the Democratic Conservatives' charges of military despotism and executive imperialism. They demanded a return to the traditional system of local law enforcement not only because of their states' rights philosophy, but also because of their belief that local law enforcement was the only salvation of civil liberty in the United States, as they defined civil liberty. The impact of federal law enforcement on race relations reinforced these attitudes. Southern Democratic Conservatives believed that the maintenance of white domination over blacks was essential to their personal liberty. Senator Reverdy Johnson expressed this connection among politics, political philosophy, and racism in an impassioned plea to the United States Circuit Court at Columbia, South Carolina: "in the name of justice and humanity, in the name of those rights for which our fathers fought, you cannot subject the white man to the absolute and unconditional dominion of an armed force of a colored race."[30]

The composition of juries added to the vulnerability of the federal courts to charges of partisanship. Restricting jury lists to members of the dominant political party was a common practice in many nineteenth-century courts. In the Enforcement Acts cases, however, the composition of the juries had important political consequences. Democratic Conservatives uniformly refused to indict Klansmen when they sat on grand juries or to convict them when they sat on petit juries. To ensure "impartial" jury determinations, venires had to be assembled in ways that excluded Democratic Conservatives. This meant that juries were comprised essentially of Republicans. This also meant that blacks not only served on juries, but also that they often comprised majorities. Southern white racists, who were incensed that black witnesses were even allowed to testify against them, regarded blacks sitting in judgment of them as an intolerable affront to their dignity. Democratic Conservatives viewed the racial and political composition of federal juries as evidence of the government's partisan motives in Enforcement Acts prosecutions and its determination to win convictions regardless of the guilt or innocence of the accused. What was common practice in other places constituted proof of judicial persecution and injustice in the minds of Democratic Conservatives. Federal authorities were thus caught in an unresolvable dilemma. To open venires to Democratic Conservatives and Klan sympathizers effectively precluded the possibility of securing indictments and convictions of the guilty. But, limiting juries to "honest and impartial" men who supported the enforcement of federal laws was interpreted as court packing, which undermined the legitimacy of the federal courts among many of the most influential people in the South.[31]

Because the Enforcement Acts trials were so inherently political, even the resolution of seemingly apolitical legal questions carried political implications. For example, the federal rules of evidence prohibited husbands and wives from testifying in behalf of each other in federal cases. This rule was challenged in Enforcement Acts cases in Mississippi. Defense counsel claimed that this rule did not apply in Mississippi because an 1862 federal statute provided that the procedural rules of the forum state should be used in federal cases at common law, equity, and admiralty law. Mississippi permitted spouses to testify in each other's behalf. This issue was raised because defense witnesses who were closely related to defendants frequently perjured themselves to provide defendants with alibis. The prosecution was at a loss to counter such perjured testimony because crimes were usually committed at night "and under the additional protection of disguised and disciplined caution, and direct testimony…" was difficult to procure. Judge Hill ruled in favor of the defense and allowed wives to testify in behalf of their husbands. "The advantage therefore gained by the defendants under this ruling," wrote United States Attorney E. P. Jacobson, "is exceedingly serious." In itself, this issue was apolitical. However, in the context of these cases, it carried serious political implications because it so substantially affected their outcome.[32]

The judicial process throughout the United States generally was held in low esteem at this time. Jurors were thought to be incompetent, even in the federal courts. Federal judges complained that the most intelligent members of the community evaded jury duty because they regarded it as burdensome and inconvenient. The courts ended up with the least qualified members of the community who could often not comprehend the law, the arguments of opposing counsel, or the nuances of commercial disputes. Judges repeatedly petitioned Congress to enact legislation requiring a literacy test as a basic qualification for federal jurors.[33]

Not only in the South were attorneys and judges regarded as venal, partisan, self-interested, and corrupt. *The New York Times* reported that the city courts of New York were demoralized because of the "chicanery, favoritism and corruption" of the lawyers and judges who used the courts to advance their personal interests. Former Supreme Court Justice John Archibald Campbell blamed the public for the debased condition of the judiciary because of its tolerating "corruption maladministration, partiality in courts—worthlessness in juries, & [regarding] government only as a means of exploitation…."[34]

Participants in Klan trials were sometimes accused of acting for self-aggrandizement. Judge Bond claimed that Senator Reverdy Johnson exploited the South Carolina Klan trials as a springboard into the White House. The fact that Senator Johnson's son was the United States marshal responsible for federal law enforcement in these cases gives a dissonant sound to the senator's charges of despotic disregard for civil liberty on the part of federal officers. However, whether he was attempting to advance himself to the White House is another matter all together. More credible are Judge Bond's intimations concerning his judicial brother, District Judge George S. Bryan. South Carolina Democrats purportedly offered Judge Bryan the governorship if he would support their position on legal questions raised in the trials. Whether Bryan was induced by their lure is uncertain. But, Judge Bond was convinced that the "democrats have hold of him... & persuade him to be a stick between our legs at every step." When defense counsel began to enter motions to quash the indictments, Bond wrote to his wife:

> This will be the beginning of my troubles with old Bryan. I went to him the other day & frightened him half to death. I stormed at him & told him, if he wanted his salary increased (you know he is always talking about that) he had just better [not] keep the court sitting doing nothing but posing about the smallest matter in the world day after day. He caved right in...I am sick of him & altogether disgusted & he is with me.

Bryan did disagree with Bond on the scope of constitutional authority to enforce civil rights and forced the cases to the Supreme Court.[35]

The participation of legal officers in partisan political activities intensified the politicization of the judicial process. Attorney General Akerman continued his active involvement in the Georgia Republican Party, and he traveled around the country in support of Republican candidates for office. When he was offered the chairmanship of the Georgia State Republican Committee, he declined because he was too distant to be effective and because "such an appointment might expose the committee to the reproach of being a mere executive agency." Nonetheless, he apparently did not feel that the office of attorney general would in any way be compromised.[36]

United States marshals and attorneys also openly participated in politics. They saw no impropriety in actively campaigning for Republican candidates for federal, state, and local offices. In fact, one's political connections were an essential condition for appointment to, and retention of, these offices. Department of Justice officers continually reassured the attorney general of their political loyalty. Nor were they above using the federal courts for political advantage. United States Marshal Stephen B. Packard, for example, found the District Court at New Orleans an effective instrument in aiding his custom house gang's struggle to win the governorship in 1873 for William P. Kellogg against Henry C. Warmoth. Benjamin H. Bristow was so disgusted with the politics of his office as United States attorney at Louisville that he wanted to resign in 1869.[37]

The incident involving District Judge Bryan shows that federal judges were not immune to politics either. While Judge Bryan's behavior represented blatant self-interest, judges were political in other ways. Political campaigning within their districts was a common practice. They evidently felt no need to hide their political affiliations. The United States district judge for Virginia, John Underwood, was notoriously partisan. He even went so far as to use his court-room as a meeting place for the Republican organization in his area. Of course, not all judges shared this rather loose conception of judicial propriety. Circuit Judge Emmons eschewed politics and bent over backwards to avoid the taint of partisanship in his courtroom. However, he still found no impropriety in the selection of judicial officers and jurors on the basis of party affiliation. District Judge Hill avoided party politics in Mississippi, but because he felt "that a faith-ful and impartial administration of the Constitution and laws, as the only judge in the State was as much as could reasonably be required of one man."[38]

The very manner in which federal judges perceived the function of their courts politicized them. Judges assumed that their essential role was to enforce the statutes enacted by Congress in the ways in which Congress intended them to be implemented, so long as the laws did not obviously conflict with the Constitution. Judges therefore functioned as instruments of congressional will. However, the Enforcement Acts and the Reconstruction Amendments had been adopted along purely partisan lines. Republican congressional majorities enacted them over the vehement opposition of Democratic minorities. They were enacted for the purpose of protecting citizens' civil and political rights. But, the citizens who were to be protected were primarily Republicans in the South, and the persons from whom they needed protection were Democrats. In imple-menting the Enforcement Acts, therefore, judges, intentionally or not, func-tioned as instruments of a Republican-controlled Congress. This partisan quality of the judicial enforcement of civil rights was so evident to contemporaries that attorneys, judges, and the public referred to the legal reasoning supporting the constitutionality or unconstitutionality of these laws as the Republican or the Democratic interpretation. Related legal questions were commonly discussed and resolved in the courts and in the public forum not only on the basis of commitment to racial equality and legal and political philosophy, but also on the basis of party affiliation.[39]

Political scientists have for some time studied the influence of sociopolitical factors on a judge's behavior on the bench. These studies have demonstrated that a judge's background and familiarity with the community he serves affect his behavior on the bench. They suggest that the longer and the more involved the connection between the judge and the community the more likely and the more strongly will he conform to and reflect local values, attitudes, interests, and objectives in his decisions. Pressures to conform to local interests and perspectives increase when a judge is native to his district and has participated in local and state politics before his judicial appointment.[40]

These studies provide insights into the political context of the federal judges' actions during Reconstruction. Of the eleven district judges who were involved in Enforcement Acts cases, only one, Richard Busteed, was a recent immigrant to his district. Eight were native to their districts while two, Busteed and John Erskine, were born in Ireland. One judge, John Underwood, was born in New York state although he had moved to Virginia in 1832. Judge Erskine had moved to Florida in 1832 before settling in Georgia in 1855. At least nine of these judges had been involved in politics before their appointment to the bench. Only Judge Underwood had been an abolitionist before the Civil War and a known Radical Republican after the War. Judge Ballard of Kentucky was noted for his dedication to federal law and, until 1872 at least, the civil rights of blacks.

None of these judges had been appointed by President Grant. Four judges, George W. Brooks of North Carolina (1865), George S. Bryan of South Carolina (1866), John Erskine of Georgia (1866), and Robert A. Hill of Mississippi (1866) were appointed by President Andrew Johnson. Five judges, Bland Ballard of Kentucky (1861), Richard Busteed of Alabama (1863), John Jackson, Jr., of West Virginia (1861), Connally F. Trigg of Tennessee (1862), and John Underwood of Virginia (1863) were appointed by President Abraham Lincoln. Two judges, John Cadwalader of Pennsylvania and Humphrey Howe Leavitt of Ohio, were appointed before the Civil War. Judge Cadwalader was appointed by President James Buchanan in 1858, and Judge Leavitt was appointed by President Andrew Jackson in 1834. All of these district judges, then, had been appointed to the federal court long before the Enforcement Acts were enacted, and most if not all of them had been appointed by presidents who were, or probably would have been, opposed to the acts' implementation.[41]

All of the judges except Busteed and Underwood were well accepted and respected by local elites in their districts. Judge Underwood was unpopular because of his blatant Radical republicanism. Judge Busteed, disliked by both Southern Democratic Conservatives and Republicans, was resented because of his political charlatanism and frequent and extended absences from his district. With three exceptions, these district judges favored states' rights over federal authority, and they were either opposed to the policies of the Grant administration or were Democrats or both. Only Judges Ballard, Hill, and Underwood were committed to the goals of congressional Reconstruction. One can understand the caution with which United States attorneys brought Enforcement Acts cases before district judges. Nor is it difficult to understand why they felt that district judges were less reliable than the circuit judges in these cases.

Only three federal circuit judges were involved in Enforcement Acts prosecutions in the early 1870s. Their actions illustrate the influence of sociopolitical factors on judicial behavior. Since Congress established the circuit courts in 1869, the circuit judges were all appointed by President Grant. Hugh Lennox Bond, born in Baltimore, was raised and educated in New York City. He returned to Baltimore after college and settled and married there. A member of the American Party in the 1850s, he, together with Henry Winter Davis, became one of the founders of the Republican Party in Maryland. Not only was he against slavery, but he also favored equal rights. As a judge of the Baltimore Criminal Court he assisted Freedmen's Bureau attorneys in litigation challenging the legality of discriminatory indenture contracts. He consistently supported black education and voting rights. Having demonstrated his Radical Republican credentials, he was appointed to the Fourth Circuit in 1869 by President Grant. One historian has suggested that the president appointed Bond because he felt that Bond was particularly well suited to try Ku Klux Klan cases.[42]

Not much is known about the other two circuit judges, Halmer H. Emmons and William B. Woods. Judge Emmons seems not to have been involved in politics before his appointment. A native of Michigan, he was appointed to a circuit that comprised two border states, Kentucky and Tennessee, and two Northern states, Indiana and his home state. Because he resided outside the South, he maintained a Northern identity, which enabled him to avoid many of the Southern Conservative pressures to which other federal judges were exposed. Judge Woods was also a Northerner by birth and background. His home state was Ohio. He distinguished himself in the Union army during the Civil War despite the fact that he was a prominent Ohio Democrat who had opposed President Lincoln. However, he became an ardent Republican after the Civil War in his adopted state of Alabama. Before his appointment to the federal bench, Woods engaged in cotton planting, various business ventures, and the practice of law in addition to playing a leading role in the Alabama Republican Party. His appointment to the Fifth Circuit was crucial to Enforcement Acts prosecutions, because the Fifth Circuit encompassed the states of the Deep South in which many of the cases arose.[43]

Circuit judges were more committed to the vigorous enforcement of federal laws than were the district judges. They had been Republicans before coming on the federal bench. They had been appointed by a Republican president and given a mandate to enforce federal laws. They were relatively insulated from local pressures, and they were more disposed by circumstance and inclination to apply federal authority even in the face of local opposition than were district judges. Little wonder that United States attorneys preferred to bring their cases before circuit judges. But the federal judicial business depended more on district judges than circuit judges. Circuit judges had to travel over several states and divide their time among many more courts than did the district judges. Moreover, district judges held court more often and for longer periods than did circuit judges. United States Attorney D. T. Corbin of South Carolina, for example, determined that the circuit judge of the Fourth Circuit could not possibly hold court in each district of his circuit every year. Consequently, from their perspective, United States attorneys were forced to bring their cases before the least reliable federal judges.[44]

Legal historian Kermit L. Hall demonstrated that these courts accommodated both federal law and local interests. That federal judges were expected to be sensitive to local, regional, and sectional interests gave their courts a democratic flavor. The participation of judicial appointees in local politics before their elevation to the bench reinforced this democratic quality. Hall asserts that party organization "acted as a link between the priorities of a national administration and the needs of local constituencies serviced by the lower federal courts." However, the infusion of partisanship and localism into the federal courts that provided such a link before the Civil War subjected them to severe strains during Reconstruction. The priorities of the Grant administration were in direct and irreconcilable conflict with local Southern Conservative interests. After the Civil War, party affiliation became a scalpel severing national policy and dominant local interests. Federal district judges were in the untenable position of having to please two irreconcilable constituencies.[45]

These opposing pressures already have been discussed with respect to Judge Bryan in South Carolina. Bryan's reluctance vigorously to enforce federal law against the Ku Klux Klan in 1871 was consistent with his posture generally on the bench. Secretary of the Treasury Hugh McCulloch complained to Attorney General William Evarts in 1868 that Judge Bryan was too lenient in Revenue Act cases. According to Louis F. Post, law clerk to United States Attorney Corbin, Judge Bryan was as undesirable personally as he was as a judge. "It may be disrespectful to criticize the behavior of a Judge, and bad taste to speak harshly of an old man," he wrote as a correspondent of the New York *Tribune* during the Ku Klux Klan trials at Columbia, South Carolina,

> but if there are exceptional cases, he certainly is one. Judge Bryan, on the Bench, is weak, vacillating, ignorant, and old-womanish; and it may not be

amiss to add that he is far from being always courteous to his presiding brother, and his whole bearing as associate Justice is marked by bad taste in the highest degree.

United States Attorney Corbin tried to avoid bringing Enforcement Acts cases before Judge Bryan, he explained to Senator George F. Edmunds, chairman of the Senate Judiciary Committee in 1872, because "[a]ll the causes heretofore attempted to be brought before the Court, have failed." Judge Bond also found that "all the negro population abjuring Judge Bryan look to me for protection as well as do the poorer class of whites."[46]

Judge Connally F. Trigg of Tennessee represented an even more serious threat to federal law enforcement. Federal legal officers complained that he was a states' rights sympathizer who had little loyalty to the United States government. He was accused of failing to enforce the federal revenue laws in good faith, of going to great lengths to dismiss cases in favor of defendants, of releasing prisoners, of refusing to hear Enforcement Acts cases, and of failing to hold court regularly. The United States attorney at Nashville, R. McPhail Smith, complained to Attorney General Akerman in 1871 that "the Federal Courts in his hands in this State amount to very little." The United States marshal, L. B. Eaton, told Circuit Judge Emmons in even more emphatic terms that "[t]he simple truth is that the enforcement of the 14th and 15th Amendments and of the revenue laws in this state rests solely upon your presence, firmness and courage." United States Attorney Smith so desperately wanted to avoid Judge Trigg that he offered to pay the expenses if another judge could be brought from another district to sit on the federal court at Nashville.[47]

The political posture of Judge Richard Busteed of Alabama was more elusive and more variable. He was a political chameleon who not only changed political affiliations between the Democratic and Republican Parties over time, but also his publicly stated opinions contradicted his private views. Despite the abundant evidence of Ku Klux Klan terrorism presented in his court, he publicly disclaimed any knowledge of the Klan's existence in Alabama or of any threats to personal rights in that state. However, in private conversations with federal legal officers he not only conceded the Klan's existence and terrorism, but he also recommended that additional federal legislation be enacted to make all violations of personal rights crimes against the United States and punishable in the federal courts. Judge Busteed was obviously playing on both sides of the Klan issue; he could thus appease local power wielders and federal legal officers.[48]

Federal legal officers sometimes encountered difficulties in enforcing civil rights even when the district judge supported federal authority and the

Enforcement Acts. No one disputed the commitment of Judge Hill of Mississippi to protect personal rights and to advance Republican policies. Yet, legal officers complained of his leniency in Enforcement Acts cases. The problem, according to Deputy Marshal Allen P. Huggins, was Judge Hill's "known weakness." "Sometimes the Ku Klux in the people will break out," Huggins informed Attorney General Akerman in 1871, "and the Court is so completely overawed that I do not see much chance for justice to be meted out to these fiends in human shape." As a Mississippian who was active in local politics before his appointment to the federal bench by President Johnson, Judge Hill's leniency and weakness in Ku Klux cases is not surprising. Moreover, he suffered from an exaggerated need to be accepted by the legal community of his district. On the other hand, much can be said in support of Judge Hill's desire to avoid alienating local elites. He commented to Solicitor General Bristow, "I know that unless these laws are enforced in such a manner as to bring to their support the moral influence of the sober right thinking men of the State it will be a failure...." Herein lay the essential problem the federal courts confronted in the South: the impossibility of accommodating national law and local interests when these two were in opposition to one another. Not surprisingly, Attorney General Akerman informed United States Attorney E. P. Jacobson that his was "not the only district where the judiciary succumbs to the pressure of a local sentiment."[49]

Despite the seemingly overwhelming adverse pressures and conditions in which they operated, the federal courts generally upheld the authority of the federal government under the Enforcement Acts of 1870 and 1871. All Southern district judges upheld their constitutionality, even if reluctantly. Some opposed using them in Ku Klux Klan prosecutions. That even unsympathetic Southern federal judges opposed to the national enforcement of civil rights upheld the constitutionality of congressional civil rights legislation demonstrates how strongly held was their view that the judicial function was to implement Congress's will unless it was obviously unconstitutional. That these unsympathetic judges accepted or attributed such broad power to Congress under the Reconstruction Amendments is revealing evidence of contemporaries' understanding of the expansive scope of legislative intent and the authority of the national government under the Thirteenth and Fourteenth Amendments. This analysis suggests that the failures of the national government to enforce civil rights were due not to insufficient constitutional or legal authority but to institutional and political obstacles.

Terrorist groups such as the Ku Klux Klan and local law enforcement authorities spearheaded the continuing rebellion against federal authority. Congress attempted to put down this rebellion primarily through the judicial implementation of the Enforcement Acts. Judicial process was invoked against violent insurrection. However, by upholding and applying national authority to secure civil rights, the federal courts ensured their condemnation by local political elites. Southern spokesmen not only criticized the federal courts for venal partisanship, but they also discredited the very legitimacy of federal judicial process under national civil rights legislation. Southern Democratic Conservatives characterized the Enforcement Acts as unconstitutional invitations to executive and judicial despotism enacted by a partisan Congress for the purpose of destroying representative government and civil liberty in the South. Republicans, on the other hand, could not expect to receive justice in the local courts, which sometimes were used against them to retaliate for federal enforcement of civil rights. The federal courts thus became the new battleground of the Civil War, and their success depended greatly on the support they received from government officials in Washington. We therefore turn now to an analysis of the Department of Justice and its impact upon judicial behavior.[50]

4

The Department of Justice and Civil Rights Enforcement, 1870–1871

Congress created the Department of Justice approximately one month after the enactment of the Enforcement Act of May 31, 1870. This administrative reform enlarged the attorney general's office and centralized the legal business of the national government within it. By creating a permanent staff of attorneys, Congress expected the new executive department to handle the nation's legal affairs more efficiently and effectively and to eliminate the need to hire outside counsel. These changes reportedly represented a savings of $1,000,000 per year. A massive problem of criminal law enforcement in certain Southern states soon confronted the enlarged and reorganized attorney general's office. The largest and most consuming area that engaged the new department was the protection of civil rights. Overcoming the almost insurmountable obstacles described in the previous chapter, federal legal officers successfully enforced the civil rights acts of 1870 and 1871 against Ku Klux Klan terrorism. Despite their success, or perhaps because of it, the attorney general largely abandoned civil rights enforcement in 1873 in an effort to reduce mounting departmental expenses. The history of the Justice Department's response to the challenge presented by the Ku Klux Klan has not been fully explored. Yet, the extent to which department officers and federal judges attempted to enforce civil rights reveals much about the commitment of federal legal officers to civil rights enforcement during Reconstruction.[1]

The Department of Justice was inaugurated with a new attorney general. President Grant's first attorney general, E. Rockwood Hoar, resigned his office just days before Congress passed the bill creating the department. In addition to the respect he enjoyed for his legal abilities, Hoar was noted for his integrity and nonpartisanship in conducting the legal affairs of the government. His successor, Amos T. Akerman, also was esteemed for his legal abilities, but he was more controversial. Born in New Hampshire and educated at Dartmouth College, Akerman moved to Georgia where he studied law under John McPherson Berrian, a former United States senator and attorney general under President Andrew Jackson. Akerman strongly opposed secession at the outbreak of the

Civil War, but he later served in the Confederate government for eighteen months. At the conclusion of the war, he helped to organize the Republican Party in Georgia, although Congress did not remove the disabilities he incurred as a Confederate governmental officer until 1869. As a Republican, Akerman suffered proscription and social ostracism because of his switch in political loyalties. His ardent republicanism was also the reason for his appointment as United States attorney for Georgia just months before President Grant elevated him to the position of attorney general in June 1870.[2]

The man appointed as the solicitor general was another ardent Republican with Southern ties, Benjamin H. Bristow of Kentucky. Relatively unknown outside of his home state, Bristow came to President Grant's attention because of his role in party politics and his efforts in behalf of the civil rights of blacks as United States attorney at Louisville. Grant initially offered him the position of assistant attorney general, but Bristow declined the appointment because the salary of $5,000 was too low. The position of solicitor general carried an extra $2,500 per year, still an income lower than that of a successful attorney, but apparently high enough to persuade Bristow to join the Grant administration.[3]

Thus, the two highest legal officers of the United States were personally and politically committed to the goals of congressional Reconstruction. Bristow had already demonstrated his commitment to civil rights as United States attorney for Kentucky; Akerman was about to demonstrate his commitment as attorney general. Allen Trelease has suggested that the reason for Akerman's unswerving desire to destroy the Ku Klux Klan and his efforts to punish its criminal members was because he personally had been endangered by this organization in Georgia. That, together with his firsthand experience of Georgia politics, helps to explain the firm stand he took against the Ku Klux Klan. He knew that federal authorities had to take vigorous action if lawlessness was to be stopped and if the Republican Party was to survive in the South.[4]

Nevertheless, Akerman preferred to leave the administration of criminal justice to the states, because local authorities had traditionally performed this function. Akerman's attitude was typical of nineteenth-century federal legal officers even in regard to federal criminal law. Prior to the Civil War, United States attorneys general gave only passing attention to the enforcement of federal criminal laws. United States attorneys were allowed to enforce federal law as they saw fit. This prosecutorial discretion was attractive when it came to Klan crimes because they were unlike violations of any previous federal laws. The protection of persons and property from violence was a radically new function Congress thrust upon federal legal officers for which they were ill prepared institutionally and professionally.

"The difficulty," Attorney General Akerman informed Alabama United States Attorney John A. Minnis in February 1871,

> is that the United States government is not so constituted as to be able to reach outrages of this character with due efficiency. The State governments are designed to be the regular and usual protectors of person and property, and when they fail in this, through the indisposition of officials, or private citizens, it is hard to accomplish the result in any other way.[5]

Yet, when the new Department of Justice was organized, the Klan's criminality was so pervasive that local law enforcement authorities in several Southern states were unable to provide even the semblance of criminal law enforcement. Military action and the imposition of martial law were probably the most effective means of bringing Klansmen to account. But, state legislatures refused to invoke martial law, and state governors were reluctant to call out militia to combat the Ku Klux Klan. Instead, state officials looked to the federal government for protection. Congress responded in 1870 and 1871 with civil rights legislation aimed specifically at the Klan. The enforcement of this legislation required a significant departure from the attorney general's traditional inaction in federal criminal law enforcement.

Attorney General Akerman nevertheless quickly prompted federal legal officers to enforce civil rights. One month after he took office, Akerman issued a circular to all United States attorneys, marshals, deputy marshals, and commissioners with instructions to implement the Enforcement Act of May 31, 1870. He informed them that the statute

> makes it your special duty to initiate proceedings against all violators of the act. You will, therefore, whenever you receive from any source credible information that this law has been violated, take prompt measures for the arrest and effectual prosecution of the guilty party.

Akerman repeated these instructions to legal officers individually and complimented them when they energetically enforced the law. He even urged the federal marshal in San Francisco to prosecute vigorously all persons who discriminated against the Chinese there in violation of the Enforcement Act.[6]

Despite the attorney general's promptings, the act was not vigorously enforced in 1870. Only forty-three cases were prosecuted under the Enforcement Act that year. Of these, however, thirty-two resulted in convictions. Five cases resulted in acquittals, and six were *nolle prosequi.* Generally, the number of Enforcement Act cases were few, but, compared to the average for all federal criminal cases in the United States, they resulted in substantially higher conviction rates (74% as against 53%) and lower *nolle prosequi* rates (14% as against 8%). The acquittal rate, however, was also slightly higher for Enforcement Act cases than for all criminal cases (12% and 8%, respectively).[7]

The Enforcement Act was relatively unenforced in 1870 because the disincentives far outweighed the incentives. As has already been discussed, federal legal officers often were reluctant or unwilling to enforce federal criminal laws. Moreover, state legal officers traditionally exercised jurisdiction over crimes against personal rights. To make these areas of law enforcement high priorities, federal legal officers had to assume a different attitude toward the functions and duties of their offices. In addition, as the previous chapter noted, merely establishing that crimes had been committed, or that crimes had been committed by members of the Ku Klux Klan, was difficult. Victims frequently were unwilling to bring charges or to testify against their assailants. Even when they were willing, victims were usually poor black country people who had been terrorized by white gangs that were often led by leading citizens. Legal officers were reluctant to involve themselves in such situations, particularly when the very existence of the Klan and its crimes was so vehemently denied by the Southern press and politicians. Legal officers who shared the political views and racial prejudices of Southern Democratic Conservatives used these denials to justify prudent inaction. The political context and practical difficulties of civil rights enforcement would have discouraged even sincerely committed legal officers. Under these circumstances, the attorney general had to do more than merely announce a policy of civil rights enforcement to get legal officers in the field to protect civil rights.[8]

Still, 271 prosecutions were pending in the federal courts at the end of 1870. Many of these cases were brought in Northern states. However, the bulk of these cases, some 190 (70%), were instituted in one state, Tennessee. The federal district courts disposed of four other cases in this state in 1870, two by convictions and two by *nolle prosequi.* The low rate of disposal (2%) in these Enforcement Act cases was consistent with the disposal rate of criminal cases generally in Tennessee. Only 17% of the total criminal docket was cleared in 1870, leaving 83% for 1871. This was considerably lower than the average disposal rate for all federal judicial districts in the United States. On the average, 41% of the criminal docket of the federal courts was disposed of in 1870, and 59% was carried over into 1871. These statistics tend to confirm the criticism of federal legal officers in Tennessee about District Judge Connally F. Trigg's antipathy towards enforcing federal law.[9]

Federal inaction bred greater local violence. As Klan violence increased in the spring and summer of 1871, so did the urgings of the attorney general to bring violators of federal criminal law to justice. Akerman again admonished United States attorneys to institute prosecutions "whenever you find that the Enforcement Act, or the Civil Rights Act, has been broken…." He stated that these laws were to be vigorously enforced "against all parties who may be guilty." The attorney general was attempting to fill the void created in criminal law enforcement by the collapse of local authorities with a federal administration of criminal justice. His policy went beyond the goals of stopping further Klan violence and destroying the Ku Klux Klan. Akerman's objective was to bring to justice all persons involved in Ku Klux crimes.[10]

The attorney general believed that peace could be restored only by directing the full force of federal power against criminals:

> It [is] my individual opinion that nothing is more idle than to attempt to conciliate by kindness that portion of the southern people who are still malcontent. They take all kindness on the part of the Government as evidence of timidity, and hence are emboldened to lawlessness by it. It appears impossible for the Government to win their affection. But it can command their respect by the exercise of its powers. It is the business of a judge to terrify evil doers, not to coax them.

Experience in Georgia and North Carolina supported this draconian approach to law enforcement, for federal officers' appeasement of the Klan in these states merely led to greater lawlessness. Relying on this experience, Akerman concluded: "The policy of coaxing those of our people who are unfriendly to the Government has utterly failed hitherto."[11]

Men of high position and stature who committed crimes were not to be spared the embarrassment and inconvenience of defending themselves in a federal court of law. On the contrary, federal legal officers were to "make special efforts to subject them to the vengeance of the law." Expressing the belief that the conviction of a few leading citizens would most effectively end lawlessness, Akerman and Bristow urged subordinates to make examples of them. "The higher the social standing and character of the convicted party," Solicitor General Bristow instructed the United States attorney in North Carolina, "the more important is a vigorous prosecution and prompt execution of judgment."[12]

However, the enormity of prosecuting all offenders of the federal civil rights laws was simply beyond the capacity of the Justice Department's legal force in the South. When Enforcement Acts cases were added to the persistently accreting workload of the federal courts, federal legal officers pleaded for help. Requests poured into the attorney general's office for special assistant counsel, investigators, clerks, and stenographers to aid in the preparation and adjudication of cases. So did calls for military assistance to make arrests, to hold prisoners for trial, and to protect government witnesses and officers while the federal courts tried defendants.[13]

At first, the attorney general rejected requests for special assistance even when they came from cabinet officers such as Secretary of War William Belknap and Secretary of the Treasury George Boutwell. The reason was twofold. One of the reforms intended by the creation of the Department of Justice was the elimination of special assistant counsel. Consequently, the statute establishing the department prohibited the employment of such assistance unless the legal issues were of such a highly specialized nature that ordinary legal officers were unable to handle them. The second reason for this policy was the lack of money to employ such assistance. "It will be difficult," Attorney General Akerman explained in rejecting a request for aid from District Judge Hill in July 1871, "if not impossible in view of the general increase of the business of the country to sustain the Courts through the current fiscal year upon the present appropriations. Hence, the strictest economy is a necessity." As legal officers became enmeshed in bringing Klansmen to justice, their repeated failure to secure requested assistance caused some to feel abandoned. A United States deputy marshal in Mississippi, Allen P. Huggins, lamented: "Attorney General it is too bad to let us fight this thing against all the public opinion as single handed as we are. We need more force enough to inspire respect and command order...."[14]

The attorney general was not impervious to the difficulties that confronted his legal officers in the South. He urged Congress to enact a special appropriation for the purpose of hiring detectives to investigate civil rights violations and to assist in bringing prosecutions in the South. The Department of Justice thus would take the initiative in instituting civil rights prosecutions. He explained that such investigators were needed because the victims of Ku Klux crimes "are for the most part, poor and ignorant men, who do not know how to put the law in motion, or who have some well-grounded apprehension of danger to themselves from the attempt to enforce it." Congress appropriated $20,000 for these purposes in June 1871, and the attorney general quickly asked H. C. Whitley, chief of the Secret Service, to employ "capable and trusting persons" who would willingly go to the South and assist in the investigation of civil rights crimes. However, President Grant diverted substantial amounts of the appropriation to New York City to preclude election frauds by Democrats. The funds available for federal officers in the South were exhausted within five months.[15]

Congress appropriated other funds to employ lawyers to assist in the preparation and trial of civil rights cases. Whereas the attorney general previously had declined requests for legal assistance, by November 1871 he not only approved such requests, but he also made unsolicited offers of such aid to United States attorneys engaged in Enforcement Acts prosecutions. Apparently the increase in Ku Klux crime stimulated a greater determination in the Grant administration and Congress to bring the criminals to justice.[16]

The willingness to employ special legal assistance nevertheless was limited by financial considerations. Funds were simply insufficient to meet the needs of federal attorneys. For example, United States Attorney John A. Minnis required $10,000 for additional attorneys in Ku Klux Klan trials in Alabama. Akerman responded that the requested amount was simply too great for a budget of $2,000,000 that had to be distributed among all the federal judicial districts of the nation. To use $10,000 in one class of cases in one portion of one state was simply impossible. However, the attorney general did authorize one half of the requested amount, and Congress subsequently appropriated an additional $1,000,000 for judicial expenses.[17]

Political considerations were almost as great a problem as the lack of funds. Democratic Conservatives in the North and South denied that the Ku Klux Klan existed, and they insisted that reports of Klan terrorism were presidential and Republican exaggerations and falsehoods. Thus, while legal officers in many areas of the South desperately struggled to put down armed insurrection, administration officials and their Republican supporters struggled to convince the public, particularly in the North, that the Klan did exist and that the prosecutions of its lawless members were not despotic persecutions of Southern political opponents. This helps to explain why Attorney General Akerman urged the United States attorneys to prosecute civil rights violators for the purpose of exposing their crimes, even when there was no hope of securing convictions. Judge Robert A. Hill reported some success in persuading Mississippians of the Klan's existence in that state. "Our investigations," he informed Solicitor General Bristow in July 1871, "have shown the public that there does exist in certain portions of the State an organization dangerous to life, liberty, and the pursuit of happiness, a fact before not generally believed."[18]

Public disbelief in the necessity of these prosecutions, combined with the extraordinary expenditures they required, exposed the Grant administration to charges of boondoggling. Legal officers were paid fees based upon the number of cases they tried. Witnesses were given per diem and travel expenses. The more cases that were brought before the federal courts, the more money legal officers earned. The more witnesses the government used in its prosecutions, the greater its potential patronage. Democratic Conservatives charged that federal legal officers were using the pretext of civil rights violations for political and economic self-interest. Sensitive to these charges, Attorney General Akerman cautioned federal attorneys to remember "that the execution of the Enforcement Laws must be, and must appear to the country to be, entirely free from any plausible suspicion that they are used for the purpose of advancing any private pecuniary interest."[19]

Political considerations complicated the selection of special assistants. Some legal officers sought to deflect partisan criticism from themselves and the courts by appointing leading Democrats to assist in Ku Klux Klan prosecutions. United States District Attorney Jacobson, for example, recommended the appointment of local attorneys in Mississippi who were opposed to the Grant administration and the Enforcement Acts, for

> their connection with the cases will go far to repress from the prosecution the complexion of political design with which the Administration is generally charged by a large class of this people, and which may prejudice the government before the jury.

He added that these lawyers "will probably carry the jury on which ever side retained." Other legal officers disagreed with this strategy. United States Attorney Minnis of Alabama counseled Attorney General Akerman that "[t]he lawyers generally have taken strong ground against these laws, and I cannot afford to be encumbered with a lawyer who will not cordially enter into the Spirit of the law." The danger in hiring sympathetic attorneys was that they most likely would be Republicans, which would highlight the partisan appearance of the trial.[20]

The attorney general opted for assistant counsel who were committed to federal law enforcement at the risk of appearing partisan. Therefore, he recommended the appointment of local attorneys who were sympathetic to the Enforcement Acts, because Republicans were "more likely to have their hearts in their work." At the same time, he cautioned against using the courts for purely partisan purposes or even giving the appearance of judicial partisanship.[21]

Detectives and assistant attorneys were not the only extraordinary aid required for Ku Klux Klan prosecutions. Because of the important constitutional questions raised, stenographers were needed to record the voluminous depositions and pretrial testimony, as well as the proceedings of the trials themselves. Accurate transcripts were also needed to demonstrate the very necessity of the trials in the face of Democratic Conservative criticism. Additional deputy marshals and federal troops often were required not only to restore peace, but also to arrest defendants, to protect witnesses, to execute judicial orders, and, in some areas, to enable the federal courts to function at all. When added to the "ordinary" costs of prosecutions, these extraordinary expenses raised the costs of prosecuting violators of the Enforcement Acts to staggering amounts. Judge Bond estimated the "fearful" expenses of the month-long South Carolina Ku Klux Klan prosecutions in 1871 at $200 per hour. Although over four hundred defendants were scheduled for trial, the court was able to try only five.[22]

With the attorney general instructing legal officers to prosecute violators of the Enforcement Acts and providing additional financial, legal, and military resources for this purpose, prosecutions under these laws increased markedly in 1871. The total number of Enforcement Acts cases handled by the federal courts rose by a dramatic 630% (from 43 cases to 271 cases). Although convictions increased, acquittals and *nolle prosequi* cases rose by even greater percentages. Therefore, the conviction rate for Enforcement Acts cases dropped over 30% from the previous year (from 74% to 41%), and this rate was 10% lower than the 51% conviction rate for other criminal cases in 1871. The acquittal rate remained about the same (12% in 1870 and 15% in 1871), and this rate was comparable to the acquittal rate for all crimes (18%) in 1871. However, the *nolle prosequi* cases rose by 30% (from 14% to 44%) over the previous year, and the 1871 *nolle prosequi* rate was 13% higher than the *nolle prosequi* rate for other crimes (which was 31%). Furthermore, the courts disposed of 63% of other federal criminal cases in 1871, but they completed only a fourth of the Enforcement Acts cases in that year. The lower conviction rate, the higher *nolle prosequi* rate, and the lower case completion rate for Enforcement Acts cases reflect the extraordinary difficulties these cases presented to federal judges, attorneys, and marshals. Federal legal officers may have directed much greater effort to Enforcement Acts prosecutions in 1871, but they were far less effective here than they were in other areas of federal criminal law enforcement.

These aggregates, however, are misleading. Most Enforcement Acts cases were instituted in 1871 in Alabama, Mississippi, North and South Carolina, and Tennessee. Eighty-two percent of the 1,193 Enforcement Acts cases brought in 1871 were begun in these states. North and South Carolina heard most of these cases (20% and 36%, respectively). United States Attorney D. H. Starbuck in North Carolina was extraordinarily successful in federal criminal prosecutions that year. He won convictions in 75% of the cases that were disposed of in his district. Little wonder that, with all of the difficulties involved in these prosecutions, he felt entitled "to the gratitude and thanks of the law abiding people everywhere and especially of the Republican or Union Party of the nation which it was the purpose of this daring conspiracy to destroy." Starbuck was equally successful in increasing convictions and reducing acquittals and *nolle prosequi* cases in other criminal prosecutions, even though the number of criminal cases that were tried in his district increased 243%. At the same time, the proportion of cases that were carried over into 1872 also was reduced, although the actual number of cases pending increased slightly. This extraordinary record is explained in large part by the combined determination of United States Attorney Starbuck and United States Circuit Judge Hugh L. Bond to enforce the federal criminal laws.[23]

The performance of United States Attorney Daniel T. Corbin of South Carolina in criminal prosecutions was significantly poorer than Starbuck's. Judicial information for 1870 is unavailable for South Carolina, so a comparison of 1871 with that year cannot be made. In 1871, however, Corbin succeeded in winning convictions in only 5 trial cases, though 49 other convictions resulted from confessions. These 54 convictions represent a conviction rate of 48%, slightly above the average for all Enforcement Acts cases. However, the acquittal rate in South Carolina of 34% was significantly higher than the acquittal rate of 15% for all Enforcement Acts cases. If these ratios are applied only to tried cases, Corbin's conviction rate drops to 12% (5 divided by 43) and his acquittal rate skyrockets to 88%.[24]

The poor record in South Carolina was due to a number of factors. Democratic Conservatives decided to concentrate their legal opposition to the Enforcement Acts in the South Carolina federal courts. Corbin's opposing counsel, therefore, were two of the most outstanding constitutional lawyers of the day, Senator Reverdy Johnson and former Attorney General Henry Stanbery. Moreover, Ku Klux violence was more virulent and widespread in South Carolina than in any other state in that year. Only in South Carolina did the president suspend the writ of habeas corpus under the Ku Klux Klan Act of 1871. The Klan controlled several counties in the northwestern portion of the state. Intimidation of witnesses was great, and the sheer volume of potential cases was staggering. Consequently, the difficulties that confronted federal legal officers in the pretrial investigation and preparation of these cases as well as in the courtroom proceedings were greater in South Carolina than in any other state. Yet, more cases were instituted there than anywhere else (390), and more cases were completed in this state than in any other (112). At the same time, Corbin *nolle prosequi* relatively few of these cases (20). Corbin's handling of other federal criminal cases reflected the strain of these Enforcement Acts prosecutions. His conviction rate in these cases was a poor 33%, his acquittal rate a somewhat high 26%, and his *nolle prosequi* rate of 41% was 10% higher than average. By the end of 1871, the burden of the month-long trial of those 5 convicted defendants was reflected in the 278 cases involving some 420 persons that had to be carried over into 1872. Apart from the difficulties confronting Corbin, his attitude toward the trials to a significant degree accounted for his poor performance. Unfavorable to the policy reflected in the Enforcement Acts, he was careful to separate himself from that policy in court. The bungling manner in which he presented these cases before the court reflected this attitude. Corbin's abilities as an attorney are seriously challenged by his performance in these trials.[25]

Most Ku Klux Klan cases remained untried at the end of 1871 in the states in which most Enforcement Acts cases were instituted. Seventy-six percent were carried over into 1872. Not one such case was settled in Alabama or Mississippi. In these two states, trials were delayed by constitutional challenges to the Enforcement Acts and the inability of legal officers to prepare cases for trial. United States attorneys in all five states generally failed to dispose of as many criminal cases as their counterparts in other states. Sixty-six percent of the criminal cases in these states were carried over into 1872, whereas the average for all judicial districts was only 41%. Similarly, these states had poorer rates of conviction and higher rates of cases that were *nolle prosequi*. However, the legal officers in these states reduced the acquittal rate 4% below the average of 18%. Aggregates for these states show that, while federal legal officers there were generally less successful in bringing cases to trial, in convicting defendants and in clearing judicial criminal dockets, they actually performed better in Enforcement Acts cases than they did in other criminal cases. However, the aggregates do not reflect the high degree of success with which United States Attorney Starbuck performed in North Carolina and the comparatively poor showing of United States attorneys in South Carolina and Tennessee.[26]

By the end of 1871 Akerman realized that the judicial process was incapable of reaching every offense and every offender. In his annual report for that year, he referred to the South Carolina cases and declared:

With the caution and deliberation which the law wisely observed in criminal proceedings, it is obvious that the attempt to bring to justice, through the forms of law, even a small portion of the guilty in that State must fail, or the judicial machinery of the United States must be increased. If it takes a court over one month to try five offenders, how long will it take to try four hundred, already indicted, and many hundreds more who deserve to be indicted?

To a lesser extent, these observations were applicable to other states as well.[27]

As the inability of the federal judiciary in South Carolina to prosecute every offender of the Enforcement Acts became evident at the end of 1871, the attorney general was forced to change his objectives and purposes there. Attorney General Akerman's original policy of assuming the administration of justice in Ku Klux Klan cases gave way to a more modest policy of selective prosecutions. Ringleaders and those who "contributed intelligence and social influence to these conspiracies," along with persons who had committed "acts of deep criminality," were to be prosecuted as soon as possible. Individuals "whose criminality is inferior to that of the first class," but still great enough "to require some visitation from the law" were to be released on bail and tried later. Finally, those persons who had been unwilling participants in these conspiracies and did not participate in violent crimes were to be spared punishment if they demonstrated "penitence for their offenses, and a determination to abstain from such crimes in the future." A confession of their crimes was an adequate demonstration of their penitence, but their confessions were to be kept on file just in case they did not "bear themselves as good citizens henceforth."[28]

The original goal of administering criminal justice in Ku Klux Klan cases remained in effect in other states. But, in South Carolina federal legal officers were content merely to try to stop the violence and break up the Ku Klux Klan. The overwhelming number of cases there forced a shift in policy from punishing past crimes to preventing future ones. Furthermore, this more modest policy of civil rights enforcement better complemented United States Attorney Corbin's unsympathetic attitude toward the Enforcement Acts.

Akerman feared that the selective Ku Klux prosecutions in South Carolina held potential dangers. He worried that prosecuting only a few of the criminals might be interpreted by the Klan as a weakening of the government's will to enforce law and order, or, worse, as a capitulation to terrorism. In either case he believed that the Klan might be encouraged to continue and even increase its criminality. He cautioned United States Deputy Marshal Charles Prossner: "As long as these bad men believe you are unable to protect yourselves, they will cherish the purpose of injuring you as soon as the hand of

the Government shall be withdrawn." He urged United States Attorney
Corbin to do nothing that might appear to be faltering. Nor did he fail to see
the same implications in other states where the courts were utterly unable to
try all cases. The ability to bring to trial only a portion of civil rights violations rendered convictions all the more imperative. Thus, he confided the
hope that "our friends will be cautious in prosecuting under these laws, and
make sure that the facts bring the case under them before proceeding. A prosecution which fails is apt to react unfavorably." Consequently, if legal officers
could not try all cases, they were to strive to prosecute the best as well as the
most important cases.[29]

The enormous difficulties that confronted them discouraged even the most
committed federal legal officers. For example, while he was in Raleigh, North
Carolina, trying Ku Klux Klan cases in June 1871, Judge Bond wrote his wife that
"I am going to stay here and fight Ku Klux if it takes all Summer." By September,
however, he began to hope that some policy could be devised that would merely
put an end to Klan atrocities. "I am only anxious to devise a method to do so,"
he wrote again from Raleigh, "for all I want is an acknowledgement of its existence & of its nefarious character—that it is suppressed." He expressed impa-
tience at the snail's pace of the litigation. He wrote three months later from
Columbia, South Carolina during the trial of Ku Klux there that "if we go on this
way it will take till the next Presidential election to clean them out." Though his
sights were lowered, Judge Bond nevertheless was determined to punish as many
defendants as he could. "If all the defense try here is my want of patience," he
told his wife, "I shall see that it don't avail." With a dramatic flair, he concluded:
"I shall stay them out if it costs me my life." Even with judges who were as determined as Judge Bond, legal officers concluded that the federal courts "are utterly
inadequate" to secure person and property. This caused Attorney General
Akerman to wonder,

> whether, if in 1867, I had foreseen the strength of the prejudices to be encoun-
> tered, I should have had the courage to enter the field on this side, which I
> believed both expedient and right, I cannot say, but, having entered, I was not
> disposed to recede, though hard pressed by many adversaries, and sometimes
> sorely tried by those whom the necessities of the case made my comrades.

He was forced to grudgingly admit in November of 1871 that the Ku Klux
Klan was "too much even for the United States to undertake to inflict adequate
penalties through the courts."[30]

Growing difficulties in the North amplified the problems in the South. Northern interest in civil rights enforcement in the South was flagging by November 1871. The attorney general urged legal officers to expose Klan atrocities "and the rebellious utterances of some of the prominent leaders" in the hopes of demonstrating the gravity of Ku Klux crimes and reviving the declining interest of Northerners in the problems of the South. "If the people of the North really understood it," he told General Alfred Terry, "there would be an outbreak of indignation unparalleled since April 1861." He expressed the belief that if the country knew only half the truth about the Klan, it would "sustain what has been done there, and [would] insist that Congress shall furnish, and that the Executive shall apply, remedies still more energetic." Exposure of Ku Klux Klan terror thus became an important goal of civil rights enforcement. Akerman identified several sources of the growing Northern disinterest. "The feeling here," he wrote to a political confidant, "is very strong that the Southern republicans must cease to look for special support to congressional action." The federal protection of civil rights appeared to be too partisan to be considered an appropriate governmental function. At a time when political scandal occupied so much of the public's attention, it smacked too much of political corruption. It was easy to view civil rights enforcement in the South as another aspect of administration corruption since Democrats so vehemently insisted that it was. Furthermore, the North simply was turning its attention to other issues. As 1871 drew to an end, the attorney general complained that "[t]he Northern mind being active and full of what is called progress, runs away from the past. My apprehension is that they are not aware that the Southern people are still untaught in the elements of the Republican creed." Under these circumstances, Akerman ruefully concluded "that Congress will be indisposed to make any changes in the national courts that would secure their efficiency in suppressing this conspiracy."[31]

Shortly after expressing these views, Attorney General Akerman resigned his office. The circumstances surrounding his resignation are as mysterious as the resignation was sudden. He undoubtedly was asked to resign, or was forced to that decision, because he felt that he could not explain the reasons for this action "without saying what perhaps ought not be said." Some observers have suggested that his resignation was triggered by the Grant administration's unwillingness to pursue a more energetic civil rights enforcement policy. There is some reason to consider this a possibility. Akerman was probably more dedicated to a strict enforcement of civil rights laws in the South than other members of the administration, including the president, who had made the curtailment of government expenses and the reduction of the public debt high priorities. Grant's administration was also under fire for corruption, venal partisanship, extravagance, waste, military despotism, and tyranny, and prosecutions under the Enforcement Acts fed the fires of that criticism. The desire for peace and normality by granting amnesty to Southerners and restoring home rule to the South was gaining support among members and leaders of the president's party in 1871. The attorney general's policy was in conflict with this growing Northern demand to terminate the federal enforcement of civil rights and interference in Southern affairs. Some contemporaries thus believed that Akerman's resignation presaged a curtailment in civil rights enforcement. This surmise was given additional credence by the simultaneous resignation of the solicitor general, another known civil rights exponent, and by the appointment of Akerman's successor, George H. Williams, who was hardly noted for his interest in the cause of civil rights.[32]

Still, Akerman's resignation appears to have been unrelated to differences over civil rights enforcement. Politics may very well have accounted for his leaving office, but the politics of economics and finance were probably more influential than the politics of civil rights. The attorney general had long been unpopular with many congressional Republicans because of decisions he made concerning interest payments due the government from the Union Pacific Railroad. At any rate, civil rights enforcement policy almost surely was not the issue that forced Akerman from office. In the last days as attorney general, he confided that the "President, I am sure, is resolute in his determination to protect the friends of the Government at the South." He also believed that his successor would continue the policy of vigorous Klan prosecutions that he had inaugurated. His confidence was not betrayed, for civil rights prosecutions were not curtailed after he left office. In fact, the number of prosecutions actually increased the following year.[33]

Although they were burdened with the onus of Klan prosecutions, federal legal officers were gratified by the effect they were having on the Ku Klux Klan. At the beginning of 1872, federal officers felt that they were on the verge of destroying the Klan. They also were heartened by the sharp curtailment of violence that had resulted from their efforts. The fear of prosecution not only restored peace, but it also motivated Klansmen to confess their crimes in the hopes of gaining leniency. "They all plead guilty...," Judge Bond found, "[i]f you only won't hang them...." The United States attorney's ambivalence notwithstanding, federal prosecutions in South Carolina had so demoralized members of the Ku Klux Klan there that its leaders issued orders to stop all Klan activity.[34]

The federal authorities were winning the war against the Klan, despite their inability to prosecute every criminal offender. A few prosecutions with a high probability of convictions seemed to have had a more beneficial effect than bringing many cases indiscriminately. United States Attorney Minnis, for example, prosecuted only six cases in Alabama, but he won convictions in five. Thus, he happily reported that the federal court was "demoralizing and carrying terror to these lawless K. K. Klans." The essential factor in breaking up the Klan seems to have been the federal government's resolve to "declare war" upon it. It was the perceived determination of the government to punish wrongdoers as much as the actual success of selective federal prosecutions that struck terror in the hearts of Klansmen. United States Attorney Corbin reported at the end of 1872 that although 1,000 indictments were pending in the United States Circuit Court for South Carolina, only the prosecution of the leaders was necessary to restore peace and order to the state. Judge Bond shared this view, which he expressed to his wife: "We have broken up Ku Klux in North Carolina. Everybody now wants to confess & we are picking out the top puppies only for trial." Significantly, the successes of the Justice Department were earned within Attorney General Akerman's more modest policy of determined but selective civil rights enforcement.[35]

Although the Ku Klux Klan was on the verge of collapse, terrorism and violence were not completely eradicated. Federal legal officers expressed the belief that the continued vigorous enforcement of federal civil rights laws was absolutely essential to maintain the peace and prevent future violence. According to United States Attorney G. Wiley Wells, the Klan in Northern Mississippi was merely biding its time until the federal government let up in its prosecutions so that it could resume its wave of terror. Any leniency in enforcing the law, he felt, would revive the Klan and violence. Corbin similarly predicted that an orgy of terror would ensue in South Carolina unless the government continued to demonstrate its determination to mete out justice. Minnis feared that the mere failure of the Republican Party to renominate the president in 1872 would be interpreted by Alabama Klansmen as evidence of faltering in the North that "would revive their hopes and encourage new outrages...." Judge Bond observed that if federal enforcement power was curtailed in South Carolina, he "would not live in this State 24 hours if I were a republican...." The restoration of peace on a permanent basis, legal officers believed, depended on continued energetic prosecutions under the Enforcement Acts.[36]

The optimism engendered by federal prosecutions of the Klan thus rested on a tenuous basis at best. The prosecutions had not eliminated violence and intimidation as instruments of political action, to say nothing of the racism and parochial prejudice from which these political tools were fashioned. United

States Attorney Wharton added another insight into the problem when he observed that in Kentucky "and in all the Southern States there exists a public sentiment which justifies the taking of human life upon very small pretext," whether the life was that of a black or a white person. While a general tradition of lawlessness undoubtedly accounts in part for the Ku Klux Klan, a Texas federal marshal identified a more fundamental and distinguishing characteristic of the Klan when he reported that "[i]n their hearts the rebellion has never been 'crushed out.'"[37]

Although the criminality of the Ku Klux Klan was exposed in federal trials during 1871, Southern apologists persisted in their support of it in 1872. They continued to oppose and impede federal legal officers who were struggling to enforce federal laws. Rather than conceding the criminality of Ku Klux violence, Southern Democratic Conservatives viewed Klansmen as defenders of Southern nationalism and excoriated federal officials for martyring them in their judicial "persecutions." They insisted that the Klan was not the cause of Southern violence, but that the organization was reacting defensively to the violence that was actually caused by federal interference in Southern communities. In their opinion, peace would be restored only when the federal authorities restored law enforcement to the people of the South. Even Southerners who condemned Ku Klux violence believed that the Enforcement Acts instigated lawlessness, and that peace, law, and order would be restored only when the federal government ceased its unwarranted and unconstitutional intrusion into Southern life.[38]

The vituperation of the Southern conservative press and mind intimidated federal witnesses and jurors. It also generated continued assaults upon them and legal officers. Though violence was reduced to minimal levels during 1872, federal legal officers still performed their duties in danger. The threat of violence was still great enough in some areas of Alabama and Mississippi to require military protection and assistance for the operation of federal officers and the judicial process.[39]

With the need for civil rights enforcement as great as ever, some question was raised as to whether vigorous civil rights enforcement would be sustained in light of growing Northern opposition. Furthermore, the president faced reelection in 1872, and his policies and actions were usually calculated to curry votes. Southern Democratic Conservatives, and particularly Ku Klux victims of Akerman's radicalism who so strongly desired a more conciliatory administration, largely interpreted Akerman's resignation as a harbinger of a more congenial presidential posture toward the South during the election year of 1872. However,

Justice Department officers believed that continued vigorous civil rights enforcement was essential to the peace and security of Southern Republicans even though they seem to have succeeded in destroying the Klan. The Grant administration's civil rights enforcement policy was, therefore, a critical factor in shaping the political life of the South.[40]

5

The Department of Justice and the Retreat from Civil Rights Enforcement, 1872–1873

Before his appointment as attorney general, George H. Williams represented the frontier state of Oregon in the House of Representatives. As a congressman, he earned a reputation for crass partisanship rather than for judiciousness and commitment to principle one might expect of the chief legal officer of the United States. His appointment as attorney general in late 1871 thus fueled speculation that President Grant was gearing up for the forthcoming presidential election. Indeed, Grant's biographer concluded that the change in attorneys general was a political maneuver intended to satisfy a Pacific Coast demand for cabinet representation. Further, this change encouraged Southern Democratic Conservatives who sought to bargain politically with the president for leniency toward the South.[1]

The new attorney general left no doubt, however, that he fully supported his predecessor's policy of civil rights enforcement and that he intended to continue it. He informed federal legal officers that

> [t]he Department has no intention of abandoning proceedings against any persons who may have rendered themselves answerable to the laws of the United States....Wherever parties have been charged with crimes it is the wish of the Department that the District Attorney...vigorously prosecute them to a conviction. It is my intention as far as it may be in my power to see that the laws of the United States are faithfully carried out and the parties offending against them properly punished.

Williams expressed to District Judge Busteed his belief that vigorous federal civil rights enforcement would restore peace, law, and order in the South. Consequently, he prodded the foot-dragging United States attorney in Atlanta, Georgia, John D. Pope: "I am sure it is only necessary to apprise you of such criminal acts to cause them to be inquired into and prosecuted with diligence and earnestness." He even authorized United States Attorney Minnis to assume the prosecution of certain cases in which Alabama state authorities already had begun to bring defendants to justice.[2]

Like Akerman, Williams soon learned that an all-out effort to enforce federal laws was unrealistic because of budgetary limitations. The original appropriations of $2,000,000 for fiscal 1872 was increased by another $1,200,000 just before the fiscal year ended, and these amounts still fell some $300,000 short of expenses incurred that fiscal year. Some dedicated legal officers even subsidized court expenses out of their own private funds, sometimes without expectation of repayment. When repayment was made, delays of a year or more were not uncommon. Still, Attorney General Williams recognized the need to employ additional legal counsel in Ku Klux cases. He authorized the United States attorneys in North and South Carolina to hire assistant attorneys in the spring of 1872, even though the department's court funds had been completely depleted.[3]

The attorney general authorized expenditures beyond the congressionally approved budget in the expectation of an additional deficiency appropriation. Congress, however, was not as accommodating as Williams expected; it failed to authorize additional funds through the rest of calendar 1872. Confronted in the summer of 1872 with escalating judicial expenses and an uncooperative Congress, he began to issue directives to curtail expenses with increasing urgency and firmness. He also began to accuse federal legal officers of excess and waste. Although Williams recognized that the hundreds of Ku Klux prosecutions in states such as South Carolina necessitated increased court costs, he nevertheless insisted that "the exercise of rigid economy" by legal officers could substantially reduce their expenses. He could not understand, therefore, how judicial expenses could legitimately have increased "so enormously" in the Southern states, and he concluded that such increases represented "the most unwarrantable extravagance." Williams's directives to curtail judicial expenses thus took on increasingly menacing tones.[4]

Williams also believed that "a very large portion" of these costs was due to corruption and abuse. Federal commissioners and marshals were beyond the attorney general's control, and they determined the number of cases heard and the expenses incurred by the federal courts. They and the United States attorneys earned only nominal salaries; most of their income was derived from fees. They therefore had an interest in multiplying the number of prosecutions instituted in the federal courts. The attorney general believed that the government was paying unnecessarily for "frivolous and vexatious prosecutions" that were brought by these legal officers to increase their incomes. In addition, witnesses were paid a per diem of $2 to $3, and Williams believed that large numbers of witnesses were often brought long distances unnecessarily. Many of these persons either did not testify at all, or, if they did testify, their testimony contributed nothing of importance. Although he admitted he had little or no evidence to support these claims, he implicitly attributed these abuses primarily to Enforcement Acts cases.[5]

The accuracy of the attorney general's charges is very difficult to prove or disprove. His annual reports did not include judicial expenses for the respective judicial districts until 1872. Exact comparisons with previous years is therefore impossible. However, total judicial expenses for fiscal 1872 were only $40,387 greater than those for fiscal 1871. This represented a 1% increase. Unless judicial districts in Northern states had sharply reduced their expenses, judicial costs in the South could not have increased very significantly. Furthermore, in those states having the highest number of Ku Klux cases, the number of cases the courts handled rose by 119% (315) in 1871 over the previous year and again by 77% (446) in 1872. South Carolina reported almost twice as many cases handled by the courts (105) in 1872 than the previous year. North Carolina reported 68 fewer cases disposed of in 1872 than in 1871. This difference was due primarily to the removal of Enforcement Acts cases to the newly created Western District and the decision of the United States attorney to await the return of Circuit Court Judge Bond to try these cases. The federal courts in Mississippi disposed of five and one-half times more cases in 1872 (488) than they did in 1871 (74). The rate of increase in prosecutions in these states was substantially greater than the overall rate of increase in judicial expenses. This would tend to contradict the attorney general's charge that prosecutions were being brought in these states extravagantly. On the other hand, judicial districts in states other than these five experienced a 9% decline in the number of cases handled by the courts (474). While this evidence is insufficient definitively to support any conclusions, it does suggest that judicial districts with the highest incidence of Enforcement Acts cases were not extravagant or corrupt unless one assumes that these prosecutions were brought frivolously and unnecessarily.[6]

Statistics for 1873 show that these judicial districts continued to function economically. In fiscal 1873, total judicial costs for all districts declined below fiscal 1871 levels. This represented a 1.5% ($45,464) decrease in judicial expenses. Judicial districts having the largest number of Ku Klux cases experienced a 26% ($191,959) reduction in expenditures while the number of cases they handled continued to rise by 13% (135). This increase was due essentially to prosecutions in North Carolina. However, other judicial districts reduced the number of cases handled by 47% (2,132), but their expenditures for court expenses dropped only 6% ($146,495). The reduction of court costs, however, was even greater for the five states of greatest Enforcement Acts prosecutions. In North Carolina, expenditures dropped 25% ($45,585), while cases handled by the courts rose 202% (370). Although North Carolina's performance was not typical of the other judicial districts with high incidents of Enforcement Acts prosecutions, these statistics support the conclusion that these prosecutions were not primarily responsible for waste, extravagance, and mounting judicial expenses. In fact, the courts in these states appear to have been more economical and more effective than average.

The effectiveness of Enforcement Acts prosecutions is more obvious when they are compared to other federal criminal prosecutions. For 1872, the number of cases handled by all federal courts (5,593) remained about the same as in 1871 (5,621). However, in those states with the largest number of Enforcement Acts prosecutions, the number of cases handled rose 77% (from 579 to 1,025). In other states that number declined 9% (from 5,042 to 4,568). Enforcement Acts cases accounted for most of the increase in cases handled in Enforcement Acts states. Enforcement Acts prosecutions rose 217% (339) while the increase in other criminal cases was 25% (107).

In Enforcement Acts states, convictions in Enforcement Acts cases rose 300% (336), in other criminal cases 7% (20), or 82% (356) in all. In other states, all convictions dropped 3%. The conviction rate for Enforcement Acts cases in Enforcement Acts states rose from 48% (112) in 1871 to 56% (448) in 1872, which was about average for all criminal cases in all federal judicial districts. However, the acquittal rate in Enforcement Acts cases dropped sharply in Enforcement Acts states from 19% (44) in 1871 to only 6% (47) in 1872, which was substantially below the average acquittal rate of 15% for all criminal cases in all states. The conviction rate of 33% (340) and acquittal rate of 19% (190) in other criminal cases in Enforcement Acts states were much poorer. United States attorneys in Enforcement Acts states thus markedly increased the number of cases handled by the federal courts, the number of Enforcement Acts convictions, and decreased the number of acquittals. By doing so, however, they sacrificed their effectiveness in other criminal cases.

The number of Enforcement Acts cases that were *nolle prosequi* in these states also rose sharply by 299% (233) in 1872. Still, this represented only a 5 percentage-point increase (from 33% in 1871 to 38% in 1872) in the proportion of *nolle prosequi* cases to all cases handled. However, the proportion of Enforcement Acts cases that were *nolle prosequi* was 10% lower than the proportion of other criminal cases that were *nolle prosequi*. Federal authorities in Enforcement Acts states had a greater tendency to *nolle prosequi* cases than their counterparts in other states. This tendency, however, was not another cost of effectiveness in Enforcement Acts prosecutions. Those states in which courts handled the greatest number of prosecutions had the lowest rates of *nolle prosequi* cases. The states of Alabama and Tennessee primarily accounted for the high rate of *nolle prosequi* cases: only 18% (36) and 17% (233) of the cases were handled by the courts. The federal district judges in both of these states were notorious for their absenteeism and unwillingness to hold court and to enforce federal law generally. It is not surprising that these states had large numbers of *nolle prosequi* cases.

Mississippi and South Carolina were extraordinarily successful in Enforcement Acts prosecutions during 1872. Mississippi accounted for 73% (356) of all Enforcement Acts convictions and South Carolina accounted for 19% (86). Legal authorities in Mississippi achieved a 73% conviction rate while those in South Carolina won an astounding 90% of their cases by conviction. South Carolina's success probably was due to United States Attorney Corbin's instructions to prosecute only the best cases. Authorities in Mississippi maintained their high conviction rate while disposing of most of their criminal cases; 56% (490) of the Enforcement Acts cases were heard by the courts, while 44% (385) were carried over into 1873.

The disposal rate was quite the reverse in South Carolina. While most of the cases resulted in convictions, the court handled only 7% (96) of the cases and 93% (1,207) were carried over. This low disposal rate is explained partially by the stiff opposition Corbin encountered in pretrial preparation and in court. He also undoubtedly tried to avoid bringing these cases before Judge George S. Bryan who sat in Judge Bond's absence. This may also explain why Corbin devoted relatively more time to the prosecution of other criminal cases. The desire to have Judge Bond on the bench in Enforcement Acts prosecutions also explains United States Attorney Starbuck's unwillingness to try Enforcement Acts cases in North Carolina solely before Judge George W. Brooks or Judge Robert P. Dick of the newly created Western District.[7]

The number of Enforcement Acts cases handled by the federal courts continued to rise in 1873, though more modestly than in 1871 and 1872. The total increase in Enforcement Acts cases handled by all federal courts in 1873 was 6% (from 505 to 537). However, this relatively modest increase becomes more significant when one considers that the total number of other criminal prosecutions heard by all federal courts declined by 40% (from 5,088 to 3,059).

The increase in Enforcement Acts cases that were tried occurred almost completely in Enforcement Acts states. These states also accounted for a 20% increase (from 530 to 636) in other criminal cases handled by the courts.

In Enforcement Acts states the number of convictions in Enforcement Acts cases increased 3% (from 448 to 461), but acquittals increased 34% (from 47 to 63). Convictions in other criminal cases increased 36% (from 340 to 462) while acquittals declined 8% (from 190 to 174) in these states. In other states, the total number of convictions dropped 53% (from 3,610 to 1,702), acquittals decreased 23% (from 958 to 734), and the total number of cases tried declined 47% (from 4,568 to 2,436). In Enforcement Acts states, the total number of convictions rose 17% (from 788 to 923), acquittals remained unchanged (at 237), and the total number of cases heard by the courts increased 13% (from 1,025 to 1,160). However, in all states, the conviction rate in Enforcement Acts cases dropped sharply from 53% (456) in 1872 to 36% (469) in 1873. This decline was comparable to the general drop in the conviction rate in other criminal cases from 54% (3,942) to 40% (2,156) for all judicial districts.

The sharp decline in the conviction rate in Enforcement Acts cases was due to the significant increase in the number and rate of *nolle prosequi* cases, not to fewer convictions. Whereas *nolle prosequi* Enforcement Acts cases in 1872 represented 41% (351) of the cases disposed, in 1873 they represented 59% (767) while the number of convictions and acquittals rose by similar amounts (13 and 19, respectively). Consequently, if *nolle prosequi* cases are excluded, 90% (456 of 505 cases) of Enforcement Acts cases heard by all the courts resulted in convictions in 1872, while 87% (469 of 537 cases) resulted in convictions in 1873. The same explanation holds for the decline in the conviction rate in other criminal cases. The increase in *nolle prosequi* cases also accounts for the rise in the proportion of Enforcement Acts cases that were disposed (31% [856] in 1872 to 40% [1,304] in 1873). Overall, then, Enforcement Acts states were more effective in criminal law enforcement than were other states. Although legal officers in Enforcement Acts states overall tended to be as effective in the courtroom, their effectiveness in Enforcement Acts prosecutions began to decline because of an increased tendency to *nolle prosequi* cases. This rise in the number and rate of *nolle prosequi* cases was due to instructions from Attorney General Williams.

Mississippi was once again responsible for much of the effectiveness in Enforcement Acts prosecutions. Over one-third of Enforcement Acts convictions were won in this state. However, North Carolina resumed its prosecutions of the Ku Klux Klan and won most of the convictions under the Enforcement Acts in 1873. Fifty-six percent (263) of all Enforcement Acts convictions were won in North Carolina. Mississippi and North Carolina combined to account for 95% (447) of all Enforcement Acts convictions that year. Federal attorneys in Mississippi almost doubled their overall conviction rate by winning 69% (184 of

234) of all cases they tried. Federal attorneys in North Carolina won a phenomenal 98% (263 of 269). However, success in the courtroom was offset somewhat by proportionately fewer Enforcement Acts cases being tried. In Mississippi, 53% (307) were carried over to 1874 and in North Carolina 74% (862) were pending at the end of 1873. Although federal attorneys in Mississippi won 184 convictions, that number was still 48% lower than the 356 they had won the previous year. The 263 convictions in North Carolina cannot be compared to 1872 because circumstances precluded the trial of Enforcement Acts cases in that year.

The resumption of Enforcement Acts prosecutions in North Carolina, therefore, mainly accounts for the overall increase in the number of cases tried in Enforcement Acts states in 1873. With the exception of Alabama, the other Enforcement Acts states experienced a decline in the number of Enforcement Acts cases and other criminal cases heard by the courts from 842 cases to 607 cases or 28%.

The reduced effectiveness of federal legal officers reflected Attorney General Williams's insistence on reduced judicial expenditures and clemency in Enforcement Acts cases. Because of the vast number of Ku Klux crimes and the stringent limitations on human and financial resources, the federal courts could prosecute only a small proportion of Enforcement Acts violations. The prosecutions that were instituted, however, usually ended in convictions.

Although the federal courts had been given an almost impossible task to perform in redressing civil rights violations, they accomplished their job exceedingly well. The decline in their effectiveness and in the number of Enforcement Acts prosecutions was due to the attorney general's decision to reduce judicial expenditures, not to changing judicial theories or the inabilities of federal legal officers. Judicial expenditures admittedly had to be closely supervised to keep them within available appropriations. But, given the relative efficiency of the federal courts in those states in which most of the Enforcement Acts prosecutions were brought, the attorney general's criticism of those prosecutions as excessively costly suggests that he used financial exigency as an excuse for curtailing civil rights enforcement. At the very least, one must wonder about the sincerity of his commitment to enforcing civil rights. The declining effectiveness in Enforcement Acts prosecutions apparently was due more to changes in the Grant administration's policy of civil rights enforcement than to faltering efforts of federal legal officers in Enforcement Acts states.[8]

Still, judicial expenditures had to be curtailed in light of inadequate appropriations for judicial expenses. If the rate of expenditure in the federal courts during the early part of the fiscal year 1873 had continued throughout the year, judicial expenses would have greatly exceeded judicial appropriations. As early as July 1872, Williams warned that funds would soon be exhausted unless spending was reduced. In December of that year, he informed Congressman James A. Garfield that judicial appropriations had been exceeded and that judicial expenses were being paid out of unexpended funds of the previous year. In response, Williams issued a circular to all United States marshals exhorting them to use the "strictest economy" in the expenditure of public funds and to use every possible means to trim judicial expenses.[9]

The shortage of funds placed the Department of Justice and its field representatives in an untenable situation. Departmental funds were dispensed at an accelerating rate. Whereas the appropriations for fiscal 1872 had been consumed by February 1872, appropriations for fiscal 1873 were gone even before the calendar year began. Although this spending trend probably was attributable to a legitimate increase in judicial business, the attorney general's solution to escalating costs was to economize. This made it impossible for United States attorneys effectively to carry out their responsibilities, particularly for those engaged in Enforcement Acts prosecutions. Given increasing dockets and the vast number of witnesses required in Enforcement Acts cases, court expenses could not be curtailed significantly without sacrificing achievement. Yet, the attorney general insisted upon a vigorous civil rights enforcement policy. This policy of vigorous prosecutions and judicial economy placed department legal officers in a dilemma they could not long endure.[10]

A resolution of the dilemma was signaled in September 1872. Former Confederate vice president Alexander H. Stephens tried to persuade Attorney General Williams to extend clemency to convicted violators of the Enforcement Acts. Hearing of Stephens's request, Major Lewis Merrill urgently petitioned Williams to reject all pleas for clemency. Merrill claimed that, because of the administration's policy of prosecuting only those individuals who had committed the most heinous crimes, clemency already had been extended inadvertently since the government had tried so few of the Ku Klux terrorists. He insisted that clemency would induce the Klan to go on a rampage of terror.[11]

Williams did reject Stephens's request for clemency, but he did so with an implied promise of future clemency. Admitting that Enforcement Acts prosecutions "impose upon the President an unpleasant duty, and one which he would if consistent with his official obligations gladly avoid," the attorney general announced a conditional change in the administration's civil rights enforcement policy: "[w]hen the President is satisfied that the danger from Ku Klux violence has ceased and that such unlawful associations have been abandoned, he will be

ready to exercise executive clemency in all cases in the most liberal manner."
Apparently the Klan accepted Williams's offer of peace because the election of
1872 was the most violence-free election during the entire period of
Reconstruction.[12]

Sensing the weakening in the administration's resolve, United States Attorney
Corbin, in an apparent change of heart, recommended that the administration
reaffirm the enforcement policy Ackerman had adopted a year earlier for South
Carolina. Apparently fearful of the consequences of further erosion of civil
rights enforcement, he argued against dropping prosecutions completely. If notorious murderers were not prosecuted, he cautioned, the Klan would interpret this
inaction as a license to murder. The threat of punishment had effectively
restrained the Ku Klux. Besides, dropping prosecutions just after an election,
Corbin observed, was impolitic. Doing so would give credence to those who
claimed that the prosecutions had been instituted for purely partisan purposes.
Yet, he suggested some reduction in federal enforcement as a way of improving
the relationship between federal legal officers and local authorities so that the
latter willingly might assume the burden of punishing civil rights violators.
This suggestion was curious because Corbin's experience gave him no grounds
for thinking that local authorities would assume the burden. On the contrary,
experience demonstrated the futility of expecting local authorities in the South
to protect Republicans.[13]

If Corbin was trying to head off a greater diminution in the Justice
Department's civil rights enforcement policy, he failed. "My desire," Attorney
General Williams informed the South Carolina United States attorney near the
end of 1872, "is that the pending prosecutions be punished only as far as may
appear to be necessary to preserve the public peace and prevent future violations of the law." Williams's "desire" represented another fundamental change
in the Justice Department's civil rights enforcement policy. Originally, the
department had tried to administer criminal justice in all Ku Klux cases. At the
end of 1871, Attorney General Akerman recognized the impossibility of achieving this goal. Hence, he attempted to prosecute only the most notorious and
important cases. A year later, Attorney General Williams suggested that of the
relatively few cases that had been selected for prosecution, fewer still should
actually be brought to trial.[14]

This policy was broadened beyond South Carolina to include all judicial districts. Legal officers were told to shun all Enforcement Acts violations except
those that could not be avoided. Officers who previously had been encouraged
to enforce civil rights vigorously were now exhorted to prosecute only those

crimes that had to be brought to trial. The administration's civil rights policy was changing from one of energetic civil rights enforcement to one of circumscribed enforcement.

During the spring and summer of 1873 the Justice Department completely abandoned civil rights enforcement. Instead of actually prosecuting violators of the Enforcement Acts, the government merely threatened prosecution, hoping that this would deter the Ku Klux from resuming its terror. This policy was enunciated in stages that began with an answer to a question raised by United States Attorney Andrew J. Evans in April 1873. Evans informed the attorney general that several Ku Klux prosecutions were pending before the federal court at Tyler, Texas. He asked Williams if he could dismiss the cases in view of the "enormous expense" they would entail and the probability of acquittal. Williams willingly consented. Further, he told Evans not to prosecute any cases unless the crime involved was a flagrant violation of the law *and* the probability of conviction was strong. He stated:

These prosecutions as a general rule are carried on to enforce an observance of the law of the United States and protect the rights of citizens; but when those ends are accomplished, it is not desirable to multiply suits of this description as they tend to keep up an excited state of feelings, and are a great expense to the United States.

Clearly, the administration had lost interest in redressing rights violations. Token cases were to be instituted to maintain the fiction that the national government would protect the rights of its citizens.[15]

The attorney general selected North and South Carolina to test this new policy of tokenism in April 1873. He instructed legal officers there to suspend all Enforcement Acts prosecutions for the current term of the federal courts to see if there was any need to proceed with prosecutions at all. Williams clung to the fiction that civil rights violations would "be prosecuted as heretofore," although he conceded that

[all] that is desired upon this subject is that Ku Klux and other similar combinations of persons, shall be abandoned, and the rights of all persons respected, and when this is done obviously there will be little need for proceeding any further with criminal prosecutions under said acts.

The attorney general was attempting to buy off the Klan with a policy of appeasement.[16]

By June, the administration was in full retreat from its original civil rights enforcement policy. Having selectively suspended prosecutions, Williams now ordered the cessation of future arrests under the Enforcement Acts unless he approved them. His intention was "to suspend these prosecutions, except in some of the worst cases with a hope that the effect will be to produce obedience to the law, and quiet and peace among the people."[17]

The reversal of the administration's civil rights enforcement policy was completed one month later. A delegation of leading Southern Conservatives paid a visit to the president at his summer retreat at Long Branch, New Jersey. Carrying a letter of introduction from United States District Judge George F. Bryan of South Carolina, they hoped to persuade President Grant to expand his new policy to include clemency for past offenses and pardons for convicted offenders. They gave the president the assurances of peace that he sought, so he accommodated them. Williams informed the delegation that the administration's newly found leniency stemmed from

> the belief that the Ku Klux Klan have, through said convictions, been almost if not altogether broken up, and that those, who were concerned in, or sympathized with, them have come to see the folly, wickedness and danger of such organizations. You have been pleased to say to me, and similar assurances have been given by others seeking the same object, that executive clemency at this time, in the Ku Klux cases would tend to remove many causes of uneasiness and irritation now existing and conduce generally to the public peace and tranquility, and the proposed action is taken in reference to such cases with the full expectation that these assurances will be verified.[18]

Implementation of the new policy of clemency was left to the discretion of federal legal officers, but this discretion created a political dilemma. The Justice Department expected that Enforcement Acts prosecutions would be exceptional. Federal legal officers who instituted even seemingly authorized prosecutions, however, were vulnerable to criticism and censure. The attorney general's angry inquiries into allegedly unauthorized arrests by Justice Department officials demonstrated Williams's acute sensitivity to complaints lodged against conscientious legal officers. He assumed that complaints against arresting officers were valid. Moreover, he made the officers prove that the arrests were consistent with departmental policy. If they succeeded, he neither commended nor supported them in their efforts. Consequently, the officers functioned within a hostile administration reminiscent of the Johnson years. It was safer, easier, and more politic to avoid Enforcement Acts prosecutions. Consequently, United States attorneys recommended the suspension of docketed cases even though they knew that this probably would lead to future violence and terrorism. After they had risked the danger and expended the energy, time, and money to fulfill their responsibilities, the suspension of these cases was a bitter pill for legal officers to swallow. To be criticized and censured by their superiors for doing their duty made their jobs intolerable. Some tendered their resignations. Others abandoned their efforts to enforce civil rights.[19]

These federal officers had been highly successful in enforcing the civil rights acts of 1870 and 1871. Their performance is all the more noteworthy given the exceedingly difficult obstacles that confronted them. Although large numbers of criminals escaped punishment, a high percentage of cases that were brought to trial under the Enforcement Acts resulted in convictions. These federal prosecutions were so effective that they virtually destroyed the Ku Klux Klan. However, they did not completely eliminate political terrorism. Chances of complete success would probably have been greater if Congress and the president had recognized Klan terrorism as rebellion and used the military to quash it. Legal officers instead were directed to put down insurrection through the judicial process. Their efforts were frequently heroic and demonstrated their commitment to enforcing congressional civil rights legislation. Their success also demonstrates that, within the limitations inherent in the judicial process, the laws themselves provided legal officers with sufficient authority to protect civil rights, even in the face of vehement and widespread resistance of Southern whites. When they were on the threshold of eliminating political terrorism, the attorney general ordered a halt to Enforcement Acts prosecutions and thus undermined the effectiveness of the civil rights laws. We will never know if the continued vigorous prosecutions under the Enforcement Acts would have secured civil rights in the South more permanently.

The Grant administration abandoned civil rights enforcement in the summer of 1873 despite the warnings of its legal officers about the effect leniency would have on the resumption of crime and violence. The cynicism of this policy is suggested by the attorney general's awareness of the consequences of eliminating federal efforts to protect civil rights. In the fall of 1873, he declared that a federal court's ruling against the constitutionality of the Ku Klux Klan Act of 1871 would encourage crime. Former Solicitor General Bristow agreed. The administration nevertheless embraced the propaganda of Southern Democratic Conservatives that law enforcement bred crime and that the absence of law enforcement produced peace, law, and order. The president and attorney general were apparently susceptible to this paradoxical argument because of the political priorities they had established and the political realities that confronted them. Beset with crunching financial woes, vulnerable to continuing charges of despotic, wasteful, corrupt and overly centralized government, and confronted with increasing Northern opposition to federal interference in Southern affairs, the fanciful logic of Southern Conservatives proved irresistible. The easiest way to rebut all of these charges while alleviating problems of finance and shifting political sentiment in the North was to give up power, curtail government oper-ations, and reduce government spending. The administration would thereby reap the additional political benefits from contributing toward rapprochement with the South. Each of these interests was served by ending civil rights enforcement.[20]

6

The Judicial Administration
of Civil Rights Enforcement,
1870–1872

The determination of the federal government's civil rights enforcement policy, to a large extent, lay with the federal courts. The Justice Department would have been powerless to protect civil rights if federal judges simply had held civil rights legislation unconstitutional. At the same time, the administrative and political problems peculiar to the administration of criminal justice by the federal courts complicated the judicial resolution of these novel constitutional issues. Judges, too, had to change their understanding of their role as officers of the federal government. They not only bore the responsibility of deciding whether constitutional law permitted the United States to assume these powers and functions, but they also carried the additional burden of providing the legal theories that either justified or precluded the national protection of civil rights.

Judicial interpretations of the authority of the federal government to enforce civil rights supported the vigorous efforts of Justice Department officers to secure civil rights. The legal theories justifying the exercise of sweeping authority over civil rights by the national government was analyzed in Chapter 1. That analysis focused on judicial interpretations of national citizenship, the nationally enforceable rights of American citizens, and the scope of national authority to enforce the rights of American citizens. Federal judges and most state appellate judges equated United States citizenship under the Thirteenth and Fourteenth Amendments with the status of freemen; they equated the nationally enforceable rights of American citizens under these amendments to the natural rights of freemen; and they interpreted these amendments as giving Congress the necessary authority to secure these natural rights. The assumption on which these interpretations were predicated, an assumption that was sometimes judicially expressed but was often implied, was that the Thirteenth and Fourteenth Amendments revolutionized citizenship in the federal Union by making national citizenship primary and state citizenship derivative of, and secondary to, national citizenship. Judges understood these amendments as giving Congress and the federal courts primary authority over citizens and citizens' rights.

Judges understood this authority to be virtually limitless. This understanding was expressed by Judge Busteed when he proclaimed that the Fourteenth Amendment gave Congress the authority "to pass police laws to operate within the political limits of a State to the exclusion of the police regulations of any State, and to punish the violations of such laws...." He upheld federal jurisdiction in all prosecutions involving combinations of two or more persons "to injure or oppress" another individual "in any matter affecting life, liberty or the pursuit of happiness." The United States attorney for Alabama, John A. Minnis, however, thought that, as a matter of policy, only politically or racially motivated crimes should be punished in the federal courts.[1]

This seemingly boundless scope of national authority over personal rights posed troublesome jurisdictional questions for federal judges. These judges struggled to find a legal theory to uphold what they regarded as constitutionally and legislatively authorized jurisdiction over these crimes without supplanting state criminal laws or eliminating the criminal jurisdiction of state courts. The judges could have declared the civil rights laws unconstitutional. That they engaged in the jurisdictional struggle at all shows that they accepted the primacy of federal authority over citizens' rights.

The perplexity of District Judge Hill illustrates the jurisdictional dilemma Enforcement Acts prosecutions presented to federal judges. He was confronted in June 1871 with the problem of delineating national and state jurisdiction over the murder of Alexander Page of Mississippi. Twenty-eight men were indicted under sections 6 and 7 of the Enforcement Act of 1870. They were charged with conspiracy to deprive the deceased of his life and liberty with the intent to deny him rights secured by the Constitution and laws of the United States under section 6 of the statute. They were also charged under section 7 with murder as the means by which they deprived the deceased of his rights to life and liberty. The defendants petitioned the court for their release under a writ of habeas corpus. The petition claimed that they were being held illegally since the crimes with which they were charged did not constitute offenses against the Constitution and laws of the United States. The basis of their claim was that the rights to life and liberty were not nationally enforceable rights of United States citizenship. Hence, the violations of these rights as charged in the indictment were offenses against the laws of the state of Mississippi that were cognizable only in the courts of that state.[2]

Judge Hill was troubled about how to handle the questions presented in the defendants' habeas petition. He expressed his anxiety in a letter to Attorney General Akerman. He described these legal issues as "the most delicate and difficult questions that have perhaps ever been presented to the Courts of the Country, determining the line between the National and State jurisdiction under the Constitution and these laws passed for the enforcement of the rights of citizens."[3]

Nevertheless, Judge Hill rejected the defendants' habeas petition and upheld the indictment. His ruling paralleled the reasoning of the federal judges discussed in Chapter 1. Declaring that natural rights were made nationally enforceable rights of citizenship under the Fourteenth Amendment, he concluded that Congress had the power to secure these rights through legislation punishing criminal violations of these rights. The Enforcement Act of 1870 was an authorized exercise of this legislative power. He resolved the jurisdictional conflict by closely adhering to the wording of the act's sixth section in defining the offenses for which defendants could be punished in the federal court under the act. To constitute a federal crime under section 6, Judge Hill ruled,

> there must have been a banding together, or conspiracy, between two or more persons, or two or more persons must have gone, in disguise, upon the public highway, or upon the premises of another, with intent to deprive some citizen of the United States...some right or privilege secured under the Constitution or laws of the United States.

Since the indictment defined the offenses according to these specifications, it was valid under section 6 of the Enforcement Act. The defendants were bound over for trial along with some two hundred other individuals who were indicted under the 1870 act during that term of the federal court at Oxford.[4]

Judge Hill had greater difficulty with section 7 and the charge of murder as the means by which the conspiracy was implemented. Section 7 provides that, if in the act of violating section 6 any other "felony, crime, or misdemeanor" is committed, the violation of section 6 shall be punished according to the penalties prescribed by state law for these other crimes. Judge Hill observed that murder was an offense under state law alone. The crime of murder therefore could be tried only in the state courts because the federal government cannot assume jurisdiction belonging to the states unless concurrent jurisdiction is conferred by law.

However, Judge Hill upheld section 7 and the charge filed under it. He ruled that the defendants were not being tried for murder under section 7 even though the indictment charged them with having murdered the victim as the means by which they deprived him of his rights to life and liberty in violation of section 6 of the Enforcement Act. He reasoned that section 7 did not create an offense for

which defendants could be tried. Rather, it provided a method for judicially determining an appropriate sentence for conviction of the crimes defined in section 6,
namely, depriving the citizen of his rights or privileges secured by the
Constitution or laws of the United States.

Judge Hill's opinion on this point represented a serious breach of constitutional law. Before a defendant may be charged with already having committed a
crime in furtherance of another crime for which he is being tried, he first must
have been duly convicted of the original crime. Therefore, a court may not convict a defendant of depriving a victim of life by virtue of his having murdered
the victim unless he was first convicted of the murder. In the case before Judge
Hill, the federal indictment charged the defendants with murder, an action that
was defined as a crime under state statutes. On conviction of the civil rights violation that was the consequence of the murder, the defendants were to be punished according to state statutes as if they had committed the crime of murder.
Since they had not been convicted of murder in a state court, they were being
punished for a crime for which they had not been tried. Alternatively, the federal
court would appear to be trying the defendants for the state-defined crime of
murder. That the jury verdict of guilty would specify the crime as the deprivation of life and liberty rather than as murder may be a distinction without a difference. Under the latter theory, the federal court would be trying the
defendants unconstitutionally for a state offense that was punishable alone in
the state courts. Judge Hill seems to have been aware of the difficulties with his
ruling, for he stated that he had "very serious doubts" that the penalties provided
in section 7 could be imposed if they extended to life or limb. He left that
question unresolved.[5]

Although he affirmed this decision in another case at Jackson, Mississippi, the
following month, Judge Hill expressed misgivings over its content and over the
novel involvement of the federal courts in the administration of criminal justice
that his ruling prescribed. Uncertain whether his opinion adequately preserved
state criminal jurisdiction, he requested the approval of Solicitor General
Benjamin H. Bristow. Bristow did not answer.[6]

Even though Hill confessed that he was "unable to perceive the distinction
between this holding, and that of...[Judge Woods's] Court in Ala...." delivered
weeks earlier, he feared that Circuit Judge William B. Woods would disapprove of
his decision. He may have feared Woods's disapproval because of the practical
difficulties his ruling presented in Enforcement Acts prosecutions of Ku Klux.
Government attorneys had to carefully word indictments to charge, and to
gather the evidence to prove, that a conspiracy had been entered into, or an act

had been committed with the intention of depriving the victim of a right of national citizenship. Proving intent, however, is one of the most difficult jobs of the prosecuting attorney. Nevertheless, this interpretation of federally punishable crimes against personal rights was not created out of whole cloth. Judge Hill merely applied the language of the Enforcement Act in a literal fashion.[7]

The administration of criminal justice thus plagued United States attorneys with jurisdictional problems as they attempted to draw up indictments under the Enforcement Acts. For example, E. C. Jacobson, United States attorney at Jackson, Mississippi, shortly after Judge Hill's ruling, expressed uncertainty to Attorney General Akerman over the sufficiency of merely alleging conspiracy and intent to deprive a citizen of his nationally secured civil rights. The case before him involved an attempt to deprive the victim of his nationally enforceable right to life. Jacobson's difficulty was in distinguishing the federal crime of assault with intent to deprive the victim of his life from the state crime of assault with intent to murder. His tentative solution was to determine if the crime stemmed from racial or political prejudice. Since racial prejudice was present in this case, he "amended the indictment by laying intent to have been to deprive the injured person of 'his *equality* of right to life' (or liberty, as the case required) secured to him by the Constitution of the United States." Skeptical whether this qualification would obviate the jurisdictional difficulty, he nevertheless added it because it introduced "a feature in the intent relieving the case from the appearance of an offence purely cognizable in the State Courts," since state criminal codes also included crimes of intent.[8]

Attorney General Akerman's response was supportive, but not very instructive. The federal administration of criminal justice was simply too new for anyone to have the answers to these questions, he replied, and federal legal officers would just have to proceed on a trial and error basis. "A few experiments," he suggested, "will demonstrate where the dangers are."[9]

How to distinguish between ordinary crimes and federally punishable violations of personal rights continued to trouble Judge Hill and United States Attorney Jacobson. Jacobson explained to the attorney general that his district was inundated with criminal cases because the public "seemed to take it for granted, from the popular name of one of the acts at least, that every deed of violence where disguise was used, was specially intended to be reached by the statute." Judge Hill apparently was satisfied that the presence of political or racial motives in committing what would otherwise be felonies under the state criminal statutes brought the offenses within federal jurisdiction. His problem was to find some way of distinguishing crimes that came before him in which such motives could not be averred. Jacobson still doubted that criminal violations of the rights to life, liberty, and property could be brought within federal jurisdiction "where the deed varied from a common-law offence only in that it proceeded from prejudice on account of difference of politics or race." He was uncertain whether this difference was sufficient to distinguish federal offenses from ordinary crimes. He undoubtedly joined Judge Hill in wishing that the Supreme Court would finally settle these and the other difficult questions arising from federal civil rights enforcement. It is ironic that the legal difficulties federal officers encountered in enforcing civil rights stemmed less from having too little authority than from having been given more authority than they knew how to apply.[10]

The first case challenging the constitutionality of the Enforcement Act of 1870 to reach the United States Supreme Court, *United States v. Avery*, originated in South Carolina. The crime had been committed by a group of Ku Klux who raided the home of a black person out of racial and political animus, robbed him of his weapons, and killed him. United States Attorney Corbin felt the need to consult Attorney General Akerman as he prepared the indictments for the Ku Klux trials at Columbia, South Carolina, in 1871. Corbin's question stemmed from the novelty of "setting up constitutional guarantees in an indictment. The specific rights involved were the Second Amendment right to keep and bear arms and the Fourth Amendment right to be secure from unreasonable searches and seizures. However, Corbin expressed no difficulty in charging the defendants with the murder that was committed in the process of violating the provisions of the Enforcement Act of 1870.[11]

Akerman's response was more definite this time. He questioned whether the Fourth Amendment guarantee against unreasonable searches and seizures applied to "an irregular and unofficial seizure," for he thought it referred only to "those made under color of official authority." But he was not certain of this and suggested that Corbin would do well to make the point. "Upon the right to bear arms," he added, "I think you are impregnable—and I think that under the Fourteenth and Fifteenth Amendments you will be able to sustain counts for a violation of the right of free political action." Corbin also had thought that the Fourth Amendment guarantee against unreasonable searches and seizures applied only to governmental officials, but, on reflection, he changed his mind and concluded that "this ought not, and never was intended, to be its full scope." While he was still uneasy about charging violations of rights in an indictment, he thought it was necessary to do so in order to protect the rights.[12]

Another case originally had been selected to test the constitutionality of the Enforcement Act of 1870. This case revealed the savage brutality of the Klan.

A night raid was made on the home of a black Republican by the name of Amzi Rainey. Klansmen fired upon Rainey and his family while his wife was holding a young child in her arms. They shot his older daughter in the head after they attempted to rape her. Rainey was saved from death only by promising that he would never again vote the Republican ticket.[13]

The defendants were charged with violating the Enforcement Act of 1870 in an eleven-count indictment. They were specifically accused of conspiring to injure, oppress, intimidate, and threaten Rainey with the intent to hinder and prevent him from freely exercising his constitutionally guaranteed rights to vote, to be secure against unreasonable searches and seizures, to the equal protection of the law, and to equal privileges and immunities. They were also charged with assault, breaking and entering, burglary, and robbery committed in the act of depriving Rainey of his nationally secured civil rights.[14]

The first count of the indictment was different from the other ten. It merely alleged the existence of a conspiracy to deprive citizens of their right to vote free from racial discrimination. It failed to specify the means by which citizens were so deprived or to identify the victims. United States Attorney Corbin probably was prompted to include this count by the experiences of United States Attorney D. H. Starbuck in North Carolina. The first large-scale prosecutions of Ku Klux had occurred in that state, and they had resulted in forty-nine convictions despite the fact that Starbuck also labored under uncertainties concerning indictments because of the novel nature of Enforcement Act violations. He had been able to prove to the satisfaction of Circuit Judge Hugh L. Bond, who was already predisposed to convict the guilty, that the Ku Klux Klan constituted a widespread conspiracy dedicated to destroying free elections through violence and intimidation. Starbuck thus was enabled merely to charge the defendants with being Klan members to make them liable to prosecution. Since Judge Bond was the circuit judge for South Carolina as well, Corbin may have attempted to gain the same advantage in South Carolina.[15]

Starbuck, however, had not been opposed by such expert counsel as Senator Reverdy Johnson, and former Attorney General Henry Stanbery. White supremacists in South Carolina established a public fund to retain Johnson and Stanbery to defend Klansmen and to challenge the constitutionality of the Enforcement Act of 1870 up to the United States Supreme Court. These eminent lawyers challenged the indictment in a pretrial motion. Stanbery opened arguments for the defense. His brief made three essential points. He argued, first, that the Fifteenth Amendment did not constitute a general guarantee of the right to vote. Rather, it merely protected black Americans in their right to vote in federal elections free from racial discrimination. He insisted that the amendment offered no protection in local or state elections. Stanbery's second point addressed the jurisdictional issue that plagued Judge Hill and United States Attorney Jacobson in Mississippi. Stanbery argued that the allegations of robbery and assault were not charged as overt acts of the conspiracy, but as separate and autonomous offenses. If they occurred at all, he insisted, they occurred for the purpose of robbing and assaulting Rainey, not for the purpose of preventing him from voting. He concluded, therefore, that these charges alleged offenses against the laws of the state of South Carolina that were cognizable in her courts alone. In his third point, which carried the greatest implications for the theory of national civil rights enforcement authority, Stanbery insisted on the narrow, states' rights legal tradition in interpreting federal authority. Conceding that natural rights were recognized by the Constitution of the United States, he maintained that "[t]he well established doctrine is, that the recognition of these rights in the Constitution is *a restriction upon the Federal authority.*" (Emphasis added.) Natural rights were protected not by federal authority, therefore, but by the state governments. Even where the state was incapable of protecting citizens against strong combinations, he argued, federal authority may be used only to assist the state in executing state statutes. He concluded that the Constitution prohibited the federal courts from intervening directly in the process of law enforcement.[16]

Senator Johnson's brief is more revealing for what it omitted than for what it actually contained. He prefaced his argument with the states' rights view of the federal Union and emphasized the principle that the national government is a government of delegated powers, while all residual powers remain in the states. However, he did not use this theory of American federalism in support of narrow interpretations of the Reconstruction Amendments. Nor did he unambiguously interpret these amendments narrowly. For example, he stated that the Thirteenth Amendment "does nothing but abolish slavery. It removes from the limbs of the slave the shackles by which he had formerly been controlled. Every right, therefore, belonging to a freeman, as a freeman," he added, "is his—literally his." He curiously failed to argue that the amendment did not empower Congress to secure these rights of freemen. He allowed to stand the implication of broad civil rights enforcement authority expressed in the latter statement. Nor did he discuss the authority to enforce civil rights under the Fourteenth Amendment or the nature of the privileges and immunities it secured. He merely asserted that the Fourteenth Amendment conferred citizenship and that the right to vote was not among the rights it secured. Again failing to dispel the implication that Congress possessed the authority to protect the rights of citizens, Senator Johnson based his case on the proposition that suffrage was not such a right.[17]

One possible explanation for Senator Johnson's implied concession of the broad scope of the Fourteenth Amendment may be found in the views he expressed in the United States Senate during the civil rights debates of 1866. At that time, he acknowledged Congress's power to protect the fundamental rights of citizenship. His explicit comments to the court about the charge of assault and battery suggest that he still held this view in 1871. His insistence that the Enforcement Act did not authorize this charge was based on the statute's language rather than on the absence of constitutional authority in Congress to punish such infringements of citizens' civil rights. Indeed, he declared that if the Enforcement Act had provided that the crimes alleged in the indictment were federal crimes when they were committed in the act of violating its provisions, those crimes would have been punishable in the federal courts. Since the Enforcement Act did not so specify, those alleged crimes remained offenses against the laws of the state alone. Senator Johnson's argument before the court does not appear to have been a mere legal strategy. He expressed similar views concerning the scope of the Ku Klux Klan Act of 1871 in a speech delivered before a gathering of Baltimore Democrats in November 1871.[18]

The government's case was opened by South Carolina's attorney general, D. H. Chamberlain, who had been retained as assistant counsel. Chamberlain offered rejoinders to the charges of lack of specificity and other technical weaknesses of the indictments. On the more substantive issues, he denied that the indictments alleged offenses against the criminal laws of the state. His reasoning paralleled that of Judge Hill's in interpreting section 7 of the 1870 act. Chamberlain argued that, in specifying crimes such as burglary as the means by which federal rights were violated, the prosecution was merely trying to provide a method of fixing the penalty for the federally punishable offense of depriving a citizen of his rights. The crime for which the defendants were being charged, therefore, was a conspiracy to deprive a citizen of his rights, not the state, created felony that was committed to further the conspiracy. He disclaimed any federal jurisdiction over ordinary offenses against the criminal laws of the state. Chamberlain espoused the nationalist interpretation of constitutional law to maintain that the rights infringed by the defendants are nationally enforceable rights. He reasoned that the recognition of rights by the Constitution conferred upon Congress the power to secure these rights. Noting that even defense counsel had conceded that natural rights, such as Bill of Rights guarantees, were constitutionally recognized rights of citizenship, he insisted that Congress was thereby empowered, concurrently with the states, to secure the personal rights of citizens from crimes such as assault, robbery, and unreasonable searches and seizures. Chamberlain, in turn, conceded that the wording of the Fifteenth Amendment did not clothe citizens with the right to vote. He nevertheless insisted that the amendment conferred suffrage on black citizens as a practical matter and pointed to the Enforcement Act of 1870 as evidence of the intent of the amendment's framers to do so.[19]

United States Attorney Corbin concluded the government's case. He was troubled by the ambiguity in the wording of the Fourteenth and Fifteenth Amendments and was peculiarly unwilling to insist on an interpretation of these amendments favorable to the government's cause. His remarks, then, were a puzzling blend of the broad nationalist and the narrow states' rights legal traditions.[20]

Like Chamberlain, Corbin observed that opposing counsel had conceded that natural rights such as Bill of Rights guarantees were rights secured to citizens by the Constitution. In a rather cleverly reasoned argument, he concluded that as the state governments possessed the power to enforce these rights by virtue of their bills of rights, so may the national government by virtue of the Fourteenth Amendment.

Nonetheless, Corbin's more expansive analysis of the amendment revealed the influence of the narrow legal tradition that viewed national guarantees of personal rights as mere prohibitions against governmental infringements. He argued that the Bill of Rights had been incorporated into the Fourteenth Amendment, but he assumed that the amendment merely applied the prohibitions of the Bill of Rights against the national government to the state governments. Conceding that the only appropriate legislation Congress could enact under the amendment had to be directed against state officers and institutions, he lamely suggested that Congress could nevertheless punish private individuals because it was Congress's prerogative to determine what constitutes legislation appropriate to the protection of citizens' rights from state infringements. Possibly embarrassed by the weakness of his argument, he told the court that he wanted to do no more than assert the proposition and let the court determine the meaning of the Fourteenth Amendment. Corbin made similar comments about the Fifteenth Amendment. Though he asserted that the Fifteenth Amendment secured the right to vote, he nevertheless conceded the possibility that it secured suffrage only against racial discrimination committed by the states.

Corbin provided a possible explanation for bungling the presentation of the government's cause in his comments concerning the Enforcement Act of 1870.

Characterizing the law as an indirect, inconvenient, and ill-advised method of securing the rights of citizens, he repeatedly disassociated himself from the policy it reflected. "I do not like the policy of the Act. I do not like the method. It has given me an exceedingly great amount of annoyance," he complained to the court. And, with an air of grudging acceptance, he declared, "but still it is there, and I am here to enforce the policy of the law, not 'my policy.'" Corbin rejected the opportunity presented to him in these trials to formulate an effective and persuasive brief for the authority of the national government to enforce civil rights. He instead completely deferred to the court's discretion in determining the meaning and scope of the constitutional provisions upon which civil rights enforcement policy was based. Although this function ultimately belonged to the court, in this case, the court was forced to perform it unaided by the government's legal officer.[21]

Arguments were concluded on December 6, 1871, and the decision was returned by the court the next day. The government was fortunate to have Judge Bond join District Judge George S. Bryan on the bench, for Bond's commitment to civil rights compensated somewhat for Corbin's clumsy presentation of its cause. Judge Bond apologized for rendering a hasty decision, but he explained that the urgency created by the enormous number of defendants and witnesses who were present for these trials compelled him to decide quickly. He brushed aside defense arguments to quash the blanket charge of conspiracy to infringe voting rights that comprised the first count. He found that the charge and the law upon which it was based were sufficiently definite. Further, he held the charges to be constitutional under the Fifteenth Amendment, which he interpreted according to the broad nationalist tradition. He acknowledged that the amendment's wording declared that the states may not deprive a citizen of the right to vote on grounds of race, color, or previous condition of servitude. But, like Justice Bradley and Judge Woods, he maintained that

> Congress may have found it difficult to devise a method by which to punish a state which, by law, made such distinction, and may have thought that legislation most likely to secure the end in view which punished the individual citizen who acted by virtue of a state law or upon his individual responsibility.

Judge Bond held that Congress's legislative power to secure the right to vote by punishing individuals who infringed that right was unlimited. He stated that, "in the line of its purpose, congress is the sole judge of its appropriateness." [22]

However, he was unwilling to apply the same broad nationalist reasoning to congressional power to enforce the Fourth Amendment. Instead, he applied the narrow legal tradition that depicted the Bill of Rights as mere limitations upon governmental authority. Consequently, he quashed the count charging a violation of the Fourth Amendment guarantee against unreasonable searches and seizures. The Fourth Amendment, he declared, "has long been decided to be a mere restriction upon the United States itself." In his efforts to reconcile conflicting legal traditions, he placed the guarantee outside the corpus of rights that are granted and secured by the Constitution. "The right to be secure in one's house is not a right derived from the constitution," he observed, "but it existed long before the adoption of the constitution, at common law, and cannot be said to come within the meaning of the words of the act 'right, privilege, or immunity granted or secured by the constitution of the United States.'" Judge Bond thus characterized the guarantee against unreasonable searches and seizures as a common law right rather than a natural right of freemen secured by the Fourteenth Amendment as a right of United States citizenship. He failed even to mention the Fourteenth Amendment and its impact on congressional power to enforce the Bill of Rights. The haste with which he rendered his decision may have prevented him from giving thoughtful consideration to the changes rendered by the Fourteenth Amendment in the national government's authority to enforce fundamental rights.[23]

Judge Bond quashed nine of the eleven counts. Five were thrown out because they failed to allege that Rainey was qualified to vote or that he was deprived of that right as secured by the Constitution. The count alleging that Rainey's Fourth Amendment rights were infringed was struck down for obvious reasons. Two counts were quashed because they lacked specificity. The judges divided over the allegation of burglary, so those counts were withdrawn and replaced with the charge of murder in order to try the case on its merits and later certify it to the Supreme Court. The court upheld two of the counts, the first charging a general conspiracy to deprive citizens of the right to vote and the last charging a conspiracy to specifically injure Rainey on account of his having voted for a particular candidate in a specific congressional election. The defendants pled guilty to the charges, and the case was certified to the United States Supreme Court under the name of James William Avery. Avery was Grand Cyclops of the Klan for York County, South Carolina, and a prosperous merchant there.[24]

One week later, United States Attorney Corbin again tried to persuade the court to accept federal jurisdiction over Bill of Rights guarantees in an Enforcement Act prosecution. In *United States v. Mitchell*, Corbin charged the defendants with conspiracy to deprive citizens of their Second Amendment right to keep and bear arms. Stanbery and Senator Johnson protested that the court had already decided that Bill of Rights guarantees were restrictions upon Congress and not authorizations of legislative enforcement of fundamental rights. They reminded the court that it had already held that violations of Bill of Rights guarantees did not constitute offenses under the Enforcement Acts. Corbin rejoined by distinguishing between Second and Fourth Amendment guarantees. Using Judge Bond's concepts, Corbin argued that the right to keep and bear arms, unlike the guarantee against unreasonable searches and seizures, was not a common law right but one granted and secured by the Constitution of the United States. Senator Johnson denied this seemingly specious and artificial distinction and insisted that the right to keep and bear arms and the conditions under which it was to be exercised were to be determined and secured by the states. Both Stanbery and Senator Johnson agreed that Bill of Rights guarantees were among the privileges and immunities secured by the Fourteenth Amendment, but they insisted that these guarantees could be secured under the amendment only against the states.[25]

Judge Bond either accepted Corbin's distinction between the Second and Fourth Amendments, or, after more thoughtful deliberation than he had previously given, changed his mind concerning the jurisdiction of the federal courts over Bill of Rights guarantees. He upheld the charge that alleged a violation of the Second Amendment and the government's authority to enforce that guarantee. However, Judge Bryan disagreed. Hence, the case was certified to the Supreme Court on that point and on the question of whether a felony under local law could constitute a federally punishable offense under the Enforcement Acts. Corbin urged Attorney General Williams to get a ruling from the Supreme Court as soon as possible because of the great number of cases and defendants who were affected by these issues. The Supreme Court decided the questions expeditiously. The case was argued on March 19 and 20, 1872, just months after it was certified, and the Court returned its decision the day after arguments were concluded.[26]

To have a case brought before and decided by the Supreme Court so quickly shows its importance. However, the manner in which the case was handled by the government and decided by the Court reveals their unwillingness to resolve the issues raised. The attorney general himself presented the case before the Supreme Court. He argued on highly technical grounds that the Court did not have jurisdiction to decide it on its merits. The Court agreed with Williams and refused jurisdiction on the grounds that it could not take cognizance of cases involving motions to quash indictments when the motions, as in this case, were preliminary in nature and subject to the discretion of the lower court. The ruling was somewhat ironic. The precedent upon which it was based had been written by Chief Justice Salmon P. Chase, who dissented from the majority opinion in this case.[27]

Subsequent attempts to get the Supreme Court to decide the issues also failed despite the repeated efforts of Senator Johnson to bring cases before it. The attorney general expressed astounding indifference to these test cases. He asserted that he did not "perceive that the questions presented in them are of such pressing public importance as to require immediate decision." The importance of the issues presented in these cases was too obvious for Williams to have believed this statement.[28]

The attorney general evidently wanted to avoid a final determination by the Supreme Court. This might have been a reasonable strategy. Federal district and circuit court judges had already upheld the constitutionality of the civil rights legislation enacted by Congress, and the government's enforcement program was able to proceed uninhibited on the basis of these rulings. At best, the Supreme Court could only affirm these lower court rulings. At worst, it could reverse them. Why jeopardize the government's civil rights enforcement program in litigation that risked all that had been won in the lower federal courts with little, if any, return? The Court's use of technical points of law to avoid a determination of the broader constitutional questions that were presented in these cases suggests that the Court was unwilling to decide the scope of federal authority to enforce civil rights.

Through 1872, therefore, the lower federal courts continued to bear the responsibility for determining the constitutionality and scope of national authority to enforce civil rights in the face of local opposition. The anxiety judges felt in bearing this responsibility is suggested in Judge Hill's regret over the Supreme Court's failure to decide a test case on its merits: "it would have thrown such light on all the questions here, that I could proceed with more safety…." District judges understandably wanted to shed some of this responsibility. More ominously, Judge Hill interpreted the Court's unwillingness to decide these issues as "an indication against the jurisdiction claimed and so far given by the Court here…."[29]

Discomfiture and uncertainty notwithstanding, federal legal officers and judges consistently upheld broad civil rights enforcement authority through 1872. Up through that year, only two district judges had declared any of the civil rights acts unconstitutional. They were John Cadwalader, Democrat of

Philadelphia, Pennsylvania, and Bland Ballard, Republican of Louisville, Kentucky. All of the other district judges in the Southern states upheld the statutes' constitutionality even though some of them were reluctant to enforce them. Judges in those states unanimously upheld congressional authority to secure civil rights, including Bill of Rights guarantees in most instances, as rights of United States citizenship. Although this authority created problems in fixing jurisdictional lines that preserved state authority over ordinary crimes, federal judges recognized a federal criminal police power that they applied to private citizens as well as public officials. Asserting a virtually unlimited authority to punish criminal offenses against civil rights, federal attorneys and judges sharply increased the number of convictions under the Enforcement Acts in 1871 and again in 1872, and they reached an apex in convictions in 1873. The federal judiciary thus succeeded where local law enforcement authorities failed, namely, in curtailing and eventually destroying the Ku Klux Klan. Especially in light of the circumstances under which they labored and despite the relatively few cases that came to trial, federal judges in the early 1870s were decidedly more successful in enforcing civil rights than the more recent federal judges who were charged with dismantling the Jim Crow system.[30]

Still, federal legal officers and judges anxiously looked to the Supreme Court of the United States to legitimize the nationalistic constitutional doctrines espoused in the federal courts to protect civil rights. On the other side, Democratic Conservatives looked to the Supreme Court with equal anticipation in the hope that the highest Court in the land would correct what they perceived to be a corruption of American federalism. Everyone knew that the Supreme Court would ultimately decide the constitutional scope of federal civil rights enforcement authority. But, with federal legal officers doing what they could to punish civil rights violators, with the lower federal courts providing legal sanctions for national civil rights protection, the public became increasingly conscious of the powerful role the Supreme Court was to play in determining public policy during Reconstruction.

7

The Supreme Court as
Legislature: The Judicial
Retreat from Civil Rights
Enforcement

T he United States Supreme Court first explained its understanding of the
theory and scope of the federal government's authority to enforce civil
rights in April 1873. The Court's initial interpretation of congressional civil
rights legislation occurred the previous April when it explored the scope of the Civil
Rights Act of 1866 in *Blyew v. United States*. By 1872 and 1873, the national political balance had shifted from what it had been in 1866, and the climate was no
longer favorable to civil rights enforcement. The political forces in Congress that
produced the Reconstruction civil rights enactments were fragmented. Many of the
political leaders and the shapers of public opinion who earlier had supported civil
rights protection were now opposed to Republican Reconstruction policies that
included the national enforcement of civil rights. Democratic Conservatives had
regained much of their respectability and power in national as well as local politics.
They, along with Liberal Republicans, exerted effective pressure upon the president
to curtail the exercise of federal power and to restore home rule in the South. The
Grant administration, struggling against charges of extravagance, corruption, and
military despotism, was waffling in its determination to protect civil rights in the
South. Northerners longed to forget the strife of the Civil War and Reconstruction.
As Attorney General Akerman put it in December 1871, the Northern mind was
"active and full of what is called progress...."[1]

The first civil rights case decided by the Supreme Court on its merits tested
the constitutionality of a federal prosecution for murder under the Civil Rights
Act of 1866. The case originated in 1868 when two white men, John Blyew and
George Kennard, brutally axed to death and mutilated the bodies of several
members of a black family in Lewis County, Kentucky. The ensuing investigation
by local authorities resulted in indictments for murder, and the defendants were
committed to the Lewis County jail to await trial at the next session of the
county circuit court. However, United States marshals removed the defendants
from local custody and placed them under federal arrest. Blyew and Kennard
were tried for murder before Judge Bland Ballard in the United States District
Court at Louisville. They were convicted and sentenced to death.[2]

The executions were delayed to allow defense counsel, B. H. Stanton, to petition the district court for a motion in arrest of judgment challenging the federal court's jurisdiction over the prosecution. Stanton's argument highlighted the fundamental conflict between federal and state jurisdiction over criminal violations of civil rights that later plagued federal judges and attorneys in prosecutions under the Enforcement Act of 1870. He noted that murder was a crime under the laws of Kentucky. It was not an offense under the laws of the United States. He insisted, therefore, that the prosecution of state-defined crimes in the federal courts was an unconstitutional usurpation of the state's exclusive jurisdiction over offenses against its laws. He observed that, if the Kentucky legislature were to repeal the statute defining murder to be a crime, the federal court would be placed in the untenable position of prosecuting a crime without a statute defining it as such.[3]

Judge Ballard upheld federal jurisdiction. He ruled that the Thirteenth Amendment incorporated the personal rights to life, liberty, and property into the nationally enforceable rights of American citizenship, and that the Civil Rights Act was enacted to protect these rights. Since murder and other crimes against persons and property violate these basic rights, the federal courts may constitutionally exercise jurisdiction over their punishment. He conceded that Congress had not enacted a criminal code that recognized such offenses as crimes under federal law. Judge Ballard circumvented this problem by interpreting the congressional intent behind the Civil Rights Act as authorizing the federal courts to try and punish civil rights violations according to the laws of the states in which the offenses were committed. This legal reasoning is somewhat analogous to other interpretations of the Civil Rights Act of 1866 as prescribing a concurrent jurisdiction over civil rights that permitted the states a role in establishing the conditions under which civil rights were to be exercised and enjoyed.[4]

Judge Ballard's decision was perceived by the Kentucky press as a usurpation of the state's exclusive authority to enforce its own laws. The Louisville *Courier-Journal* complained:

> If the State has the right to say what are crimes, as no one disputes, it has a right to punish them. The power to administer State laws, and punish crimes committed under State laws, was never given to the Federal Government, and the action of the Federal authorities at Louisville in this case is a bold, unmitigated and wanton usurpation.

The Maysville *Bulletin* noted that Judge Ballard's decision was based on Justice Swayne's *Rhodes* opinion of the year before, and the editor warned that it gave the federal courts "the whole power of the State, to administer by its own courts its own criminal laws." National jurisdiction over the administration of local justice represented the deepest penetration of national power into state authority. It therefore provided states' rights advocates with the specific issue they could present to the United States Supreme Court in their persistent resistance to the national government's definition of American federalism. They looked to the Supreme Court to establish the predominance of states' rights over national authority. The Maysville *Bulletin* thus urged the state government to employ the most learned counsel it could find to bring a test case to the Supreme Court to vindicate the usurped rights of the state.[5]

The Kentucky government needed little prodding. Following the recommendation of the governor, the state legislature appropriated funds to challenge the constitutionality of the Civil Rights Act of 1866 up to the Supreme Court of the United States with the hope of reversing what they perceived to be a revolutionary centralization of judicial power. The attorneys they retained to defend their states' rights-centered version of federalism included one of the foremost lawyers of his day, President James Buchanan's attorney general, Jeremiah S. Black, and the locally prominent Isaac Caldwell. However, the attorneys were at first reluctant to use *Blyew* as the test case because they feared that the atrocious cruelty of the crime of which the defendants were so incontrovertibly guilty would compromise their cause and the issues they wanted resolved. In the end it very well may have been the notoriously adverse facts that recommended this case as the one to challenge the Civil Rights Act of 1866, for it was the case on which they carried their challenge to the Supreme Court. Once the case selection was made, United States Attorney Bristow urged the attorney general to advance the case as quickly as possible in view of the great number of similar cases that were pending before the federal district court. Despite Bristow's urgent plea for an early decision, the petitioners' counsel successfully delayed oral argument for two years.[6]

The Supreme Court heard oral argument in February 1871. Opposing counsel made the arguments concerning federal civil rights enforcement authority that had been made in the lower courts since 1866. Neither Caldwell nor Black argued that the fundamental rights to life, liberty, and property were not federally enforceable rights of citizenship. On the contrary, their case was based on the theory that the Civil Rights Act was unconstitutional precisely because Congress attempted to revolutionize the constitutional structure of the Union by legislating to protect civil rights by conferring primary criminal jurisdiction on the federal courts. Invoking the narrow states' rights legal tradition concerning national powers, they insisted that the Thirteenth Amendment did not authorize such legislation because it merely abolished slavery. They also complained that the exclusive jurisdiction conferred by the statute upon the federal courts in cases in which a party claimed that his rights were not enforceable in the local courts would eliminate state jurisdiction over local crimes.[7]

Caldwell resurrected *United States v. Ortega* by using another theory to challenge federal jurisdiction. *Ortega* held that a criminal prosecution was a case that affected only the defendant and the state. In *Blyew*, the government claimed jurisdiction under the provision of the Civil Rights Act that gives jurisdiction to federal courts over "causes" affecting persons who are denied or cannot enforce certain rights in the state courts. If the only persons affected by a criminal prosecution are the defendants and the state, Caldwell reasoned, then the Civil Rights Act could not confer jurisdiction on the federal court because the black victims of the crime were denied the right to testify in the state court, as the government claimed. The black victims were not persons affected by the prosecution, according to *Ortega*. There was a problem in this argument, however. Justice Swayne had already rejected it as circuit justice by ruling that *Ortega* did not apply to the Civil Rights Act because *Ortega* referred to criminal "cases" while the statute referred to criminal "causes." Swayne ruled that the victims of a crime were persons affected by a criminal cause or prosecution within the meaning of the Civil Rights Act. In pressing the point, though, Caldwell presented it for review by the Supreme Court.[8]

Both Black and Caldwell attempted to persuade the Court of the impracticability as well as the unconstitutionality of the administration of criminal justice by the federal courts. They skillfully used the floodgate theory to argue that the application of the Civil Rights Act to this kind of prosecution would inundate the federal courts with every case in which a party claimed he could not enforce or redress his rights in the local courts. They tried to alarm the Court with the revolutionary consequences that would follow if it affirmed the constitutionality of the Civil Rights Act. Caldwell sounded the alarm that earlier had been expressed by states' rights-oriented judges when he warned that, "if Congress has lawfully passed this [statute], then they have the power, to be exercised at will, to cover the entire ground of legislation touching civil and political rights."[9]

The government's case was presented by Benjamin H. Bristow, who had been appointed solicitor general of the United States. Earlier, as United States attorney at Louisville, Bristow had successfully defended the constitutionality of the Civil Rights Act and federal jurisdiction in this case as well as the *Rhodes* case in 1867. He held the distinction of being almost the only United States attorney to attempt the systematic enforcement of civil rights under the Civil Rights Act. He was well suited, therefore, to argue the government's position before the Supreme Court.

Bristow reduced the issues before the Court to two questions: Did the Civil Rights Act confer upon the federal courts jurisdiction over the crime of murder when committed by a white person upon a black person? If so, did Congress possess the constitutional authority to confer such jurisdiction? Bristow insisted that the Civil Rights Act did give the federal courts concurrent jurisdiction over civil rights and criminal causes when citizens were unable to enforce their rights in the state courts. He claimed federal jurisdiction in this case on the grounds that black citizens in Kentucky were denied the right to give evidence in the courts of the state in any case in which a white person was a party. Answering the objection raised by Stanton in the district court concerning the exclusivity of state jurisdiction over violations of the state's criminal code, Bristow argued that the Civil Rights Act incorporated the common law as modified by the constitutions and laws of the states. Federal courts were authorized to secure civil rights by trying offenses against the laws of the state because "Congress made the common law and state statutes the law of the United States," at least in those criminal and civil cases in which persons were unable to enforce their rights in the state courts.[10]

Bristow recognized that the power of Congress to give federal courts jurisdiction in criminal cases, as well as the constitutionality of the Civil Rights Act itself, rested on the Court's interpretation of the Thirteenth Amendment. He argued the broad nationalist interpretation of the amendment expressed by Justice Swayne and other federal judges. Since the Thirteenth Amendment abolished slavery, Bristow reasoned, it constituted a positive guarantee of the natural rights that "belong to all free men in every free government." He concluded that Congress possessed the power to "confer on all citizens those rights which…are…essential to the perfect enjoyment of freedom…." Thus, the Civil Rights Act was constitutionally enacted "in the interest of freedom and civil liberty, under a radical change in the fundamental law."[11]

The legal debate over the enforcement of civil rights begun by Congress in early 1866 finally came before the highest Court in the land. The legal and political consequences of the Court's decision were immeasurably greater at the time of the Court's deliberation in 1871 than they were when the *Blyew* case originated in 1868. During the interim, Congress had enacted additional and more sweeping

civil rights statutes that more explicitly conferred direct jurisdiction on the federal courts over offenses that were similar to the murders in the *Blyew* case. The
Enforcement Acts of 1870 and 1871 did not require a showing that the victim of
the crime could not enforce some right in the local courts before a federal court
could assume jurisdiction. These statutes directly conferred jurisdiction on the
federal courts by defining certain offenses as federal crimes punishable exclusively in the federal courts. Moreover, the federal administration of criminal justice had expanded beyond Kentucky and had become essential to the
preservation of law and order in areas of the South that were overwhelmed with
Ku Klux terrorism. While *Blyew* was pending before the Supreme Court, lower
federal courts were upholding the constitutionality of the administration of
criminal justice under the Enforcement Acts of 1870 and 1871 in decisions that
paralleled others asserting the primacy of national authority over citizens and
citizens' rights. The Supreme Court's acceptance or rejection of this radical legal
theory thus held grave implications for the Grant administration's civil rights
enforcement policy and the course of Southern politics.[12]

The Supreme Court deliberated for more than one year. Just days before
announcing its decision in *Blyew* on April 1, 1872, the Court manifested its unwillingness to resolve these broad constitutional questions. It dismissed the first case
to present it with these issues on narrow procedural grounds rather than consider
the issues raised by the constitutional challenge to Ku Klux prosecutions that
emerged from South Carolina.[13]

Although the Court was unable to avoid a decision on the merits in *Blyew*, it
nevertheless sidestepped questions concerning the national government's
authority over the administration of criminal justice. It therefore succeeded in
limiting the impact of its decision to the scope of one section of the Civil Rights
Act of 1866. The Court's ruling on the Civil Rights Act was a compromise that
upheld the act's constitutionality but eliminated the jurisdiction conferred on
the federal courts over criminal prosecutions of whites for crimes committed
against blacks. However, in upholding the Civil Rights Act of 1866, the Court
failed to affirm explicitly the broad legal theory of national civil rights enforcement authority applied by the lower federal courts. Consequently, the Court
failed to address, much less resolve, the urgent questions concerning the nature
and scope of the national government's authority to secure civil rights.

At least two explanations may account for the Court's reticence. It may have
wanted to avoid expressing a legal theory of civil rights enforcement based on
the Thirteenth Amendment when the Fourteenth Amendment had become the
primary constitutional authority for congressional civil rights legislation.

Indeed, it may have wanted to avoid explicitly embracing the radical constitutional theory of national civil rights enforcement it would have had to affirm in upholding the constitutionality of the Civil Rights Act of 1866 on the basis of the Thirteenth Amendment.[14]

The Court's opinion instead addressed narrow and technical issues and, with respect to those issues, it largely followed the arguments of Black and Caldwell. Speaking through Justice Strong, the Court rejected Justice Swayne's decision in *Rhodes* to the extent that it ruled that a criminal prosecution for a public offense was a cause affecting the victim of the crime. On the contrary, Strong concluded that "the only parties to such a cause are the government and the persons indicted." If federal jurisdiction could be invoked by merely claiming that potential witnesses, albeit victims of the crime, were precluded from giving evidence because of their race or color, Strong reasoned, "there is no cause either civil or criminal of which those courts may not at the option of either party take jurisdiction…." The federal courts could be saddled with any suit, even those involving only white parties, whenever one of the parties alleged that a black person might be an important witness. Strong expressed disbelief that Congress intended to exercise national authority in this way.[15]

At the same time, the Court concluded that the Civil Rights Act was intended to afford black citizens the protection of the federal courts by giving those courts jurisdiction over cases in which a black citizen's "personal, relative, or property rights" could not be enforced in the state courts. The Court therefore upheld federal jurisdiction over criminal cases in which blacks were defendants and could not enforce their rights in the state courts. The Court interpreted the Civil Rights Act as giving jurisdiction to federal courts when a party to the cause merely claimed that his rights were infringed by, or could not be enforced or redressed in the state courts. The petitioner did not have to first exhaust the state's appellate process. However, these concessions to national civil rights enforcement authority were offset by the elimination of a vast area of protection that had been exercised by the federal legal and judicial officers in Kentucky. Blacks would have to look to hostile local legal officers and judges to prosecute crimes committed against them.[16]

Justice Bradley, joined by Justice Swayne, wrote a stinging dissent. To say, as the majority did, that prosecutions such as the one before them were not within the scope of the Civil Rights Act, Bradley declared, was "a view of the law too narrow, too technical and too forgetful of the liberal objects it had in view." In his opinion, those liberal objectives were to give to the federal courts jurisdiction in cases such as the instant one and to provide a remedy whenever "the State refuses to give one; where the mischief consists in inaction or refusal to act, or refusal to give requisite relief...." Although he conceded that the "technical parties" to a criminal prosecution were the defendant and the government, Bradley looked beyond technicalities and insisted that the prosecution was a cause that affected the victim. He chided the majority for effectively depriving blacks of the right to testify and thereby subjecting them to "wanton insults and fiendish assaults," that would render "their lives, their families, and their property unprotected by law" and "brand them with a badge of slavery." He warned that the Court's decision would invite "vindictive outlaws and felons to rush upon these helpless people and kill and slay them at will, as was done in this case."[17]

Because the Supreme Court's decision represented a compromise that resolved few of the major questions concerning the authority of the federal government to enforce civil rights, it satisfied no one. Judge Ballard reacted with sarcasm: "Blessed are they who expect little for they shall not be disappointed. But if Congress meant what the Court say they meant is not all of their legislation which relates to the negro a mockery?" He underscored the point with a hypothetical consequence of the ruling:

> Think of the President using the army & navy not to capture the desperado who has committed numberless outrages on the negro & who sleeps secure under State laws, but to arrest the poor negro & drag him before the United States to be there tried & punished with high ceremony!!!

Ridicule might vent feelings of anger, but it did not alleviate the real difficulties that flowed from the decision. Future prosecutions of white offenders under the Civil Rights Act were virtually eliminated. Previously convicted defendants could not only gain release from prison, but they also conceivably could have sued the responsible federal legal officers for false imprisonment. Solicitor General Bristow therefore responded positively to suggestions for their pardon. All of the defendants who had been convicted under the Civil Rights Act at the previous term of the United States District Court for Kentucky had their sentences set aside.[18]

Still, the decision conceded more to civil rights proponents than their harsh criticism allowed. The Court upheld the Civil Rights Act of 1866, which could be interpreted as an implicit acceptance of the broad nationalist interpretation of congressional authority under the Thirteenth Amendment. At the very least, the decision conceded to the national government a constitutionally prescribed role in securing civil rights under that amendment. These concessions were potentially significant victories for proponents of civil rights, particularly since Congress had enacted additional legislation under the broader Fourteenth Amendment to counteract the growing menace posed by the Ku Klux Klan. Consequently, John Marshall Harlan speculated that Black and Caldwell would find their fees reduced since "the Democracy are [not] at all jubilant over the result."[19]

Thus, the legal and political impact of the *Blyew* decision was ambiguous. There seems to be no record explaining why the Court refused to resolve the questions surrounding the scope of the federal government's authority to enforce civil rights.

The Supreme Court selected the *Slaughter-House Cases* as the instrument for its interpretation of national civil rights enforcement authority. The *Slaughter-House Cases* were argued in February 1872, just weeks before the Court dismissed one civil rights case on narrow procedural grounds and decided *Blyew* without resolving the constitutional issues of civil rights enforcement. The litigants were white butchers and a New Orleans slaughter-house corporation rather than blacks and Klansmen. The Supreme Court's selection of a case involving the civil rights of Southern white butchers as the occasion for its initial determination of the national government's authority to secure civil rights is more than ironic. This decision appears to have been a masterful political stratagem of the Court enabling it to decide politically explosive legal questions in a seemingly nonpolitical way. The Court thereby resolved many of the legal issues inherent in the national protection of civil rights outside the political context that made their resolution so urgent and controversial.[20]

Apart from their civil rights implications, the *Slaughter-House Cases* reveal some of the political tensions associated with the economic development of nineteenth-century America. Located next to the cattle ranges of Texas, New Orleans was one of the cities through which animal products were transported to the nation's growing urban populations. As with industry generally, meat-packing was beginning to develop a modern corporate structure. Control over the industry was becoming centralized in the hands of a few businesses. Complementing and stimulating the centralization of control over meatpacking was the growing concern over health and sanitation that was reflected in government-prescribed reforms designed to establish standards over the processing and distribution of food for human consumption. Several municipalities around the United States enacted ordinances during the Civil War era confining the processing of meat products to areas outside of their population centers and under standards established by their legislative bodies.[21]

The creation in 1869 of the Crescent City Stock Landing and Slaughter House Company by the Louisiana state legislature was typical of economic and political trends in other parts of the country. Legislatures in New York and Massachusetts chartered similar corporations, giving them monopolistic control over the slaughtering of animals, and state appellate courts upheld these measures. However, the process of establishing the Louisiana corporation was distinctive; it was riddled with blatant corruption, bribery, graft, and economic self-interest. The butchers who were adversely affected by the corporation felt a double injustice. They were deprived of their own slaughterhouses, and they were forced to ply their trade on the premises of a corporate monopoly for a fee. The monopoly introduced the corporate form of business structure to the area's meatpacking industry and presaged the butchers' demise as artisans and sole proprietors. It also represented a notorious example of a favored interest group receiving special privileges through the political corruption of the Republican-controlled state legislature. Given the circumstances that led to the creation of the slaughterhouse, the butchers and the New Orleans community generally were blinded to the genuine health and sanitation benefits that it might have presented to the city. Opposition to the monopoly as the creation of a corrupt Republican legislature, then, was stimulated by partisanship as well as by the portend of adverse economic implications for established economic groups.[22]

The complicated and, at times, absurd history of the battle in the local courts among the butchers, the monopoly, and the state of Louisiana has been ably told by Professor Charles Fairman. It is enough to mention that the various parties to the suits won conflicting and contradictory court orders from various state district courts in the city of New Orleans. The butchers won a court order permitting them to continue slaughtering animals as they had before the enactment of the law establishing the monopoly. The monopoly won an injunction against the butchers and an order requiring the butchers to use the facilities of the monopoly as provided by the 1869 statute. The state of Louisiana was enjoined from building the facilities that were authorized by the law for slaughtering animals, while it in turn won a court order restricting the slaughtering of animals to those facilities. The Supreme Court of Louisiana finally upheld the constitutionality of the statute and the corporation in April 1870, but its decision did not end the litigation.[23]

When the Louisiana Supreme Court ruled against them, the butchers brought their case into the United States Circuit Court at New Orleans. They hoped to win an injunction to prevent the city police from enforcing a local court injunction against the butchers that prohibited them from slaughtering animals in places other than the facilities of the corporation. The enforcement of this injunction against the butchers created a severe meat shortage in New Orleans and prompted public meetings to explore alternative solutions to the food crisis. Needless to say, public interest in the outcome of the judicial fight was keen. Great public pressure, mostly for a ruling favorable to the butchers, was exerted on the newly appointed circuit justice, Joseph P. Bradley, and circuit judge William B. Woods. Aware of the urgency created by the meat shortage, Justice Bradley ordered the corporation to answer within two days the brief filed by the butchers on June 6, 1870.[24]

Oral arguments were presented on the designated day. A packed courtroom was on hand to hear Justice Bradley's decision two days later. This case "excites more general interest just now than any other," the New Orleans *Daily Picayune* commented, because of its importance to the city's meat supply. Public reaction to the circuit court's application of the nationalist theory of civil rights enforcement authority to strike down the constitutionality of the slaughterhouse and to enforce the butchers' civil rights demonstrates that the decision's impact upon Reconstruction political issues was not evident to the public.[25]

The city's conservative white community praised Justice Bradley's strongly nationalistic opinion. The Democratic New Orleans *Daily Picayune* complimented Justice Bradley and Judge Woods as persons "involved with a high sense of uprightness, and a stern purpose to administer law impartially." The suspicion with which the people of Louisiana initially had regarded them was replaced with "universal respect for their learning, intelligence, courteous official manner, and regard for law in their decision." However, the Republican New Orleans *Times* caustically criticized Justice Bradley for his ignorance of the scope of federal authority, which, in the editor's opinion, Bradley stretched beyond accepted judicial limits to "a vast and indefinite extension of the power and authority of the judicial department of the Government." The 800 shares of stock the newspaper's editor held in the corporation may have motivated him to castigate Bradley for going out of his way to bring the case within the authority of the Constitution and laws of the United States and thereby "'convert our judges into constitution makers and amenders, with full power to lay down and proclaim what are the "civil rights" of men....'" The only New Orleans newspaper that commented on the implications of Bradley's ruling for the national enforcement of black civil rights was the New Orleans *Bee*. The paper described the opinion as "'one of the most luminous expositions of American constitutional law....'" The editor of this black newspaper asserted that not even the great Chief Justice John Marshall or Justice Joseph Story "'ever uttered grander principles than did Justice Bradley yesterday, from the bench of the United States Circuit Court.'"26

The practical effect of Justice Bradley's decision was to permit the butchers to continue their unrestricted slaughtering of animals and to enjoin the corporation from bringing any new suits against them. However, the ruling did not stop New Orleans District Judge Henry C. Dibble, a Republican, from enforcing a preliminary injunction against the butchers that was won by the state attorney general in the Louisiana Supreme Court before Justice Bradley's ruling in the federal court. Judge Dibble was outraged by Justice Bradley's revolutionary ruling, which he thought subverted the integrity of the state judiciary. Preserving the integrity of the state judiciary was perhaps less important than preserving the incorporator's investment in the monopoly. Its stock plummeted from $30 a share to $15 and remained below $25. Concern over the value of their investment plagued the incorporators throughout the litigation.27

The confused political impact of the *Slaughter-House Cases* is manifested by the attorneys who represented the litigants and by the positions they argued before the Supreme Court. Legal counsel for the butchers were led by a former justice of the United States Supreme Court who resigned his seat as a states' rights Southerner when his native Alabama seceded. John Archibald Campbell now argued the broad nationalist theory of national civil rights enforcement authority that was associated with Northern Republican supporters of civil rights. The corporation's counsel included a Radical Republican who argued for a more narrow interpretation of this authority. Democratic Conservatives and others who opposed the slaughterhouse corporation as a monopoly created by a corrupt Republican-controlled Louisiana legislature embraced the nationalist theory of civil rights enforcement authority associated with the Republican Party, while Republicans and others who wanted the slaughterhouse invoked a more states' rights-oriented theory of civil rights enforcement authority associated with Democratic Conservatives. Under these circumstances, the Court could decide the constitutionality of the politically controversial national administration of criminal justice in Ku Klux prosecutions without actually sitting in judgment of it, or of even giving the appearance of its having done so.28

The United States Supreme Court heard oral argument in the *Slaughter-House Cases* on February 4, 1872. Campbell presented his legal position within the context of the recent history of the Civil War. Arguing that the war was a constitutional struggle between national supremacy and state sovereignty, he stated that the Northern victory was translated into law and incorporated into the United States Constitution through the Thirteenth and Fourteenth Amendments. He interpreted these amendments as lodging the locus of sovereignty in the national government and, with it, primary authority to regulate and secure the natural rights of citizens. The same point was argued by Campbell's cocounsel, J. A. Q. Fellows, who quoted from the congressional debates leading to the adoption of the Civil Rights Act of 1866 and the Fourteenth Amendment as authority for this position. Campbell's brief paralleled the interpretations of national civil rights enforcement authority under the Thirteenth and Fourteenth Amendments expressed by federal and most state appellate judges since 1867.[29]

However, Campbell overstated his case and thereby provided the Court with grounds for rejecting his argument. He interjected a concept of dual citizenship that characterized national and state citizenship as separate statuses under distinct and exclusive jurisdictions. He therefore implied that the Fourteenth Amendment's prohibitions against state infringements of citizens' rights were absolute. His curt recognition of the states' police power to regulate the natural rights of national citizenship was obviously negated by the emphasis he placed on the exclusivity of national and state jurisdictions over the rights of their respective citizens. Indeed, Campbell drew such an absolute and impenetrable line of separation between national and state authority and jurisdiction that the states' police power, as it had traditionally been exercised, appeared to have been transferred to the national government. To decide the case on this view of dual federalism, the Court either would have had to sanction a revolutionary and seemingly impracticable transfer of absolute and exclusive police powers from the states to the national government or accept a virtually exclusive state authority over natural rights. Opposing counsel were quick to pick up this implication of Campbell's argument and drive home the point, successfully as it turned out.[30]

The corporation's case was argued by Republicans Thomas J. Durant and Senator Matthew H. Carpenter. They focused on the economic aspects of the case rather than the implications it held for a redefinition of American federalism. They insisted that the law establishing the corporation did not create a monopoly because it did not prevent the butchers from plying their trade. Rather, it merely regulated the way in which they prepared meat for human consumption to protect the health and safety of consumers. They reminded the Court of the long-established state practices of regulating the manufacture of certain products and of conferring special privileges in corporate charters. A ruling for the butchers, they concluded, would not only impede the states from licensing trades and products and regulating them, but it also would destroy the corporation as a viable form of business organization.[31]

Like defense counsel in *Blyew*, the corporation's counsel did not argue that natural rights were not protected by the United States Constitution. This line of argument would have been the strongest one for the corporation. But, this point would have been difficult for Senator Carpenter to press. Representing Myra Bradwell before the same Court two weeks earlier, he had argued that natural rights were secured by the Fourteenth Amendment. He also had expressed this interpretation of the amendment in the United States Senate the previous spring in support of the Ku Klux Klan Act of 1871. However, he discarded this interpretation of the amendment after the Supreme Court's decision in these cases.[32]

The similarities between the corporation's argument and that of the defendants in *Blyew* were not necessarily accidental. Jeremiah S. Black had been retained by the corporation, but, for some unknown reason, he failed to appear for oral argument. He may have suggested his strategy to Durant, for the latter used the floodgate theory argued by Black and Caldwell in *Blyew*. Durant warned the Court that if it adopted Campbell's and Fellows's interpretation of national authority, it would assume "a jurisdiction over every case there can be imagined in every court in every State in the Union." Justice Samuel F. Miller noted this danger in his *Slaughter-House* opinion. The points emphasized by Durant were wisely geared to justices who felt increasingly burdened with backlogged dockets, who called for judicial reforms to curtail its jurisdiction and relieve it of much of its workload, and who were struggling to determine the proper relationships of the national and state governments to each other and to their respective citizens. Still, Durant provided the Court with a legal rationale for upholding the corporation's charter as a legitimate police regulation without having to interpret the Fourteenth Amendment so narrowly as to undermine national civil rights enforcement.[33]

That neither the Democratic Conservative defense counsel in *Blyew* nor the Republican corporate counsel in the *Slaughter-House Cases* proffered interpretations of the Thirteenth and Fourteenth Amendments that placed the natural rights of citizenship outside the protective authority of the United States government suggests the degree to which the primacy of national citizenship and, with it, the primacy of the national government's authority to secure civil rights had become associated with these amendments. F. J. Pratt, president of the corporation, instructed Black to inform him "ahead of all others" if Black succeeded in his "'flank movement' and defined the Fourteenth Amendment in our favor...." Black's failure to submit and argue a brief in the *Slaughter-House Cases* may have been due to his failure to devise a "flank movement" around the Fourteenth Amendment.[34]

The Supreme Court succeeded where Black failed in circumventing the scope of the Fourteenth, as well as the Thirteenth, Amendment. However, it struggled with the case for more than a year before Justice Miller announced the 5–4 decision on April 14, 1873.

Miller's opinion was a curious and contradictory mixture of nationalist Republican assumptions about Reconstruction and the need for national protection of civil rights that led to the adoption of the Fourteenth Amendment and of narrow conclusions that reflected the ideas of states' rights Democratic Conservatives concerning the scope of authority it conferred upon the national government to protect civil rights. Justice Miller's opinion overturned the growing body of judicial interpretations of the impact of the Thirteenth and Fourteenth Amendments upon American constitutionalism as fixing sovereignty in the nation and as establishing the primacy of national citizenship and the concomitant national authority to secure the civil rights of American citizens.

The majority's immediate overriding concern seems to have been the preservation of state police powers from what they perceived as a potential usurpation by the national government. Justice Miller expressed a rigidly exclusionary concept of national and state powers to hold that the regulation of slaughterhouses was within the exclusive jurisdiction of the state and that Congress could not interfere with this state regulatory authority. He adopted this part of the opinion from former Justice Campbell's characterization of national and state powers as exclusive of one another. The opinion rejected other points made by Campbell regarding the monopolistic character of the corporation established by the Louisiana statute. Rather, it held that the corporation did not unconstitutionally engross trade, for, as the corporation's counsel had argued, the butchers were not prevented from plying their trade. They were merely required to slaughter animals for human consumption under conditions constitutionally prescribed by the state legislature. In short, the Louisiana law regulating abattoirs was a constitutionally authorized exercise of the state's police power.[35]

Having resolved the immediate legal issues before it, the Court could have ended its consideration of constitutional law by upholding the Louisiana abattoir statute and the corporation established under it. However, the Court seized the opportunity to examine the other legal issues raised by the butchers' counsel concerning the constitutional structure of the federal Union. "No questions so far reaching and pervading in their consequences," Justice Miller proclaimed, so profoundly interesting to the people of this country, and so important in their bearing upon the relations of the United States to each other, and to the citizens of the United States, have been before this court during the official life of any of its present members.[36]

The answers Justice Miller gave to the questions concerning the constitutional impact of the Civil War and Reconstruction on American federalism were of profound significance. But their significance lay more in the Court's reversal of the constitutional developments in the nation's courts than in the changes they suggested had occurred in American constitutionalism. In order to defend its states' rights views, the majority minimized the development of federalism during the Civil War and Reconstruction.

Miller premised his constitutional theories on an inaccurate history of the Civil War. He asserted that the war's primary objective was the abolition of slavery. He completely ignored President Lincoln's official characterization of the Civil War's primary objective as preserving the political integrity of the Union by establishing the North's idea of national sovereignty over the South's idea of state sovereignty by which the Confederate states had justified secession. The majority was driven to this historical inaccuracy in order to separate the nation's authority to abolish slavery and guarantee freedom from the constitutional authority to secure the fundamental rights of freemen. Although Miller described the Thirteenth Amendment as "the main and most valuable result" of the Civil War, he undermined its value by eliminating much of the power attributed to it by federal judges. He interpreted it as a mere abrogation of chattel slavery as Democratic Conservatives and opponents of national civil rights enforcement had unsuccessfully argued for seven years in the lower federal courts. Miller conceded that the amendment was a "grand yet simple declaration of the personal freedom of all the human race within the jurisdiction of this government...," but, he ignored lower federal court precedents concerning its import. He concluded that it did not give Congress the constitutional authority to secure the freedom it guaranteed by protecting the personal rights of which that freedom consists. He also ignored the obvious contradiction this view of the Thirteenth Amendment posed for the Court's decision of the previous year sustaining the constitutionality of the Civil Rights Act of 1866, which had been enacted to enforce the Thirteenth Amendment.[37]

Miller similarly interpreted the Fourteenth Amendment more narrowly than had lower federal court judges. He again predicated his interpretation upon a misinterpretation of history. He noted that black Americans were intended to be the primary beneficiaries of the amendment's guarantees because of unyielding Southern refusals to respect black civil rights so "that their freedom was of little value...." However, Miller overemphasized the racial context of the Fourteenth Amendment and concluded that it was applicable almost exclusively to blacks and other racial minorities who suffered from similar kinds of racial discrimination. In so narrowing the amendment's application to racial discrimination, he was able to minimize its impact on federal citizenship. He asserted that it merely reversed the Supreme Court's *Dred Scott* decision of 1857 by admitting blacks to citizenship and thus prevented the Southern states from re-enslaving blacks. However, Miller again ignored the lower court decisions that had interpreted both the Thirteenth and Fourteenth Amendments as applicable to whites as well as blacks. To have conceded this broader application of these amendments would have undermined the plausibility of the Court's view of the minimal constitutional impact of the Civil War on the nature of federal citizenship.[38]

It is in Miller's interpretation of citizenship that the Court's solicitude for states' rights is most clearly evident. He casually declared that the distinction between national and state citizenship "is clearly recognized and established." And, just as these two statuses were distinct and clearly understood, so were the rights that comprised them and the jurisdiction of the national and state governments over their citizens and citizens' rights. Not only were their jurisdictions distinct, but they were also exclusive of one another. In asserting that the Fourteenth Amendment was virtually inapplicable to white Americans who were already citizens, and in interpreting it as merely admitting black Americans to the citizenship that white Americans had always enjoyed, Miller was able logically to conclude that the amendment did not effect any changes in the nature of citizenship and authority over citizens' rights.[39]

The interpretation of federal citizenship the Court adopted attributed to the states exclusive primary authority over the fundamental rights of American citizens. Recognizing that the term, "privileges and immunities," which the Fourteenth Amendment purported to secure, was defined by Justice Bushrod Washington in his 1823 opinion in *Corfield v. Coryell* as "those rights which are fundamental," Miller agreed that it embraced "nearly every civil right, for the establishment and protection of which organized government is instituted." Miller nevertheless concluded that, with only a few exceptions, "the entire domain" of these natural rights "lay within the constitutional and legislative power of the states, and without that of the Federal Government." In short, the rights apparently secured by the Fourteenth Amendment's privileges and immunities clause were not secured by it at all, for these rights pertained to the rights of state citizenship, not to those of national citizenship. In ascribing exclusivity to the authority of the national and state governments over the rights of their respective citizens, Miller virtually placed the natural rights of American citizens beyond national authority and emasculated the amendment's citizenship and privileges and immunities clauses. More immediately, in placing these rights within state authority, he enabled the states to accomplish precisely what he said the amendment was intended to prevent: the destruction of the civil rights of American citizens.[40]

If the fundamental rights of freemen constituted the rights of state citizenship, what were the rights of national citizenship? Justice Miller enumerated as privileges and immunities of United States citizenship the right of habeas corpus, the right to petition the national government for the redress of grievances, the right to use the seaports and navigable waterways of the United States, the right to pass through and engage in trade in any of the states of the Union, and the right to the protection of the national government when on the high seas or in a foreign country. It is no small anomaly that Miller asserted that the United States government could not do for its citizens within its jurisdiction what he claimed it was authorized to do for them beyond it.

One might ask how Justice Miller could interpret the privileges and immunities of national and state citizenship in a manner that was so at odds with lower federal court precedents. On a theoretical level, Miller incorrectly assumed that the natural rights of citizenship were generally recognized as rights of state citizenship before the ratification of the Fourteenth Amendment. Given this assumption, he asserted that the transfer of authority over these fundamental rights was too revolutionary a constitutional change in American government not to have been clearly expressed by Congress. "Was it the purpose of the Fourteenth Amendment," he wanted to know

> by the simple declaration that no State should make or enforce any law which shall abridge the privileges and immunities of citizens of the United States, to transfer the security and protection of all the civil rights which we have mentioned, from the States to the Federal Government? And where it is declared that Congress shall have the power to enforce that article, was it intended to bring within the power of Congress the entire domain of civil rights heretofore belonging exclusively to the States?

His answer was a resounding "NO!" If the framers of the Fourteenth Amendment had intended such revolutionary changes, he declared, that intention would have been clearly expressed. Yet, he did not look to the legislative history of the Fourteenth Amendment to discover whether such intentions had been expressed. Instead, he merely asserted without supporting evidence that Congress did not intend such revolutionary changes in American constitutionalism.[41]

Justice Miller's interpretation of federal citizenship is remarkable for several reasons. His assumption of the prior existence of a well-defined and distinct separation between national and state citizenship is contradicted by the ambiguity that characterized views of federal citizenship before the adoption of the Reconstruction Amendments. His assertion that the primacy of state authority over the natural rights of citizens was well established and recognized is contradicted by the predominant antebellum view of citizenship and the post–Civil War judicial interpretations of citizenship under the Reconstruction Amendments. That the Court adopted this view of citizenship, so at odds with prevailing legal theories and without citing any supporting authority, was astonishingly bold. It was especially so, in light of the profound political and constitutional consequences it entailed, and since none of the opposing counsel had argued its adoption. Justice Miller perhaps attempted to assuage the expected criticism of this decision when he observed that the justification for a judicial determination "is not always the most conclusive which is drawn from the consequences urged against the adoption of a particular construction of an instrument...." He thus confessed the majority's refusal to sanction those revolutionary consequences for American politics, law, and constitutionalism that the lower federal courts had already declared were inherent in the Thirteenth and Fourteenth Amendments. Justice Miller made this clear when he rationalized that

> when, as in the case before us, these consequences are so serious, so far reaching and pervading, so great a departure from the structure and spirit of our institutions; when the effect is to fetter and degrade the state governments by subjecting them to the control of Congress, in the exercise of powers heretofore universally conceded to them of the most ordinary and fundamental character; when in fact, it radically changes the whole theory of the relations of the State and Federal Governments to each other and of both these governments to the people; the argument has a force that is irresistible, in the absence of language which expresses such a purpose too clearly to admit of doubt.

Interestingly, the lower federal courts were more willing to embrace these revolutionary constitutional theories than was the Supreme Court. These roles were just the reverse of those taken by the lower federal courts and the Supreme Court during the civil rights revolution of the 1950s and 1960s.[42]

Theoretical rationalizations of legal doctrine are also means to achieve political objectives. The Court's decision may thus be explained in terms of its political goals. Miller was quite explicit about the majority's desire to resist the nationalizing impact of the Civil War by redefining American federalism as a states' rights-centered dual federalism. As a matter of legal theory, Miller speculated that if the Reconstruction Amendments empowered Congress to protect the fundamental rights of citizens, Congress thereby could curtail the legislative powers of the states and their "most ordinary and usual functions." This national power, he feared, would result in the replacement of state authority with national authority. He insisted that the majority did not see "in those Amendments any purpose to destroy the main features of the general system." On the contrary, the statesmen of the nation "still believed that the existence of the States with powers for domestic and local government, including the regulation of civil rights, the rights of person and property, was essential to the perfect working of our complex form of government…."[43]

The decisions and activities of the lower federal courts and other branches of the national government may elicit some skepticism about the Court's concern for the continued existence of the states and their functions. Federal judges were able to preserve ordinary state jurisdiction over fundamental rights while carving out concurrent national authority. Congress had expressed its desire to preserve the states' powers and functions while providing the protection of personal rights that the states failed to offer. The Department of Justice and the federal courts despaired of punishing more than the most notorious violations of the congressional civil rights acts; to think they would even consider assuming the local administration of criminal and civil justice is absurd. In light of the administrative and judicial history of civil rights enforcement, one is forced to conclude that the United States Supreme Court simply refused to allow the national government to assume the function of enforcing the fundamental rights of its citizens. This is not to say that the Court shared the political objectives and values of Democratic Conservatives of the South. Yet, the Court appears to have been more concerned about preserving the states' regulatory functions and police powers than in establishing national authority to protect the civil rights of black Americans. It achieved its purpose by articulating a states' rights-centered theory of American federalism. It rationalized its theory by raising a false danger to the continued existence of the states' police powers through a fallacious concept of exclusivity in national and state authority.

In addition to its ostensible commitment to states' rights, the Court also was troubled apparently by the specter of overloaded dockets. To concede national authority over civil rights, Miller ominously predicted,

> would constitute this court a perpetual censor upon all legislation of the States, on the civil rights of their own citizens, with authority to nullify such as it did not approve as consistent with those rights, as they existed at the time of the adoption of this Amendment.[44]

Hence, Miller gratuitously interpreted the Fourteenth Amendment's equal protection clause in an unnecessarily restrictive way. He suggested that the equal protection clause applied specifically, and therefore, only to state laws "which discriminated with gross injustice and hardship against them [blacks] as a class...." Only state laws that discriminated and were unjust and imposed great hardship upon blacks as a class came within the scope of the equal protection clause. One need only note that this interpretation of equal protection of the laws virtually precluded the national government from protecting or enforcing citizens' rights when local authorities failed, or were unwilling, to do so. It is no less ironic than it is remarkable that a Northern Republican–controlled Supreme Court should have incorporated into the Constitution an interpretation of the Reconstruction Amendments that approximated the views of Democratic Conservatives and thereby established the doctrinal basis for undermining the scope and effectiveness of national civil rights enforcement authority for almost one hundred years.[45]

Four of the nine members of the Supreme Court rejected the majority's decision and the historical and legal analysis on which it was based. Their dissents were tinged with stinging rebukes that manifested their belief that the majority's decision was not simply a difference of opinion, but that it was clearly wrong and improper. Their indignation undoubtedly stemmed, in part, from the legal theory of national civil rights enforcement authority that had been expressed in the courts of the United States up to the time of this decision, a theory they generally reflected in their dissents.

Ironically, Democrat Stephen J. Field espoused the broad nationalist and natural rights interpretation of the Thirteenth and Fourteenth Amendments and national civil rights enforcement authority associated with the Republican Party. Field quoted from congressional debates to argue that these amendments established the primacy of national authority over citizens and citizens' rights. He recalled the ambiguous and conflicting definitions of the nature of federal citizenship before the Civil War. The Reconstruction Amendments, he insisted, removed that ambiguity. The Thirteenth Amendment not only abolished slavery, but it also guaranteed to all citizens the natural rights of freemen. Furthermore, under the Fourteenth Amendment, Justice Field asserted, a "citizen of a State is now only a citizen of the United States residing in that State." He concluded, therefore, that the natural rights that "belong to him as a free man and a free citizen, now belong to him as a citizen of any State." He added that these rights "do not derive their existence from its [the state's] legislation, and cannot be destroyed by its power." On the contrary, the Fourteenth Amendment "places them under the guardianship of the national authority." Using rhetoric and constitutional theory reminiscent of the abolitionists before the Civil War and the Radical Republicans after the Civil War, Field explained that the amendment was "intended to give practical effect to the Declaration of 1776 of inalienable rights, rights which are the gift of the Creator, which the law does not confer, but only recognizes." If this was not the result achieved by the amendment, he scoffed, then "it was a vain and idle enactment, which accomplished nothing, and most unnecessarily excited Congress and the people on its passage."[46]

It would be a mistake to conclude that Justice Field embraced the nationalistic constitutional doctrines he expressed in his dissent for the same political objectives as civil rights proponents. His concern focused on what he regarded as an improper use of political power by the Louisiana legislature to create a corporate monopoly that violated citizens' nationally protected right "to pursue one of the ordinary trades or callings of life...." Field rejected the rigid exclusivity of national and state powers in this area of civil rights enforcement advanced by the majority. He insisted that the Supreme Court had the obligation to oversee the manner in which the states exercised their police powers, because the states "cannot be permitted to encroach upon any of the just rights of the citizen, which the Constitution intended to secure against abridgement." Field argued for a nationalistic and centralizing idea of American federalism as a limitation upon the abusive exercise of state powers.[47]

The legal reasoning and political values expressed in Field's opinion evince the paradoxical compatibility between a theory of broad national civil rights enforcement authority and nineteenth-century American opposition to big government. Expressing his Democratic political values and commitment to a liberal laissez faire political system, Justice Field asserted a doctrine of broad national powers over states' rights in the interest of curtailing governmental interference with individual liberties. This analysis suggests that Liberal

Republicans who opposed the use of national governmental powers did not necessarily base their opposition on the philosophical purity of liberal political theory and values.[48]

The two other dissenting opinions were written by justices who earlier had affirmed the broad nationalist interpretation of national civil rights enforcement authority while riding circuit. Justice Bradley's broad nationalist interpretation of the Fourteenth Amendment was predicated on a different view of Civil War and Reconstruction history than that described by Miller. Bradley argued that the amendment reflected the nationalism generated by the era. "[It] was an attempt to give voice to the strong national yearning for that time and that condition of things," he recalled, "in which American citizenship should be a sure guaranty of safety…in the full enjoyment of every right and privilege belonging to a free man, without fear of violence or molestation."[49]

Miller's opinion presented Bradley with an opportunity to refine his views about citizenship, the rights of citizens, and the respective authority of national and state governments to enforce these rights. Bradley rejected the distinction Miller made between national and state citizenship. Because Americans inherited traditional rights and privileges from their English forebears, Bradley reasoned, citizenship "has certain privileges and immunities attached to it…," and "these privileges and immunities attach as well to citizenship of the United States." He explained that "to say these rights and immunities attach only to state citizenship, and not to citizenship of the United States, appears to me to evince a very narrow and insufficient estimate of constitutional history and the rights of men, not to say the rights of the American people."[50]

Bradley therefore disputed Justice Miller's observations concerning the comity clause and Justice Washington's interpretation of the privileges and immunities it secured:

> [B]oth the clause of the Constitution referred to, and Justice Washington in his comment on it, speak of the privileges and immunities of citizens in a State, not of citizens of a State. It is the privileges, and immunities of citizens, that is, of citizens as such, that are to be accorded to citizens of other States when they are found in any State; or as Justice Washington says: "privileges and immunities which are, in their nature, fundamental; which belong, of right, to the citizens of all free governments."

Bradley specified the rights to life, liberty, and property, the right to choose one's calling in addition to Bill of Rights guarantees as some of the rights of

United States citizenship. He further maintained that even if a person was not a citizen of any particular state, he could lay claim to these rights as a citizen of the United States.[51]

Justice Bradley was not troubled by the "dire consequences" presented by the recognition of broad national civil rights enforcement authority. He did not think that this broad national power would interfere unduly with the civil and criminal affairs and laws of the states or abolish "the state governments in everything but name," because little if any legislation was required to implement the amendment. He also rejected the concept of exclusivity in the powers of the national and state governments over civil rights, and instead asserted that these powers were concurrent and coequal. A more pressing concern was the prospect of logjammed dockets in the federal courts suggested by Justice Miller. But, even here, Bradley minimized his concern with the observation that, as questions relating to these fundamental rights arose in the courts, they would become so well defined and so well recognized and secured that violations would decrease along with the necessity of litigating in the federal courts. Should this power over civil rights increase the business of the federal courts, he suggested, Congress could alleviate the burden by providing for additional and more efficient courts. He closed his comments with a reproach to the majority:

> The great question is, what is the true construction of the Amendment? When once we find that, we shall find the means of giving it effect. The argument from inconvenience ought not to have a very controlling influence in questions of this sort. The national will and national interest are of far greater importance.[52]

Justice Noah H. Swayne expressed a view of legislative intent similar to Bradley's. He had been the first justice to judicially examine and assess the intent of the framers of the Civil Rights Act of 1866 and the Thirteenth Amendment in an 1867 opinion he apparently wrote after consulting with the author of the Civil Rights Act, Senator Lyman Trumbull, to determine its legislative intent. Acknowledging the existence of dual citizenship, Swayne nevertheless recognized a concurrent federal authority over natural rights, which he insisted constituted nationally enforceable rights of national citizenship. The rights peculiar to state citizenship were those special privileges given by a state to its citizens. However, even these could be enjoyed by citizens of the other states, in Swayne's opinion, by virtue of the comity clause. The comity clause thus conferred upon citizens of the United States an equality of state-conferred rights. He sharply criticized the majority for its fear of federalism presented by this novel and great power. He retorted that "the novelty was known and the measure deliberately adopted," and insisted that "any government claiming to be national" that lacked the authority to secure the rights of its citizens was "glaringly defective." Turning directly to the majority's opinion, Justice Swayne censured his judicial brothers for defeating "by a limitation not anticipated, the intent of those by whom the instrument was framed and of those by whom it was adopted. To the extent of that limitation it turns, as it were, what was meant for bread into a stone." Reserving his most acerbic criticism for last, he proclaimed that the United States Supreme Court "has no authority to interpolate a limitation that is neither expressed nor implied. Our duty is to execute the law, not make it ..."[53]

The dissenters' accusations that Miller misinterpreted legislative intent was supported by reactions to his opinion in Congress. Some of the framers of the Fourteenth Amendment roundly criticized the opinion on the floor of Congress in 1873. George S. Boutwell, William Lawrence, Benjamin F. Butler, Timothy O. Howe, and Robert S. Hale insisted that the framers in 1866, as well as their Democratic opponents, recognized that they were assuming authority to protect the natural rights of freemen, and that they thereby produced the revolution in American federalism that Justice Miller claimed they could not have intended. James G. Blaine expressed the same view in his memoirs when he stated that the Supreme Court had deprived the amendment of the power Congress intended it to have.[54]

The Court must have known the debilitating consequence its decision would have on the efforts of Department of Justice officers to enforce civil rights in the federal courts of the South. The editor of the American Law Review, for example, satirized the decision's impact upon President Grant's Southern policy by noting

> that, while the executive department keeps Casey in New Orleans, and sends its soldiers to regulate the internal politics of Louisiana, the judicial department remits to people of that State, to its courts and legislature, the custody of the privileges and immunities of its citizens.[55]

Justice Miller, for one, was conscious of the eviscerating impact his opinion had upon the president's Southern policy. When Chief Justice Salmon P. Chase died shortly after the decision, Justice Miller became the front-runner to fill the vacancy. His legal acumen and experience on the bench made him the favorite of the nation's bar. However, the position went to Morrison R. Waite after Roscoe Conkling, George H. Williams, and Caleb Cushing either refused nomination or withdrew after their nominations were sent to the Senate. Justice Miller blamed his *Slaughter-House* decision and the intrigue of Justices Bradley and Swayne for his being passed over by the president. He lamented to Justice David Davis that this "will not be the first time that the best and most beneficial public act of a man's life has stood in the way of his political advancement." Reviewing the appointments of Chief Justices John Marshall, Roger B. Taney, and Chase, Miller complained that the position had "always been the reward of political, I may say partisan services." Disclaiming any partisanship in his behavior on the Court, he added, "it is perhaps looking for too much to expect Grant with these examples before him, to look alone to the voice of the profession or to the qualifications of the nominee."[56]

Some newspaper editors also saw the Court's ruling as a challenge to presidential policy. The Chicago *Tribune* called the decision a needed check "upon the determination of the Administration to enforce its policy and to maintain its power, even at the expense of the constitutional prerogatives of the States." The New York *World* suggested that the reason the Court was not more forceful "in declaring this sound doctrine is to be accounted for by their consciousness that they were running counter to the impetuous hostility of the Republican Party to the constitutional rights of the States."[57]

However, the decision's impact on the politics of Reconstruction was not generally perceived. Considering its importance, it aroused surprisingly little controversy in the newspapers around the country. Curiously, the New Orleans newspapers hardly noticed it. One explanation for this indifferent reaction was suggested by M. F. Taylor when he wrote that the decision was not generally understood. Public reaction reinforces the contention of this study that the Court consciously may have chosen the *Slaughter-House Cases* to express its view of national civil rights enforcement authority as the safest way to resolve the intensely political and controversial constitutional issues created by Republican Reconstruction policies and legislative enactments.[58]

The absence of controversy is also partially explained by the support the decision gave to the growing opposition of erstwhile Republican proponents of civil rights to the continuation of national interference in Southern affairs. The constitutional formulation of that political opposition included a reaffirmation of the primacy of state authority over citizens' rights. Those political policies could be defeated by eliminating the legal authority under which actions were taken to achieve them.

The disaffection of Republican support from Republican policies is evident from an analysis of the Republican press. Such an analysis reveals that the legal doctrine enunciated in *Slaughter-House* served other Republican political goals. The Chicago *Tribune*, for example, strongly applauded the Court's decision in an editorial that demonstrated that the paper's desire to control monopolies in Illinois had displaced its earlier passion to protect civil rights in the South. The timing and conclusions of the Court's decision were most propitious to states that were steeped in antimonopoly ferment. Paradoxically, the Supreme Court's sanction of a state-created monopoly in Louisiana implicitly acknowledged the state's power to destroy monopolistic controls in Illinois. The *Slaughter-House* decision was therefore consistent with the *Munn* ruling four years later that upheld Illinois's antimonopoly Granger Laws.[59]

The revitalization of states' rights was crucial to the success of Northern states in their struggle to cope with the stresses of industrialization and urbanization. The importance of the decision to the North, then, was not that it sustained a state-created monopoly, nor that it curtailed national civil rights enforcement authority. Rather, its importance to the North was that it endorsed the state police power necessary to control the growing concentrations of monopolistic power of rising business. Noting these implications, the Chicago *Tribune's* editor declared that the decision would put "a quietus upon the thousand-and-one follies seeking to be legalized by hanging on to the Fourteenth Amendment." He endorsed the states' rights emphasis of the ruling by asserting that, although the amendment was understood by its framers and the public at large as securing to blacks the rights enjoyed by whites, "it had no power to interfere with municipal relations, however unjust in themselves, or with previously-existing state rights...." The amendment "only had binding force when the State sought to deprive the negro of his rights."[60]

The *Tribune's* hearty support of states' rights in 1873 stands in sharp contrast to the position it took in 1866 when it insisted on the necessity to interfere with municipal regulations to protect civil rights. In a May 1866 editorial, the *Tribune* dared the "copperheads" to campaign on "the proposition that local legislation shall have the opportunity to abridge the rights of the citizens, as to deprive any person of life, liberty or property without due process of law." It claimed that "Republican stumpers" wanted "no better fun than taking off the hides of Copperheads on that issue...." Yet, in his approval of the *Slaughter-House* decision, the editor stated in 1873 that it was "only recently that...the people have sought to override the acts of State Governments by appeal to the provisions of this Amendment." The Court's ruling had been required to check the centralizing tendencies of the national government that cut so deeply into the prerogatives of the states. "The Supreme Court has not spoken a moment too soon," it concluded, "or any too boldly, on this subject."[61]

The Nation also reversed its support for the national protection of civil rights through a curious recollection of legislative history. In 1866 it proclaimed that protection of the personal rights of the freedmen was "the first duty of the Government" and insisted that "Congress is directly invested with full power to legislate to this end ..." by virtue of the Thirteenth Amendment. The revolution wrought by conferring the "legal condition of free citizens" on four million slaves was secured, the editor proclaimed, when the guarantees of the Civil Rights Act of 1866 were incorporated into the Constitution by the Fourteenth Amendment.[62]

Yet, *The Nation* withdrew its support of congressional Reconstruction and federal civil rights enforcement as early as 1869. The reasons given for its change in policy were the "corruption, injustice and ineptitude" of the Republican governments of the Southern states. The following year, this erstwhile defender of civil rights condemned Justice Bradley's circuit court ruling in the *Slaughter-House Cases*. The focus of *The Nation's* criticism was not civil rights protection. Rather, the paper criticized the decision's impact upon patents, railroads, canals, in short, every private franchise in the nation. Seeing no distinction between the slaughterhouse monopoly and other corporate grants, *The Nation* feared that, under this ruling, corporate charters would be perceived as conferring special privileges that benefited private individuals rather than the public and that most corporations would be declared unconstitutional. Few corporations would withstand such a test, it predicted, and it hoped that a ruling that was so detrimental to the economic interests of the United States would be rejected by the Supreme Court.[63]

The Nation's hopes were fulfilled in 1873. It observed that the *Slaughter-House* decision demonstrated that the Supreme Court "is recovering from the War fever, and is getting ready to abandon sentimental canons of [constitutional] construction." While it emphasized how the decision saved "almost every franchise in the United States" from destruction, it also commented on its civil rights implications. Contradicting the views it held in 1866, *The Nation* in 1873 condemned the butchers' contention that the civil rights of citizens were brought under the protective power of the national government by the Fourteenth Amendment. It characterized that notion as a "monstrous conclusion," and declared that the national protection of civil rights "would put an end to federal government, do away with state courts, laws and constitutions, and throw pretty much the entire business of the country into the hands of Congress and the officials of the United States." Public reaction to *Slaughter-House* evinces Attorney General Akerman's observation of December 1871 that Northern support for civil rights protection in the South was being replaced by a greater interest in "progress."[64]

Some congressmen and senators also reversed their support for Republican objectives of civil rights enforcement. These Republican supporters of civil rights in 1866 manifested a curiously selective recollection in the 1870s of what they had intended in their earlier legislative efforts to secure civil rights. Congressman James A. Garfield, for example, opposed the Ku Klux Klan Act of 1871 because he insisted that the authority to protect natural rights was one of the powers of the states, and it remained a state power despite the Fourteenth Amendment. He recalled that in 1866 Congressman John A. Bingham had opposed the Civil Rights Act of 1866 precisely because Bingham believed that Congress did not possess the power to protect the natural rights that that legislation was intended to secure. Congressman Garfield reminded Bingham that when Bingham introduced his proposed constitutional amendment to confer that power upon Congress, it was rejected for a more limited proposal that merely prohibited the states from infringing citizens' rights.[65]

Congressman Garfield's excursion into legislative history inadvertently supported the point he was attempting to disprove. In claiming that Congressman Bingham opposed the Civil Rights Act because it was intended to protect natural rights, he unwittingly conceded that congressional intent in enacting the law was actually broader than the intent he claimed led to the proposed Fourteenth Amendment. He did not explain why Congress would enact a law to protect natural rights over the president's veto with the expected result of irrevocably splitting the president and Congress politically, but limit a proposed constitutional amendment to prohibitions against the states. Nor did he offer to explain how the law and the amendment could be so fundamentally different in scope when their framers, and the public generally, thought of them as identical in scope and meaning.[66]

The extent of Garfield's reversal is clear when one contrasts the views he expressed in 1871 with those he stated in 1866. In 1866, he said that he intended to "see to it that, hereafter, personal rights are placed in the keeping of the nation...," and that the rights to life, liberty, and property shall "no longer be left to the caprice of mobs or the contingencies of local legislation." He stated that Congress "must make American citizenship the shield that protects every citizen, on every foot of our soil." He spoke these words in support of Senator Lyman Trumbull's Freedmen's Bureau Bill, which he declared was "one of the means for reaching this desirable result." The other means undoubtedly included the Civil Rights Act of 1866 since it was regarded as a twin of the Freedmen's Bureau Bill and was intended by Senator Trumbull to make permanent and nationwide the temporary protection offered by the Freedmen's Bureau Bill in the South.[67]

Congressman Garfield did complain in 1866 that the Fourteenth Amendment did not go as far as he would have liked. But, his complaint was not that the proposed amendment did not protect natural rights or that it was limited to state action; rather, he would have added to the protection provided to natural rights the same protection over voting rights. He stated that if suffrage was not itself a natural right, it was so crucial to the enjoyment of natural rights and their security that it was virtually a natural right and should be included among the other natural rights secured by the Fourteenth Amendment. He also acknowledged in 1866 that the amendment incorporated the Civil Rights Act to protect the statute from being repealed. Garfield's biographer has concluded that in 1866 the congressman had adopted a "thoroughgoing nationalism that would have made even Marshall and Webster turn over in their graves and that might have done credit to Theodore Roosevelt himself." Observing that Garfield believed "that Congress could and should enter within the limits of the individual State to protect all persons against injustice," his biographer concluded that Congressman Garfield's views were in the mainstream of Republican policy in 1866.[68]

Senator Lyman Trumbull, author of the Civil Rights Act of 1866, also made a weak and rather unpersuasive attempt to deny the past. Despite the statements he made in 1866 expressing his intention to secure all of the natural rights of all American citizens, he insisted in 1871 that his Civil Rights Act and the Fourteenth Amendment that incorporated it applied only to racially discriminatory state legislation. Further, in 1866, he had attempted to persuade Congressman Samuel Shellabarger to withdraw another bill Shellabarger had introduced to secure natural rights absolutely. Trumbull insisted that his Civil Rights bill accomplished this purpose. In 1871, however, Trumbull was equally insistent that this Civil Rights Act and the Fourteenth Amendment applied only to black Americans and merely secured to them an equality in state-conferred rights, and then only against discriminatory state laws. The fundamental rights of citizens, he declared in opposition to the proposed Ku Klux Klan Act, remained under the authority of the states. The Fourteenth Amendment, he insisted, had "not changed an iota of the Constitution as it was originally framed, in that respect."[69]

This reversal of Republican supporters of civil rights enforcement even affected the federal judiciary. The one federal court in which the Civil Rights Act of 1866 was enforced with any significance in the 1860s was Judge Bland Ballard's District Court in Louisville, Kentucky. He concurred in the broadly nationalistic

Rhodes opinion penned by Justice Swayne in 1867. He subsequently issued his own rulings that interpreted national civil rights enforcement authority as broadly. Judge Ballard's court and the Civil Rights Act were of primary importance in prosecuting whites who committed crimes against blacks in Kentucky.[70]

By the early 1870s, however, federal legal officers in this overwhelmingly Democratic state had grown weary of prosecuting ordinary crimes committed against black victims, and they longed to be relieved of this burden. In a February 1872 charge to a grand jury, Judge Ballard used Kentucky's legislative recognition of the right of blacks to testify in all state cases as an excuse to eliminate the jurisdiction over criminal cases that he had been exercising since 1866 under the Civil Rights Act. He also declared unconstitutional those portions of the Ku Klux Klan Act of 1871 that "invests this court with jurisdiction of offenses against the States." Although he recognized the natural rights of citizens as the rights secured by the Fourteenth Amendment's privileges or immunities clause, he nevertheless asserted that "to the State governments was left all matters relating to the citizen, the protection of his life, liberty and property." He stated that this "form of government has not been changed." In an apparent repudiation of the jurisdiction he exercised under the Civil Rights Act in trying crimes committed by whites against blacks, he denied that the federal courts possessed jurisdiction even if the state courts did not bring the offenders to justice. "If we can try offenses committed by marauders who go about committing outrages, because the State Courts do not punish," he explained, "then we can absorb to ourselves the jurisdiction of the whole criminal law of the State for the same reason...." Ballard anticipated subsequent Supreme Court decisions by narrowing the authority of the federal government to secure civil rights under the Fourteenth Amendment to state statutes that were racially discriminatory on their face.[71]

Furthermore, by the end of 1872 the Grant administration signaled a change in civil rights enforcement policy. It announced to United States attorneys that only those cases that were so outrageous and notorious that prosecutions could not be avoided were to be brought in the federal courts. By the summer of 1873, the administration abandoned its efforts to enforce civil rights by ordering the cessation of new prosecutions under the Enforcement Acts and extending executive clemency and pardons for past offenses. While the *Slaughter-House* decision was not responsible for this change in administration policy in 1873, it was certainly parallel to the shift in the nation's attitude towards civil rights enforcement that had prompted the administration to curtail its efforts to secure civil rights. However, it was directly responsible for subsequent judicial rulings that abolished essential constitutional authority on which the Department of Justice depended to enforce civil rights. The *Slaughter-House* decision served as judicial precedent for decisions that halted later efforts by the Grant administration to protect civil rights when it revived its policy of vigorous civil rights enforcement to combat the renewal of Southern terrorism in 1874. *Slaughter-House,* therefore, was a turning point in Reconstruction. The remainder of this study analyzes the political and legal consequences of *Slaughter-House.*[72]

8 The Judicial Curtailment of Civil Rights Enforcement, 1874–1875

The legal impact of the *Slaughter-House Cases* on the constitutional history of Reconstruction was not immediately clear to contemporary observers. Indeed, its impact on federal regulatory powers was interpreted in various and sometimes contradictory ways. One legal commentator, for example, condemned the decision because he feared that it would impede efforts to regulate monopolies. At the same time, another praised it because it affirmed the nation's authority to engage in such regulation.[1]

While the *Slaughter-House* decision was generally perceived as a revitalization of states' rights and a corresponding diminution in national authority, it left unanswered many questions relating to national civil rights enforcement authority. The decision, after all, involved a legal conflict between white butchers and a corporation rather than the protection of Southern blacks and white Republicans with which most lower federal court interpretations of the Fourteenth Amendment were involved. The Supreme Court's emasculation of the amendment's citizenship and privileges and immunities clauses so contravened the virtual unanimity of lower federal court interpretations that contemporaries plausibly could have assumed that the Supreme Court did not intend its ruling to apply to civil rights violations arising from racial and political vendettas.

Even if one concedes the emasculation of these clauses as constitutional authority for national civil rights enforcement generally, the due process and equal protection clauses of the Fourteenth Amendment remained unexplored by the courts. The power to enforce civil rights that was eroded by the Supreme Court's interpretation of the respective rights of dual citizenship might conceivably have been restored through the due process and equal protection clauses. Indeed, it was upon the equal protection clause of the Fourteenth Amendment that congressional supporters of the Civil Rights Act of 1875 based Congress's constitutional authority to proscribe racial discrimination in places of public accommodations. Some of them even cited the *Slaughter-House* decision in defense of the bill's constitutionality.[2]

Because of its uncertain impact on national efforts to protect the civil rights of Southern blacks and white Republicans, the *Slaughter-House* decision permitted federal judges to interpret in contradictory ways the constitutional authority upon which these efforts depended. Some judges circumvented or simply ignored the ruling as they continued to exercise national civil rights enforcement authority as they had before *Slaughter-House*. Others cited the decision as precedent to void national civil rights enforcement authority.[3]

The legal theory deduced from Miller's opinion that characterized national civil rights enforcement authority more narrowly than judges previously had defined it eventually prevailed in the federal courts. This restrictive interpretation of national civil rights enforcement authority brought to a jarring halt the Justice Department's struggle to combat the renewal of Ku Klux terrorism in 1874. Inhibited by adverse judicial rulings, Attorney General Williams ordered United States attorneys to stop bringing prosecutions under the Enforcement Acts of 1870 and 1871 until the Supreme Court clarified the Justice Department's authority to secure civil rights. The department never again enforced civil rights in the South under President Grant, in part because the Supreme Court's awaited clarification of national authority to secure the civil rights of Southern blacks was not announced until 1876. This decision limited enforcement of the Fourteenth Amendment to violations committed by the states and eliminated the jurisdiction over civil rights that the lower federal courts originally had been exercising.

Although the *Slaughter-House* decision complemented the Grant administration's political decision to curtail Justice Department enforcement of civil rights, the attorney general did not welcome judicial rulings that undermined the department's constitutional authority to protect civil rights. For example, Judge Ballard declared the Ku Klux Klan Act of 1871 unconstitutional in his charge to the jury in an October 1873 civil suit that was brought under the Civil Rights Act of 1866. Although he acknowledged the impropriety of declaring a statute unconstitutional in a charge to the jury, particularly when the statute was not involved in the case, Judge Ballard nevertheless disallowed the jurisdiction the statute purported to give to his court to punish what, in his opinion, were offenses against state laws punishable exclusively in the courts of the state. Judge Ballard's action brought immediate angry denunciations from Attorney General Williams as well as Judge Ballard's political ally, former Solicitor General Bristow, for treating the "legislation as a nullity without a careful and painstaking consideration of the subject…." Williams expressed incredulity over Ballard's opposition "to the suppression of the disorder now existing in Kentucky…."[4]

Other judges also declared the 1871 statute unconstitutional. In another of the ironies of this history, the case that ultimately decided the constitutionality of national authority to protect citizens' rights under this legislation, like *Slaughter-House,* arose in Louisiana. The circumstances of the case, *United States v. Cruikshank,* involved a level of violence tantamount to a localized civil war in what was perhaps the bloodiest racial conflict in Louisiana history.[5]

The Grant Parish massacre was, in part, the product of the confusion following the state elections of 1872. Both the Conservatives, led by the incumbent governor, Henry C. Warmoth, and the Republicans, led by gubernatorial challenger William P. Kellogg, claimed victory. For a time Louisianans experienced the political anomaly of having two governors and two legislatures claiming and exercising governmental authority. Both claimants to the office of governor appointed election returning boards whose functions included the appointment of parish judges and sheriffs. The Conservative Warmoth board appointed Alphonse Cazabat and Christopher Columbus Nash to the positions of judge and sheriff of Grant Parish, which is located in the central portion of the state. At the time of his appointment to the office of sheriff, Nash was awaiting trial for the political murder of a white Republican leader in the area. The Republican Kellogg board appointed R. C. Register and Daniel Shaw to these offices.

The two pairs of appointees each claimed to be the legitimate officeholders and maneuvered to gain possession of the parish courthouse. The Republicans Register and Shaw succeeded in occupying it, and they reinforced it with armed supporters determined to retain possession. On Easter morning, April 13, 1873, a "veritable army" of "old time Ku Klux Klan" led by the Conservatives Cazabat and Nash stormed the courthouse. Conflicting accounts of what transpired prevent a complete narrative of the fighting, but federal investigators sent from New Orleans reported that the Conservative white forces had committed shocking atrocities. At least sixty freedmen were killed after they had surrendered, and their bodies were mutilated and left to rot in the parching sun. One of the federal deputy marshals was so affected by the slaughter that he could only compare it to the massacre at Fort Pillow. Federal investigators reported that the Conservatives viewed the conflict over the local political offices as a "test of white supremacy," and they were joined by men from surrounding parishes in a determined effort to restore white rule. Government investigators put the onus of blame for the violence on the white Conservatives. They concluded that the Conservatives had massacred the black Republicans in a political vendetta motivated by racial hatred.[6]

The Justice Department's reaction to the massacre reflected the administration's ambivalence toward civil rights enforcement. The massacre was simply too notorious to ignore. So, the attorney general departed from his evolving policy of nonenforcement of civil rights and instructed the United States attorney at New Orleans, James R. Beckwith, to "spare no pains or expense to cause the guilty parties to be arrested and punished...." He supported this instruction with authorization for the use of troops and special detectives to assist in conducting the investigation and in making arrests.[7]

The attorney general's support quickly diminished when he was informed of the amount of assistance required by the magnitude of the violence. Beckwith and the United States marshal estimated that they would need some 150 soldiers to arrest between 300 and 400 defendants who scoured the countryside in armed bands prepared to resist arrest. Many had already fled to Texas to avoid arrest. Williams sharply pared down his expectations because the prosecution of all the defendants was impracticable within the limited amount of military and financial resources the Grant administration was willing to commit. He radically revised his instructions by directing the United States attorney to select only 6 to 12 of the leaders for trial. The attorney general was apparently less interested in vindicating federal law and the dead victims of criminal violence by bringing offenders to justice than in merely discouraging future crimes. He observed that "the conviction of the prominent men and leaders would have all the desired effect to vindicate the law and induce the future observance of it by the people." United States Attorney Beckwith implored the attorney general to authorize a more vigorous enforcement of the law. He explained that he had never been connected with the prosecution of a crime "so revolting and horrible in the details of its perpetration and so burdened with atrocity and barbarity." Beckwith's supplications won the attorney general's promise to discuss the matter with President Grant, but, if he did, he failed to inform Beckwith. The administration's decision to prosecute only a fraction of those responsible for the crimes represented cynical tokenism.[8]

On June 16, 1873, the federal grand jury at New Orleans indicted 97 defendants and accused each defendant of 32 violations of sections 6 and 7 of the Enforcement Act of 1870. The first 16 counts charged that they banded together and conspired to deprive Levi Nelson and Alexander Tillman, "being citizens of the United States of African descent, and persons of color," of various rights secured by the Constitution of the United States. The specific rights included the right of assembly; the right to keep and bear arms; the right to protection against deprivation of life, liberty, and property without due process of law; the right to the full and equal benefit of all laws and proceedings for the security of persons and property; and the right to vote. Beckwith seemed to be experimenting with the language of specific counts, perhaps because of the uncertain impact of *Slaughterhouse* on national civil rights authority. Some counts specified the federally enforceable rights that were infringed, while one count merely used the general phrase "rights, privileges, immunities and protection granted and secured to them as citizens of the United States and of Louisiana." The counts also varied with respect to the intent charges. The defendants were accused of conspiring with "unlawful and felonious intent and purpose," with the intent of hindering, and conspiring to infringe, the victims' rights secured to them "by reason of their race and color, and because they were of African descent, and persons of color." The last 16 counts charged the defendants with murder in pursuing the conspiracy charged in the first 16 counts. They also were charged with oppressing the victims for having voted in the November 1872 election. While the circumstances of the crime were singular, the indictment was similar to so many others that had been upheld in the federal courts prior to April 1873.[9]

Despite the number of defendants indicted, United States Attorney Beckwith complied with the attorney general's instructions and selected only 9 for the trial that began on February 23, 1874. Louisiana Conservatives decided to use this case to challenge the constitutionality of federal prosecutions of Ku Klux-type crimes. Public donations and a benefit opera organized by prominent citizens of New Orleans yielded sufficient funds to retain four lawyers to represent the defendants. Two of the four, R. H. Marr and E. John Ellis, were leaders of the Louisiana Conservative Party. Ellis was a member of the House of Representatives who would play an instrumental role in negotiating the removal of federal troops from Louisiana in 1877. The other two defense counsel were William R. Whitaker and D. S. Bryan.[10]

The trial took two months. A certain symmetry characterized the trial before it was given to the jury, for two days were required to impanel the jury and two days were required to make closing arguments while two weeks were needed to examine some 280 witnesses. The witnesses included local political leaders and state officers such as state legislators. Significantly, Circuit Judge Woods presided, and, in his charge to the jury, he asserted that every right mentioned in the indictment was secured by the Constitution and laws of the United States. His apparent defiance of the Supreme Court is perhaps explained by his characterization of the case as one of grave importance not only to the defendants and people of Louisiana, but to the people of the United States as well. The jury evidently appreciated the import of the case, for it deliberated for approximately six weeks. However, it acquitted one defendant and failed to reach a verdict as to the others.[11]

The remaining eight defendants were retried within one month. When the trial began on May 18, Justice Bradley was on the bench with Judge Woods at the request of defense counsel. The defense's strategy was to challenge the constitutionality of the Enforcement Act of 1870, and they hoped to divide Bradley and Woods for the purpose of having the case certified to the United States Supreme Court. Immediately after the jury was impaneled, Marr entered a pretrial motion to quash the indictment on the grounds that the statute was unconstitutional. His argument was based on the Supreme Court's *Slaughterhouse* opinion, parts of which he read to the court. However, Bradley refused to decide this issue with the trial pending because the issues it raised were too grave to be decided hurriedly. He instructed counsel to proceed with the trial, and, if it resulted in convictions, the court would then consider a motion in arrest of judgment based on Marr's argument. He also promised to certify the case to the Supreme Court if he and Woods divided.[12]

Examination of witnesses again required two weeks, but closing arguments filled four days. The reason for the excessively long closing arguments, in the opinion of United States Attorney Beckwith, is that Justice Bradley fell into a trap laid by defense counsel by permitting the defense to argue against the constitutionality of the Enforcement Acts to the jury. This procedure was highly unusual. This time, however, the jury reached a verdict as to all of the defendants, and after only three days. Three of the defendants were found guilty of conspiracy as charged in the first 16 counts of the indictment, but not guilty of murder as charged in the second 16 counts. The other five defendants were acquitted.[13]

Beckwith was understandably discouraged with the poor results of two trials that stretched over four months and consumed so much of his physical and emotional energy and personal and financial well-being. He and other federal officials were under constant attack by the local conservative press during the trials, which emphasized the political and racial complexion of the grand and petit juries in its insistence that the prosecutions were politically motivated proceedings before a politically biased court. "The trial has been unpleasant in the extreme," Beckwith complained to Attorney General Williams, "and my health has been impaired by three weeks trial in this sweltering climate." That only three of nine defendants were convicted led him to the pessimistic conclusion that the federal judiciary was unable "to make law respected." "This difficulty will be more marked in the future, as the jury which rendered the beggarly verdict in the last trial is intimidated," he warned, "and I doubt if another jury can be found with courage enough to convict under any pressure of proof." The problems that confronted the federal courts in enforcing civil rights in 1874 had not diminished from earlier years. In fact, they were about to get worse.[14]

As anticipated, defense counsel entered motions in arrest of judgment based upon the unconstitutionality of the Enforcement Act of 1870. Reflecting the influence of Justice Miller's views of the Fourteenth Amendment, Marr argued that the Enforcement Act was unconstitutional because the rights it attempted to secure were rights of state citizenship and under the exclusive jurisdiction of the states. He also maintained that the crimes it punished were offenses against state criminal laws alone and punishable only in the courts of the states. In short, Marr insisted that the statute attempted to give the federal courts jurisdiction over crimes that were within the exclusive domain of the states. United States Attorney Beckwith expected Justice Bradley, on whom he lost little love, to affirm the defense's position and declare the law unconstitutional. The common opinion in New Orleans was that the *Slaughter-House* decision rendered the Enforcement Acts unconstitutional and that Bradley wanted to certify the case to the Supreme Court.[15]

Bradley had to leave New Orleans before he was prepared to decide the issues raised by Marr, but he promised to return with his decision within two weeks. True to his word, he was back in New Orleans to announce his decision on June 27. As United States Attorney Beckwith feared, Bradley upheld the defense's motion in arrest of judgment in an opinion that declared unconstitutional sections 6 and 7 of the Enforcement Act of 1870 and voided the indictment for vagueness and for failing to charge crimes punishable under federal law.[16]

The *Slaughter-House* decision forced Bradley to change some of his earlier views concerning national civil rights enforcement authority. Confronted with a diminution in the scope of the Fourteenth Amendment because of the Supreme Court's interpretation in *Slaughter-House*, Bradley reasoned his way into contradictory and anomalous interpretations of the Thirteenth and Fifteenth Amendments in an apparent attempt to preserve federal jurisdiction over civil rights.

Bradley prefaced his interpretation of the Reconstruction Amendments with a reassertion of the broad nationalist view of constitutional interpretation. Citing *Prigg v. Pennsylvania,* as had so many other judges before him, he asserted "that Congress has power to enforce by appropriate legislation, every right and privilege given or guaranteed by the Constitution." However, Bradley modified this interpretation by immediately limiting its scope with the condition that the "method of enforcement, or the legislation appropriate to that end, will depend upon the character of the right conferred."[17]

Since Bradley's original interpretation of the Fourteenth Amendment's privileges and immunities clause as securing the natural rights of citizenship had been rejected by the Supreme Court, he was forced to reinterpret the clause. In changing "the character of the right[s] conferred" by the privileges and immunities clause, Bradley also changed his view of the "method of enforcement" it authorized. The Fourteenth Amendment did not secure the civil rights of citizens themselves, he noted, because these rights are protected and enforced by the particular state of which the individual is a citizen. Rather, the amendment "only guarantees that they shall not be impaired by the state, or the United States, as the case may be," since the sole right secured by the Fourteenth Amendment's privileges and immunities clause is the security from governmental infringements of fundamental rights. Consequently, "there can be no constitutional legislation of congress for directly enforcing the privileges and immunities of citizens of the United States by original proceedings in the courts of the United States...." Rather, Congress may merely "provide a preventive or compensatory remedy or due punishment ..." for state infringements of these rights. "The affirmative enforcement of the rights and privileges themselves...belongs to the state government as a part of its residuary sovereignty."[18]

Bradley's interpretation of the amendment's due process clause was virtually indistinguishable from his interpretation of its privileges and immunities clause. It, too, "is a guaranty of protection against the acts of the state government itself ..., not a guaranty against the commission of individual offenses ...." Therefore, the remedies Congress may provide must be directed to the denial of due process by the state. The amendment does not authorize "congress to perform the duty which the guaranty itself supposes it to be the duty of the state to perform, and which it requires the state to perform." Bradley concluded that the "duty and power of enforcement take their inception from the moment that the state fails to comply with the duty enjoined, or violates the prohibition imposed." Under this interpretation, it was discriminatory state action rather than the infringement of a personal right that constituted a violation of the Fourteenth Amendment and that gave the federal courts jurisdiction over the offense.[19]

Bradley did not mention the Fourteenth Amendment's equal protection clause. This omission is perhaps explained by the equal protection nature of his interpretation of the amendment's privileges and immunities and due process clauses as directed exclusively to state infringements of citizens' rights. Bradley thus read into the Fourteenth Amendment a state action interpretation that virtually reduced it to an equal protection guarantee against racially discriminatory state legislation. The strengthening of the equal protection clause of the Fourteenth Amendment was a consequence of the emasculation of its privileges and immunities clause.

That *Slaughter-House* was responsible for Bradley's novel interpretation of the Fourteenth Amendment also is evinced by his interpretations of the Thirteenth and Fifteenth Amendments. Bradley attributed profound significance to the absence in the language of the Thirteenth Amendment of any references to the states. More than a mere "prohibition against the passage or enforcement of any law inflicting or establishing slavery ...," he observed, the amendment "is a positive declaration that slavery shall not exist. It prohibits the thing." Bradley asserted that, in prohibiting slavery, the Thirteenth Amendment affirmatively conferred on Congress "the power to give full effect to this bestowment of liberty. ..." Since "the character of the right" conferred was liberty itself, Congress was authorized to legislate directly and fully to secure liberty. He therefore upheld the constitutionality of the Civil Rights Act of 1866 and its grant of citizenship and punishment of individuals who interfered with the rights of citizens. He characterized the statute as appropriate and legitimate legislation to achieve the constitutionally authorized end of securing liberty. He quickly cautioned, though, that the amendment "does not authorize Congress to pass laws for the punishment of ordinary crimes and offenses...."[20]

The way Bradley distinguished between ordinary crimes punishable by the states alone and nationally punishable civil rights violations was his second novel interpretation of national civil rights enforcement authority. To be nationally punishable, the offense must have been motivated by racial animus. Neither the amendment nor the Civil Rights Act was explicitly limited to racial discrimination, nor were they interpreted as applying only to racially discriminatory infringements of fundamental rights until the Supreme Court's *Slaughter-House* decision. To a significant degree, the protection of white citizens' rights under the Thirteenth and Fourteenth Amendments became casualties to the Supreme Court's recognition of the primacy of state authority over citizenship and limitation of these amendments to racial discrimination.

The impact of the *Slaughter-House* decision on Bradley's interpretation of the Fourteenth Amendment is demonstrated even more clearly by his interpretation of the Fifteenth Amendment. Bradley acknowledged that, like the Fourteenth Amendment, the Fifteenth is worded as a negative prohibition of state infringements of voting rights. Moreover, the Fifteenth Amendment explicitly prohibited racially discriminatory state denials of voting rights. He nevertheless concluded that the Fifteenth Amendment "confers a positive right, which did not exist before." It conferred upon blacks the "right not to be excluded from voting by reason of race, color or previous condition of servitude...." Since it conferred a positive right, the Fifteenth Amendment authorized Congress "to pass laws to directly enforce the right and punish individuals for its violations, because that would be the only appropriate and efficient mode of enforcing the amendment." Bradley emphasized that the amendment did not just apply to state action with the declaration that it conferred upon Congress "the power to secure the right not only against the unfriendly operation of state laws, but against outrage, violence, and combinations on the part of individuals, irrespective of the state laws." He saw "no essential incongruity in the coexistence of concurrent laws, state and federal, for the punishment of the same unlawful acts as offenses both against the laws of the state and the laws of the United States." Racial animus was again the factor that distinguished nationally punishable voting rights infringements from those punishable by the state.[21]

Questions arise as to why and how Bradley could have interpreted the Fifteenth Amendment as reaching beyond state action when he interpreted the similarly worded Fourteenth Amendment as applicable only to discriminatory acts of the state. Doctrinally, the crucial difference was Bradley's interpretation of the Fifteenth Amendment as conferring and, therefore, directly securing a right itself and of the Fourteenth Amendment as not conferring any civil rights and, therefore, not directly securing rights but only a prohibition against governmental infringements of rights. However, this was a distinction that Bradley was forced to read into the amendments, since they are similarly worded as prohibitions against the states. Bradley attempted to rationalize his interpretation of the Fifteenth Amendment by explaining that it contained a double negative that created a positive right "to be exempt from the disability of race, color, or previous condition of servitude, as respects the right to vote." The Fifteenth Amendment, however, does not contain a double negative any more than the Fourteenth Amendment. It appears that Bradley applied to the Fifteenth Amendment the analysis he originally had applied to the Fourteenth but that he no longer could apply to the Fourteenth because of *Slaughter-House*. Because the Supreme Court had not as yet interpreted the Fifteenth Amendment, Bradley still was free to interpret it broadly. Thus, he declared that when the Fifteenth Amendment provides that the right to vote shall not be denied by the state, it means that the right shall be enjoyed. Consequently, the only legislation that would give effect to this amendment is legislation that directly enforces the right by punishing individuals who infringe it.[22]

Bradley found in the Thirteenth and Fifteenth Amendments much of the authority to enforce citizens' rights that the Supreme Court had extirpated from the Fourteenth. He declared that "any outrages, atrocities, or conspiracies, whether against the colored race or the white race" that were motivated by racial hatred were within the jurisdiction of the United States. Ordinary crimes were within the sole jurisdiction of the state unless "the state, by its laws, denies to any particular race equality of rights, in which case the government of the United States may furnish a remedy and redress to the fullest extent and in the most direct manner."[23]

Nonetheless, the recoupment of federal authority to enforce civil rights was incomplete. The Fourteenth Amendment was narrowed to proscribe only racially discriminatory state action. The Thirteenth and Fifteenth Amendments were interpreted as applying to infringements of rights *by* private individuals, but only infringements motivated *by* racial animus. Infringements of civil and political rights that were not racially motivated could be punished in federal courts only if state statutes were racially discriminatory.

The nuances of Bradley's constitutional analysis were not clearly understood by contemporaries, but the end result certainly was. He dismissed the indictment in *Cruikshank* because it attempted to punish the defendants for infringing rights that the national government could not directly protect and because it failed to charge that the offenses had been committed with the intent to deprive the victims of their rights because of their race, color, or previous condition of servitude.[24]

United States Attorney Beckwith was irate over the decision. "It is clear from the printed copy of his opinion," he complained to Attorney General Williams, "that he never had read the indictment, but has taken some person's statement of its substance." Beckwith's essential objection to the decision was that Bradley "exhibited a determination to demolish the law where he...[felt] equal to the task, and to demolish the indictment where he...[could not] wrestle successfully with the law," and that he failed to shed any light upon how a good indictment could be framed. United States Attorney John A. Minnis also complained that the ruling seemed to suggest that the Enforcement Acts protected only voting rights. "It is absolutely necessary that these Acts should extend to the protection of civil rights, through or by the Courts of the United States," he insisted, because to leave them to the state courts would render them worthless. Southern Republicans were understandably demoralized by Justice Bradley's decision.[25]

Louisiana Conservatives, however, were delighted. The New Orleans *Daily Picayune*, which had praised Bradley's nationalistic interpretation of the

Fourteenth Amendment in the *Slaughter-House Cases,* found his *Cruikshank* decision narrowing the Fourteenth Amendment and national civil rights enforcement authority equally laudatory. It joyfully informed its readers that the decision "virtually annuls and arrests all the proceedings in the Grant Parish prosecutions," which the editor insisted had been "conducted with a partisan virulence that has naturally excited the profound sympathies of our people for the accused...." Looking beyond *Cruikshank,* the editor anticipated that the decision would put an end to the troublesome meddling of United States Attorney Beckwith and Judge Woods in Louisiana elections. The editor's optimism was due in part to his belief that Bradley's opinion was the "authentic exposition" of the statute, since he noted that Bradley had returned to Washington, D. C., during his two week absence and consulted with his brethren on the Supreme Court. Beckwith apparently shared this view of the decision's impact upon the government's ability to secure civil rights, for he predicted that the decision would "cost five hundred lives between this time and November."[26]

Bradley decided another case around the time of *Cruikshank* that further eroded civil rights enforcement authority under the Civil Rights Act of 1866. This case concerned white juries in the state courts of Texas. While Texas statutes extended to black citizens the right to serve as jurors, blacks were effectively excluded from local juries because the process of selecting venires was generally in the hands of Democrats. In certain places, some of the very individuals who were responsible for crimes against blacks and who should have been tried for them were instead put on the juries that were to punish the crimes, according to reports of federal legal officers. Similar problems affected federal juries. Blacks were unable to receive justice in the state and federal courts even during the period of Republican rule in Texas, from 1867 to 1872, despite attempted reforms. The situation worsened after Conservatives won control of the state government.[27]

The case that was presented to the United States Circuit Court, *Texas v. Gaines,* involved an alleged politically and racially motivated prosecution of Matthew Gaines, a prominent black state senator and Republican leader. Gaines was charged with bigamy and was about to be tried in the local court at La Fayette County, Texas, when he applied for removal of the case to the federal district court under section 3 of the Civil Rights Act of 1866 on the grounds that he could not receive the full and equal benefit and protection of the laws because of racial and political prejudice against him. He alleged that the prosecution itself was nothing more than a racial and political vendetta to destroy his political influence. Judicial precedents and practice clearly supported Gaines's application for removal. However, the local court rejected his petition, and he was tried and convicted. He then appealed to the Republican-controlled Texas Supreme Court, and it reversed the judgment of the local court and directed it to remove the case as requested.[28]

In the district court, Gaines moved to quash the indictment, but the United States attorney, Andrew J. Evans, a black Republican, surprisingly asked the court to dismiss the case for want of jurisdiction. Evans's motion placed Gaines in the novel position of having to persuade the federal court to enforce his rights over the opposition of the United States attorney. Evans's opposition to Gaines's cause seems to have been motivated more by political considerations than by legal principles. Although Evans had been appointed to his office as a Republican in 1872, he became a Fusionist candidate for the state legislature to which he was elected in 1878. At the time of Gaines's case, he was connected to Democratic Party leaders by marriage, and he was one of the few Republicans holding an office in the Texas federal courts. He reportedly held his office as a sinecure and had no interest in furthering the fortunes of the Republican Party. Furthermore, by opposing jurisdiction, Evans could gain additional political advantage with the attorney general because he could meet the latter's demand to curtail judicial expenses and prosecutions.[29]

Bradley rejected Gaines's petition in an opinion that was riddled with contradictions. On the one hand, Bradley premised his interpretation of the Civil Rights Act of 1866 on the Supreme Court's 1872 ruling that only black defendants in criminal cases have the right to remove cases from the state to the federal courts under section 3. He then interjected an additional qualification on the right of removal. He asserted that mere denial of the right to a fair trial, even because of racial prejudice, was insufficient to remove a state prosecution to a federal court. The right must be denied in a particular manner, he stated; it must be denied by reason of a racially discriminatory state statute. Yet, the rationale he offered for this departure from the general understanding and practices of federal legal officers was based on a contradictory premise that actually conformed to those earlier interpretations and practices. "It must be remembered," Bradley cautioned, "that the privilege of removal is thus guaranteed to every citizen of the United States, as well white as black."[30]

Bradley could not have meant that a white defendant who was denied the right to the testimony of a black defense witness was entitled to removal. The Supreme Court had held in *Blyew* that witnesses to and, indeed, even the victims of crimes were not parties to the prosecution; the only parties were the government and the defendant. Therefore, the only party to a criminal prosecution who could claim removal under the Civil Rights Act, the Court concluded, was a black defendant. It is not likely that Bradley would have forgotten or overlooked this holding, because he had written a bitter dissent to it.[31]

Moreover, when the Supreme Court narrowed the right of removal under the Civil Rights Act to black defendants alone, it did not hold that only cases involving racially discriminatory state laws could be removed. On the contrary, the Court expressly noted that the statute was enacted to protect black Americans from rights infringements resulting from racial prejudice. The Court interpreted the Civil Rights Act as conferring jurisdiction on the federal courts when a defendant claimed that rights were infringed by, or could not be enforced or redressed in, the state court. A defendant could remove his case at any stage of the proceedings when he could demonstrate that he was unable to get justice in the local courts. Neither the judicial interpretations of, nor the practice in the lower federal courts under, the Civil Rights Act recognized the state action limitation Bradley now read into it. There is a bitter irony in this. Bradley had objected to the Supreme Court's limitation of the statute's right of removal to black defendants. Now, when a black defendant sought to invoke this right, Bradley restricted it even more by requiring that the petitioner's motion be based on a racially discriminatory statute.[32]

Bradley's opinion in *Gaines* also contradicted his decision in *Cruikshank*. In *Cruikshank*, Bradley virtually stated that the Civil Rights Act applied only to black Americans. He also explicitly held that the statute protected blacks from racially motivated actions of private individuals, from the inaction of public officials as well as from racially discriminatory state statutes. These contradictions, so obvious in retrospect, cry out for explanation.[33]

Bradley seemed to be struggling to reconcile contradictory judicial interpretations of the authority of the national government to enforce civil rights under the Thirteenth and Fourteenth Amendments on the one hand, and to delineate national and state jurisdiction over civil rights on the other. In interpreting the Fourteenth Amendment in *Slaughter-House,* the Supreme Court had affirmed unambiguously the primacy of state authority over the enforcement and protection of citizens' rights. The function of the national government under this theory was to ensure that the state was racially impartial and fair to all citizens. The main question that this theory raised is the extent to which the national government would interfere with the states' authority to ensure impartiality and fairness before the law.[34]

However, the Thirteenth Amendment, as Bradley understood it, contradicted this theory of national civil rights enforcement authority. He construed the

Thirteenth Amendment as securing liberty itself; it was not just a guarantee of the equal protection of liberty under state law. Hence, the Thirteenth Amendment encompassed the virtually unlimited authority to enforce and protect civil rights that the Supreme Court had rejected in its emasculation of the Fourteenth Amendment. These conflicting theories somehow had to be reconciled.[35]

In his *Cruikshank* and *Gaines* decisions, Bradley elaborated a theory of national civil rights enforcement authority that was based upon the diminished theory of the Fourteenth Amendment. Bradley seems to have been forced by the *Slaughter-House* decision to limit national authority to protect civil rights to state action as a way of delimiting the lines of national and state jurisdiction over civil rights and of curtailing the national oversight of state civil rights enforcement. In *Gaines,* he justified this diminution in national power with the assertion that "litigants, especially of the criminal class," would flood the federal courts if they were permitted to remove their state prosecutions on the mere allegation that they could not get a fair trial in the state court, regardless of how fanciful the allegation.[36]

Bradley must have known that Senator Gaines was not "of the criminal class" and that his petition was not a groundless legal tactic to escape deserved punishment. Bradley was well aware that blacks were effectively prohibited from serving on juries in the Texas courts. Attorney General Williams brought the problem to Bradley's attention and asked him to devise some means of resolving it. Nothing was done to rectify the injustice. Bradley also must have been aware of the notorious efforts of Texas Conservatives to remove Radical Republicans, such as Gaines, from state office. Yet, his decision in *Gaines* effectively precluded the federal courts from providing the justice black defendants were denied in the local courts. It also contributed to the expulsion of Matthew Gaines from the Texas Senate.[37]

However meritorious Gaines's petition might have been, Bradley evidently believed he could not grant it without continuing the extensive involvement of the federal courts in the administration of criminal justice that his brothers on the Supreme Court had rejected. The limitation of federal jurisdiction to cases involving state action was not predetermined by the legal theory of the *Slaughter-House* decision. However, it was mandated by the states' rights-oriented focus of the opinion. In restricting national authority over civil rights to a guarantee of racially impartial state statutes, Bradley effectively precluded the federal courts from intruding into local affairs to a greater extent than the Supreme Court would tolerate.

The impact of Bradley's decisions was felt beyond Louisiana and Texas. It reached across the South and into the nation's capital. During the summer of 1874 his *Cruikshank* ruling was widely publicized as a decisive blow to national civil rights enforcement authority. Democratic Conservatives became increasingly confident that the permanent elimination of Enforcement Acts prosecutions was at hand. Republican fears mounted that the Supreme Court would declare these laws unconstitutional or at least interpret them so narrowly that their effectiveness would be destroyed. This added to the fears Republicans already held for their personal safety because of the administration's policy of leniency and clemency. Federal legal officers predicted that these rulings, combined with the administration's weakened resolve, would constitute an irresistible invitation to white supremacist Democratic Conservatives to renew their political and racial terrorism.[38]

The violence anticipated by prescient federal officials exploded in the wake of Bradley's decisions. The period of relative calm won by the federal prosecutions during the years 1871 to 1873 was shattered in August 1874 when violence, terrorism, and intimidation became so widespread that contemporary observers described the mayhem as a new phase in the South's rebellion against national authority begun in 1861. Organized bands of guerrillas patterned after the Ku Klux Klan sprang up to overthrow Southern Republican governments and restore white rule. In some areas of the South, local government gave way to conditions of near anarchy reminiscent of the period 1870–1871.[39]

Governor Kellogg informed Attorney General Williams that leaders of the so-called White League in Louisiana believed that Justice Bradley "acted on inspiration received from the Administration" when he quashed the indictments and released the prisoners in the Colfax Massacre prosecutions. He complained that the administration's policy of leniency, "taken in connection with the decision of Judge Bradley releasing the Grant Parish murderers, has had a very bad effect," for the White League was confident that the national government would refrain from intervening in Louisiana affairs. United States Attorney Beckwith shared the governor's fears; he also reported that the *Cruikshank* decision "has led to serious and lamentable consequences and is still accepted by those engaged in that Massacre as conclusive against jurisdiction of the federal courts."[40]

Similar reports poured into the attorney general's office from other Southern states. Judge Richard Busteed could not conceal his panic when he informed Williams of the political murder of a prominent carpetbag Republican leader in Alabama. He insisted that forceful federal action was required to stop "the inauguration of the carnival of blood," which the judge characterized as "the first fruits of the pardons secured by Alabama Congressmen for the Ku Klux before me... ." If federal protection was not provided, he warned, "the life of every prominent Northerner who belongs to the Republican party will be in danger from way-side assassination." Judge Busteed, who was from New York, resigned from the bench two months after Attorney General Williams responded that he did not see how the murder could be brought within federal jurisdiction. Apparently, Judge Busteed's resignation was prompted by more than the threat of impeachment.[41]

United States Attorney Nick S. McAfee of the Southern District of Alabama confirmed Judge Busteed's warnings with even more alarming reports. Announcing the revival of a Ku Klux reign of terror, McAfee admonished that if the government abandoned Republicans "to work out their salvation as best they may," and if Democrats became aware of the government's abandonment, "it will be a little while till the American citizenship will be, in Alabama, the veriest mockery of a name without a right recognized by a dominant Democracy (rebels still) or capable of enforcement." The chairman of the Alabama Republican Executive Committee similarly complained that the combination of the president's Southern policy and Justice Bradley's adverse ruling led Democrats to believe "that the results which they endeavored to effect by the Ku Klux conspiracy, can now be effected surely and with impunity...; the old Ku Klux organization of Alabama has been revived...," he lamented. The belief was widespread in the state that "any man may murder a Republican, for political reasons without the slightest reason to fear that he will be punished, but with every reason to believe that he will be applauded for the act."[42]

This flow of reports eventually persuaded Williams that vigorous civil rights enforcement was again required to put down political terrorism. Noting that the political assassinations of Republicans "are becoming quite too frequent in the Southern States, and forebode evil times," he concluded that Republican fortunes in the upcoming fall elections would depend upon the federal protection of voters. Williams issued a circular letter on September 3, 1874, to the federal marshals in Alabama, Kentucky, Louisiana, South Carolina, and Tennessee exhorting them "to proceed with all possible energy and dispatch to detect, expose, arrest, and punish the perpetrators of these crimes." He added, "to that end, you are to spare no effort or necessary expense." He also informed them that troops would be provided to assist them. Within eighteen months of its inception, the administration's policy of clemency and leniency collapsed, and it seemed to return to the original policy of all-out civil rights enforcement inaugurated under Attorney General Amos T. Akerman in 1871.[43]

Nonetheless, United States attorneys who had been reprimanded for being too conscientious in enforcing civil rights were very cautious in embarking on this change in the administration's policy. United States Attorney G. Wiley Wells, for example, wanted assurance that the attorney general would support his prosecution suspects who intimidated black Mississippi voters in the 1874 election. Williams was annoyed that Wells would doubt his support. "You are expected by this Department to prosecute all violations of the laws of the United States with all the energy and ability you can command," he admonished. Yet, his instructions included a typically paradoxical statement of policy. He cautioned Wells against involving the government in "groundless or frivolous prosecutions which are not only an annoyance and an irritation to the people but are a matter of great expense to the United States." Then, in complete contradiction, he suggested that Wells prosecute only two or three of the most prominent leaders, provided that he had enough evidence for certain conviction.[44]

Contradictory instructions were sent to legal officers throughout the states affected with Ku Klux-type crime. The administration apparently wanted to enforce the laws of the United States and protect citizens without incurring expenses and without irritating the individuals who were directly and indirectly responsible. What appeared to be a revival of the Justice Department's original policy of unrestrained civil rights enforcement turned out to be an ambiguous modification of its more recent policy of highly selective enforcement of civil rights. Federal legal officers soon discovered that their efforts to enforce federal laws were ineffectual.[45]

Very few violations of civil rights were punished under the Grant administration anywhere in the South after 1874. Violence and fraud characterized the fall 1874 elections, but federal authorities could do little to check this lawlessness. Conservative terrorists were no longer fearful of punishment in the federal courts, and, with the organization and power they had established, they uninhibitedly intimidated Republican voters. Conditions were so poor in Louisiana that federal legal officers there had to communicate with Washington in code and feared that their lines of communication would be cut. Evincing a siege mentality characteristic of belligerent armies during wartime, United States Attorney Beckwith informed the attorney general that federal officers "are surrounded by an armed camp with a force exceeding by far the federal land forces now in the City [of New Orleans]." "Anarchy in January is inevitable," he predicted. Neither federal nor state law was respected in the state because neither could be enforced against the White League. Threatened with personal violence and unable to protect himself, his health impaired, his private law practice ruined because of the prosecution of the Colfax Massacre case, Beckwith asked to be relieved of his office and tendered his resignation in December 1874.[46]

Conditions in Mississippi were similar. United States Attorney W. W. Dedrick reported "that Mississippi was in a condition of more thorough and effective armed insurrection against the Constitution and laws of the United States than in 1861 when she raised the flag of rebellion." Expressing the desire to enforce the laws of the United States, he questioned "how much relief can be afforded through the channels of the Courts in the present attitude of the Courts towards certain acts of Congress...." Judge Hill advised him that recent rulings in the federal courts placed these outrages beyond federal jurisdiction, and he was instructed not to begin any new prosecutions under the Enforcement Acts until the Supreme Court resolved the uncertainties of federal civil rights enforcement authority. "It is clear to my mind," Judge Hill observed, "that the judgment of our unseat republican jurists and Statesmen is now against Federal interference in such cases, but to leave it to the State authorities and the good sense of the people."[47]

The administration's revivification of civil rights enforcement in September 1874 was quickly aborted. Attorney General Williams instructed United States Attorney Beckwith as early as October not to take any further action in the Colfax Massacre case, or in any other cases that involved the same questions of law arising under the Enforcement Acts until the Supreme Court decided those issues. Similar instructions were sent in May 1875 to United States Attorney W. W. Murray in Tennessee, who urged the attorney general to permit him to prosecute the defendants in the Gibson County murders. Although he agreed that the murderers should be punished, Williams responded "that prosecutions under the enforcement acts at this time will amount to very little so long as the questions before the Supreme Court remain undecided." He ordered a general suspension of Enforcement Acts prosecutions in Tennessee "until it is known whether the Supreme Court will hold them to be constitutional or otherwise."[48]

Federal civil rights enforcement in 1874 and after was strikingly different from that of the previous years. Earlier, Justice Department officers assumed jurisdiction over civil rights enforcement with confidence in their constitutional authority. Federal judges broadly applied federal jurisdiction over civil rights. The Supreme Court's *Slaughter-House* ruling undermined the constitutional theory that permitted federal legal officers to interpret their powers so broadly. Thereafter, many judges retreated from the expansive interpretations of constitutional authority they earlier had believed were the intended meaning and scope of national authority to enforce civil rights. United States District Judge William F. Giles of Maryland, for example, observed in 1876 that the

Slaughter-House decision deviated from the "mere literal meaning" of the Fourteenth Amendment by calling "the attention of the people of this country to the distinction between rights that belonged to citizens of the states, and the rights which belonged to the citizens of the United States as such." Although he thought it was shameful that federal authority could not punish racially motivated crimes, Circuit Judge Halmer H. Emmons nevertheless charged a Memphis federal grand jury in March 1875 that they could not assert such authority to indict persons suspected of having committed such crimes:

> In view of the judgments of the Supreme Court already rendered, that a crime perpetrated by one citizen of Tennessee upon another, when it consists in the violation of some right which is enjoyed solely as the citizen of the state, depends in no degree upon the national constitution…

While some federal judges, such as Circuit Judge Hugh L. Bond, circumvented the *Slaughter-House* decision and applied the original broad nationalist concept of civil rights enforcement authority, most federal judges limited their jurisdiction to cases involving state action.[49]

By 1875, uncertainties concerning federal jurisdiction disposed the federal courts and the Department of Justice decidedly against attempting to enforce civil and political rights. District Judge John Erskine refused to try any Enforcement Acts cases in the absence of a circuit judge. Another federal district judge ruled that a racially discriminatory tax structure did not violate federal laws, while still another denied the right of three black soldiers to remove their prosecutions from a local court to the federal court because state laws did not discriminate. Judge Hill's directive to United States Attorney Dedrick against further Enforcement Acts prosecutions was broadened to include all federal legal officers and grand juries. By the spring of 1875, doubts concerning the scope of national civil rights enforcement authority prompted the Justice Department to suspend all prosecutions under the Enforcement Acts. In May 1875, Edwards Pierrepont, Williams's successor as attorney general, even suspended prosecutions of violations of federal laws committed by state officers who had acted under state laws. He was fearful that even these cases did not fall within federal jurisdiction.[50]

By the fall of 1875, then, the administration made no pretense of its capitulation to the political and legal climate that was clearly hostile to the federal enforcement of civil and political rights. "The whole public are tired out by these annual autumnal outbreaks in the South," Attorney General Pierrepont retorted to Mississippi Governor Adelbert Ames's request for federal troops to put down violence, "and the great majority now are ready to condemn any interference on the part of the Government." Manifesting the era's spirit of self-help individualism and laissez faire, he cynically suggested that Mississippi Republicans demonstrate to the rest of the nation that they "have the courage and the manhood to fight for their rights, and to destroy the bloody ruffians who murder the innocent and unoffending freedmen." The president's entire cabinet endorsed this attitude. In light of the consistent failure of local authorities to protect political and racial minorities, this attitude constituted a cynical abandonment of Southern Republicans, white and black. But, it was possible to hide the irresponsibility of this abandonment of erstwhile political allies with the expedient rationalization provided by adverse judicial rulings concerning national authority to enforce civil rights. Instead of continuing prosecutions until legal questions were resolved by the Supreme Court, the Justice Department and the lower federal courts suspended them. It was clear to observers that the Supreme Court held the power to decide these questions of public policy, and attention focused on it. But, Southern Republicans peered with waning hopes.[51]

9

The Reinstitution
of Decentralized
Constitutionalism: The
Supreme Court and Civil
Rights, 1876

In 1876 the United States Supreme Court finally consented to resolve the decade-long judicial struggle over the scope of national civil rights enforcement authority. In retrospect, the Supreme Court's interpretations of the Reconstruction Amendments as guarantees of the civil rights of black Americans appear to have been predetermined by its 1873 *Slaughter-House* decision and Justice Bradley's 1874 opinion in *Cruikshank*. Both counsels' arguments and the Court's 1876 decisions were predicated upon the legal assumptions of these opinions. While hindsight is almost always clearer than foresight, the states' rights emphasis of most federal court civil rights decisions after 1873 combined with the Grant administration's cessation of civil rights enforcement must have suggested to contemporaries the probable outcome of the Supreme Court's deliberations.

However predictable the outcome, the need to resolve the constitutional questions surrounding the congressional civil rights program prompted proponents as well as opponents to seek a quick resolution in the Supreme Court. The Court's interpretation of the Reconstruction Amendments as they applied to black Americans would affect national policies. An adverse ruling could diminish the constitutional authority that permitted the Department of Justice and the federal courts to intervene in Southern affairs. The elimination of that authority held grave implications for the department's political fortunes and the subsequent nature of race relations. Defense counsel desired an early hearing because of the uncertain fate of their clients and their rising expectations of a favorable decision. United States attorneys urged the attorney general to advance civil rights cases on the Supreme Court's docket despite their pessimism about achieving a favorable decision. The Supreme Court yielded to the litigants' entreaties and accelerated the process by which the cases involving these issues were heard.[1]

The Court's determination of the authority of the federal government to enforce voting rights became entwined with its authority to enforce civil rights. Terrorist assaults on Southern blacks and white Republicans usually occurred during electioneering. As Judge Hill noted, the Fifteenth Amendment's protection of voting rights potentially could serve as the constitutional authorization for federal intervention to protect Southern Republicans in the place of diminished authority under the Fourteenth Amendment. However, in their arguments before the Supreme Court, counsel on both sides advanced legal theories that characterized voting rights and civil rights enforcement authority in similar ways. The Supreme Court interpreted these amendments and their respective scopes with a great degree of similarity. The history of voting rights before the Supreme Court, therefore, provides some insights into the Court's interpretation of national authority to secure civil rights under the Fourteenth Amendment.

The case that tested the scope of national voting rights enforcement authority, *United States v. Reese*, grew out of the January 1873 Lexington, Kentucky, municipal elections. State statutes required voters to pay a $1.50 capitation tax to the city collector, who issued a receipt that had to be presented to election registrars before the elector was allowed to vote. However, the Lexington city collector effectively disfranchised black voters by refusing to accept their offers to pay the tax. When they presented themselves at the polls on election day, registrars of election refused to allow them to vote because they did not have the necessary tax receipt. Kentucky Republicans believed that Lexington election officials purposefully used the tax in a conspiracy to disfranchise black voters.[2]

A committee of Kentucky Republicans led by United States Attorney G. C. Wharton decided to invoke the power of the federal courts to combat this official disfranchisement. Attorney General Williams supported this decision after the committee consulted with him in the nation's capitol. The federal grand jury at Louisville indicted two Lexington inspectors of election, Matthew Foushee and Hiram Reese, in February 1873 for alleged violations of the Enforcement Act of 1870. The first count charged them with refusing to receive the vote of William Garner, a qualified voter "of African descent," because of Garner's failure to produce the city collector's receipt showing that he had paid the capitation tax. The second count charged that defendants agreed not to allow black voters to vote without the requisite tax receipt with intent to deprive them of their right to vote because of their race and color, and that they demanded the tax receipt from Garner in pursuit of this agreement in order to deprive him of his right to vote because of his race and color. The third count charged that the inspectors wrongfully refused to accept Garner's affidavit stating that he had offered to pay the required tax, but that his offer was refused by the city collector because of his race and color. The fourth count simply charged that the defendants refused to receive Garner's vote because of his race and color.[3]

Counsel for Reese demurred that the indictment did not charge an offense punishable under the Enforcement Act of 1870 or within the jurisdiction of the federal courts. They claimed that Garner's mere offer to pay the tax was insufficient to discharge him from the statutory requirement of actually paying it, because the city collector's refusal to accept Garner's offer of payment did not satisfy the statutory obligation. Therefore, the defendants lawfully refused to allow Garner to vote because of his failure to meet the statutory qualifications for voting.[4]

The importance of the Lexington case is reflected in the attention it received from supporters and opponents of national civil rights enforcement. The local conservative press sensationalized the trial and complained that the defendants were oppressively wrenched from their homes in Lexington and dragged all the way to Louisville at great expense to themselves and the government to stand trial before strangers rather then before their neighbors. The case was portrayed as a politically motivated persecution of Democrats by vindictive Republicans who invoked "the aid and vengeance of their ever willing friend, the Federal Court" in an effort to prevent responsible individuals from being judges of election. According to these accounts, the bases of the arrests and charges were falsehoods and perjured testimony of Republicans who sought to overturn the election results. The federal courts and the Justice Department were again confronted with politically explosive prosecutions that rendered them vulnerable to accusations of partisanship.[5]

Attorney General Williams supported the Republicans' cause by authorizing special assistants. He allowed Wharton to hire two special prosecutors, William C. Goodloe and future Supreme Court justice John Marshall Harlan. Williams also sent to government counsel a copy of Justice William Strong's opinion in a similar case decided in the United States Circuit Court for Delaware just weeks before the Supreme Court's *Slaughter-House* decision. The Delaware case was a criminal prosecution of a local tax collector who was charged with violating the Enforcement Act of 1870 by preventing black voters from becoming qualified to vote by a variety of means. The collector was tried and convicted, and his attorney filed a motion in arrest of judgment on the grounds that the law was unconstitutional. This action gave Justice Strong an opportunity to interpret the scope of the Reconstruction civil rights enforcement program.[6]

Justice Strong became the third justice of the United States Supreme Court to explore the legal theory encompassed in the Reconstruction Amendments. Like his predecessors, he adopted the broad nationalist interpretation of these amendments. He held that, despite their negative wording, these amendments recognized substantive rights, and, therefore, were positive guarantees of the substantive rights of liberty, citizenship, and political participation that gave Congress the necessary authority to secure civil and political rights against any interference or infringement. However, the utility of this powerful expression of the primacy of national civil and political rights enforcement authority was undermined by the growing public awareness of other decisions restricting national authority over basic rights to an equal protection guarantee against racially discriminatory state action.[7]

The Lexington case was not argued before the federal Circuit Court at Louisville until November 1873. Judge Bland Ballard delayed arguments until Circuit Judge Halmer H. Emmons could participate in the decision because of the "gran constitutional questions" it raised. Ballard and Emmons divided on the first three counts. Ballard found that counts one and three were faulty for failing to charge that the defendants acted with the intent of depriving Garner of his voting rights because of his race and color. He found that count two could not stand because it was based upon section 4 of the 1870 Enforcement Act, which he thought was unconstitutional since it was intended to punish private individuals as well as governmental officials who interfered with citizens' right to vote absent a racially discriminatory intent. He held that the Fifteenth Amendment, which purportedly was authority for section 4, applied only to the racially discriminatory actions of state officers. However, he joined Emmons in upholding the fourth count. United States Attorney Wharton did not want to go to trial on that count alone. Consequently, the case was certified to the United States Supreme Court on a division of opinion in the circuit court.[8]

The significance attributed to the case by the Grant administration is suggested by the rare appearance of the attorney general to argue it before the Supreme Court on January 13, 1875. If Southern Republicans were to have any meaningful participation in political life, state officers, such as the defendants in this case, simply would have to be subject to prosecutions in the federal courts for such overt violations of black citizens' right to vote. Therefore, Williams argued for the broadest scope of protection that could be brought within the amendment's state action prohibition. He insisted that the amendment protected the voting rights of all citizens; that it protected their right to vote in state and local as well as national elections; that it protected voting rights from state action whether the action was in the form of a racially discriminatory statute enacted by the legislature, of a state officer acting under authorization of a discriminatory statute, of a state officer acting in violation of state authority, or of the failure of state officers to protect citizens against the interference with their voting rights by private individuals. In the last situation, Williams argued, the Fifteenth Amendment conferred jurisdiction on the national government to punish the private offender. The rulings of both Strong in *Givens* and Bradley in *Cruikshank* supported the government's position. Williams concluded, then, that the motion to quash the indictment should be denied.[9]

B. F. Bucknor argued the case for the defendants. He quoted freely from the congressional debates leading to the adoption of the Fifteenth Amendment to insist that the framers of the Fifteenth Amendment intended to preserve the states' primary authority over voting rights originally conferred upon them by the United States Constitution. He asserted that the Fifteenth Amendment was intended merely to protect black citizens against infringements of their state-conferred right to vote resulting from racially discriminatory acts of the state. He narrowly restricted the scope of state action to racially discriminatory statutes enacted by the state legislature. He submitted a separate brief that specifically rebutted Justice Bradley's *Cruikshank* interpretation of the Fifteenth Amendment as conferring upon Congress authority directly to enforce voting rights by punishing state officials for alleged violations. Bucknor reasoned that the state can act in its official capacity only through the legislature; therefore, the actions of state officers did not constitute official acts of the state. Consequently, the Fifteenth Amendment did not reach the actions of state officers, particularly when they acted to implement racially impartial state statutes. He conceded that the amendment's prohibition against state discrimination was a tacit recognition of the preexistence of the right to vote. Federal judges had made this observation in concluding that this negative prohibition against state infringement of the right to vote was a recognition of the right by the United States Constitution that gave Congress the authority directly to enforce the right in whatever manner it deemed appropriate. Bucknor, however, rejected this conclusion by insisting that the right to vote existed prior to the ratification of the Fifteenth Amendment by virtue of the state's grant of the right to qualified citizens.[10]

Two important conclusions of law followed from Bucknor's analysis. Since the state granted the right to vote, the state possessed primary authority to enforce the right. If this right is recognized as a state-conferred right in the Fifteenth Amendment's prohibition against state infringement, then the mere constitutional recognition of the right is insufficient to confer upon Congress the requisite authority directly to enforce the right as previously held by federal judges.

Bucknor concluded that the Enforcement Act of 1870 was unconstitutional, first, because it attempted to punish the enforcement of racially discriminatory state statutes and racially discriminatory actions of state officers as well as the actions of private individuals who interfered with citizens' voting rights. Second, the statute was unconstitutional because it purported to punish voting rights infringements even when the infringements did not stem from a racial motive. Hence, the indictment based on this statute should be quashed.

Bucknor also argued that the indictment itself was bad. Interpreting the Fifteenth Amendment as only protecting black voters against racially discriminatory state action, he insisted that any state infringements of the right to vote must be motivated by reasons of race, color, or previous condition of servitude to constitute offenses under the amendment. The indictment against Reese was bad, he concluded, because it did not aver, nor did the government show, that their refusal to allow Garner to vote was motivated by racial prejudice.

If defense counsel in *Cruikshank* intended it, connecting the civil rights case and the scope of the Fourteenth Amendment to the voting rights case and the scope of the Fifteenth Amendment was a brilliant strategy. Aspects of each amendment could be applied to the other to produce a narrow theory of national authority to enforce citizens' rights that was applicable to both amendments. The theory of state action became the linchpin that joined the similarly worded amendments. The Supreme Court had already suggested, and Justice Bradley had already held, that the Fourteenth Amendment was applicable only to discriminatory state statutes. This narrow view of the Fourteenth Amendment could be read into the Fifteenth Amendment to curtail the more expansive interpretation of the latter amendment proclaimed by Bradley and Strong. If state action limited the Fourteenth Amendment's application to racially discriminatory statutes, state action logically would have the same limiting effect on the applicability of the Fifteenth Amendment, Justices Bradley's and Strong's earlier circuit court opinions notwithstanding. Consequently, Bucknor argued a narrow theory of state action in interpreting the Fifteenth Amendment, and defense counsel in *Cruikshank* amplified the argument in interpreting the Fourteenth as well as the Fifteenth Amendments.[11]

The Fifteenth Amendment also served to rationalize the Supreme Court's dicta in *Slaughter-House* suggesting a narrow state action interpretation of the Fourteenth Amendment. The Court had declared that the Fourteenth Amendment was intended almost exclusively to protect black Americans from racially discriminatory state laws. The amendment, however, is not limited on its face to racial discrimination. However, the Fifteenth Amendment is explicitly directed to racially motivated violations of voting rights. The explicit application of the Fifteenth Amendment to blacks and racial discrimination could be used more convincingly to limit the application of the Fourteenth Amendment to racial discrimination.

Moreover, substantial evidence was available to argue that Congress's intent with respect to the Fifteenth Amendment was merely to provide black Americans with protection from voting rights denials rather than to provide a general guarantee of voting rights to all Americans. This view was supported not only by the language of the amendment and explicit statements of the framers in congressional debates, as Bucknor argued in *Reese,* but also by the long-recognized primacy of state authority over voting rights. These considerations could have been applied to strengthen the Supreme Court's conclusion in *Slaughter-House* that the Fourteenth Amendment was not a direct guarantee of civil rights. The legal theories elaborated by counsel in *Cruikshank* expressed these relationships between the two amendments. Interpreting both amendments as mere prohibitions against racially discriminatory state action and narrowly equating state action to state statutes deprived them of the expansive authority that was earlier attributed to them by the courts of the United States.

Legal arguments of both defense and prosecution in *Cruikshank* evince the great impact of *Slaughter-House* on the understanding of the Fourteenth Amendment as a guarantee of equal protection of the law. The Supreme Court's 1873 interpretation of the amendment established a concept of the amendment that has withstood subsequent attempted alternative interpretations. Consequently, the decision in *Slaughter-House* concerning the personal rights of white workers pointed to the outcome of the Court's decision in *Cruikshank* concerning the personal rights of black citizens.

As in *Reese,* the government's argument in *Cruikshank* was again presented by Attorney General Williams along with Solicitor General S. F. Phillips. However, they capitulated to the opponents of national civil rights enforcement, for they failed to propose a legal theory supporting the broad authority of the national government to enforce civil rights. Williams and Phillips made no attempt to offer an interpretation of the Thirteenth and Fourteenth Amendments that was favorable to national civil rights enforcement or to provide a legal theory supporting the constitutionality of section 6 of the Enforcement Act of 1870 under which the indictment in *Cruikshank* was brought. They conceded defeat on fourteen of the sixteen counts of the indictment under which the defendants stood convicted. They based the government's case on counts fourteen and sixteen, which charged the defendants with feloniously conspiring "'to injure, oppress, threaten, and intimidate'" named citizens of the United States with the intent "'to *prevent and hinder'*" such citizens in the free exercise and enjoyment of their right to vote in any election and "'of each, every, all and singular the several rights and privileges granted or secured to…[them] by the Constitution and laws of the United States….'" They abandoned the effort to defend the other counts charging the defendants with infringing specific Bill of Rights guarantees of freedom of assembly and the right to keep and bear arms, and Fourteenth Amendment guarantees to due process and equal protection.[12]

The contrast in the government's argument before the Supreme Court in 1875 to the broad pre-*Slaughter-House* interpretations of the Reconstruction Amendments and civil rights statutes is striking. The Supreme Court's and Justice Bradley's interpretations of the Fourteenth Amendment seem to account for Williams's and Phillips's strategy. These decisions placed the fundamental rights of citizenship and Bill of Rights guarantees beyond the scope of the Fourteenth Amendment's privileges and immunities clause. They also placed racially motivated infringements of citizens' rights by private individuals beyond the amendment's due process and equal protection guarantees. In short, the Supreme Court's interpretation of the Fourteenth Amendment seemed to limit its application to racially discriminatory state action, which was not involved in this case.

The government therefore shifted its argument to a theory of civil rights enforcement under the Fifteenth Amendment. This theory was reasonable since the Supreme Court had not as yet interpreted the scope of the power of the federal government to enforce voting rights, and Justice Bradley had interpreted this power broadly enough to provide authority for these prosecutions. Still, the state action interpretation of the Fourteenth Amendment in *Slaughter-House* was nonbinding *obiter dicta* in a case that was easily distinguishable from *Cruikshank*. The attorney general's failure even to attempt to offer an alternative theory of the Fourteenth Amendment to preserve the broad authority over civil rights is difficult to understand. It is also tragic. Black Americans did not have their "day in court" because the attorney general of the United States did not present the Supreme Court with legal theories of civil rights enforcement most favorable to their cause. This failure virtually ensured that the Supreme Court would adopt a states' rights interpretation that narrowed the scope and diminished the effectiveness of the Fourteenth Amendment to protect the rights of black Americans.

Equally difficult to explain is the government's failure to proffer a legal theory of civil rights enforcement under the Thirteenth Amendment. Williams and Phillips argued for the constitutionality of the count charging the defendants with infringing rights of citizens secured by the United States Constitution. This suggests that they may have hoped that the Supreme Court would broaden its concept of nationally enforceable rights of citizens or to elucidate a legal theory of national civil rights enforcement that was broader than that expressed in *Slaughter-House*. Bradley had provided such a theory under the Thirteenth Amendment in his decision in the court below.

Three possible explanations may account for Williams's and Phillips's failure to base their case, at least in part, on the Thirteenth Amendment. First, the 1870 statute was primarily enacted to implement the Fifteenth Amendment. Legislation, however, may be upheld as constitutional if authorization can be found in any portion of the Constitution. Furthermore, the 1870 statute reenacted the Civil Rights Act of 1866, which offered evidence that it was based as much upon the Thirteenth as the Fifteenth Amendment. If the Court had been willing to adopt Bradley's and other federal judges' interpretations of the Thirteenth Amendment, the relevant sections of the 1870 statute conceivably could have been upheld.[13]

This observation raises the second possible explanation. The attorney general and solicitor general may have been convinced that the Supreme Court was unwilling to recognize the legal theory of national civil rights enforcement implicit in the case under any theory. Bradley certainly had not used the Thirteenth Amendment as authority for the statute in the circuit court, and his opinion was regarded in New Orleans as an expression of the views of his judicial brothers whom he was thought to have consulted before writing it. The Grant administration seemed to express pessimism about the Supreme Court's consideration of its civil rights enforcement activities when it ordered Justice Department officers to cease those activities until the Supreme Court evaluated their constitutionality.

Nonetheless, Williams's and Phillips's failure even to attempt to present a legal theory of civil rights enforcement under the Thirteenth Amendment raises a third and more cynical explanation. The administration may have welcomed a Supreme Court decision that precluded the civil rights enforcement efforts that had become so politically debilitating. The Justice Department could withdraw gracefully from an undesirable policy under the semblance of a judicial mandate. Yet, in basing its case on a theory of voting rights enforcement power, the administration not only could avoid winning more authority than it cared to exercise, but it also possibly could preserve enough legal authority to punish rights violations that were potentially politically rewarding, such as violations arising from elections and the exercise of political power. Whatever the explanation, the government's brief offered no legal theory of civil rights enforcement; it was directed primarily at justifying the legal and procedural adequacy of the language of those counts of the indictment Williams and Phillips chose to defend.

The government's anemic argument was sharply contrasted by the elaborate and various theories presented by the defense. The seven attorneys who represented the three defendants predicated their legal theory of national civil rights enforcement authority on a states' rights concept of American federalism as modified by their conservative conception of the Civil War and Reconstruction. Their view of American federalism and recent American history contradicted that expressed by federal judges prior to 1873, but it was consistent with the view expressed by a majority of the United States Supreme Court. The defense's legal arguments again demonstrate that the *Slaughter-House* decision was clearly imprinted on *Cruikshank*.

Defense counsel repeatedly reminded the Court that the issues posed by this case held grave implications for the nature of American federalism. They characterized the primary issue to be decided by the Court as whether "power has been conferred upon Congress to protect individual citizens by punitive legislation, against the violation of these [civil] right [*sic*] by individuals." "In this aspect," John Archibald Campbell observed in complete contradiction to the position he had argued before the Court in *Slaughter-House*, "this cause is one of surpassing interest, and on its determination depends either the maintenance of the government upon its ancient foundation, or a radical change in its entire structure." David S. Bryan agreed "that no greater or more important case was ever brought before a court for judgment…. In truth, the [local self-] government which our fathers formed for themselves and their children, is on trial in this case."[14]

Using the theory offered by the Supreme Court to opponents of national civil rights enforcement, defense counsel elaborated a states' rights view of American federalism that preserved local self-government as they conceived it. Bryan expressed the defense's fundamental premise when he stated that the regulation and enforcement of such fundamental rights as Bill of Rights guarantees "belongs to the *police* authority of the State, and it is a necessary power to be exercised by the State for the peace of society and the safety of life and property[.]" Equally important was their second assumption that this power was one "that the States have always exercised from a time before the General Government was formed until the present, without gainsaying or dispute."[15]

The defense's argument is an interesting example of the interplay between history and legal theory in trial advocacy. Implicit in Bryan's historical argument for the primacy of state authority over citizens and citizens' rights is a state sovereignty conception of American federalism. David Dudley Field, brother of sitting Supreme Court Justice Stephen J. Field, also appealed to history. The Founding Fathers, Field observed, established the national government as a government of limited powers delegated to it by the Constitution of the United States. All residuary powers of government were reserved by the states. He and his colleagues insisted that the authority over citizens' fundamental civil rights was retained as an "essential attribute of the sovereignty of" the states. R. H. Marr supported this position by citing a number of pre–Civil War cases, beginning with *Barron v. The Mayor and City Council of Baltimore,* that held that Bill of Rights guarantees are limitations upon the national government, not affirmative grants of legislative authority to enforce and protect the fundamental rights of citizens. Defense counsel reasoned from this doctrine to the conclusion that the Constitution of the United States, as it was originally framed, reserved to the sovereign states exclusive authority over citizens' civil rights. They audaciously asserted as an undisputed fact of legal history what was actually the states' rights position in a hotly contested and unresolved antebellum constitutional question of federal power.[16]

Field proffered a conservative theory of constitutional interpretation and a conservative view of recent American history that, if accepted, unamendably riveted this state sovereignty theory of American federalism onto the Constitution. He asserted that the recent amendments to the Constitution did not transfer the states' sovereign power over citizens' rights to the national government. He characterized the Civil War as an American struggle to abolish slavery and establish the indestructible unity of the nation as it had existed before the war, as a union of sovereign and independent states. Further, he interpreted the constitutional amendments that the nation had ratified to ensure the freedom of the liberated slaves within this concept of the Civil War. These amendments, therefore, left undisturbed the states' "plenary power over the subject" of citizens' rights and merely provided that the states "should make no discrimination to their disadvantage."[17]

Defense counsel denied the possibility that the Reconstruction Amendments could have conferred concurrent authority over citizens' rights upon the national government. This conclusion was predicated on two assumptions. The first is that Americans wanted to preserve a states' rights-centered federalism. The second assumption is that the concession to the national government of any enforcement authority over citizens' rights was incompatible with the continued existence of sovereign and independent states. There could be "no middle ground between giving Congress plenary power over the subject of those fundamental rights, and giving it none," Field insisted, because the laws of Congress would "supersede or exclude legislation by the States upon the same subject, the United States would stand as the universal law giver of the country, and the laws of the States would dwindle to the dimensions of corporation ordinances or regulations of county supervisors." Concede this congressional power, Field warned, and the "substance of American constitutional government, as received from the Fathers, will have gone, and the forms will not be long in following."[18]

Field's colleagues also sounded this danger of revolutionary constitutionalism if the Court upheld broad national authority over civil rights. Campbell asserted that the recognition of such power in the national government would lead to the "entire subversion of the institutions of the States and the immediate consolidation of the whole land into a consolidated empire...." American government will "have been completely revolutionized," Marr admonished the Court, "by the mere conferring of power upon Congress to enforce the prohibitions of the recent Amendments." Relying on Miller's parallel conclusion in *Slaughter-House* and his conservative historical assumptions about the nature of the Civil War, Field insisted "that such was not, and could not have been the intention of the American people, in sanctioning these amendments...." Deploring the revolutionary constitutional consequences of the primacy of national authority over the enforcement of citizens' fundamental rights, Field added that these amendments "should not be thus interpreted, even if the natural significance of their language were, as it is not, favorable to such an interpretation."[19]

Defense counsel reached four conclusions from their limitation of the scope of the Fourteenth Amendment to racially discriminatory state action. Equating the state to the legislature and state action to legislation, they reasoned that national civil rights enforcement authority was triggered by, and could only be directed against, racially discriminatory state statutes. Consequently, "the natural, the true, and the only constitutional mode of enforcement is by judicial remedies..." declaring the state statute void. Moreover, since the Fourteenth Amendment merely prohibits the states from legislating in a racially discriminatory manner, national authority does not apply if a state merely fails to protect citizens' civil rights. State inaction, in other words, "*is no cause for federal action.*" Nor may the national government proceed against state officers or private individuals who violate citizens' rights. Relying on the Supreme Court's 1871 decision in *Collector v. Day,* Field argued that the national government could not punish state officers for failing to enforce, or for violating, citizens' rights because the national and state governments "'*are separate and distinct sovereignties,* acting separately and independently of each other, within their respective spheres.'" Federal prosecutions of state officers "would be incompatible with the independence of the State[s]...," which, counsel argued, is "essential to the sovereignty...of the States." Similar considerations would preclude federal prosecutions of private individuals who infringed citizens' basic rights. The protection of citizens' civil and political rights is a part of the states' police powers, and, "in relation to these," Campbell insisted, "THE AUTHORITY OF A STATE IS COMPLETE, UNQUALIFIED, AND EXCLUSIVE." In short, the national government could not constitutionally interfere with, or assume, the states' exclusive jurisdiction over the administration of criminal justice.[20]

The 1870 Enforcement Act and the indictment brought under it were void, defense counsel insisted. The rights that were allegedly violated were within the exclusive jurisdiction of the states. The offenses that were charged were offenses against the sovereignty of the states. The power and function of redressing these rights and punishing these wrongs, therefore, were exclusive and essential attributes of the sovereignty of the states. Indeed, the very existence of the states depended upon their retaining control of the administration of criminal justice and enforcement of citizens' civil and political rights. Since congressional authority generally is limited by the express and implied prohibitions of the Constitution, Field observed, Congress cannot, "under color of preventing a state from doing certain things, destroy the State, or any of its essential attributes." Not only is Congress thus limited, but also none of the departments of the national government "has, expressly or by implication, power to destroy any essential attribute of the sovereignty of" the states. Field thereby cleverly confused a theory of congressional authority under the Reconstruction Amendments with a more general principle of constitutional interpretation to insist that the Enforcement Act of 1870 was unconstitutional. However, the more important basis of the defense's position was that Congress's attempt directly to protect civil and political rights so intruded upon the sovereign powers of the states that it threatened their very existence. Their legal argument had come full circle.[21]

The issues raised in this case were too important for the defense to rely exclusively upon points of law. Although he conceded that "political argument addressed to the Supreme Court would of course be out of place," Field could not resist remarking that anyone who "has carefully watched the political events of the last decade must have seen a constant and constantly accelerated movement towards the organization and cumulation of Federal authority." However well meaning were the persons responsible for this steady accretion in national powers, they nevertheless acted, in Field's opinion, "in obliviousness of the truth that every new power added to the Nation is just so much subtracted from the states." Marr agreed that recent events had disrupted fundamentally American conceptions of federalism and that the "time has come when the line of demarcation between State and Federal power must be plainly defined, and maintained with a steady and an even hand, lest it be obliterated and utterly lost, to the ruin of our institutions." In what could be interpreted as a bold invitation to the Supreme Court to assume a new function in formulating public policy, Marr declared that "[t]his duty now devolves upon this Court, the great conservative department of the government, made independent by the Constitution. Let us hope," he implored, "that the conclusion of the Court, in the Slaughter House cases, will never be disturbed...." If that hope was dashed and congressional authority to enact statutes such as the 1870 act was accepted, then, Bryan concluded, "[t]he original or inherent rights of the States are crushed out and absorbed by a great central power—a revolution has been accomplished, brought about by an Act of Congress and a judicial decree."[22]

In *Cruikshank* and *Reese,* the Supreme Court was presented with legal questions whose importance greatly transcended the immediate issues in the cases. The resolution of those legal questions concerning the power to enforce civil and political rights would define anew the constitutional structure of the American federal union by determining the primacy of national or state authority over the fundamental rights of Americans. In resolving these legal questions, the Court would be sanctioning or rejecting congressional Reconstruction. Ultimately, then, the Court's review of the Fourteenth and Fifteenth Amendments and the Enforcement Act of 1870 allowed it to determine public policy.

Chief Justice Morrison R. Waite delivered the opinions in both *Reese* and *Cruikshank* on March 27, 1876. He wrote a relatively short opinion for the majority in *Reese* that quashed the indictment and found sections 3 and 4 of the 1870 Enforcement Act to be unconstitutionally overbroad. The chief justice affirmed his earlier ruling in *Minor v. Happersett* and held that the Fifteenth Amendment did not confer a general right to vote. Rather, it merely provided an "exemption from discrimination in the elective franchise on account of race, color, or previous condition of servitude." He concluded, therefore, that the third and fourth sections of the Enforcement Act of 1870 were unconstitutional because they attempted to punish every wrongful infringement of the right to vote, not only infringements that resulted by reason of race, color, or previous condition of servitude. He also declared unconstitutional the provision in the law that required election officials to permit potential voters to vote upon their affidavit stating that they had been wrongfully denied the opportunity to meet prescribed conditions for voting. "A citizen should not unnecessarily be placed where, by an honest error in the construction of a penal statute, he may be subjected to a prosecution for a false oath," he reasoned, "and an inspector of election should not be put in jeopardy because he, with equal honesty, entertains an opposite opinion." This provision was too ambiguous to stand the test of constitutionality, in the opinion of the chief justice. However, he implicitly rejected the defense's narrow interpretation of state action. Even so, he concluded that the indictment was faulty because it was based upon an unconstitutional statute.[23]

Justice Nathan Clifford wrote a concurring opinion that elaborated other reasons why the indictment should be quashed. Clifford stated that the indictment failed to meet the requirement of all indictments, namely, that they allege every element of the offense as defined by the relevant statute. He found the four counts of the indictment deficient because they did not allege that Garner was a qualified voter at the time he had attempted to vote; that they did not aver that the rejection of Garner's offer to pay the capitation tax resulted from the wrongful act of the city collector; that they did not specify all of the facts and circumstances that constituted the offense; and that the term "offer" to pay the tax was too vague, uncertain, and indefinite to know what Garner's "offer" was and whether it was sufficient to constitute a wrongful denial of the opportunity to pay the tax.[24]

Justice Ward Hunt alone dissented, and he wrote an opinion in which he rebuked his judicial brethren. He described the majority's criticism of the wording of the indictment as "almost ridiculous" and accused them of sacrificing good sense to technical niceties in striking down the relevant sections of the Enforcement Act. He censured the majority for unnecessarily declaring these sections unconstitutional. He claimed this declaration was *obiter dicta* since the majority had quashed the indictment because of its faulty technical construction. Hunt found the indictment sufficient under the 1870 statute, and he found the 1870 statute sufficient under the Fifteenth Amendment, even though he interpreted the amendment as applying only to state action. However, he rejected Bucknor's narrow theory of state action for a broad theory that "include[d] the acts of all who proceed under the authority of the State." Hunt's was the only analysis of state action in the two cases.[25]

Chief Justice Waite's opinion in *Cruikshank* was more elaborate than his *Reese* opinion. He prefaced his remarks concerning the specific issues presented in *Cruikshank* with a discussion of the nature of American federalism and the division of powers between the national and state governments. His prefatory comments affirmed the antebellum states' rights view of American federalism. He betrayed an unyielding determination to perpetuate that view of the federal division of powers over civil rights, for he ignored the antebellum nationalist view of federalism as well as the vast changes in American federalism that resulted from the Civil War and Reconstruction. Instead of exploring the impact of these events upon the Constitution, the chief justice leapfrogged back in time to the Founding Fathers and the purposes and ideas they held concerning the federal union. Paralyzing the historical process of constitutional development, he based his interpretation of American federalism in 1876 on those pristine ideas as he understood them.

In a federal union such as the United States, Waite began, the people owe their allegiance to, and can demand protection from, two governments, the national and the state. He quickly cautioned that there need be no conflict between the powers and functions of the two governments, since they were "established for different purposes, and have different jurisdictions," and therefore represented different parts of a "complete government." "The powers which one possesses, the other does not," the chief justice declared in an overstatement of the absolute separation of national and state powers.[26]

Waite then characterized the respective powers and functions of the national and state governments from the states' rights view of American federalism. He asserted that the powers of the national government are delegated powers, defined and limited by the Constitution of the United States. All other governmental powers "are reserved to the States or the people." Relying upon the cases cited in Marr's brief, he declared that Bill of Rights guarantees are not enforceable by the national government because that authority was originally reserved by the states, and "it has never been surrendered to the United States." Similarly, the natural rights of citizens, such as the rights to life and liberty, were also reserved to the exclusive jurisdiction of the states. "The very highest duty of the States, when they entered into the Union under the Constitution," Waite admonished, "was to protect all persons within their boundaries in the enjoyment of those 'unalienable rights with which they were endowed by their Creator.' Sovereignty for this purpose rests *alone* with the States."[27]

The chief justice based this view of the primacy of state authority over citizens' rights on two theories. The first was a theory of constitutional delegation. For the Constitution to affirmatively authorize Congress directly to enforce a right, the right must have been "granted by the Constitution," or it must be "dependent upon that instrument for its existence." Since the existence of the natural rights of citizens predated the formation of the Union, they were not granted by, nor did they depend upon, the Constitution for their existence.[28]

The second theory was a convoluted concept of the kind of legislative powers Congress was capable of acquiring. "No rights can be acquired under the Constitution or laws of the United States," Waite proclaimed, "except such as the Government of the United States *has the authority to grant or secure.*" (Emphasis added.) Since the Founding Fathers reserved to the states the authority to protect the fundamental rights of citizens, that authority could not be acquired by the national government or deleted from the states except by explicit delegation by the Constitution. "It is now too late," Waite asserted, "to question the correctness of this construction." It was not the rights secured by the Constitution that determined what rights Congress was constitutionally authorized to enforce; rather, it was the chief justice's understanding of the original purposes and powers of the national government that became the determining factor. The chief justice's conservative states' rights theory of American constitutionalism rejected the revolutionary impact of the Reconstruction Amendments that previously had been recognized by federal judges and legal officers. Instead, he imposed his understanding of the intent of the Founding Fathers concerning the division of federal powers in 1787 to conclude that the Reconstruction Amendments did not amend the Constitution by conferring upon Congress authority directly to enforce the civil and political rights of American citizens.[29]

Having already concluded that the Constitution had not been amended to redistribute national and state powers over civil rights, Waite's interpretation of the Fourteenth Amendment was a foregone conclusion. He did not believe that the amendment conferred upon the national government any authority directly to secure natural rights or to punish criminal infringements of those rights. Adopting the Democratic Conservative interpretation of the Bill of Rights as limitations upon government, the Chief Justice asserted that the Fourteenth Amendment simply furnished "an additional guaranty against any encroachment by the States upon the fundamental rights which belong to every citizen as a member of society." Since the Fourteenth Amendment could not be applied directly against private citizens, the indictment against the defendants was invalid. Furthermore, the offenses it charged were within the exclusive jurisdiction of the states. Although Waite refrained from explicitly declaring the Enforcement Act of 1870 to be unconstitutional, that implication was so strong that any observer was forced to conclude that the law was unconstitutional insofar as it attempted to punish private individuals who violated the civil rights of other citizens. These crucially important declarations of federal civil rights law, however, were *obiter dicta*. The Court had voided the indictment because it was "too vague and general" and, therefore, "not good and sufficient in law." The chief justice thus extended to the area of black Americans' civil rights, in *obiter dicta*, the narrow states' rights interpretation of the Fourteenth Amendment espoused by Southern Democratic Conservatives that the Supreme Court, also in *obiter dicta*, had engrafted upon the Fourteenth Amendment in *Slaughter-House*.[30]

More serious anomalies tainted the Supreme Court's interpretation of the Fourteenth Amendment as it applied to the rights of black Americans. The Court had held in *Slaughter-House* that the amendment was intended almost exclusively for the protection of the rights of black Americans. The central legal question decided in *Slaughter-House* was whether it conferred upon the national government primary authority over civil rights. Yet, the Supreme Court had refused earlier to decide this question when it was presented initially in cases involving alleged violations of the civil rights of black Americans. The Court consciously chose instead to decide this crucial question in the *Slaughter-House* case, a case involving alleged violations of white Americans' civil rights in a context that the Court acknowledged had not been contemplated by the amendment's framers. The consequence of the Court's case selection was that its consideration of the scope of protection offered by the Fourteenth Amendment to black Americans was preempted by its decision in *Slaughter-House*. The Court similarly preempted its consideration of the scope of the Fifteenth Amendment's protection of blacks' voting rights with its initial interpretation of this amendment in another case whose context was beyond that contemplated by the amendment's framers, *Minor v. Happersett*. Furthermore, the Court interpreted the scope of the Fourteenth Amendment's protection of the civil rights of black Americans without even having been presented with the legal theories that were most favorable to the interests of black Americans. The Supreme Court's handling of the Fourteenth, and, apparently, the Fifteenth Amendments suggests that its decisions were a calculated effort to reverse the constitutionally centralizing thrust of the Civil War and Reconstruction.

The public reacted to *Reese* and *Cruikshank* as welcome correctives to the centralization of power that was brought about by congressional Reconstruction. Republican and Democratic Conservative newspapers applauded the *Reese* and *Cruikshank* decisions for their alleged judiciousness, impartiality, and wisdom. The Supreme Court was lauded for restoring the public's confidence in the national judiciary by correcting the imbalance in federal powers created by a misguided Congress striving to maintain unworthy and corrupt politicians in public office. The obviously devastating consequences for desperately needed national civil rights protection in the South were rationalized away by a cynical justification of the decisions. The opportunity for renewed terrorism in the South was characterized as merely an apparent injurious effect of the decisions. The Court's reaffirmation of the "traditional" division of federal powers was more important because it was in the best interests of all Americans. Equally remarkable was the press's acceptance of the Supreme Court's interpretation of the statutes and amendments that differed so fundamentally from the meaning that uniformly had been attributed to them by federal, and most state, judges.[31]

How can the Supreme Court's emasculation of national civil rights enforcement authority be explained? Apparent public approval does not offer a satisfactory explanation. Nor do accepted legal theories of American federalism alone adequately explain the Court's action. A partial explanation was the need to redefine the scope and limits of national and state powers because of the disruptions to federalism caused by the Civil War and Reconstruction and the modernizing forces of industrial capitalism. Changing needs and novel situations produced by the integration and nationalization of American life demanded a restructuring of the lines of national and state authority. Stanley Kutler has demonstrated that the Supreme Court's response to legal questions relating to American federalism was "pragmatic in nature and attuned to the justices' conception of the economic and social needs within the federal system." Kutler argues that since the justices were neither states' rights advocates nor nationalists, they looked favorably upon state police powers while they remained "alert to the possibility that such legislation could unduly burden the national market or the instrumentalities of the national government."[32]

The decisions of the Supreme Court during Reconstruction nevertheless were at least partially consistent with prior rulings. The Court desired to preserve the judicially established powers of the respective governments of the United States and of the states in considering legislative applications of those powers to new situations. It refrained from diminishing or departing from preexisting constitutional principles and definitions of national and state powers whenever it believed it could avoid doing so. The Supreme Court's rulings, then, were conservative during an age of far-reaching changes in the conditions of American life. However, the Court was guided by two overriding principles in its application of established legal doctrines to new situations. When it decided conflicts between national and state authority and jurisdiction, it carefully considered whether the power in question was essential to the functioning of the national or state governments as governmental agencies. It was also guided by the principle that many of the respective powers of the national and state governments are exclusive.

Essentiality and exclusivity, concepts applied by the Supreme Court in its civil and political rights decisions, were determining factors in the Court's decisions relating to federalism in other areas of law during the period. An 1869 case, for example, involved a clash of the right of the states to charter corporations, the property rights of state-chartered banks, and the authority of Congress to regulate the currency. The Supreme Court interpreted broadly Congress's exclusive authority to regulate the currency in sustaining a federal lax levied against state bank notes. The Court conceded that the tax discriminated against state bank notes in favor of national bank notes and therefore infringed the power of the states to charter corporations. Yet, it upheld the tax because it was deemed to be essential to Congress's functioning as regulator of the national currency. The Court thus gave precedence to congressional authority to regulate the currency over the right of the states to charter corporations and to protect the property rights of state banks.[33]

Although the Court upheld a federal tax on state bank notes, it struck down a federal tax upon the incomes of state officials two years later. Speaking for the Court, Justice Samuel Nelson declared "that the means and instrumentalities employed for carrying on the operations of their [the states'] governments for preserving their existence, and fulfilling the high and responsible duties assigned to them in the Constitution, should be left free and unimpaired...." He added that without this protection "no one of the States, under the form of government guaranteed by the Constitution could long preserve its existence." Justice Nelson applied a nationalist ruling of Chief Justice John Marshall that had struck down a state tax levied against a nationally chartered bank to void a national tax upon state officials. He also based his opinion on the theory that the national and state governments are "separate and distinct sovereignties, acting separately and independently of each other, within their respective spheres." If one compared this case, which voided a federal tax on state officials' income, with the case upholding a federal tax on state bank notes from the perspective of nationalism versus states' rights, they would appear inconsistent. However, if they were analyzed from the perspective of essentiality and exclusivity, they would appear to be consistent.[34]

Exclusivity in national and state powers was a basis for the Court's decisions in several cases involving state regulation of interstate commerce. In one case, the Court struck down a state tax levied against freight carried by railroads engaged in interstate commerce. Justice William Strong affirmed Congress's exclusive power over interstate commerce in an opinion that echoed the 1852 decision in *Cooley v. Pennsylvania Port Wardens*. He declared "that whenever the subjects over which a power to regulate commerce is asserted are in their nature national, or admit of one uniform system or plan of regulation, they may justly be said to be of such a nature as to require exclusive legislation by Congress."[35]

However, the Court applied the principle of exclusivity in Congress's authority over interstate commerce with flexibility. It allowed the states to use their police powers to regulate interstate commerce whenever it considered state regulation to be essential to the functioning of state government. The constitutional principle that permitted the states to regulate interstate commerce was again taken from the *Cooley* decision. The Court declared that the states may regulate interstate commerce when the subject of the regulation was local in nature and Congress had not already legislated. While the Court voided a state tax on freight carried by railroads engaged in interstate commerce, it upheld another state tax imposed on the revenues of an interstate railroad. Justice Strong explained in the latter case that the power to tax "may be essential to the healthy existence of state governments and the Federal Constitution ought not to be so construed as to impair, much less destroy, anything that is necessary to their efficient existence."[36]

In a similar vein, the Court affirmed a principle enunciated in the *License Cases* of 1847 and upheld a state tax levied against wholesalers engaged in the sale of interstate goods. The specific issue presented to the Court was whether local wholesalers who sold imported goods in unbroken packages were subject to local sales and other taxes. In upholding the tax, Justice Samuel Miller observed that the

> merchant of Chicago who buys his goods in New York and sells at wholesale in the original packages, may have his millions employed in trade for half a lifetime and escape all state, county and city taxes; for all he is worth is invested in goods which he claims to be protected as imports from New York.

If the merchant could thus escape local taxes, Justice Miller concluded, "the grossest injustice must prevail, and equality of public burdens in all our large cities is impossible."[37]

The Supreme Court sacrificed doctrinal consistency in its desire to uphold state laws that it considered essential to a proper exercise of state police powers. In one of the most important cases of the decade, it upheld state statutes regulating the operation of grain elevators in Illinois and other states and held that the storage of grain, even when the grain was sold to buyers in other states, was only indirectly involved in interstate commerce. Grain elevators were considered to be local businesses that were subject to the regulatory authority of the states until Congress legislated on the subject. The Court was evidently unconcerned with the apparent contradiction with its own definition a year earlier that "commerce" is "intercourse for the purpose of trade in any and all its forms." It circumvented the principle of exclusivity in federal powers to accommodate what it considered to be state police powers that were essential to the states' function of promoting commercial progress.[38]

However, the Court did not give the states *carte blanche*. It struck down a New York law that required a bond of $300 or a cash payment of $1.50 for every immigrant coming into the country through its ports. The Court declared that the law went beyond the legitimate purpose of indemnifying the state against pauperized immigrants. It also voided a California statute that imposed a bond of $500 upon "lewd and debauched" women who entered the state from foreign countries. The Court saw through this thinly veiled discrimination against female Chinese immigrants. It characterized the bond as "systematic extortion of the grossest kind" and declared that the determination of criminal, lewd, and debauched interstate passengers was a function of the national, not of the state governments. Although the Court upheld other state taxes levied against wholesalers dealing in interstate goods, it struck down a Missouri tax on such goods because it considered the tax to be a discriminatory burden on those goods since locally produced goods were not similarly taxed. In this case, the Court emphasized the inhibiting effect of the tax on interstate commerce.[39]

In these cases, the Supreme Court exhibited a desire to preserve principles of constitutional law while it also strove to preserve the powers it considered essential to the functioning of the national and state governments. These same concerns and principles were present in its *Slaughter-House, Reese,* and *Cruikshank* decisions. To a large extent the Court was impeded by its conservatism and logic from sanctioning the radically new congressional applications of civil rights enforcement authority. The Court's concerns expressed in these other decisions predisposed it to emasculate these far-reaching powers over civil rights because those powers previously had been exercised by the state governments. In the opinion of the Supreme Court, Congress had assumed an area of authority that was essential to the existence of the states as independent governments. The Court expressed the fear that a recognition of Congress's concurrent authority over civil rights would destroy the states and change the nature of American federalism beyond recognition.

The Court's revival of states' rights reflected attitudes and views expressed in legal commentaries on the Fourteenth Amendment. Legal writers feared that the Civil War and congressional Reconstruction had pushed the nation too far toward centralized government. William L. Royall reported in 1878 that "the minds of patriotic men were filled with alarm at the centralizing tendency of the government...and...the prospect that the ancient landmarks of the states were to yield before the advancing strides of an imperial despotism." He suggested that "patriots" rejected a broad interpretation of the Fourteenth Amendment because "privileges and immunities" were thought to "include every conceivable right," and, if Congress possessed the authority to secure those rights, then that authority "would give Congress the constitutional power to legislate in respect to every matter which ought to be under exclusive state control, and would practically obliterate all state lines, and make one central government in Washington."[40]

The Supreme Court's unwillingness to accept the primacy of national authority over civil rights, then, was not simply the product of racism. It expressed the fear that its recognition of the primacy of national authority over civil rights enforcement might result in the national government's replacing the state governments in the actual administration of law, both civil and criminal. The Court seemed to have been unable to devise a theory for primary national civil rights enforcement authority that would have permitted the states to continue to fulfill functions that the Court believed were essential to the survival of American federalism.

One endangered state function that the Court deemed essential to the well-being of the Union was the regulation of the economy. Northern reform during the 1870s focused to a great degree upon state regulation of what the public perceived as monopolistic control of important segments of the economy by large corporations, particularly the railroads. Antimonopolists agitated for state regulation of corporate practices, mergers, and, in the case of railroads, rates charged to shippers. At the same time, states were assuming increasing control over professions, such as the practice of medicine, trades and occupations, the manufacture of dangerous substances, and the sale of alcoholic beverages through licensing requirements. The *Slaughter-House Cases* involved such state regulation.[41]

The states' legal authority to regulate economic activities was based on their police powers. States claimed the constitutional power to regulate economic activities as part of their authority to promote the health, safety, and welfare of their citizens. Moreover, they claimed the authority to engage in such regulation even though it restricted the exercise of fundamental rights because of their authority to determine conditions under which these rights could be enjoyed and exercised.[42]

The opponents of such state regulation largely based their legal arguments on a natural rights legal theory. They claimed that such state regulation violated corporations' and individuals' fundamental rights. If these rights were recognized as nationally enforceable rights, then the states could be precluded from exercising a regulatory function that the Chase and Waite Courts had deemed essential to the existence of the states and the prosperity of the nation. Invoking the theory of exclusivity, corporations argued that state economic regulation infringed rights that were protected under the United States Constitution. Thus, national civil rights enforcement authority could be applied to negate state regulatory power. This legal theory was the butchers' argument in *Slaughter-House*. Indeed, the doctrine of substantive due process that the Supreme Court adopted in the 1890s to void state regulation of property rights originated with the butchers' argument, which the Court rejected in *Slaughter-House*. The Court's rejection of the primacy of national civil rights enforcement authority in *Slaughter-House*, therefore, provided the legal foundation for its affirmation of state economic regulation under the police power in *Munn*.[43]

Within this context, *Slaughter-House* also ordained the outcome in *Cruikshank*. Once the Supreme Court affirmed the primacy of state authority over the butchers' fundamental rights, it could not easily assert the primacy of national authority over the fundamental rights of the freedmen. This difficulty was due to the absence of a legal theory that might distinguish between the two and to nineteenth-century political values and political realities.

Nineteenth-century legal theory did not readily offer a theoretical basis for the primacy of national authority over the rights of black Americans as distinguished from the rights of white Americans. American liberalism abhorred artificial classifications among, and favored treatment of, similarly situated groups. To single out blacks for special treatment after their transition from slavery to freedom would have been contrary to predominant values of equal opportunity and self-reliance. This was particularly true in this era of European immigration because "Americans" regarded Southern and Eastern European nationalities as inferior, along with blacks. Black Americans, then, were no more entitled to special treatment than "inferior" immigrants.[44]

Nor did nineteenth-century legal theory distinguish between the economic rights of corporations and workers and the personal rights of individuals. To the nineteenth-century mind, property rights were central to American freedom because personal freedom and independence were thought to be inextricably connected to the ownership of property. Nineteenth-century Americans did not place greater value upon noneconomic rights, such as First Amendment guarantees, than they did upon property rights. The contrary was true. Justice Harlan Fiske Stone's 1937 "preferred freedoms" distinction between personal rights and economic rights would not have made much sense to Americans in the 1870s.[45]

If the Court had affirmed primary national civil rights enforcement authority, it would have been presented with difficult problems of legal theory. The Court would have been required to devise some theoretical basis for distinguishing between national and state authority over civil rights. Such a theoretical distinction might have been impossible in light of the Court's assertion of the mutual exclusivity in national and state powers. The Court's legal theory of American federalism placed civil rights under the exclusive authority of either the nation or the states. The Court believed that, at a functional level, the administration of justice was simply too central to the states and too difficult for the nation to undertake. The Court's principles of exclusivity and essentiality in the distribution of federal powers may have rendered impossible its recognition of the primacy of national civil rights enforcement authority.

Problems of legal theory may have been unsolvable even if the Court had recognized a concurrent national and state authority over civil rights violations. The theories worked out by federal judges and United States attorneys that attempted to distinguish between federal crimes and ordinary crimes may not have been sustainable in all situations. The tenuousness of distinguishing federal crimes by virtue of the intent of the offender is suggested by the existence of state crimes of intent. For example, it is difficult to perceive the difference between the federal crime of assault with intent to deprive the victim of his or her nationally protected right to life and the state offense of assault with intent to kill. Moreover, trying the same defendant for the same act under the parallel offenses in the federal and the state courts would seem to violate the spirit, if not the letter, of the Fifth Amendment guarantee against double jeopardy.

Requiring state action to violate nationally enforceable civil rights avoided these difficult problems of legal theory and federalism. Moreover, it was easier to administer and enforce in the federal courts. Racially discriminatory state action was a relatively convenient and facile legal theory for defining the scope of national civil rights enforcement authority. The presence or absence of racially discriminatory state action, particularly in the form of discriminatory statutes, was a relatively simple means for determining whether national authority was applicable to an alleged civil rights violation. Furthermore, this theory possessed the additional allure of justifying the preservation of the states as the primary guarantors of civil rights by providing a legal remedy that offered the appearance of a national guarantee that the states would perform this function with fairness and impartiality.

Still, James G. Randall long ago observed that principles of constitutional law frequently serve as rationalizations to achieve desired political and social goals. Randall's observation is applicable here, for the Court had devised theories of constitutional law that established concurrent jurisdiction between the national and state governments in areas of law, such as interstate commerce, that seemed to be within the exclusive authority of one or the other. Legal theory alone, therefore, does not account for the Court's rejection of the primacy of national authority over civil rights. In addition to the intricacies of legal theory, political considerations prompted the Court to reach its decisions in *Slaughterhouse* and *Cruikshank*.[46]

Concerns over judicial administration motivated the Court to curtail national civil rights enforcement authority. Burgeoning case loads and backlogged dockets pressured the justices to cut back the exploding scope of federal jurisdiction. Legal journals observed that the docket of the Supreme Court was two years in arrears, and they foresaw little hope of improvement without judicial reform. Justice Miller publicly declared that the problem of overworked judges was so acute that it endangered the very viability of the federal judiciary. Diminishing federal jurisdiction was one of the reforms he proposed. The state action theory curtailed federal jurisdiction and, therefore, could be viewed as a reform in judicial administration.[47]

The state action theory served interests of federal comity as well as judicial efficiency. Predicating national authority over civil rights upon racially discriminatory state action served to minimize the intrusion of the federal courts into the state administration of justice. Indeed, restricting state action to racially discriminatory state statutes avoided federal inquiries into the impartiality of the local administration of justice and consequent evidentiary problems and complicated and vexatious trials. Federal courts thus could be completely relieved of the protection of civil rights if the states replaced their racially discriminatory statutes with racially impartial ones and avoided blatant racial unfairness in other respects. The state action theory of national civil rights enforcement authority thereby could curtail jurisdictional clashes between federal courts and local authorities and contribute to the improvement in the relationships between federal and local officials. Ultimately, then, the Court's civil rights rulings facilitated the healing of the breaches caused by the Civil War and accelerated the return to normality.[48]

The elimination of primary federal jurisdiction over civil rights served other political purposes. The enforcement of civil rights in the federal courts exposed and intensified the political aspects of the judicial process. Curtailment of this function produced a corresponding depoliticization of the federal courts. The elimination of national enforcement of civil rights thus paradoxically improved the reputation of the federal courts among white Americans and contributed to the public's acceptance of judicial authority. It deprived Democratic Conservatives of the opportunity to use judicial decisions as evidence of partisanship in the Southern federal courts, for they could no longer claim that the courts merely implemented the political will of Republican-controlled Congresses. Furthermore, the Supreme Court's decisions diminished the need to select federal juries on the basis of political affiliations, for its decisions largely eliminated the possibility of federal prosecutions of Democratic Conservatives on behalf of Republicans. The state action theory contributed to the restoration of the legitimacy of the federal judiciary by precluding functions performed, and legal theories espoused, by the federal courts that were vehemently opposed by dominant local groups. This theory helped the Southern federal courts again accommodate both national policies and local interests.

By the mid-1870s, the Northern public understood civil rights enforcement to be a partisan device to buttress waning Republican interests in the South. The idealism of the 1860s that motivated Republican-inspired legislation to secure the freedom of the former slaves appeared to have been replaced during the Grant administration by the president's venal self-interest in protecting the Republican Party. Even some Northern Republicans who earlier had supported civil rights enforcement had come to oppose such a perceived abuse of power. In a formalistic way, state action limitations of the Fourteenth Amendment could be rationalized as providing impartial justice by placing blacks and whites, Republicans and Democratic Conservatives on the "same" basis before the law. All races and all parties would have to look to local legal institutions to enforce and redress their rights. However, this equality before the law would be an equality in form, not an equality in substance.

These political and administrative benefits, then, were based upon political priorities that relegated the protection of black rights to a relative unimportance. The black American was the primary beneficiary of national guarantees of civil rights. The black American was therefore the main victim of their destruction. The far-reaching civil rights enforcement authority that judges in earlier cases found in the Reconstruction Amendments was ultimately destroyed by the growing disinterest in the plight of black Americans. National enforcement of civil rights presented the Supreme Court with difficult problems of legal theory and federalism. The Court failed to find solutions to these problems that preserved effective national authority to protect citizens' rights. This judicial failure was partially due to the temper of the times. The racism, economic self-interest, partisanship, and liberal ideology that characterized the political order of the 1870s promoted a callous disregard among Northern Republicans toward Southern violent oppression of black Americans. The Supreme Court reflected this political order in emasculating the Reconstruction civil rights program in the 1870s.

Notes

Introduction to the Fordham University Press Edition

1. George Santayana, *Reason in Common Sense*, vol. 1, *Life of Reason or the Phases of Human Progress* (New York: Charles Scribner & Sons, 2nd ed., 1936): 284.

2. This view of the framers' understanding of the Thirteenth and Fourteenth Amendments is taken from my earlier work, dating back to my doctoral dissertation in 1971, which was published in 1987. See Robert J. Kaczorowski, *The Nationalization of Civil Rights: Constitutional Theory and Practice in a Racist Society, 1866–1883* (New York, 1987); *ibid.*, "Revolutionary Constitutionalism in the Era of the Civil War and Reconstruction," *New York University Law Review* 61 (1986): 863; *ibid.*, "To Begin the Nation Anew: Congress, Citizenship, and Civil Rights After the Civil War," *American Historical Review* 92 (1987): 45; *ibid.*, "The Enforcement Provisions of the Civil Rights Act of 1866: A Legislative History in Light of *Runyon v. McCrary*," *The Yale Law Journal* 98 (1989): 565. There is an enormous literature on this subject. The following are representative of other interpretations: Jacobus ten Broek, *Equal Justice Under Law* (New York, 1965); Charles Fairman, *Reconstruction and Reunion, 1864–88, Part One* (New York, 1971); Harold M. Hyman, *A More Perfect Union: The Impact of the Civil War and Reconstruction on the Constitution* (New York, 1973); Michael Les Benedict, *A Compromise of Principle: Congressional Republicans and Reconstruction, 1863–1869* (New York, 1974); Herman Belz, *Emancipation and Equal Rights: Politics and Constitutionalism in the Civil War Era* (New York, 1978); Raoul Berger, *Government by Judiciary: The Transformation of the Fourteenth Amendment* (Cambridge, 1977); Michael Kent Curtis, *No State Shall Abridge: The Fourteenth Amendment and the Bill of Rights* (Durham, NC, 1986); William E. Nelson, *The Fourteenth Amendment: From Political Principle to Judicial Doctrine* (Cambridge, 1988); Earl M. Maltz, *Civil Rights, The Constitution, and Congress, 1863–1869* (Lawrence, KS: University Press of Kansas, 1990); Akhil R. Amar, *The Bill of Rights: Creation and Reconstruction* (New Haven, CT, 1998); Xi Wang, *The Trial of Democracy: Black Suffrage and Northern Republicans, 1860–1910* (Athens, GA, 1997). The most comprehensive and best general history of Reconstruction, which includes informative treatment of its constitutional dimensions, is Eric Foner, *Reconstruction: America's Unfinished Revolution, 1863–1877* (New York, 1988).

3. Ch. 114, 14 Stat. 27 (1866).

4. Allen W. Trelease, *White Terror: The Ku Klux Klan Conspiracy and Southern Reconstruction* (New York, 1971).

5. Ch. 114, 16 Stat. 140 (1870); Ch. 22, 17 Stat. 13 (1871).

6. William Gillette and Xi Wang attribute the failure of rights enforcement to the logistical, financial, and human deficiencies recounted in this book. William Gillette, *Retreat From Reconstruction, 1869–1879* (Baton Rouge, LA, 1979); Xi Wang, *The Trial of Democracy: Black Suffrage and Northern Republicans, 1860–1910* (Athens, GA, 1997). For

studies that attribute the failure to inadequate legal authority, see Kermit L. Hall, "Political Power and Constitutional Legitimacy: The South Carolina Ku Klux Klan Trials, 1871–1872," *Emory Law Journal* 33 (1984): 936; Lou Falkner Williams, "The South Carolina Ku Klux Klan Trials and Enforcement of Federal Rights, 1871–1872," *Civil War History* 39 (1993): 47–66; Lou Falkner Williams, *The Great South Carolina Ku Klux Trials, 1871–1872* (Athens, GA, 1996); Richard Zuczek, "The Federal Government's Attack on the Ku Klux Klan: A Reassessment," *South Carolina Historical Magazine* 97 (January 1996): 47; Richard Zuczek, *State of Rebellion: Reconstruction in South Carolina* (Columbia, SC, 1996). Professor Gillette reports complaints from federal attorneys about judges' rulings in Ku Klux Klan prosecutions, but it is not clear from his account whether they were complaining because judges interpreted the Reconstruction Amendments narrowly or because they made procedural rulings that benefited defendants. In addition to the evidence presented in this book, Stephen Creswell's account of the success of federal prosecutions in Mississippi contradicts Hall's, Williams', and Zuczek's conclusions regarding the state action interpretation of the Reconstruction Amendments. Stephen Cresswell, "Enforcing the Enforcement Acts: The Department of Justice in Northern Mississippi, 1870–1890," *Journal of Southern History* 53 (August 1987): 421–40.

7. *Slaughter-House Cases*, 83 U.S. (16 Wall.) 36 (1873).

8. *United States v. Cruikshank*, 92 U.S. (2 Otto) 542 (1875).

9. Ch. 114, 18 Stat. 335 (1875); *Civil Rights Cases*, 109 U.S. 3 (1883).

10. Wang, *The Trial of Democracy*; Robert M. Goldman, *"A Free Ballot and a Fair Count" The Department of Justice and the Enforcement of Voting Rights in the South, 1877–1893* (New York, 2001); Stanley Hirshon, *Farewell to the Bloody Shirt: Northern Republicans and the Negro, 1877–1893* (Bloomington, IN, 1962); Vincent P. DeSantis, *Republicans Face the Southern Question: The New Departure Years, 1877–1897* (Baltimore, 1959).

11. The discussion of the Fifteenth Amendment and state action has benefited from the perceptive analysis of Michael Les Benedict. See Michael Les Benedict, "Preserving Federalism: Reconstruction and the Waite Court," *Supreme Court Review* (1978): 39–62. Nevertheless, I disagree with Benedict's conclusions that the framers of the Reconstruction Amendments were committed to a "State-centered nationalism" that limited the Reconstruction Amendments' guarantees of citizens' rights only to state action and, measured against the framers' intentions, that the Waite Court was remarkable for the degree to which it sustained national authority to protect rights rather than for the degree to which it curtailed those rights. See *United States v. Reese*, 92 U.S. 214 (1875); *Ex parte Siebold*, 100 U.S. 371 (1880); *Ex parte Clarke*, 100 U.S. 399 (1880); *Ex parte Yarbrough*, 110 U.S. 651 (1884); *James v. Bowman*, 190 U.S. 127 (1903); *Ex parte Virginia*, 100 U.S. 339 (1880); and *Virginia v. Rives*, 100 U.S. 313 (1880). The Court held that the act of a state official who acted in violation of state law was not state action. *Barney v. City of New York*, 193 U.S. 430 (1904).

12. *Plessy v. Ferguson*, 163 U.S. 537 (1896). A. Leon Higginbotham, Jr., *Shades of Freedom: Racial Politics and Presumptions of the American Legal Process* (New York, 1996); Michael J. Klarman, *From Jim Crow to Civil Rights: The Supreme Court and the Struggle for Racial Equality* (New York: Oxford University Press, 2004); Charles Lofgren, *The Plessy Case: A Legal-Historical Interpretation* (New York, 1987); C. Vann Woodward, *The Strange Career of Jim Crow* (New York, 3rd edition, 1974).

13. See Richard Ayers, *The Promise of the New South: Life After Reconstruction* (New York, 1992); W. Fitzhugh Brundage, *Lynching in the New South: Georgia and Virginia, 1880–1930* (Urbana, 1993); W. Fitzhugh Brundage, ed., *Under Sentence of Death: Lynching in the South* (Chapel Hill, 1997); William Cohen, *At Freedom's Edge: Black Mobility and the Southern White Quest for Racial Control, 1861–1915* (Baton Rouge, 1991); Philip Dray, *At the*

Hands of Persons Unknown: The Lynching of Black Americans (New York, 2002); Glenda E. Gilmore, *Gender and Jim Crow: Women and the Politics of White Supremacy in North Carolina, 1896–1920* (Chapel Hill, 1996); J. Morgan Kousser, *The Shaping of Southern Politics: Suffrage Restriction and the Establishment of the One-Party South, 1880–1910* (New Haven, 1974); Leon Litwack, *Trouble in Mind: Black Southerners in the Age of Jim Crow* (New York, 1998); C. Vann Woodward, *Origins of the New South, 1877–1913* (Baton Rouge, 1951); Joel Williamson, *The Crucible of Race: Black-White Relations in the American South Since Emancipation* (New York, 1984); George C. Wright, *Racial Violence in Kentucky, 1865–1940: Lynchings, Mob Rule and "Legal Lynchings"* (Baton Rouge, 1990).

14. *Brown v. Board of Education*, 347 U.S. 483 (1954). Richard Kluger, *Simple Justice: The History of* Brown v. Board of Education *and Black America's Struggle for Equality* (New York, 1976); Mark Tushnet, *The NAACP's Legal Strategy Against Segregated Education, 1925–1950* (Chapel Hill, 1987); Mark Tushnet, *Making Civil Rights Law: Thurgood Marshall and the Supreme Court, 1936–1961* (New York, 1964).

15. The activities of these organizations and leaders are recounted in many biographies and histories. For example, see Taylor Branch, *Parting the Waters: America in the King Years, 1954–63* (New York, 1989); Clayborne Carson, *In Struggle: SNCC and the Black Awakening of the 1960s* (Cambridge, 1981); David Garrow, *Bearing the Cross: Martin Luther King, Jr., and the Southern Christian Leadership Conference* (New York, 1986); August Meier and Elliott Rudwick, *CORE: A Study in the Civil Rights Movement, 1942–1968* (New York, 1973); Adam Fairclough, *To Redeem the Soul of America: The Southern Christian Leadership Conference and Martin Luther King, Jr.* (Athens, GA, 1987).

16. Hugh Davis Graham, *The Civil Rights Era: Origins and Development of National Policy, 1960–1972* (New York, 1990); Carl M. Brauer, *John F. Kennedy and the Second Reconstruction* (New York, 1977); Mark Stern, *Calculating Visions: Kennedy, Johnson, and Civil Rights* (New Brunswick, NJ, 1992); Robert Dallek, *Flawed Giant: Lyndon Johnson and His Times, 1961–1973* (New York, 1998); Michael R. Belknap, *Federal Law and Southern Order: Racial Violence and Constitutional Conflict in the Post-*Brown *South* (Athens, GA, New Edition, 1995).

17. Quoted in Dallek, *Flawed Giant: Lyndon Johnson and His Times, 1961–1973*, 112; Michael J. Klarman, *From Jim Crow to Civil Rights: The Supreme Court and the Struggle for Racial Equality* (New York, 2004): 363, 221.

18. *Heart of Atlanta Motel v. United States*, 379 U.S. 241 (1964); *Katzenbach v. McClung*, 379 U.S. 294 (1964); *South Carolina v. Katzenbach*, 383 U.S. 301 (1966); *Jones v. Alfred H. Mayer Co.*, 392 U.S. 409 (1968). Stern, *Calculating Visions*, 231–232.

19. Graham, *The Civil Rights Era*, 320, 382; Richard Reeves, *President Nixon: Alone in the White House* (New York, 2001): 117–119, 159, 166–167, 192, 238, 303–304, 317–318; Stern, *Calculating Visions*, at 705; James T. Patterson, *Grand Expectations: The United States, 1945–1974* (New York, 1996): 461, 702. A special assistant to Nixon's campaign manager in the 1968 election presented statistical evidence and analysis to support his theory that the 1968 election marked the beginning of a new political cycle, "comparable in magnitude to the New Deal era which began in 1932," which would result in "a new cycle of national Republican hegemony." Experience has confirmed his theory and prediction. See Kevin P. Phillips, *The Emerging Republican Majority* (New Rochelle, NY, 1969).

20. Steven A. Shull, *American Civil Rights Policy From Truman to Clinton: The Role of Presidential Leadership* (Armonk, NY, 1999); Hugh Davis Graham, "Race, History, and Policy: African Americans and Civil Rights Since 1964," 12–39, in Hugh Davis Graham, ed., *Civil Rights in the United States* (University Park, PA, 1994); W. Elliot Brownlee and Hugh Davis Graham, *The Reagan Presidency: Pragmatic Conservatism and Its Legacies* (Lawrence, KS, 2003); Norman C. Amaker, *Civil Rights and the Reagan Administration*

(Washington, DC, 1988); Raymond Wolters, *Right Turn: William Bradford Reynolds, the Reagan Administration, and Black Civil Rights* (New Brunswick, NJ, 1996).

21. *Swann v. Charlotte-Mecklenburg Board of Education*, 402 U.S. 1 (1971); *Keyes v. School District No.1*, Denver, CO, 413 U.S. 189 (1973); *Milliken v. Bradley*, 418 U.S. 717 (1974). For informative discussions of the Swann case, see Bernard Schwartz, *Swann's Way: The School Busing Case and the Supreme Court* (New York, 1986); Davison M. Douglas, *Reading, Writing, & Race: The Desegregation of the Charlotte Schools* (Chapel Hill, 1995); Bob Woodward and Scott Armstrong, *The Brethren: Inside the Supreme Court* (New York, 1981). On the role of the federal courts in desegregating the public schools, see Jack Bass, *Unlikely Heroes* (New York, 1981); J. W. Peltason, *Fifty-Eight Lonely Men* (New York, 1961); Frank Read and Lucy McGough, *Let Them Be Judged: The Judicial Integration of the Deep South* (Metuchen, NJ, 1978); Gerald N. Rosenberg, *The Hollow Hope: Can Courts Bring About Social Change?* (Chicago, 1991); Harvie J. Wilkinson, *From Brown to Bakke: The Supreme Court and School Integration: 1954–1978* (New York, 1979).

22. *University of California v. Bakke*, 438 U.S. 265 (1978); *City of Richmond v. J. A. Croson Co.*, 488 U.S. 469 (1989); *Adarand Constructors, Inc. v. Pena*, 515 U.S. 200 (1995). Note, however, that the Supreme Court recently approved the University of Michigan Law School's affirmative action plan to achieve diversity in its student body. See *Grutter v. Bollinger*, 539 U.S. 306 (2003). However, the Court struck down the affirmative action plan used by the University of Michigan's college of arts and sciences because it did not provide individualized review of each application and made race a decisive factor for minimally qualified under-represented minority applicants; see *Gratz v. Bollinger*, 539 U.S. 244 (2003). See also *Patterson v. McLean Credit Union*, 491 U.S. 164 (1989), which diminished the scope of a provision of the Civil Rights Act of 1866 guaranteeing the right to make and enforce contracts and ruled that this provision did not afford a remedy for racial harassment. Compare *Runyon v. McCrary*, 427 U.S. 160 (1976) and *Jones v. Alfred H. Mayer, Co.*, 392 U.S. 409 (1968). See also *City of Boerne v. Flores*, 521 U.S. 507 (1997) and *United States v. Morrison*, 529 U.S. 598 (2000), which limited Congress's power to enforce the Fourteenth Amendment. Compare *Katzenbach v. Morgan*, 384 U.S. 641 (1966). For a critical assessment of the Rehnquist Court's interpretation of Congress's power to enforce the rights secured by the Fourteenth Amendment, see Robert J. Kaczorowski, "The Supreme Court and Congress's Power to Enforce Constitutional Rights: An Overlooked Moral Anomaly," *Fordham Law Review* 73 (2004): 154; *ibid.*, "The Rehnquist Court and Congress's Power to Enforce Fourteenth Amendment Rights: The History of Federal Civil Remedies the Court Overlooked," *Harvard Journal on Legislation* 42 (2005).

Chapter 1: Judicial Interpretations of National Civil Rights Enforcement Authority, 1866–1873

1. These conclusions are based upon James H. Kettner, *The Development of American Citizenship, 1608–1870* (Chapel Hill, 1978), especially ch. 10.

2. My analysis of Congress is in "Congress and Civil Rights in 1866," which will be published separately. Also see my article "Searching for the Intent of the Framers of the Fourteenth Amendment," *Connecticut Law Review* 5 (Winter 1973): 368–398; and "The Nationalization of Civil Rights: Constitutional Theory and Practice After the Civil War" (unpublished Ph.D. dissertation, University of Minnesota, 1971); Kettner, *The Development of American Citizenship*, epilogue.

3. 14 *U.S. Statutes at Large* 27.

4. For antebellum radical abolitionist natural rights theory see William M. Wiecek, *The Sources of Antislavery Constitutionalism in America, 1760–1848* (Ithaca, N.Y., 1977), ch.

11. The legal reasoning on which the constitutionality of the Civil Rights Act was based, as well as the act's constitutionality itself, was more frequently assumed than explained.

5. See, for example, *United States v. Rhodes*, 27 F. Cas. 785 (No. 16,151) (C.C. Ky. 1867); *People v. Washington*, 36 Cal. 658, 664–665 (1869); *McCulloch v. Maryland*, 17 U.S. (4 Wheat.) 316 (1819).

6. *Rhodes*, 27 F. Cas. 789, 791, 794. The Indiana Supreme Court reached the same conclusion concerning the Thirteenth Amendment conferring citizenship. *Smith v. Moody*, 26 Ind. 299, 307 (1866).

7. For an example of a states' rights rejection of nationalist civil rights theory, see n. 9. *Barron v. Mayor and City Council of Baltimore*, 32 U.S. (7 Pet.) 243 (1833).

8. The quotation is in *Washington*, 36 Cal. at 678–679; also see 36 Cal. at 683; *Mississippi v. Lewis*, in *The New York Times*, Oct. 26, 1866, p. 2; Jackson, Mississippi *Daily Clarion*, Oct. 6, 1866, p. 2; *State v. Rash*, 6 Del (1 Houst.) 271, 277–279 (1867); *People v. Brady*, 40 Cal. 198, 216–217 (1870). The California Supreme Court's broad interpretation of the authority of the federal government to enforce civil rights in its 1869 decision was rejected for the narrower states' rights interpretation in its 1870 decision. In 1873, the court returned to its 1869 position on federal authority over citizens' rights by virtue of the Fourteenth Amendment. *Van Valkenburg v. Alb Brown*, 43 Cal. 43 (1873). These shifts in the California Supreme Court's opinions were due to changes in its membership and corresponding shifts in Republican and Democratic control. *The New York Times*, Feb. 20, 1869, p. 4.

9. *Bowlin v. Commonwealth*, 65 Ky. (2 Bush) 5, 13 (1867).

10. *Rash*, 6 Del (1 Houst.) at 277 and 279; the Maryland case was not reported, but the full text of the opinion was reprinted in the Baltimore *American and Commercial Advertiser*, July 7, 1866, and the Baltimore *Sun*, July 9, 1866; Margaret Law Callcott, *The Negro in Maryland Politics, 1870–1912* (Baltimore, 1969): 18, fn. 21. A newspaper copy of the decision is entered in Edward McPherson, ed., *Scrapbook on the Civil Rights Bill*, pp. 114–115 (container 99), Edward McPherson Papers, Library of Congress, hereinafter cited as L.C.; also see *The New York Times*, July 7, 1866, p. 4. The case is discussed in W. A. Low, "The Freedmen's Bureau and Civil Rights in Maryland," *The Journal of Negro History* 37 (July 1952): 239–241. For other state appellate cases concerning Negro testimony, see *Ex parte Warren*, 37 Tex. 147 (1868); *Kelley v. Arkansas*, 25 Ark. 392 (1869); *State v. Underwood*, 63 N.C. 98 (1869).

11. See, for example, *Live-Stock Dealers' & Butchers' Ass'n v. Crescent City Live-Stock Landing & Slaughter-House Co.* 15 F. Cas. 649, 652, 653, 655 (No. 8,408) (C.C. La. 1870), hereinafter cited as *Slaughter-House Cases*; *The New York Times*, Nov. 2, 1866, p. 5; Cincinnati *Gazette*, Oct. 24, 1866, p. 1; unidentified paper, McPherson, ed., *Scrapbook on the Civil Rights Bill*, p. 122; *In re Hobbs* 12 F. Cas. 262, 264 (No. 6,550) (C. C. N. D. Ga. 1871); *Bowlin*, 65 Ky. (2 Bush) at 28–30. One exception to these expansive interpretations of congressional intent was an 1870 decision in the Democratically controlled California Supreme Court in which the court asserted that the Fourteenth Amendment "could not have been intended to authorize the Federal Government to supervise the state in the exercise of its undoubted powers." The court also interpreted the Thirteenth Amendment as limited to prohibiting state laws that enslaved persons. *Brady*, 40 Cal. at 214–217.

12. See McPherson, ed., *Scrapbook on the Civil Rights Bill*, clippings from unidentified Papers, pp. 108, 119, and 136; New York *Herald*, n.d., p. 108; Baltimore *American*, Apr. 16 1866, p. 109; Detroit *Post*, Sept. 14, 1866, p. 120; Philadelphia *Daily News*, Apr. 23, 1866, pp. 109, 110–111; also see Cincinnati *Gazette*, July 4, 1867, p. 1; *The New York Times*, May 14, 1871, p. 1; *Stevens v. Richmond, Fredericksburg and Potomac Railroad Co.* clippings in John C. Underwood, ed., *Scrapbook*, pp. 193, 203, 205, 207, John C. Underwood Papers, L.C. For

cases rejecting Negro access to public facilities under the Civil Rights Act of 1866, see in McPherson, ed., *Scrapbook on the Civil Rights Bill*, Baltimore *Gazette*, May 25, 1866, p. 111; unidentified paper, pp. 133–134. Concerning Negro access to juries, see *The New York Times*, May 8, 1867, p. 1; Aug. 9, 1867, p. 4; Aug. 30, 1867, p. 5; Oct. 17, 1867, p. 1; Oct. 20, 1867, p. 1; Underwood, ed., *Scrapbook*, p. 205; U.S. Senate, "Correspondence Relative to Reconstruction," 40th Cong. 1st sess. *Sen. Exec. Doc.* No. 14 (Serial 1308): 208–209. The application of the separate but equal doctrine to public facilities usually occurred in cases that involved the Fourteenth Amendment. See *Bertonneau v. Board of Directors of City Schools*, 3 F. Cas. 294 (No. 1,361) (C. C. La. 1878); *United States v. Buntin*, 10 Fed. 730, especially at 735–737 (C. C. S. D. Ohio 1882); *West Chester and Pennsylvania Railroad Co. v. Miles*, 55 Pa. 209, 211–213 (1867); *State v. Board of Education of Cincinnati*, 1 Wk. L. But. 139 (1867); *State ex rel. Garnes v. McCann*, 21 Ohio St. 198, 211 (1871); *People ex rel. Dietz v. Easton*, 13 Abb. Pr. 159, 164–165 (N.Y. Sup. Ct. 1872); *Ward. v. Flood*, 48 Cal. 36, 49–57 (1874); *Cory v. Carter*, 48 Ind. 327, 354–357, 359 (1874). However, the Iowa Supreme Court and, in one case at least, the Louisiana Supreme Court ruled that separate but equal was unconstitutional. *Clark v. The Board of Directors*, 24 Ia. 267 (1868); *Coger v. The North West. Union Packet Co.*, 37 Ia. 145, 155–157 (1873); *Smith v. The Directors of the Independent School District of Keokuk*, 40 Ia. 518 (1875); *Dove v. The Independent School District of Keokuk*, 41 Ia. 689 (1875); *DeCuir v. Benson*, 27 La. Ann. 1 (1875). One of the best discussions of the subject of Negro access to public facilities that also concludes that separate but equal was the common practice during this period is Howard N. Rabinowitz, *Race Relations in the Urban South, 1865–1890* (New York, 1978); also see his "From Exclusion to Segregation: Southern Race Relations, 1865–1900," *Journal of American History* 63 (Sept. 1976): 325–350. Mary S. Donovan concludes that federal law and the federal courts pressured one state to replace its racially discriminatory laws with laws that were remarkably fair and just to blacks. See her "Kentucky Law Regarding the Negro, 1865–1877" (unpublished M.A. thesis, University of Louisville, 1967).

13. *The New York Times*, Oct. 18, 1866, p. 5; Louisville *Daily Journal*, June 27, 1867, p. 2.

14. Louisville *Daily Journal*, June 28, 1867, p. 2.

15. *Rhodes*, 27 F. Cas. at 785–786. The conservative Kentucky jurist, S. S. Nicholas, wrote an extensive commentary upon Justice Swayne's opinion in which Nicholas noted that Justice Swayne rejected the notion that the Civil Rights Act merely secured an equality in state-conferred rights and observed that its protection went beyond discriminatory state law. McPherson, ed., *Scrapbook on the Civil Rights Bill*, pp. 143, 147. Also see Judge Bland Ballard's charge to the grand jury in this connection, Louisville *Daily Journal*, Oct. 3, 1867, p. 3. For other comments on Justice Swayne's *Rhodes* decision, see McPherson, ed., *Scrapbook on the Civil Rights Bill*, pp. 122, 137–142, 149. The defendants in this case were subsequently sentenced to ten years at hard labor in the penitentiary at Frankfurt. Ibid., p. 149; Louisville *Daily Journal*, Oct. 12, 1867, p. 2. Justice Swayne's opinion was reprinted in its entirety in *The New York Times*, Nov. 25, 1867, p. 2.

16. Cincinnati *Gazette*, Oct. 24, 1866, p. 1; *The New York Times*, Nov. 2, 1866, p. 5; McPherson, ed., *Scrapbook on the Civil Rights Bill*, p. 122; *Charge to Grand Jury*, enclosed in Judge Robert A. Hill to Benjamin H. Bristow, July 28, 1871, S. C. F., S. D. Miss., R. G. 60, N. A.; *Gaines v. State*, 39 Tex. 606, 612 (1873); *Blyew v. United States*, 80 U.S. (13 Wall.) 581, 593 (1871). In this case, the Supreme Court curtailed federal jurisdiction under the Civil Rights Act despite the implication of broad federal civil rights enforcement authority. The case is discussed in greater detail in Chapter 7.

17. *Rhodes*, 27 F. Cas. at 790; *Washington*, 36 Cal. at 670. However, some appellate courts declared the Civil Rights Act unconstitutional because they understood it as attempting to

supplant the states in regulating the conditions under which civil rights were to be exercised in the states. See *Rash*, 6 Del. (1 Houst.) at 275; *Brady*, 40 Cal. at 210ff.; *Bowlin*, 65 Ky. (2 Bush) 5.

18. *Rhodes*, 27 F. Cas. at 786, 788; *Washington*, 36 Cal. at 666–667, 669–670. See also the cases cited in n. 12 of this chapter.

19. *United States v. Ortega*, 24 U.S. (11 Wheat.) 467 (1826). Bristow to Senator Lyman Trumbull, Jan. 7, 1867 (container 1), Benjamin Helm Bristow Papers, L.C.; Judge Bland Ballard to Salmon P. Chase, Aug. 16, 1866 (Vol. 97), Salmon P. Chase Papers, L.C.; Ross A. Webb, *Benjamin Helm Bristow: Border Slate Politician* (Lexington, Ky., 1969): 54. Bristow had written to Senator Trumbull out of "a deep interest in the perfection and enforcement of laws for the protection of Freedmen" and a sense of obligation to inform the senator of defects in the Civil Rights Act. Bristow believed that prejudice would still prevent blacks from receiving justice in the state courts even after Kentucky's discriminatory statutes were repealed. A judicial ruling against federal jurisdiction over civil rights, therefore, would be "disastrous beyond measure," in Bristow's opinion. It is significant that Bristow, in alerting Senator Trumbull to defects in the Civil Rights Act and recommending corrective legislation, did not mention any state action limitations.

20. *Rhodes*, 27 F. Cas. at 786–787. Bristow subsequently informed the attorney general in 1869 that this decision enabled him to proceed with numerous prosecutions under the Civil Rights Act. Webb, *Benjamin Helm Bristow*, p. 60. Even with sufficient constitutional authority and the active cooperation of the Freedmen's Bureau, only a fraction of the crimes committed against blacks in Kentucky were prosecuted because of limited resources. Bristow to Trumbull, Jan. 7, 1867 (container 1), Bristow Papers, L.C.; Cincinnati *Gazette*, Mar. 21, 1868; McPherson, ed., *Scrapbook on the Civil Rights Bill*, p. 155; Victor B. Howard, "The Black Testimony Controversy in Kentucky, 1866–1872," *The Journal of Negro History* 58 (Apr. 1973): 150.

21. 16 *U.S. Statutes at Large* 140; 17 *U.S. Statutes at Large* 13.

22. The case is *United States v. Hall*, 26 F. Cas. 79 (No. 15,282) (C. C. S. D. Ala. 1871). For a discussion of events leading up to this riot, see William W. Rogers, "The Boyd Incident: Black Belt Violence during Reconstruction," *Civil War History* 21 (Dec. 1975): 309–329.

23. Joseph P. Bradley to William B. Woods, Jan. 3, 1871, Joseph P. Bradley Papers, The New Jersey Historical Society.

24. Justice Bradley to Judge Woods, Mar. 12, 1871, ibid.

25. *Hall*, 26 F. Cas. at 82. Judge Woods reached the same conclusion in *United States v. Mall*, 26 F. Cas. 1147 (No. 15,712) (C. C. S. D. Ala. 1871). The editor of the *American Law Review* thought the ruling reflected "a somewhat obscure course of reasoning." *American Law Review* 5 (July 1871): 752. However, he also thought that the inclusion of state inaction within the meaning of equal protection of the laws had merit.

26. *Hall*, 26 F. Cas. at 81.

27. Ibid., pp. 81–82; *Corfield v. Coryell*, 6 F. Cas. 546 (No. 3,230) (C. C. N.J. 1823). The Supreme Court decision that held that the determination of citizens' rights is to be made on a case by case basis is *Conners v. Elliot*, 59 U.S. (18 How.) 591 (1855). For other interpretations of privileges and immunities as incorporating Bill of Rights guarantees, see Justice Bradley to Frederick T. Frelinghuysen, July 19, 1874, Bradley Papers; *Slaughter-House Cases*, 15 F. Cas. at 652, 653; *United States v. Given*, 25 F. Cas. 1328 at 1329 (No. 15,211) (C. C. Del. 1873); and the cases discussed below. Courts generally interpreted the privileges and immunities secured to citizens by the Fourteenth Amendment and the Civil Rights Act of 1866 as the fundamental rights of citizens. See *Slaughter-House Cases*, 15 F. Cas. at 652–654; *In re Hobbs*, 12 F. Cas. at 263–264; *Given*, 25 F. Cas. 1324 at 1325 (No.

15,210) (C. C. Del. 1873) and 25 F. Cas. at 1329; *United States v. Blackburn*, 24 F. Cas. 1158, 1159 (No. 11,603) (D. C. W. D. Mo. 1874); *United States v. Cruikshank*, 25 F. Cas. 707, 711, 714, 715 (No. 14,897) (C. C. La. 1874); *Washington*, 36 Cal. at 662–664; *Van Valkenburg*, 43 Cal. at 47–48; *White v. Clements*, 39 Ga. 232, 272–273 (1869); *Ducat v. Chicago*, 48 Ill. 172, 179–180 (1868); *Smith*, 26 Ind. at 301ff.; *Coger* 37 Ia. at 155–156; *Bowlin v.* 65 Ky. (2 Bush) at 30; *Marshall v. Donovan*, 73 Ky. (10 Bush) 681, 688–690 (1874); *Hart v. Hoss & Elder*, 26 La. Ann. 90, 93, 97 (1874); *Donnell v. State*, 48 Miss. 661, 677–678 (1873); *Dallas v. Fosdick*, 40 How. Pr. 249, 256 (N.Y. Sup. Ct. 1869); *Lonas v. State*, 50 Tenn. 287, 306–307, 311 (1871).

28. *Slaughter-House Cases*, 83 U.S. (16 Wall. 36) 73–81 (1873); *In re Hobbs*, 12 F. Cas. at 264; *United States v. Canter*, 25 F. Cas. 281 (No. 14,719) (C. C. S. D. Ohio 1870); *Rhodes*, 27 F. Cas. at 788–789, 790–791. In addition, see the cases cited in nn. 11 and 12; *Mall*, 26 F. Cas. 1147; *Murrell v. State*, 44 Ala. 367 (1870). Many judges continued to hold an expansive view of federally enforceable civil rights even after the Supreme Court's *Slaughter-House* decision. Justice Bradley continued to insist that natural rights were nationally enforceable, but he acknowledged the *Slaughter-House* decision by suggesting that Congress was empowered to protect them only against state infringements. This represented a shift away from his earlier views. *Cruikshank*, 25 F. Cas. at 714. And the federal district judge for the Western District of Missouri also defined the rights of United States citizens to be natural rights, but his charge to the jury raises the possibility that he meant that the Fourteenth Amendment only secured an equality in these natural rights. The wording is ambiguous. *United States v. Blackburn*, 24 F. Cas., 1159–1160. Also see United States Supreme Court Justice Stephen J. Field's opinion in *In re Fong*, 1 F. Cas. 217, 218 (No. 210) (C. C. Cal. 1874). The Louisiana Supreme Court similarly ruled in 1874 that the Civil Rights Act of 1866 "declares who shall be citizens of the United States, what shall be their rights and privileges in the several States...," and that it "conferred upon them and vested in them all the civil rights and privileges of white persons." On rehearing, the court also said that it conferred upon blacks "the rights, and privileges which they would have under state laws if they were white persons." *Hart*, 26 La. Ann. at 93, 97.

29. For school cases using this reasoning, see *Dallas*, 40 How. Pr. at 256; *Mary Ward*, 48 Cal. at 49–50; *State ex rel. Garnes*, 21 Ohio St. at 210. For Negro testimony cases see *Rhodes*, 27 F. Cas. at 787; *Sommers v. Powell*, McPherson, ed., *Scrapbook on the Civil Rights Bill*, pp. 114–115; *Ex parte Warren*, 31 Tex.: 147; *Kelley v. Arkansas*, 25 Ark. 392; *Underwood*, 63 N.C. 98.

30. For decisions commenting upon political rights, see *Rhodes*, 27 F. Cas. at 794; *United States v. Crosby*, 25 F. Cas. 701, 704 (No. 14,893) (C. C. S. C. 1871); *Given*, 25 F. Cas. at 1325–1327; *Canter*, 25 F. Cas. 281; *United States v. Anthony*, 24 F. Cas. 829, 830 (No. 14,459) (C. C. N. D. N. Y. 1873); *United States v. Petersburg Judges of Election*, 27 F. Cas. 506, 509 (No. 16,036) (C. C. E. D. Va. 1874); *Washington*, 36 Cal. at 661–662, 670; *White*, 39 Ga. at 244, 273 ff., the dissenting opinion; *State v. Gibson*, 36 Ind. 389, 393 *Donnell*, (1871) 48 Miss. at 676–677; *Smith*, 26 Ind. at 306; *Washington*, 36 Cal. at 685–686. For cases dealing with interracial marriage, see *In re Hobbs*, 12 F. Cas. at 264; *Ex parte Kinney*, 14 F. Cas. 602 (No. 7,825) (C. C. E. D. Va. 1879); *Ex parte Francois*, 9 F. Cas. 699 (No. 5,047) (C. C. W. D. Tex. 1879); *State v. Fairston and Williams*, 63 N.C. 451 (1869); *Gibson*, 36 Ind. at 389; *Lonas*, 50 Tenn. at 287; *Green v. Alabama*, 58 Ala. 190 (1877); *Frasher v. State*, 3 Tex. Ct. App. Reps. 263 (1877). Two cases held that marriage came within the rights secured by the Constitution and laws of the United States. They were *Burns v. Alabama*, 48 Ala. 195 (1872) and *Hart*, 26 La. Ann. at 90. Even the State of Maine's antimiscegenation law was upheld by the state courts. Boston *Post*, Aug. 31, 1867, in McPherson, ed., *Scrapbook on the Civil Rights Bill*, p. 136. Also see *The New York Times*, June 13, 1869, p. 1.

31. Actions to enforce an equality in state-conferred rights were not brought in the federal courts before the Supreme Court's *Slaughter-House* decision. The reason appears to be that the civil rights asserted in the federal courts were presumed by federal judges and the petitioners to be federally protected rights of national citizenship. As such, they were directly secured by, and enforceable under, the Constitution and laws of the United States. We must look to state appellate decisions, therefore, for pre-*Slaughter-House* rulings on this point. It appears that state courts were prompted to explore this issue precisely because the natural rights of citizenship were presumed to fall within federal jurisdiction. See *Washington*, 36 Cal. at 669–670; *State ex rel. Garnes*, 21 Ohio St. at 209–211; *People ex rel. Dietz*, 13 Abb. Pr. at 164–165. When the Supreme Court restored the natural rights of citizenship to exclusive state jurisdiction, federal courts were forced to distinguish between federally enforceable civil rights and state, protected civil rights. Still, some judges continued to insist that the privileges and immunities of United States citizenship included the right to an equality in fundamental rights. See *Blackburn*, 24 F. Cas. at 1159–1160; *Petersburg Judges*, 27 F. Cas. at 507–509; *In re Fong*, 1 F. Cas. at 218; *Cully v. Baltimore & O. R. Co.*, 6 F. Cas. 946, 947 (No. 3,466) (D. C. Md. 1876); *Ward*, 48 Cal. at 50–51; *Cory*, 48 Ind. at 358; *Hart*, 26 La. Ann. at 98; *DeCuir*, 27 La. Ann. at 6.

32. Judge Bradford's opinion is cited separately as *Given*, 25 F. Cas. 1328; the quotation is at 1328–1329; for Justice Strong's opinion, see *Given*, 25 F. Cas. at 1325–1326. The United States district judge for West Virginia, John J. Jackson, Jr., was one of the first federal judges to uphold the constitutionality of the Enforcement Act of 1870. Although he was reputedly unfriendly to the policies of the Grant administration, he upheld the statute's constitutionality. His August 1870 charge to the grand jury conceived of national civil rights enforcement authority in the same broad nationalist tradition as judges who were sympathetic to national civil rights enforcement. So, too, did the United States district judge for the Southern District of Ohio, Humphrey Howe Leavitt. Appointed to the district court by Andrew Jackson in the 1830s, Judge Leavitt's interpretation of national authority in such broad terms was contrary to his Jacksonian Democratic antecedents. Judges Leavitt's and Jackson's rulings manifest the general acceptance among federal judges of the expansive understanding of the authority of the federal government to enforce civil rights. For Judge Jackson's charge, see *Charge to Grand Jury*, 30 F. Cas. 987 (No. 18,252) D. W.Va. (1870). Judge Jackson's political views were described by Judge John Underwood of Virginia in his *Charge to Grand Jury*, reported in a newspaper clipping contained in Underwood, ed., *Scrapbook*, p. 227. Judge Leavitt's opinion is in *Canter*, 25 F. Cas. 281.

Chapter 2: The Freedmen's Bureau and Civil Rights Enforcement, 1866–1868

1. See John A. Carpenter, *Sword and Olive Branch: Oliver Otis Howard* (Pittsburgh, 1964); William S. McFeely, *Yankee Stepfather: General O. O. Howard and the Freedmen* (New York, 1970); Donald G. Nieman, *To Set the Law in Motion: The Freedmen's Bureau and the Legal Rights of Blacks, 1865–1868* (Millwood, N.Y., 1980); James Sefton, *The United States Army and Reconstruction, 1865–1877* (Baton Rouge, 1967); Daniel J. Flanigan, "The Criminal Law of Slavery and Freedom, 1800–1868" (unpublished Ph.D. dissertation, Rice University, 1973).

2. Col. J. R. Lewis to Gen. C. B. Fisk, May 15, 1866, M752, Reel 33, K135, Vol. 6, 1866, BRFAL, R.G. 105, N.A.; Maj. F. W. Gilbreth to Howard, May 22, 1866, ibid., G182 (filed with K135); Gen. E. O. C. Ord to Howard, Feb. 22, 1867, ibid., Reel 41, A116, Vol. 9, 1867; Judge Robert A. Hill to Howard, Jan. 5, 1867, ibid., Reel 42, H22; Col. J. V. Bamford to Howard,

Mar. 5, 1867, ibid., Reel 43, N54; Gen. J. B. Kiddoo to Howard, Jan. 12, 1867, ibid., Reel 44, T11; Robt. Smith to Gen. Kiddoo, Oct. 30, 1866, ibid.; Col. Thomas Bayley to Col. H. A. Ellis, Nov. 15, 1866, ibid.; A. Craig to Col. Ellis, Dec. 17, 1866, ibid.; Gen. Chas. Griffin to Howard, Feb. 12, 1867, ibid., T63; U.S. Congress, 40th Cong., 2d sess., *House Exec. Doc.* No. 329 (Serial 1346).

3. Col. Lewis to Gen. Fisk, May 15, 1866, M752, Reel 33, K135, Vol. 6, 1866; Robt. Smith to Gen. Kiddoo, Oct. 30, 1866, ibid., Reel 44, Vol. 9, 1867, T11; Gen. Kiddoo to Howard, Jan. 12, 1867, ibid.; Gen. W. P. Carlin to Howard, Mar. 14 and 18, 1867, ibid., T95 and T104; U.S. Senate, "Freedmen's Affairs," 39th Cong., 2d sess., *Sen. Exec. Doc.* No. 6 (Serial 1276, Vol. 1), passim.

4. Gen. Baird to Howard, May 10, 1866, M752, Reel 33, L119, Vol. 6, 1866; Gen. J. J. Reynolds to Howard, Feb. 19, 1867, ibid., Reel 43, R24; Gen. Carlin to Howard, Feb. 12, 1867, ibid., Reel 44, T56; Robert Smith to Gen. Kiddoo, Oct. 30, 1866, ibid., T11; Howard to Stanton, Nov. 1, 1866, M742, Reel 2, Vol. 2, p. 403; BRFAL, R.G. 105, N.A. General Schofield refused to discharge a defendant who was about to be tried by military commission for the murder of a freedman despite defense counsel's argument that the defendant already had been tried and acquitted by a local court within the meaning of the United States Constitution. "Memorandum," "Case of Dr. James L. Watson," Virginia Assistant Commissioner, Letters Received, L345, Vol. 4, 1867, BRFAL, R.G. 105, N.A. Also see pp. 35–36.

5. Gen. E. M. Gregory to Ketchum, Apr. 10, 1867, M752, Reel 43, M104, Vol. 9, 1867; "Freedmen's Affairs," passim; U.S. Senate, "Correspondence Relative to Reconstruction," 40th Cong., 1st sess., *Sen. Exec. Doc.* No. 14 (Serial 1308), passim.

6. Col. Lewis to Gen. Fisk, May 15, 1866, M752, Reel 33, K135, Vol. 6, 1866; Gen. Carlin to Howard, Mar. 18, 1867, ibid., Reel 44, T104, Vol. 9, 1867; "Correspondence Relative to Reconstruction," p. 116; Nieman, *To Set the Law in Motion* , pp. 15–16.

7. U.S. Senate, "Violations of the Civil Rights Bill," 39th Cong., 2d sess., *Sen. Exec. Doc.* No. 29 (Serial 1277), pp. 12–13; the Freedmen's Bureau Bill is cited 14 *U.S. Statutes at Large* 173.

8. Oliver O. Howard, *Autobiography of Oliver Otis Howard*, Vol. 2 (New York, 1907): 283; Nieman, *To Set the Law in Motion*, pp. 16, 19, 21; Sefton, *The United States Army*, passim; Jerrell H. Shofner, *Nor Is It Over Yet: Florida in the Era of Reconstruction, 1863–1877* (Gainesville, Fla., 1974): 98, 101; Benjamin P. Thomas and Harold M. Hyman, *Stanton: The Life and Times of Lincoln's Secretary of War* (New York, 1962): 476–478; Flanigan, "The Criminal Law of Slavery and Freedom," pp. 329–333; Edson St. Clair, "Administration of Justice in North Carolina, 1865–1876" (unpublished Ph.D. dissertation, Ohio State University, 1939). Flanigan's and Nieman's studies are indispensable to anyone interested in the legal activities of the Freedmen's Bureau.

9. Howard to assistant commissioners, Sept. 19, 1866, M742, Reel 2, Vol. 2, pp. 330–334; Howard to Stanton, Nov. 1, 1866, ibid., p. 379; Col. C. C. Sibley to Howard, Feb. 16, 1867; Howard to Sibley, Jan. 30 and Feb. 20, 1867, M752, Reel 42, G33, Vol. 9, 1867; U.S. Congress, "Report of the Secretary of War," 39th Cong., 2d sess., *House Exec. Doc.* No. 1 (Serial 1285): 705–774 and passim; 40th Cong., 2d sess., *House Exec. Doc.* No. 1 (Serial 1324): 621–693 and passim; Ex Parte Milligan, 4 Wall. 2 (1866); Howard, *Autobiography*, Vol. 2, p. 285.

10. Gen. Carlin to Howard, Feb. 12, 1867, M752, Reel 44, T56, Vol. 9, 1867; Gen. Clinton Fisk to Howard, May 28, 1866, ibid., Reel 33, K142, Vol. 6, 1866; "Freedmen's Affairs"; "Report of the Secretary of War," 39th Cong., 2d sess., pp. 48–68, 733–750; Theodore B. Wilson, *The Black Codes of the South* (University, Ala., 1965).

11. Gen. Fisk to Howard, June 6 and July 28, 1866, M752, Reel 33, K149 and K171, Vol. 6, 1866; Col. Sibley to Howard, Mar. 19, 1867, ibid., Reel 42, G79, Vol. 9, 1867; Judge Hill to

Gen. L. Wood, Nov. 9, 1866, ibid., H90; Judge Hill to Howard, Mar. 5, 1867, ibid., H34; Gen. Gillem to Howard, Feb. 15 and Apr. 10, 1867, ibid., Reel 43, M85 and M114; Col. Lewis to Howard, Dec. 31, 1866, ibid., Reel 44, T61; Gen. Carlin to Howard, Feb. 12, Mar. 18, Apr. 11, and May 16, 1867, ibid., T56, T104, T130, and T164; "Freedmen's Affairs," p. 3; Judge Hill to Chief Justice Chase, Nov. 14, 1866, Vol. 97, Salmon P. Chase Papers, L.C. These perceptions of Southern racial justice have also been noted by Vernon L. Wharton, *The Negro in Mississippi, 1865–1890* (New York, 1965): 93, 135–136; and Shofner, *Nor Is It Over Yet*, p. 86.

12. Gen. Griffin to Howard, Feb. 12 and 18, 1867, M752, Reel 44, T63 and T65, Vol. 9, 1867; Gen. Reynolds to Howard, Feb. 19, 1867, and related letters, ibid., Reel 43, R24; "Freedmen's Affairs," pp. 35, 44; "Correspondence Relative to Reconstruction," passim; the annual reports of the Secretary of War and other materials cited in n. 9 above; Sefton, *The United States Army* , pp. 147–148; Nieman, *To Set the Law in Motion* , p. 76; Carpenter, *Sword and Olive Branch* , p. 135.

13. See nn. 9, 11, and 12 above.

14. Howard to Stanton, Jan. 19, 1867, M742, Reel 3, Vol. 3, p. 30.

15. See Nieman's and Flanigan's studies cited in n. 1 above for expressions of this narrow view of the power of the federal government to enforce civil rights.

16. J. S. Holt to Secretary of War, June 18, 1866, M752, Reel 33, L119, Vol. 6, 1866. This opinion was given in a case that involved a white former Bureau agent who claimed that he was being prosecuted for a crime he did not commit because of the assistance he had rendered to blacks in Louisiana. The assistant commissioner for Louisiana asked about the authority he possessed to assist the defendant in the face of the local judge's refusal to allow the case to be removed to a federal court under the Civil Rights Act. The judge, Edmund Abell, was subsequently arrested on a warrant issued by the United States commissioner for New Orleans for violating the Civil Rights Act. United States District Judge E. H. Durell quickly overruled state Judge Abell's decision. Judge Durell upheld the constitutionality of the Civil Rights Act of 1866 and ruled that it gave the federal court jurisdiction in the case. Judge Durell's decision was heartily approved by Southern Unionists who believed that "'it ensures justice at the hands of the Federal authorities.'" Quoted in *The New York Times*, July 14, 1866, p. 8. See also Gen. Baird to Howard, May 10, 1866, M752, Reel 33, L119, Vol. 6, 1866; newspaper clippings, n.t., May 9, 1866, and New York *News*, July 30, 1866, in McPherson, ed., *Scrapbook on the Civil Rights Bill*, pp. 111 and 118, respectively.

17. Gen. Davis to Maj. Ketchum, Jan. 29, 1867, M752, Reel 42, K12, Vol. 9, 1867 and nn. 10 above and 22–23 below. For a contrary view, see Nieman, *To Set the Law in Motion*, pp. 137–140. Professor Nieman identifies a United States district judge, Henry Caldwell of Arkansas, who, according to Professor Nieman, rejected jurisdiction over a case involving the murder of a black person by a white assailant even though the local authorities failed to bring the defendant to justice. Professor Nieman concludes that Judge Caldwell did not believe the Civil Rights Act authorized federal courts to intervene when state officials failed to mete out justice to those who assaulted or murdered freedmen. Nieman, *To Set the Law in Motion*, p. 139. He quotes Caldwell as saying that such a defendant ought to be punished, but that function belongs to the state courts. If the state courts "neglect to try and punish him (as I fear they will) he will go 'scott [*sic*] free.'" Quoted in ibid. The letter cited by Professor Nieman could not be located in the records of the Freedmen's Bureau, so I have not had the opportunity to evaluate its contents or Nieman's interpretation of what the letter says. An equally plausible explanation of Judge Caldwell's statement is that he was referring to the political and practical impossibility of trying outrages against blacks instead of legal or constitutional limitations. Even if Judge Caldwell did believe

the federal courts could not take jurisdiction in such cases, he was exceptional in that view. I might add that he either did not express his views in an official opinion, or, if he did, it did not get much publicity, because other federal judges failed to take notice of his views. Furthermore, Bureau officers and other federal legal officials brought criminal prosecutions in the federal court in Judge Caldwell's district and otherwise assumed jurisdiction in such cases. See "Circular No. 30," Arkansas, M979, Reel 21, Vol. 22, pp. 35–37, BRFAL, R.G. 105, N. A.; H. B. Allis to Col. Chas. H. Smith, Apr. 18, 1867, ibid., Reel 14, Vol. 138, D139; Gen. Ord to Lt. Taylor, Jan. 24, 1867, M752, Reel 41, A113, Vol. 9, 1867.

18. Maj. Vanderlip to Col. W.W. Rogers, Mar. 7, 1867, M752, Reel 41, C100, Vol. 9, 1867.

19. Ibid.; *Rhodes*, 27 F. Cas. 785. Concerning the discriminatory features of Maryland law, see Gen. Gregory to Maj. Ketchum, Apr. 10, 1867, M752, Reel 43, M104, Vol. 9, 1867.

20. Col. James V. Bamford to Howard, Mar. 15, 1867, M752, Reel 43, N54, Vol. 9, 1867; St. Clair, "Administration of Justice," pp. 88–94, 358, 382–384, 400–404. A third letter was received from Col. Sibley in Georgia. Col. Sibley to Howard, Feb. 22, 1867, M752, Reel 42, G40, Vol. 9, 1867. His concern over the scope of the Civil Rights Act arose from an interpretation of the act made by the United States attorney at Savannah, Henry S. Fitch. Fitch was an opponent of federal protection of civil rights who had a political interest in impeding federal officers from accomplishing that goal.

21. Gen. Fisk to Howard, May 18, 1866, M752, Reel 33, K135, Vol. 6, 1866; Lt. Palmer to Gen. Carlin, Feb. 20, 1867, and Gen. Carlin to Lt. Palmer, Feb. 22, 1867, ibid., Reel 44, T100; H. Exec. Doc. 329, 19–24.

22. Gen. Griffin to Howard, Feb. 12 and 18, 1867, M752, Reed 44, T63 and T65, Vol. 9, 1867; also see other materials cited in n. 12 above.

23. Reports of such prosecutions came from various parts of the South and border states. See Gen. Baird to Maj. Ketchum, July 23, 1866, M752, Reel 33, L146, Vol. 6, 1866; Gen. Ord to Howard, Feb. 4, 1867, ibid., Reel 41, A71, Vol. 9, 1867; Col. John T. Sprague to Howard, Feb. 14, 1867, ibid., Reel 42, F37; Isaac Brooks to Gen. Gregory, Jan 27, 1867, and Gen. Gregory to Maj. Ketchum, Jan. 29, 1867, ibid., Reel 43, M38; Lt. Fred S. Palmer to Gen. Carlin, Feb. 20, 1867, and Gen. Carlin to Lt. Palmer, Feb. 22, 1867, ibid., Reel 44, T100; "Circular No. 30," Arkansas, M979, Reel 21, Vol. 22, pp. 35–37; "Report of the Secretary of War," 39th Cong., 2d sess., pp. 53, 733–735, 747; "Report of the Secretary of War," 40th Cong., 2d sess., passim; Howard, *Autobiography*, Vol. 2, ch. 52; Shofner, *Nor Is It Over Yet*, pp. 83–84, 97; St. Clair, "Administration of Justice," pp. 77–94.

24. In Virginia, where state law recognized the rights of blacks, Bureau officers took cases into the federal courts when judges refused to admit the testimony of blacks in their state courts. They also performed police and judicial law enforcement functions when local officials failed to protect citizens. However, in Maryland and Mississippi, where state laws continued to discriminate against blacks, Bureau and other federal authorities refrained from using Bureau, military, and federal courts, but worked instead through the local authorities and courts. "Freedmen's Affairs," pp. 34–35, 96–97, 145–146, 165–166. The variety of offenses for which and conditions under which private persons were prosecuted under the Civil Rights Act is shown in the sources in n. 23 above and Col. Sibley to Howard, Feb. 22, 1867, M752, Reel 41, G40, Vol. 9, 1867; Gen. Davis to Maj. Ketchum, Jan. 29, 1867, ibid., K12; Gen. Burbank to Maj. Ketchum, Mar. 13, 1867, ibid., K28; Jack Fry to Gen. John Ely, Feb. 21, 1867, ibid; Capt. A. Benson Brown to Col. C. H. Fredericks, July 7, 1866, ibid.; Col. Fredericks to Gen. Davis, June 21, 1866, ibid.; Gen. Burbank to Howard, May 11, 1867, ibid., K52; Gen. Reynolds to Howard, Feb. 19, 1867, and enclosed correspondence, ibid., Reel 43, R24; Howard to Stanton, Nov. 1, 1866, M742, Reel 2, Vol. 2, pp. 394–395, 403. Maj. William Dawes to Maj. John Tyler, Arkansas, Dec. 27, 1866, M979, Reel 11, D84,

Vol. 2, 1866; Maj. Dawes to Maj. Tyler, Dec. 27, 1866, ibid., D92; newspaper clippings, n.t., July 18, 1866, and n.t., n.d., in McPherson, ed., *Scrapbook on the Civil Rights Bill*, pp. 116–117 and 134–135, respectively; Shofner, *Nor Is It Over Yet*, p. 85. Attorney General Stanbery, who opposed the Civil Rights Act, did not believe it to be limited to discriminatory laws. In an official opinion explaining the legal import of the Reconstruction Acts, he asserted that the Civil Rights Act, along with the Freedmen's Bureau Act, "made ample provision for the protection of all merely civil rights, where the laws *or courts* of the State might fail to give full, impartial protection." (Emphasis added.) Henry Stanbery, "The Reconstruction Acts," *Official Opinions of the Attorneys General*, Vol. 12 (Washington, D.C., 1868): 189. When the Reconstruction Acts went into effect in 1867, military commanders instructed subordinates to supervise local police and judicial officers, and, if they failed to provide impartial justice, military officers were to assume legal and judicial authority by arresting and trying offenders. "Correspondence Relative to Reconstruction," passim. Local commanders believed they were authorized to protect natural rights, including First Amendment guarantees, when they were infringed by state officials and private citizens out of racial or political animus; they also believed they were authorized to end discrimination in transportation facilities. Ibid., pp. 108–109, 112–113, 147 and passim; U.S. Congress, "…General and Special Orders…for the Execution of the Reconstruction Laws," 40th Cong., 2d sess., *House Exec. Doc.* No. 342 (Serial 1346): passim.

25. This conclusion is based on the annual reports of the Secretary of War for 1866 and 1867 and the Bureau correspondence cited in the notes above and below.

26. *Congressional Globe*, 39th Cong., 2d sess., p. 326, hereinafter cited as *Cong. Globe*.

27. Howard K. Beale, ed., *The Diary of Gideon Welles* , Vol. 3 (Boston, 1911): 42–44; Orville H. Browning, *The Diary of Orville Hickman Browning* , Vol. 2 (Springfield, Ill., 1933): 130; Henry Stanbery to the president, Jan. 21, 1867, M699, Reel 11, Vol. F, pp. 289–290, R.G. 60, N.A. The president and his cabinet viewed the Senate's request as an intended embarrassment to the administration and as an instrument for enhancing congressional power in its struggle with the president over Reconstruction policy. Thomas and Hyman, *Stanton*, pp. 522–524. The number of violations reported to General Howard would have been much greater than the 440 mentioned by Secretary Welles if Bureau agents had been asked to report all violations of the Civil Rights Act, especially of the first three sections, which are the heart of the statute. Instead, agents were requested to report only violations of sections 4, 8, and 9, which authorized federal officials to enforce the act and authorized the president to use federal judicial officers and the armed forces to prevent and punish violations of the act. For the reports, see Howard to Stanton, Feb. 14, 1867, M742, Reel 3, Vol. 3, pp. 67–68; E.D. Townsend to Howard, Jan. 23, 1867, M952, Reel 41, Al 13, Vol. 9, 1867, BRFAL, R.G. 105, N.A.; Gen. Swayne to Howard, Jan. 30, 1867, ibid., A57; Gen. Ord to Howard, Feb. 4, 1867, ibid., A71; Col. Sprague to Howard, Feb. 14, 1867, ibid., Reel 42, F37; Col. Sibley to Howard, Feb. 22, 1867, ibid., G40; Gen. Davis to Maj. Ketchum, Jan. 29, 1876, ibid., K12; Gen. Mower to Gen. Thomas, Mar. 14, 1867, ibid., L46; Gen Gregory to Maj. Ketchum, Jan. 29, 1867, ibid., Reel 43, M38; Gen. Scott to Howard, Feb. 12, 1867, ibid., Reel 44, S90; Gen Carlin to Howard, Feb. 12, 1867, ibid., T56; Gen. Griffin to Howard, Feb. 12, 1867, ibid., T63.

28. "Violations of the Civil Rights Act," pp. 2–11. The proceedings concerning Fincher's appeal for certiorari to the superior court are in "Documents Relating to the Imprisonment in Georgia of Reverend William Fincher, a Missionary to the Freedmen," which is filed in U.S. Congress, "Riot at Norfolk," 39th Cong., 2d sess., *House Exec. Doc.* No. 72 (Serial 1293): 67–71. A newspaper account can be found in the Boston *Advertiser*, n.d., McPherson, ed., *Scrapbook on the Civil Rights Bill*, p. 133. The Equal Rights Association worked in the interests of blacks to achieve the right to testify and to sit on

juries in state courts, the right to fair and impartial enforcement of contracts, and for the full protection of persons and property. Alan Conway, *The Reconstruction of Georgia* (Minneapolis, 1966): 72. The quote is taken from Fitch to Stanbery, Jan. 21, 1867, as reprinted in "Violations of the Civil Rights Act," pp. 4–5. Fitch's report was sent at the request of the attorney general. See Stanbery to Henry S. Fitch, Dec. 1, 1866, M699, Reel 11, Vol. F, pp. 291–292; "Violations of the Civil Rights Act," pp. 2–3.

29. "Violations of the Civil Rights Act," p. 5; Fitch to Stanbery, Jan. 22, 1867, S. C. F., Ga., R.G. 60, N.A.; John Erskine to Fitch, Dec. 12, 1866, ibid.; Col. Sibley to Howard, Feb. 22, 1867, M752, Reel 42, G40, Vol. 9, 1867; "Reports of Outrages—Savannah," Feb. 1867, M798, Reel 32, BRFAL, R.G. 105, N.A.

30. Howard to Col. Sibley, Jan. 30 and Feb. 20, 1867, M752, Reel 42, G33, Vol. 9, 1867; Fitch to O. H. Browning, Feb. 6, 1867, Series 1, Reel 26, and Fitch to Andrew Johnson, Dec. 1 and 27, 1867, Series 1, Reel 30, Andrew Johnson Papers, Columbia University Microfilm Collection. Fitch refused to bring cases into the United States Court under the Civil Rights Act because he said he could not get convictions for violations of the act. He also felt that the act would not sustain the removal of cases from the state courts into the federal courts. Since other attorneys had succeeded in doing what Fitch said could not be done, his refusal to even test the act reveals his political opposition to its enforcement.

31. "Violations of the Civil Rights Act," pp. 37–43. There is no record of the outcome of the case, but it is quite likely that President Johnson intervened to prevent the exercise of military authority because he had done so under somewhat similar circumstances in the Watson case, and he was expected to do so in another Texas case. Gen. Reynolds to Howard, Feb. 19, 1867, M752, Reel 43, R24, Vol. 9, 1867.

32. Relevant documents are included in "Violations of the Civil Rights Act," pp. 17–37; the quotation is taken from Gen. J. M. Schofield to Howard, Dec. 19, 1866, M752, Reel 40, V588, Vol. 8, 1866; the official proceedings and other records in the case are filed in Virginia, Assistant Commissioner, Letters Received, L345, Vol. 4, 1867.

33. "Violations of the Civil Rights Act," p. 30. Correspondence concerning the procedural, administrative, and political aspects of this case are in M752, Reel 40, V588, Vol. 8, 1866; Howard to Gen. Schofield, Dec. 10, 1866, M742, Reel 2, Vol. 2, p. 478; "Memorandum," in "Case of Dr. James L. Watson," Virginia, Assistant Commissioner, Letters Received, L345, Vol. 4, 1867; Jackson, Mississippi *Daily Clarion*, Jan. 1, 1867, p. 4. President Johnson also impeded civil rights enforcement by appointing military commanders in the South who were political conservatives and hostile to the federal protection of civil rights. For example, he replaced General P. Sheridan with General W. S. Hancock, who refused to use the military in criminal cases even when the local authorities requested military aid. Newspaper clipping, n.t., n.d., McPherson, ed., *Scrapbook on the Civil Rights Bill*, pp. 152–154; Charles Ramsdell, *Reconstruction in Texas* (New York, 1910): 183–185; Sefton, *The United States Army*, chs. 7–8.

34. Howard to Stanton, Nov. 1, 1866, M742, Reel 2, Vol. 2, pp. 379, 403; these conclusions are based on the sources cited in nn. 2, 3, 10, and 11 above and the discussion to which they refer and the following: Judge Hill to Gen. Woods, Nov. 9, 1866, M752, Reel 42, H90, Vol. 9, 1867; Judge Hill to Howard, Mar. 5, 1867, ibid., H34; Gen. Carlin to Howard, Mar. 14, 1867, ibid., Reel 44, T95; Lewis to Howard, Dec. 31, 1866, ibid., T61; "Freedmen's Affairs," pp. 42, 95–96; *House Exec. Doc.* No. 329, pp. 11–12, 35–38, 46–48.

Chapter 3: The Politics of Civil Rights Enforcement in the Federal Courts, 1866–1873

1. Gen. Clinton B. Fisk to Gen. O. O. Howard, May 18 and July 28, 1866, M752, Reel 33, K135 and K171, Vol. 6, 1866, BRFAL, R.G. 105, N.A.; Gen. Wager Swayne to Howard, Jan.

30, 1867, ibid., Reel 41, A57, Vol. 9, 1867; Gen. R. K. Scott to Howard, Feb. 23, 1867, ibid., Reel 44, S90; Gen. Charles Griffin to Howard, Feb. 12, 1867, ibid., T63; Col. C. C. Sibley to Howard, Mar. 19, 1867, ibid., Reel 42, G79; Howard to E. M. Stanton, Jan. 19, 1867, M742, Reel 3, Vol. 3, p. 30, BRFAL, R.G. 105, N.A.; U.S. Senate, "Freedmen's Affairs," 39th Cong., 2d sess., *Sen. Exec. Doc.* No. 6 (Serial 1276, vol. 1).

2. See President Andrew Johnson's vetoes of the Freedmen's Bureau and Civil Rights Bills in John D. Richardson, ed., *A Compilation of the Messages and Papers of the Presidents, 1787–1897,* Vol. 6 (Washington, D.C., 1900): 398–405 and 405–413, respectively. For the political machinations of the president, see LaWanda and John Cox, *Politics, Principle, and Prejudice, 1865–1866* (New York, 1963); Eric McKitrick, *Andrew Johnson and Reconstruction* (Chicago, 1960); Michael Les Benedict has persuasively argued that it was the president's obstruction of congressional policy that prompted and justified his impeachment, *The Impeachment and Trial of Andrew Johnson* (New York, 1973), while Hans L. Trefousse, arguing along similar lines, concludes that the president succeeded in defeating congressional Reconstruction policy. *Impeachment of a President: Andrew Johnson, the Blacks, and Reconstruction* (Knoxville, 1975).

3. J. L. Williamson to James Speed, May 19, 1866, S. C. F., W. D. Tenn., R.G. 60, N.A.; M. F. Pleasants to J. L. Williamson, June 2, 1866, M699, Reel 11, Vol. F, p. 39, R.G. 60, N.A.; Henry Stanbery to A. H. Garland, Feb. 5, 1867, ibid., p. 305.

4. See Stanbery to W. H. Randall, Feb. 5, 1867, M699, Reel 11, Vol. F, p. 304; J. Hubley Ashton to John Hardy, June 21, 1866, ibid., p.173; Ashton to Duff Green, Aug. 2, 1866, ibid., p. 109; Ashton to D. H. Starbuck, Sept. 22, 1866, ibid., p. 161; Ashton to Nathaniel Usher, June 22, 1865, ibid., Reel 10, Vol. E, p. 76. The quotation is from Bland Ballard to H. H. Emmons, July 7, 1870 (box 2, folder 1), Halmer H. Emmons Papers, Burton Historical Collection, Detroit Public Library.

5. These problems of increasing judicial business and limited budgets are reflected in the following: James Speed to Wm. F. Fessenden, Apr. 7, 1866, M699, Reel 10, Vol. E, pp. 472–475; Pleasants to O. H. Browning, Mar. 18, 1868, ibid., Reel 12, Vol. G, pp. 104–105; Browning to Benjamin F. Wade, Mar. 17, 1868, ibid., p. 107; Browning to L. Trumbull, June 25, 1868, ibid., pp. 190–192; E. R. Hoar to James G. Blaine, Dec. 6, 1869, ibid., Reel 13, Vol. H, pp. 131–132; A. T. Akerman to W. W. Belknap, Nov. 9, 1870, ibid., pp. 459–460. United States attorneys in Kentucky attributed most of the increased judicial business to the internal revenue laws and the Civil Rights Act of 1866, and later, to prosecutions under the Enforcement Act of 1870. Benjamin H. Bristow to W. M. Evarts, Dec. 21, 1868, and G. C. Wharton to A. T. Akerman, Nov. 7, 1870, S. C. F., Ky. The quotation is from Robert A. Hill to S. P. Chase, Aug. 16, 1868 (box 7), Salmon P. Chase Papers, The Historical Society of Pennsylvania. The theme of Republicans as reluctant nationalizers is argued by Kermit L. Hall, "The Civil War Era as a Crucible for Nationalizing the Lower Federal Courts," *Prologue* (Fall 1975): 177–186.

6. Gen. Absalom Baird to Maj. A. P. Ketchum, July 23, 1866, M752, Reel 33, L146, Vol. 6, 1866; Maj. Wm. L. Vanderlip to Lt. Col. W. W. Rogers, Mar. 7, 1867, ibid., Reel 41, C100, Vol. 9, 1867; Judge Hill to Howard, Jan. 5, 1867, ibid., Reel 42, H22; James P. Butler to Capt. Barden, Feb. 6, 1867, ibid., Reel 43, R24; Jerrell H. Shofner, *Nor Is It Over Yet: Florida in the Era of Reconstruction, 1863–1877* (Gainesville, Fla., 1974): 98. Federal judges Connally F. Trigg of Tennessee, George S. Bryan of South Carolina, and Richard Busteed of Alabama were notoriously derelict in their judicial duties and absent from their respective courts. See Chapter 4.

7. Professor Harold M. Hyman makes a similar comparison between the difficulties of civil rights enforcement in the 1860s and 1960s in *Lincoln's Reconstruction: Neither Failure of Vision Nor Vision of Failure* (Fort Wayne, Ind., 1980): 24–25.

8. Benjamin H. Bristow to John Marshall Harlan, Mar. 20, 1866 (container 14), John Marshall Harlan Papers, L.C.; John Marshall Harlan to William Belknap, Dec. 15, 1869, John Marshall Harlan Papers, The Filson Club; Bland Ballard to Lyman Trumbull, Mar. 30, 1866 (Vol. 65, reel 18), Lyman Trumbull Papers, L.C., microfilm collection; Noah H. Swayne to Rutherford B. Hayes, Jan. 10, 1870 and Apr. 27, 1871, Rutherford B. Hayes Papers, Rutherford B. Hayes Library; Ross A. Webb, *Benjamin Helm Bristow: Border State Politician* (Lexington, Ky., 1969): 51–58; Ross A. Webb, "Benjamin H. Bristow: Civil Rights Champion, 1866–1872," *Civil War History* 15 (Mar. 1969): 39–42; Victor B. Howard, "The Black Testimony Controversy in Kentucky, 1866–1872," *The Journal of Negro History* 58 (Apr. 1973): 146–147, 153.

9. W. A. Field to Bristow, May 18, 1869, M701, Reel 1, Instruction Book A-1, pp. 291ff., R.G. 60, N.A.; G. C. Wharton to Akerman, Nov. 7, 1870, S. C. F., Ky.; Cincinnati *Gazette,* Mar. 21, 1868, in McPherson, ed., *Scrapbook on the Civil Rights Bill,* p. 155; Webb, "Benjamin H. Bristow," p. 46; Howard, "The Black Testimony Controversy," pp. 146–153.

10. Bristow to Evarts, Dec. 21, 1868, and Wharton to Akerman, Nov. 7, 1870, S. C. F., Ky. Apparently states' rights Democrats also believed that a legislative recognition of equal rights was tantamount to judicial enforcement of those rights. See Victor B. Howard, "The Breckinridge Family and the Negro Testimony Controversy in Kentucky, 1866–1872," *The Filson Club History Quarterly* 49 (Jan. 1975): 37–56, and his "The Black Testimony Controversy," pp. 159–160, 164. Judge Ballard began rejecting cases involving blacks the day after the Kentucky legislature repealed its discriminatory testimony law and replaced it with a racially impartial one on January 30, 1872. He declared that the court's jurisdiction under the Civil Rights Act in such cases was eliminated with the legislative recognition of the right of blacks to testify in the state courts. See his *Charge to the Grand Jury,* Louisville *Courier-Journal,* Feb. 23, 1872, p. 3. Lewis and Richard Collins asserted that Judge Ballard had unofficially declared that he did not intend to allow such cases to continue to encumber the dockets of the federal court. Lewis and Richard J. Collins, *History of Kentucky,* Vol. 1 (Frankfort, Ky., 1966): 222, 224. The Collins' identified the case that inaugurated Judge Ballard's new judicial policy as one involving a black defendant who was charged with grand larceny in the Louisville Circuit Court. This was two months before the Supreme Court first interpreted the Civil Rights Act. The Supreme Court's interpretation would have permitted federal courts to assert jurisdiction in the kinds of cases Judge Ballard said were now outside federal judicial authority. See Chapter 7.

11. Ku Klux Klan terrorism is recounted in U.S. Congress, Joint Select Committee on the Condition of Affairs in the Late Insurrectionary States, 42nd Cong., 2d sess., *House Reports* No. 22 (Serial 1529–1541) or *Senate Reports* No. 41 (Serial 1484–1496), 13 vols., hereinafter cited as *K.K.K. Report.* The accuracy and validity of the testimony given before this committee has been challenged, but it is generally corroborated by the correspondence of the attorney general and local federal attorneys and marshals. The best secondary work on the Klan that documents its terrorism to 1872 is Allen W. Trelease, *White Terror: The Ku Klux Klan Conspiracy and Southern Reconstruction* (New York, 1971).

12. The quotations are taken from H.L.B. to Anna, June 14, 1871; n.d.; Feb. 9, 1871, Hugh Lennox Bond Papers, The Maryland Historical Society; Akerman to Gen. Alfred H. Terry, Nov. 18, 1871, pp. 138–145, Letterbooks, Vol. 1, Akerman Papers, Alderman Library, University of Virginia, microfilm copy; Akerman to James Jackson, Nov. 20, 1871, ibid., pp. 149–160.

13. Akerman to Silliman, Nov. 9, 1871, Letterbooks, Vol. 1, pp. 90–93, Akerman Papers; D. H. Starbuck to Akerman, June 28, 1871, S. C. F., N.C.; Akerman to Charles Prossner, Nov. 17, 1871, M699, Reel 14, Vol. 1, pp. 118–119; Minnis to Geo. H. Williams, Apr. 6, June

25, 1872, ibid., N. and M. D. Ala.; E. P. Jacobson to Williams, Feb. 17, 1872, ibid., S. D. Miss.; Corbin to Williams, Feb. 21, Nov. 21, Dec. 15, 1872, ibid., S.C.; Maj. Lewis M. Merrill to Corbin, enclosed in Merrill to Williams, Sept. 30, 1872, ibid.

14. Minnis to Akerman, Dec. 28, 1871, S. C. F., N. D. Ala.; Akerman to Silliman, Nov. 9, 1871, Letterbooks, Vol. 1, pp. 90–93, Akerman Papers; H.L.B. to Anna, Sept. 20, 1871 and Apr. 18, 1872, Bond Papers; Edgar Needham to Bristow, Dec. 7, 1871 (box 1), Bristow Papers, L.C.

15. Charleston *Daily Courier,* Nov. 27, 1871, p. 2; Atlanta *Constitution,* reprinted in Charleston *Daily Courier,* Oct. 24, 1871, p. 4; Louisville *Courier-Journal,* reprinted in Charleston *Daily Courier,* Apr. 25, 1871, p. 4; Detroit *Post,* Jan. 17, 1871, clipping in box 2, folder 6, Emmons Papers. A good example of the Southern Democrat's view of federal civil rights enforcement is John S. McNeilly, "The Enforcement Act of 1871 and the Ku Klux Klan in Mississippi," *Publications of the Mississippi Historical Society 9* (1906): 109–172, especially at p. 122. For a more balanced and more accurate account, see Otto H. Olsen, "The Ku Klux Klan: A Study in Reconstruction Politics and Propaganda," *The North Carolina Historical Review* 39 (July 1962): 340, especially pp. 341–343. The editor of the Charleston newspaper was mistaken about the imposition of martial law. Professor Trelease has pointed out that martial law was never authorized or imposed by the Grant administration. The Enforcement Act of 1871 authorized only the suspension of habeas corpus. *White Terror,* p. 402 and fn. 5, p. 513. Professor Otis Singletary's study of the Negro Militia during Reconstruction supports the view that the South was in rebellion, although that is not its focus or intention. See his *Negro Militia and Reconstruction* (New York, 1963).

16. The Enforcement Act of May 31, 1870, is cited 16 *U.S. Statutes at Large* 140; the Ku Klux Klan Act of April 20, 1871, is cited 17 *U.S. Statutes at Large* 13. The issue of federal administration of criminal law was explored in *Cong. Globe,* 42nd Cong., 1st sess., Senator Edmunds, pp. 567–568; Congressmen Shellabarger, p. 477; Poland, p. 514; in the *Appendix,* Willard, pp. 187–190; Burchard, pp. 312–316.

17. The congressional speeches supporting this point are too numerous to cite here. The reader is referred to p. 303, fn. 6 of the unpublished copy of this study.

18. The quotation is from Akerman to John H. Caldwell, July 22, 1871, M701, Reel 2, Instruction Book B2, pp. 289–290; the difficulties confronting legal officers are revealed in Akerman to John E. Bryant, July 28, 1871, ibid., pp. 302–303; Akerman to Prossner, Nov. 9, 1871, M699, Reel 14, Vol. I, pp. 127–128; Akerman to Thomas, Nov. 7, 1871, ibid., pp. 118–119; Minnis to Akerman, Sept. 8 and 13, 1871, S. C. F., N. D. Ala.; Bristow to Akerman, Oct. 6, 1871, ibid., Ky.; Wells to Attorney General, Jan. 1, 1872, ibid., N. D. Miss.; Jacobson to Akerman, July 18, 1871, ibid., S. D. Miss.; Judge Robert A. Hill to Bristow, July 28, 1871, ibid; Brown to Akerman, Nov. 14, 1871, ibid., S.C.; H.L.B. to Anna, Sept. 17 and Dec. 18, 1871, Bond Papers.

19. The quotation is from H. H. Wells to Williams, Jan. 23, 1872, S. C. F., Va. These dangers and obstacles were reported in H. H. Wells to Williams, Feb. 11 and 20, 1872, ibid.; F. S. Tukey to Akerman, Dec.—, 1871, ibid.; Judge Busteed to Williams, Mar. 29, 1872, ibid., N. and M. D. Ala.; Judge Hill to Akerman, Aug. 17 and 21, Sept. 5, 1871, ibid., N. D. Miss.; G. Wiley Wells to Akerman, July 15, 1871, and G. Wiley Wells to Williams, Feb. 21, 1872, ibid.; Jacobson to Akerman, July 18 and 19, Aug. 25 and 26, 1871, ibid., S. D. Miss.; the attorney general's reactions are in Akerman to B. F. Tracy, Nov. 15, 1871, M701, Reel 1, Instruction Book A1, pp. 653–654; Akerman to Jacobson, Aug. 26, 1871, ibid., Reel 2, Instruction Book B2, p. 335; Bristow to G. Wiley Wells, Sept. 19, 1871, ibid., p. 370; Akerman to H. H. Wells, Dec. 15, 1871, ibid., Reel 3, Instruction Book C, pp. 96–97; Williams to H. H. Wells, Jan. 19 and 27, 1872, ibid., pp. 146–147 and 152–154, respectively.

20. The quotation is from Allen P. Huggins to Akerman, June 28, 1871, S. C. F., N. D., Miss.; Judge Hill to Akerman, June 21, 1871, ibid., N. D. Miss.; Charleston *Daily Courier*, Nov. 11 and 25, 1871, pp. 2 and 1, respectively; *The New York Times*, Oct. 7 and Nov. 29, 1871, pp. 3 and 4, respectively.

21. Jacobson to Akerman, July 5 and Sept. 13, 1871, S. C. F., S. D. Miss.; Minnis to Akerman, Nov. 26 and Dec. 1, 1871, ibid., N. and M. D. Ala.; Starbuck to Bristow, Oct. 5, 1871, ibid., N.C.; Bristow to Starbuck, Oct. 2, 1871, M701, Reel 2, Instruction Book B2, pp. 388–389; Akerman to Corbin, Jan. 11, 1871, ibid., p. 19; Cousin C. Minahan to George, Feb. 19, [1872] (file 97), David Davis Papers, The Chicago Historical Society; H.L.B. to Anna, Sept. 28, 1871, Bond Papers; *The New York Times*, May 15 and Oct. 7, 1871, pp. 1 and 3, respectively. Federal officers sometimes risked dismissal for political reasons. See E. C. Camp to Emmons, Nov. 11, 1871 (box 1, folder 4), Emmons Papers.

22. Jacobson to Akerman, Sept. 13, 1871 and n.d., S. C. F., S. D. Miss.; Stanwood to U. S. Attorney General, Dec. 20, 1871, ibid., N. D. Miss.; G. Wiley Wells to Akerman, Dec. 11, 1871, ibid.; Corbin to Akerman, Nov. 3 and 20, 1871, ibid., S. C.; Akerman to Minnis, Nov. 11, 1871, M701, Reel 3, Instruction Book C, pp. 22–23. *The New York Times*, Sept. 9, 1871, provides a good summary of the problems faced by federal legal officers.

23. Jacobson to Akerman, Sept. 13, 1871 and n.d., S. C. F., N. D. Miss.

24. James Speed to Wm. P. Fessenden, Apr. 7, 1866, M699, Reel 10, Vol. E, pp. 472–475; Akerman to John N. Montgomery, Aug. 21, 1871, Letterbooks, Vol. 1, pp. 47–49, Akerman Papers; Akerman to James Jackson, Nov. 20, 1871, ibid., pp. 149–160. The enormity of the problem is revealed in Akerman to Silliman, Nov. 9, 1871, ibid., pp. 90–93, E. C. Camp to Judge Emmons, Oct. 9, 1871 (box 1, folder 3), Emmons Papers.

25. The quotations are taken from R. McP. Smith to Emmons, Apr. 12, 1871 (box 1, folder 1), Emmons Papers; and Emmons to Akerman, Nov. 28, 1870, S. C. F., W. D. Tenn.; a copy of this letter is in box 2, folder 6, Emmons Papers. The other points are made in R. McP. Smith to Emmons, June 9, 1871 (box 2, folder 2), Emmons Papers; Jacobson to Akerman, n.d. and Sept. 13, 1871, S. C. F., S. D. Miss.; Huggins to Akerman, June 28, 1871, ibid., N. D. Miss.

26. See *The New York Times*, July 17, 1977, section 3, pp. 1, 7.

27. Judge Emmons to Akerman, Nov. 28, 1870, S. C. F., W. D. Tenn.

28. Minnis to Akerman, Nov. 26 and Dec. 1, 1871, S. C. F., N. and M. D. Ala.; newspaper clipping from the Montgomery *State Journal*, n.d., enclosed in Minnis to Akerman, Dec. 28, 1871, ibid.; Jacobson to Akerman, Sept. 13, 1871, ibid., S. D. Miss.; *The New York Times*, Oct. 5, 1871, p. 1.

29. Wm. J. Promis to Akerman, Aug. 16, 1871, S. C. F., N. and M. D. Ala.; Minnis to Akerman, Dec. 28, 1871, ibid.; Jacobson to Akerman, Aug. 7, 1871, ibid., S. D. Miss.; Starbuck to Akerman, Oct. 5, 1871, ibid., N.C.; Corbin to Akerman, Dec. 3, 1871, ibid., S. C.; *K.K.K. Report*, Vol. 8, p. 562. The partisan character of Southern violence was a recurring theme in Attorney General Akerman's personal correspondence. Akerman to J. H. H. Wilcox, Aug. 16, 1871, Letterbooks, Vol. 1, pp. 33–35, Akerman Papers; Akerman to Blodgett, Nov. 8, 1871, ibid., pp. 83–87; Akerman to McWharton, Nov. 16, 1871, ibid., pp. 134–136; Akerman to Jackson, Nov. 18, 1871, ibid., pp. 149–160. But, sometimes the law was applied against feuding factions of the Republican Party. See Minnis to Akerman, Nov. 18, 1871, S. C. F., N., and M. D. Ala.; Akerman to Minnis, Nov. 24, 1871, M701, Reel 3, Instruction Book C, pp. 120–121.

30. Senator Johnson is quoted in the Charleston *Daily Courier*, Dec. 13, 1871, p. 4. The same point was sounded in ibid., Sept. 6, 1871, p. 2, by Senator James Doolittle in his speech to Wisconsin Democrats, and in ibid., Apr. 25, 1871, p. 4, and the reprints in ibid.

of editorials that appeared in the New York *Evening Post,* New York *Journal of Commerce,* Louisville *Courier-Journal,* Cincinnati *Enquirer,* and the Wilmington *Journal.* The Charleston *Daily Courier* agreed with these views; see ibid., Oct. 26, p. 2; Nov. 25, p. 1; Nov. 27, p. 2. Southern Conservatives also privately expressed the view that they were living through a centralizing and nationalizing revolution in American federalism. See John T. Stuart to Alex. H. H. Stuart, Oct. 30, 1872 (box 1), Alexander H. H. Stuart Papers, Alderman Library, University of Virginia.

31. Pierce to Akerman, Aug. 21, 1871, S. C. F., N. D. Miss.; Akerman to Pierce, Aug. 28, 1871, M701, Reel 2, Instruction Book B2, p. 336; H.L.B. to Anna, Nov. 26, 1871, Bond Papers; Cousin C. Minahan to George, Feb. 19, [1872] (file 97), David Davis Papers, The Chicago Historical Society; *K.K.K. Report,* Vol. 5, pp. 71–72 and Vol. 8, p. 564; for examples of newspapers' characterizations of the racial and partisan composition of federal juries, see the Charleston *Daily Courier,* Sept. 27, p. 4; Nov. 27, p. 2; Nov. 29, p. 4; Dec. 2, p. 1; Dec. 4, p. 1; and Dec. 14, 1871, p. 2; New York *World,* Dec. 26, 1871, reprinted in Charleston *Daily Courier,* Jan. 4, 1872, p. 4; clippings from the New York *Tribune,* Dec. 18, 1871 and Cincinnati *Gazette,* n.d. in Louis F. Post, ed., *Scrapbook on the South Carolina Ku Klux Trials* (container 9), Louis F. Post Papers, L.C.

32. The quotations are taken from Jacobson to Akerman, July 25, 1871, S. C. F., S. D. Miss.; Judge Hill explained his ruling in Judge Hill to Bristow, July 28, 1871, ibid.; the attorney general disagreed with Judge Hill, but could offer little help; Akerman to Jacobson, Aug. 19, 1871, M701, Reel 2, Instruction Book B2, pp. 329–330.

33. Judge Hill to Williams, Dec. 5, 1872, S. C. F., S. D. Miss.; Judge George S. Bryan to Williams, Jan. 1, 1873, ibid., S.C.; *The New York Times,* Apr. 10, 1870, p. 4; *The Albany Law Journal* 1 (Jan. 15, 1870): 36 and 3 (May 27, 1871): 330.

34. J. A. Campbell to Justice Nathan Clifford, June 25, 1871 (box 2, folder 6), Nathan Clifford Papers, Maine Historical Society; H.L.B. to Anna, Apr. 22, 1873, Bond Papers; *The New York Times,* Dec. 11, p. 4; Dec. 15, p. 4; Dec. 16, 1871, pp. 4 and 5; Dec. 5, 1868, p. 4.

35. Corbin to Akerman, Nov. 17, 1871, S. C. F., S.C.; Akerman to Corbin, Dec. 6, 1871, Letterbooks, Vol. 1, pp. 203–205, Akerman Papers; H.L.B. to Anna, Nov. 26, 1871 and n.d., Bond Papers; *The New York Times,* Nov. 11, 1871, p. 1. For a discussion of the South Carolina Ku Klux Klan cases see Chapter 6.

36. The quotation is taken from Akerman to Blodgett, Nov. 8, 1871, Letterbooks, Vol. 1, pp. 83–87; for Akerman's continuing political activities while attorney general, see his Letterbooks, Vol. 1, especially his letters to Silliman, Nov. 9, 1871, pp. 90–93; James Atkins, Nov. 29, 1871, pp. 175–180; and William Marvin, Dec. 6, 1871, pp. 209–212, and *The New York Times,* Nov. 4, 1871, p. 3.

37. Some of the partisan dimensions and activities of federal legal officers are revealed in Robert Alcorn to Williams, Aug. 12 and 22, 1873, S. C. F., S. D. Miss.; Judge Hill to Williams, Aug. 18, 1873, ibid.; Williams to Alcorn, July 8, 1873, M701, Reel 4, Instruction Book D; Bristow to Ma, Sept. 20, 1869 (miscellaneous manuscripts), Benjamin H. Bristow Papers, The Filson Club; J. M. Harlan to Bristow, Sept. 29, 1871 (box 1), Bristow Papers, L. C.; Robt. P. Dick to W. L. Scott, June 15 and Aug. 24, 1870, July 21, 1871, July 4, 1872, William Lafayette Scott Papers, William R. Perkins Library, Duke University; Alphonso Taft to Edwards Pierrepont, Nov. 17, 1870, Edwards Pierrepont Papers, The University of Iowa; Robert W. Hughes to Col. John W. Jenkins, Nov. 29, 1872, Special Collections, Columbia University; Robert W. Hughes, "Opening of the Presidential Campaign in Virginia, Speech of…Delivered at Abingdon, Va., …May 29, 1872," Morris Family Papers, Alderman Library, University of Virginia; *K.K.K. Report,* Vol. 8, pp. 562, 1155. Many of the observations made by Professor Kermit L. Hall concerning the political dimensions of

judicial appointments are applicable to federal attorneys and marshals. See his "101 Men: The Social Composition and Recruitment of the Antebellum Lower Federal Judiciary, 1829–1861," *Rutgers-Camden Law Review* 7 (Winter 1976): 199–227.

38. Bristow to Judge Underwood, May 3, 1872, M699, Reel 14, Vol. 1, pp. 313–314; clipping from the Memphis *Daily Whig & Register*, Dec. 20, 1870 (box 1, folder 4), Emmons Papers; *The New York Times*, June 19, 1868, p. 8. The quotation is taken from Judge Hill to Chief Justice Chase, Aug. 16, 1868 (box 7), Chase Papers, Historical Society of Pennsylvania; also see *The National Cyclopedia of American Biography*, Vol. 11 (New York, 1924): 521. Politics even reached up to the United States Supreme Court. Chief Justice Salmon P. Chase's desire for the White House was well known. Justice David Davis was also a presidential aspirant in 1872. Jeremiah S. Black, petitioners' counsel in the *Blyew* case, consulted with Justice Davis concerning Democratic support for Davis's candidacy just one week after Black had presented his legal arguments before the Court. The Court's decision in the case was returned one month later. J. S. Black to David Davis, Feb. 28, 1872 (file 103), Davis Papers.

39. For judges' perceptions of their roles as implementers of congressional will, see Judge Hill to Bristow, July 28, 1871, S. C. F., S. D. Miss., and *Charge to Grand Jury* enclosed in this letter; Judge Hill to Chief Justice Chase, Aug. 16, 1868 (box 7), Chase Papers, Historical Society of Pennsylvania; *Charge to Grand Jury*, 30 Fed. Cases 987 (No. 18,252) D. W.Va. (1870); *Charge to Grand Jury*, Huntsville *Advocate*, Nov. 12, 1871, clipping enclosed in Judge Busteed to Akerman, Nov. 22, 1871, S. C. F., N., and M. Ala. Congressional Republicans sought to use the federal courts to implement Republican policy; see Kermit L. Hall, "The Civil War Era as a Crucible for Nationalizing the Lower Federal Courts," *Prologue* 7 (Fall 1975): 177–186; Stanley I. Kutler, *Judicial Power and Reconstruction Politics* (Chicago, 1968); Harold M. Hyman, *A More Perfect Union: The Impact of the Civil War and Reconstruction on the Constitution* (New York, 1973): ch. 14. For attributions of political affiliations with constitutional interpretations, see Minnis to Akerman, Dec. 1, 1871, S.C. F., N., and M. D. Ala.; Minnis to Attorney General, Dec. 28, 1871, ibid.; Akerman to Blodgett, July—, 1871, Letterbooks, Vol. 1, pp. 16–17, Akerman Papers; speeches of Senator Doolittle, Charleston *Daily Courier*, Sept. 6, 1871, p. 2; Senator Thurman, ibid., Sept. 11, 1871, p. 2; and Congressman Grosbeck, ibid., Sept. 18, 1871, p. 2; and the editorial in ibid., Sept. 19, 1871, p. 2.

40. While a vast literature exists on the subject of federal judicial behavior, the work of the following scholars was the most useful for the present analysis: Stuart S. Nagel, Kenneth M. Dolbeare, Joel B. Grossman, Joseph Tanenhaus, Peter G. Fish, Sheldon Goldman, Thomas P. Jahinge, Kenneth M. Vines, Richard J. Richardson, and Clement Vose.

41. For Judge Ballard, see 30 F. Cas. 1362; Collins, *History of Kentucky*, Vol. 1, passim; James Speed to Attorney General, Aug. 28, 1869, Circuit Court Appointment Papers, R.G. 60, N.A.; John M. Harlan to the President, Dec. 15, 1869, ibid.; Geo. Hoadly to E. Rockwood Hoar, Dec. 15, 1869, ibid.; Bristow to the President, Aug. 24, 1869, ibid. For Judge George W. Brooks, see *The National Cyclopedia of American Biography*, Vol. 3 (New York, 1924): 167–168; 30 F. Cas. 1365; and J. G. de Roulhac Hamilton, *Reconstruction in North Carolina* (Gloucester, Mass., 1964, reprint of 1914 edition): 522–532, 538. The only information uncovered on George B. Bryan is in 30 F. Cas. 1365 and a clipping from the New York *Tribune*, Dec. 18, 1871, in Post, ed., *Scrapbook*, Post Papers. Information concerning Judge Richard Busteed may be found in *The New York Times*, June 17, 1867, p. 4; 30 F. Cas. 1366; James Grant and John Fiske, eds., *Appleton's Cyclopedia of American Biography*, Vol. 1 (New York, 1888): 476; *Charge to Grand Jury*, newspaper clipping in

Scrapbook, Underwood Papers, p. 227. For Judge Humphrey Howe Leavitt, see Robert C. Schenck to the President, Oct. 15, 1870, U. S. Grant Papers, Rutherford B. Hayes Library; 30 F. Cas. 1382; Dumas Malone, ed., *Dictionary of American Biography,* Vol. 11, pp. 83–84; Grant and Fiske, eds., *Appleton's Cyclopedia of American Biography,* Vol. 3 (New York, 1887): 649. For Judge Connally F. Trigg, see n. 47 below; 30 F. Cas. 1399; Will T. Hale and Dixon C. Merritt, *History of Tennessee and Tennesseans,* Vol. 2 (Chicago, 1913): 391. For Judge John C. Underwood, see obituaries in *Scrapbook,* Underwood Papers; 30 F. Cas. 391; Jack P. Maddox, Jr., *The Virginia Conservatives 1867–1879* (Chapel Hill, 1970): 11, 27, 49, 57; Moger, *Virginia,* p. 6.

42. See Hugh Lennox Bond Papers; W. A. Low, "The Freedmen's Bureau and Civil Rights in Maryland," *The Journal of Negro History 37* (July 1952): 241; Margaret L. Calcott, *The Negro in Maryland Politics* (Baltimore, 1969): 10, 18, fn. 21; Jean H. Baker, *The Politics of Continuity: Maryland Politics from 1858 to 1870* (Baltimore, 1973): 183–188, 199; *Baltimore: Its History and People,* Vols. 1 and 3 (New York, 1912): 834, 899, and 897–899, respectively; Hamilton, *Reconstruction in North Carolina, p.* 532; 30 F. Cas. 1363–1364; Malone, ed., *Dictionary of American Biography,* Vol. 2, pp. 431–432.

43. For Judge Halmer H. Emmons, see Halmer H. Emmons Papers; 30 F. Cas. 1372. For William B. Woods, see New Orleans *Daily Picayune,* Dec. 17, 1869, p. 4; 30 F. Cas. 1403; Leon Friedman and Fred L. Israel, eds., *The Justices of the United States Supreme Court, 1789–1969; Their Lives and Major Opinions,* Vol. 2 (New York, 1969): 1327–1336.

44. Corbin to Williams, Feb. 10, 1872, S. C. F., S.C.

45. The quotation is taken from Hall, "101 Men," p. 226; also see his "The Civil War Era" and "Federal Judicial Reform and Proslavery Constitutional Theory: A Retrospect on the Butler Bill," *The American Journal of Legal History* 18 (Apr. 1973): 166–184. The conclusions concerning politics and the courts during Reconstruction are the author's.

46. Evarts to McCulloch, Nov. 27, 1868, M699, Reel 12, Vol. G, pp. 308–309; Corbin to Senator George F. Edmunds, Feb. 7, 1872, enclosed in Corbin to Williams, Feb. 10, 1872, S. C. F., S.C.; H.L.B. to Anna, n.d., Bond Papers; clipping from the New York *Tribune,* Dec. 18, 1871, Post, ed., *Scrapbook,* Post Papers.

47. The quotations are from Smith to Emmons, Nov. 7, 1870 (box 2, folder 6), Emmons Papers; L. B. Eaton to Emmons, Nov. 10, 1870 (box 2, folder 2), ibid.; Trigg's poor performance as a federal judge is discussed in ibid., Emmons to C. Delano, May 26, 1870 (box 1, folder 1); Emmons to Hoar, May 26, 1870 (box 1, folder 1); H. E. Hudson to Emmons, Nov. 11, 1870 (box 2, folder 6); Hudson to Emmons, Aug. 9, 1871 (box 1, folder 3); Bateman to Emmons, Jan. 5, 1870 (box 2, folder 1) and Nov. 2, 1870 (box 2, folder 6); Smith to Emmons, Mar. 28, 1871 (box 1, folder 1); Oct. 13, 1871 (box 1, folder 3); and Nov. 5, 1871 (box 1, folder 4); Camp to Emmons, Oct. 9, 1871 (box 1, folder 3). There was some talk of impeaching Judge Trigg because of his bias against national authority. See New Orleans *Daily Picayune,* Dec. 19, 1869, p. 8. However, Judge Trigg enjoyed the favor of the Memphis, Tennessee, Bar from which he received an endorsement. Wm. H. Stephens, et al. to Connally F. Trigg, Dec. 13, 1871 (box 2, folder 3), Emmons Papers. Judge Trigg defended himself by deprecating federal legal officers. He said they were of poor quality and tried to compensate for their inability by blaming the court for inadequacies. Judge Trigg to Hoar, Dec. 3, 1869, Ebenezer R. Hoar Papers, Rutherford B. Hayes Library. He nevertheless feared that he had so alienated congressional Radicals that they intended to legislate him out of office by redistricting his judicial district out of existence. Judge Trigg to Judge Emmons, Apr. 2, 1871 (box 1, folder 1), Emmons Papers. They did not.

48. *K.K.K. Report,* Vol. 8, pp. 320–322, 562–564; Judge Busteed to Akerman, Nov. 27, 1871, S. C. F., N., and M. D. Ala.; Minnis to Akerman, Nov. 26 and Dec. 1, 1871, ibid.; Hall, "The Civil War Era," pp. 184–185. Busteed was the subject of a congressional Judiciary Committee investigation for malfeasance in office, but apparently he was exonerated. *The New York Times,* Dec. 31, 1868, p. 1.

49. Akerman to Jacobson, Aug. 18, 1871, Letterbooks, Vol. 1, pp. 44–46, Akerman Papers; Huggins to Akerman, June 28, 1871, S. C. F., N. D. Miss.; Judge Hill to Akerman, June 21, 1871, ibid.; Judge Hill to Bristow, July 28, 1871, ibid., S. D. Miss.; Judge Hill to Chief Justice Chase, Aug. 16, 1868 (box 7), Chase Papers, Historical Society of Pennsylvania; Hall, "The Civil War Era," p. 184.

50. Pierce to Akerman, Aug. 21, 1871, S. C. F., S. D. Miss.; Judge Hill to Bristow, July 28, 1871, ibid.; Maj. Lewis Merrill to Akerman, Nov. 11, 1871, ibid., S.C.; Corbin to Akerman, Nov. 27, 1871, ibid.; Akerman to Pierce, Aug. 28, 1871, M701, Reel 2, Instruction Book B2, p. 336; Akerman to Jackson, Nov. 20, 1871, Letterbooks, Vol. 1, pp. 149–160; H.L.B. to Anna, n.d., Bond Papers.

Chapter 4: The Department of Justice and Civil Rights Enforcement, 1870–1871

1. *The Albany Law Journal* 1 (May 7, 1870): 355; *The American Law Review* 5 (Oct. 1870): 159–161. William Gillette includes a discussion of the Department of Justice in his study of the Grant administration. However, his focus is an analysis of the political history of Grant's two terms. Civil rights enforcement policy and its implementation are surveyed only generally over the entire era. See his *Retreat from Reconstruction, 1869–1879* (Baton Rouge, 1979).

2. *The Albany Law Journal* 1 (Jan. 8, 1870): 13; (June 25, 1870): 491–492; (July 2, 1870): 520; 2 (July 9, 1870): 10–11; *The American Law Review* 4 (Jan. 1870): 390–395; 5 (Oct. 1870): 158–159; *The New York Times,* June 17, pp. 1 and 4; June 20, 1870, p. 1.

3. Amos T. Akerman to B. H. Bristow, July 8, 1870 (box 1), Benjamin H. Bristow Papers, L.C.; Bristow to Akerman, July 12, 1870, ibid.; W. Q. Gresham to U.S. Grant, Sept. 17, 1870, ibid.; W. Dennison to the President, Sept. 24, 1870, ibid.; Bland Ballard to Grant, Sept. 21, 1870, ibid.; *The Albany Law Journal* 2 (Oct. 20, 1870): 309.

4. Allen W. Trelease, *White Terror: The Ku Klux Klan Conspiracy and Southern Reconstruction* (New York, 1971): 402. The discussion that follows buttresses these conclusions.

5. Akerman to John A. Minnis, Feb. 11, 1871, M701, Reel 2, Instruction Book B2, pp. 57–58. For the reluctance of nineteenth-century federal legal officers to enforce federal law, see Homer Cummings and Carl McFarland, *Federal Justice: Chapters in the History of Justice and the Federal Executives* (New York, 1937): ch. 22, especially pp. 469–476, 478.

6. "Circular Relative to Rights of Citizens to Vote in the Several States," July 28, 1870, Circulars of the Attorneys General, R.G. 60, N.A.; "Circular Relative to the Enforcement of the Fourteenth Amendment," July 6, 1871, ibid. Akerman's urgings are too numerous to include them all, but, for representative examples, see Akerman to Starbuck, July 13, 1871, M701, Reel 2, Instruction Book B2, pp. 275–276; Akerman to Judge R. A. Hill, Sept. 12, 1871, Letterbooks, Vol. 1, pp. 70–71, Akerman Papers. For the Chinese cases in California see Akerman to Morris, July 29, 1870, M701, Reel 1, Instruction Book A1, p. 570, and M699, Reel 13, Vol. H, pp. 397–398; Akerman to the President, July 29, 1870, ibid., pp. 396–397.

7. The data concerning federal prosecutions used in this and the following chapters are taken from the following annual reports of the attorney general: (1870–1871) U.S. Congress,

41st Cong., 3rd sess., *House Exec. Doc.* No. 90 (Serial 1454), Appendix B; (1871–1872) and (1872–1873) U.S. Senate, 42nd Cong., 3rd sess., *Senate Exec. Doc.* No. 32 (Serial 1545), Exhibits B and D, respectively; (1873–1874) U.S. Congress, 43rd Cong., 1st sess., *House Exec. Doc.* No. 6 (Serial 1606), Exhibit B; (1874–1875) U.S. Congress, 43rd Cong., 2d sess., *House Exec. Doc.* No. 7 (Serial 1638), Exhibit B; (1875–1876) U.S. Congress, 44th Cong., 1st sess., *House Exec. Doc.* No. 14 (Serial 1686), Exhibit D; (1876–1877) U.S. Congress, 44th Cong., 2d sess., *House Exec. Doc.* No. 20 (Serial 1751), Exhibit B; (1877–1878) U.S. Congress, 45th Cong., 2d sess., *House Exec. Doc.* No. 7 (Serial 1802), Exhibit B.

Financial data used in discussing the expenses of the federal courts in this study are taken from the following annual reports of the attorneys general: (1872–1873), pp. 4–5 and Exhibit C; (1873–1874), pp. 7–10 and Exhibits E and F; (1874–1875), pp. 6–11 and Exhibits D and E; (1875–1876), pp. 11–14 and Exhibits D and L; (1876–1877), pp. 8–9 and Exhibits E and F; (1877–1878), pp. 7–18 and Exhibits D and M. These data are also taken from the following annual reports of the Secretary of the Treasury: (1870–1871) U.S. Congress, 41st Cong., 3d sess., *House Exec. Doc.* No. 5 (Serial 1452), pp. 89–93; (1871–1872) U.S. Congress, 42nd Cong., 2d sess., *House Exec. Doc.* No. 5 (Serial 1509), pp. 85–87, 89–94; (1872–1873) U.S. Congress, 42nd Cong., 3d sess., *House Exec. Doc.* No. 5 (Serial 1564), pp. 46–51; (1873–1874) U.S. Congress, 43rd Cong., 1st sess., *House Exec. Doc.* No. 5 (Serial 1605), pp. 48–49, 51–53; U.S. Congress, "Balance of Appropriations," 43rd Cong., 1st sess., *House Exec. Doc.* No. 235 (Serial 1614), pp. 4–7; (1874–1875) U.S. Congress, 43rd Cong., 2d sess., *House Exec. Doc.* No. 5 (Serial 1643), pp. 44–50; U.S. Congress, "Balances to be Re-appropriated," 43rd Cong., 2d sess., *House Exec. Doc.* No. 113 (Serial 1648), pp. 4–5; (1875–1876) U.S. Congress, 44th Cong., 1st sess., *House Exec. Doc.* No. 5 (Serial 1685), pp. 53–54, 56–58; U.S. Congress, "Deficiencies in Appropriations," 44th Cong., 1st sess., *House Exec. Doc.* No. 151 (Serial 1689), pp. 30–31; (1876–1877) U.S. Congress, 44th Cong., 2d sess., *House Exec. Doc.* No. 5 (Serial 1754), pp. 54–56, 58–61; (1877–1878) U.S. Congress, 45th Cong., 2d sess., *House Exec. Doc.* No. 45 (Serial 1806), pp. 41–43.

In compiling these data, the following inaccuracies in the reports of the attorneys general were noted:

For the year ended December 31, 1870:

Total customs cases as reported were 136; the actual total was 135 or 1 less than the reported amount.

Total Internal Revenue cases as reported were 2,272; they actually totaled 2,201 or 71 less than the reported amount.

Post office cases disposed as reported totaled 135; they actually totaled 124 or 11 less than the reported amount.

Miscellaneous cases disposed as reported totaled 782; they actually totaled 692 or 90 less than the reported amount.

The total of 3,197 used in this study for total cases disposed is 173 less than the total of 3,370 reported by the attorney general. This discrepancy is accounted for by the errors noted above.

For the year ended December 31, 1872:

Internal Revenue cases disposed as reported totaled 2,761; they actually totaled 2,760 or 1 less than the reported amount.

The total of 8,091 used in this study for total cases disposed is 1 less than the total of 8,092 reported by the attorney general. This discrepancy is accounted for by the error noted above.

Prior to the creation of the Department of Justice, records were poorly kept, or, in some cases, they were not kept at all. Even the annual reports of the attorney general sometimes contained fundamental discrepancies that went unnoticed. The standardization of record keeping and reporting and increased accountability within the Justice Department was one of the administrative reforms of the 1870s.

8. See Chapter 3.

9. This poor performance in Tennessee is also explained, in part, by the adverse conditions under which federal legal officers labored in that state. See pp. 49–50, 59.

10. Akerman to Minnis, Feb. 11, 1871, M701, Reel 2, Instruction Book B2, pp. 57–58.

11. Akerman to Jacobson, Sept. 18, 1871, Letterbooks, Vol. 1, pp. 44–46, Akerman Papers; Akerman to Caldwell, Nov. 10, 1871, ibid., pp. 113–117; Trelease, *White Terror*, pp. 191, 318.

12. Akerman to Wingate Hayes, Nov. 15, 1870, M701, Reel 1, Instruction Book A1, p. 652; Bristow to Starbuck, Oct. 2, 1871, ibid., Reel 2, Instruction Book B2, pp. 388–389.

13. See, for example, Bristow to Akerman, Aug. 8, 1871, S. C. F., Ky.; Jacobson to Akerman, July 5, n.d., Aug. 15, Sept. 13, 1871, ibid., S. D. Miss.; Judge Hill to Akerman, June 21 and 23, 1871, ibid., N.D. Miss.; G. Wiley Wells to Akerman, Aug. 21 and Dec. 11, 1871, ibid.; Starbuck to Akerman, July 9, 1871, ibid., N.C.

14. The quotations are from Akerman to Judge Hill, July 27, 1871, M699, Reel 14, Vol. 1, pp. 6–7, and Huggins to Akerman, n.d., S. C. F., N. D. Miss. Examples of the attorney general's refusal to authorize special assistance requested by cabinet officers can be found in Akerman to W. W. Belknap, Nov. 9, 1870, M699, Reel 13, Vol. H, pp. 459–460; Akerman to Geo. S. Boutwell, Nov. 8, 1870 and Jan. 17, 1871, ibid., pp. 457–458 and 577–579, respectively; although requests for special assistance were generally refused, Akerman did make exceptions when the case involved esoteric aspects of law.

15. Akerman to Congressman C. Cole, Jan. 23, 1871, M699, Reel 13, Vol. H., pp. 586–587; Akerman to H. C. Whitley, June 28, 1871, ibid., pp. 777–778; O. E. Babcock to Akerman, June 15, 1871, Letterbooks, Vol. 1, p. 348, Series 2, Reel 3, Ulysses S. Grant Papers, microfilm copy, Columbia University; Akerman to Caldwell, Nov. 10, 1871, Letterbooks, Vol. 1, pp. 113–117, Akerman papers; Gillette, *Retreat from Reconstruction*, p. 49; Albie Burke, "Federal Regulation of Congressional Elections in Northern Cities, 1871–1894" (unpublished Ph. D. dissertation, University of Chicago, 1968): 191.

16. See, for example, Akerman to Starbuck, July 6 and 13, 1871, M701, Reel 2, Instruction Book B2, pp. 260–261 and 275–276, respectively.

17. Akerman to Minnis, Dec. 26, 1871, M701, Reel 3, Instruction Book C, pp. 120–121.

18. The quotation is from Judge Hill to Bristow, July 28, 1871, S. C. F., S. D. Miss; the public's disbelief in the existence of Klan terror was noted in Minnis to Akerman, Dec. 1 and 28, 1871, ibid., N. and M. D. Ala.; Akerman to Minnis, Sept. 8, 1871, M701, Reel 2, Instruction Book B2, pp. 347–348; H.L.B. to Anna, Sept. 28, 1871, Hugh L. Bond Papers, Maryland Historical Society; *The New York Times*, July 26, 1870, p. 4; Oct. 6, p. 4; Oct. 7, 1871, p. 3.

19. The quotation is from Akerman to James R. Beckwith, Jan. 5, 1872, M701, Reel 3, Instruction Book C, p. 137. These political problems were discussed by the attorney gen-

eral in Akerman to Packard, Jan. 6, 1872, ibid., pp. 137–138; *Sen. Exec. Doc.* No. 32, p. 7; *House Exec. Doc.* No. 6, pp. 17–18.

20. Jacobson to Akerman, July 5, 1871, S. C. F., S. D. Miss; Minnis to Akerman, Dec. 1, 1871, ibid., N. and M. D. Ala.; Judge Busteed to Akerman, Nov. 22, 1871, ibid.

21. Akerman to Minnis, Nov. 11 and Dec. 26, 1871, M701, Reel 3, Instruction Book C, pp. 22–23 and 120–121, respectively; Akerman to Jacobson, July 11, 1871, ibid., Reel 2, Instruction Book B2, pp. 271–272; Akerman to Corbin, Dec. 6, 1871, Letterbooks, Vol. 1, pp. 203–205.

22. H.L.B. to Anna, Sept. 27, 1871, Bond Papers; U.S. Congress, "Annual Report of the Attorney General," 42nd Cong., 2d sess., *House Exec. Doc.* No. 55 (Serial 1510), pp. 4–5. On the need for extraordinary assistance, see nn. 13, 16, and 18 above.

23. The quotation is from Starbuck to Bristow, Oct. 5, 1871, S. C. F., N.C. Convictions carried punishments of up to six years' imprisonment and $5,000 fines. *The New York Times,* Oct. 7, 1871, p. 4; J. G. de Roulhac Hamilton, *Reconstruction in North Carolina* (New York, 1914): 577–580.

24. *House Exec. Doc.* No. 55, p. 5.

25. Ibid., pp. 4–5; *Senate Exec. Doc.* No. 32, p. 11. For a discussion of the legal implications of the South Carolina Ku Klux trials, see pp. 98–106. For Corbin's performance in pretrial motions, see pp. 126–127 below. Convictions in the South Carolina cases carried penalties ranging from three months' to five years' imprisonment and fines of $10 to $1,000.

26. Still, the 98 cases pending in North Carolina at the end of 1871 included some 930 defendants. *Senate Exec. Doc.* No. 32, p. 10.

27. *House Exec. Doc.* No. 55, p. 5. The attorney general had to refuse a request for additional federal protection to his own state because the magnitude of Ku Klux crime and the limited resources of the federal government made it impossible to maintain a meaningful federal presence everywhere in the South. Akerman to Charles Hooks, Dec. 6, 1871, M699, Reel 14, Vol. 1, pp. 179–180. He dismally confided to a friend that, although the local courts completely failed to protect persons and property, "it seems to me that it is too much even for the United States to undertake to inflict adequate penalties through the courts." Akerman to B. D. Silliman, Nov. 9, 1871, Letterbooks, Vol. 1, pp. 90–93, Akerman Papers. He nevertheless remained unflagging in his resolve to protect civil rights. He wrote to political confidant, Foster Blodgett, that "if our perverse fellow-citizens subject the Government to the necessity of either permitting the guilty to persecute the innocent, or punishing the guilty by extraordinary means, I am for the latter. . . ." Akerman to Blodgett, Nov. 8, 1871, ibid., pp. 83–87.

28. Akerman to Corbin, Nov. 10, 1871, M701, Reel 3, Instruction Book C, pp. 28–30.

29. Akerman to Charles Prossner, Nov. 9, 1871, M699, Reel 14, Vol. 1, pp. 127–128; Akerman to George F. Burnett, Dec. 1871, Letterbooks, Vol. 1, pp. 240–242, Akerman Papers; Akerman to Corbin, Nov. 16, 1871, M701, Reel 3, Instruction Book C, pp. 47–48.

30. H.L.B. to Anna, Sept. 17 and 28, Dec. 18 and 28, 1871, and n.d., Bond Papers; Akerman to James Jackson, Nov. 20, 1871, Letterbooks, Vol. 1, pp. 149–160, Akerman Papers; Corbin to Akerman, Nov. 3, 1871, S. C. F., S.C.

31. Akerman to H. P. Farrow, Nov. 25, 1871, Letterbooks, Vol. 1, pp. 162–167, Akerman Papers; Akerman to J. R. Parrot, Dec. 6, 1871, ibid., pp. 213–220; Akerman to Jackson, Nov. 20, 1871, ibid., pp. 149–160; Akerman to Maj. Merrill, Nov. 9, 1871, ibid., pp. 94–97; Akerman to Gen. Terry, Nov. 18, 1871, ibid., pp. 138–145; Akerman to Benjamin Conley, Dec. 28, 1871, ibid., pp. 272–277; Akerman to James Atkins, Nov. 29, 1871, ibid., pp. 175–180.

32. Akerman to Corbin, Dec. 15, 1871, ibid., pp. 250–253; Akerman to Conley, Dec. 28, 1871, ibid., pp. 272–278; Akerman to Silliman, Jan. 1, 1872, ibid., pp. 296–297; *The Albany*

Law Journal 3 (Mar. 4, 1871): 168; (Mar. 18, 1871): 208; 8 (Dec. 6, 1873): 358; (Dec. 20, 1873): 388; (Dec. 27, 1873): 408; 9 (Jan. 10, 1874): 21; *The American Law Review* 8 (Jan. 1874): 354–355; Louisville *Courier-Journal,* Dec. 2, 1871, p. 1; *The New York Times,* Nov. 8, 1871, p. 2; Charleston *Daily Courier,* Jan. 8, 1872, p. 2. As to the priorities of the Grant administration, see Gillette, *Retreat from Reconstruction;* B. Hesseltine, *Ulysses S. Grant: Politician* (New York, 1957); Harold M. Hyman, *A More Perfect Union: The Impact of the Civil War and Reconstruction on the Constitution* (New York, 1973). In chapter 14 of the latter, Hyman argues that Americans in this era were committed to a balanced budget and restricted government. In short, they were unredeemed liberals.

33. The quotation is from Akerman to Conley, Dec. 28, 1871, Letterbooks, Vol. 1, pp. 272–277, Akerman Papers. Akerman informed federal legal officers of his belief that Williams would continue his enforcement policies; Akerman to Minnis, Jan. 3, 1872, ibid., p. 310; Akerman to Maj. Merrill, Jan. 8, 1872, ibid., pp. 312–314.

34. H.L.B. to Anna, Apr. 11 and 14, 1872, Bond Papers.

35. H.L.B. to Anna, Sept. 21, [1871], ibid.; Minnis to Williams, June 25 and Apr. 1, 1872, S. C. F., N., and M. D. Ala.; Corbin to Williams, Nov. 2, 1872, ibid., S.C. Attorney General Williams observed in his annual report for 1872 that only fifteen new indictments were instituted in North Carolina under the Enforcement Acts, and, with three exceptions, they were for infractions committed before 1872. *House Exec. Doc.* No. 6, p.11.

36. H.L.B. to Anna. Apr. 14, 1872, Bond Papers; G. Wiley Wells to Williams, Apr. 2 and July 8, 1872, S. C. F., S. D. Miss.; Corbin to Williams, July 22, 1872, ibid., S.C.; Minnis to the Attorney General, Dec. 28, 1871, and Minnis to Williams, Apr. 1, 1872, ibid., N. and M. D. Ala.

37. Wharton to Williams, Mar. 27, 1872, S. C. F., Ky.; C. T. Garland to Williams, Apr. 1872, ibid., W. D. Tex.; A. J. Evans to Williams, Dec. 8, 1872, ibid. Also see H.L.B. to Anna, Dec. 11, 1872, Bond Papers.

38. Minnis to Williams, Jan. 10, Apr. 1, and June 25, 1872, S. C. F., N., and M. D. Ala.; Judge Busteed to Williams, Mar. 29, 1872, ibid.; David P. Lewis to Williams, July 1872, ibid.; G. Wiley Wells to Williams, Mar. 9, 1872, ibid., N. D. Miss.; Wm. F. Dowd to Bristow, Sept. 9, 1872, ibid.

39. Robert W. Healy to Williams, Feb. 26, 1872, ibid., N. and M. D. Ala.; Judge Busteed to Williams, Mar. 29, 1872, ibid.; Judge Hill to Williams, Jan. 10, 1872, ibid., N. D. Miss.; G. Wiley Wells to Williams, Jan. 16, Feb. 21, Mar. 4, and July 8, 1872, ibid.; Williams to Sec. Belknap, Jan. 17, Feb. 29, Mar. 8, and July 11, 1872, M702, Reel 1, Vol. A, pp. 454, 534, 558, 731, respectively.

40. See n. 31 above; Trelease, *White Terror,* p. 411; Hesseltine, *Ulysses S. Grant,* p. 262.

Chapter 5: The Department of Justice and the Retreat from Civil Rights Enforcement, 1872–1873

1. William B. Hesseltine, *Ulysses S. Grant: Politician* (New York, 1957): 262.

2. Williams to Maj. Merrill, July 13, 1872, M699, Reel 14, Vol. 1, pp. 370–371; Williams to Judge Busteed, Apr. 9, 1872, ibid., p. 294; Williams to John D. Pope, Feb. 23, 1872, M701, Reel 3, Instruction Book C, p. 194; Minnis to the Attorney General, Apr. 6, 1872, S. C. F., N., and M. D. Ala.

3. Williams to Starbuck, Mar. 14 and 25, 1872, M701, Reel 3, Vol. C, pp. 218, 236–237, respectively; Williams to Corbin, Mar. 25, 1872, ibid., pp. 239–240; Williams to William E. Earle, Feb. 27, 1872, M699, Reel 14, Vol. 1, p. 256. There is a discrepancy between Williams's claimed deficit of $300,000 and the surplus of $123,667 he included in his annual report for 1872. This

appears to be due to the Justice Department's borrowing from funds appropriated for fiscal 1873 and subsequent deficiency appropriations. See U. S. Senate, "Annual Report of the Attorney General," 42nd Cong., 3 sess., *Sen. Exec. Doc.* No. 32 (Serial 1545), p. 6.

4. Williams to S. T. Carrow, July 13 and 24, 1872, M701, Reel 3, Instruction Book C, pp. 385–386 and 403–404, respectively; Williams to R. M. Wallace, Aug. 27, 1872, ibid., pp. 438–439.

5. See the citations in nn. 3 and 4 above, and *Senate Exec. Doc.* No. 32, p. 7; U. S. Congress, "Annual Report of the Attorney General," 43rd Cong., 1st sess., *House Exec. Doc.* No. 6 (Serial 1606), pp. 6, 17; *The Albany Law Journal 3* (May 27, 1871): 330–331; 8 (Oct. 25, 1873): 260. The one state for which the attorney general most probably had evidence for his charges was Arkansas. Judicial expenses in that state were much higher than those of other states that disposed of more cases. For the fiscal year ended June 30, 1872, for example, Arkansas expended $284,332 in disposing of 341 criminal cases and 142 civil cases in which the United States was a party. Mississippi, by contrast, spent $143,025 in disposing of 623 criminal cases and 102 civil cases in which the United States was a party. *Senate Exec. Doc.* No. 32, pp. 4, 28–29, 34–35.

6. *Senate Exec. Doc.* No. 32, p. 10. A report of judicial expenses for the periods Mar. 1, 1867–Mar. 1, 1869, $3,437,627; and Mar. 1, 1869–Mar. 1, 1871, $4,703,457, can be found in *The Albany Law Journal 3* (Mar. 11, 1871): 200. These amounts were much lower than the annual expenditures of the courts during the 1870s. Note, too, that the number of cases reported for North Carolina as discussed by the attorney general does not correspond to the number of cases for North Carolina in his summary. See *Senate Exec. Doc.* No. 32, pp. 10 and 36.

7. *Senate Exec. Doc.* No. 32, p. 10; Corbin to Senator Edmunds, Feb. 7, 1872, enclosed in Corbin to Williams, Feb. 10, 1872, S. C. F., S.C. Judge Robert P. Dick was a native North Carolinian who, before the Civil War, was "one of the ablest and most active members of the Democratic party in the State." Until the outbreak of the Civil War, he served as United States attorney for North Carolina with the endorsement of Supreme Court Justice James M. Wayne and Governor Thomas Bragg. He served in the North Carolina Senate during the Civil War, but was appointed United States district judge for North Carolina by President Johnson. Legal disabilities stemming from the war prevented his occupying the federal bench for more than two months. He became one of the organizers and leaders of the Republican Party in North Carolina, and he was one of the North Carolina Supreme Court justices who interpreted federal civil rights enforcement authority broadly. However, he was described by Professor Hamilton as a Conservative Republican. The quotation is from L. O. B. Branch to the President, Mar. 30, 1857, United States Circuit Court Appointment Papers, R.G. 60, N.A. For Judge Dick's political background, see James M. Wayne to the President, Mar. 24, 1857, ibid.; Tho. Bragg to James Buchanan, Mar. 20, 1857, ibid.; Robt. P. Dick to W. L. Scott, June 15, 1870, July 21, 1871, July 4, 1872, William Lafayette Scott Papers, Perkins Library, Duke University; J. G. de Roulhac Hamilton, *Reconstruction in North Carolina* (Gloucester, Mass., reprint of 1914 edition, 1964): passim.

8. The remainder of this chapter discusses Attorney General Williams's changing civil rights enforcement policy. Tennessee and Alabama are exceptions to this generalization. Enforcement Acts prosecutions in Tennessee were usually *nolle prosequi*, while few cases were reportedly instituted in Alabama.

9. Williams to Zachariah Thomas, Dec. 13, 1872, Reel 3, Instruction Book C, p. 544; Williams to Carrow, July 13 and 24, 1872, ibid., pp. 385–386 and 403–404, respectively; Williams to James A. Garfield, Dec. 13 and 14, 1872, M702, Reel 2, Vol. B, pp. 79 and 85–86, respectively; "Circular Relative to Court Expenses, etc.," Feb. 12, 1873, Circulars of the Attorneys General, R.G. 60, N.A.

10. Williams to Minnis, Sept. 17, 1872, M701, Reel 3, Instruction Book C, pp. 458–459; Williams to Farrow, Nov. 26, 1872, ibid., p. 525; Williams to Packard, Dec. 3, 1872, ibid., p. 532; Williams to H. H. Wells, Jan. 7, 1873, ibid., p. 568.

11. Maj. Lewis Merrill to the Attorney General, Sept. 30, 1872, S. C. F., S.C.

12. Williams to Alexander H. Stephens, Sept. 16, 1872, M699, Reel 14, Vol. 1, pp. 429–431; concerning the peacefulness of the 1872 election, see Minnis to Williams, July 18, 1873, ibid., N. and M. D. Ala.; Beckwith to Williams, Feb. 23, 1873, ibid., La.; Jacobson to Williams, Jan. 17, 1873, ibid., S. D. Miss. Not all areas, however, were peaceful. See Evans to Williams, Dec. 6, 1872, ibid., W. D. Tex.; Packard to Williams, Nov. 16, 1872, ibid., La.; H.L.B. to Anna, Dec. 11, 1872, Bond Papers.

13. Corbin to Williams, Nov. 21, 1872, S. C. F., S.C.

14. Williams to Corbin, Nov. 26 and Dec. 7, 1872, M701, Reel 3, Instruction Book C, pp. 525 and 535–536, respectively.

15. Evans to Williams, n.d., S. C. F., W. D. Tex.; Williams to Evans, Apr. 16, 1873, M701, Reel 3, Instruction Book C, p. 696.

16. Williams to James M. Blount, Apr. 15, 1873, M699, Reel 14, Vol. 1, pp. 681–682. The *Boston Globe*, for example, reportedly announced that the attorney general had given notice that all Enforcement Acts cases would be suspended if affairs in the South continued to be quiet. Reprinted in New Orleans *Daily Picayune*, Apr. 15, 1873, p. 1.

17. Williams to Lusk, June 21, 1873, M701, Reel 4, Instruction Book D, p. 91.

18. W. D. Porter, J. B. Kershaw, and R. M. Sims to Williams, July 30, 1873, S. C. F., S.C.; Williams to Porter, Kershaw, and Sims, July 31, 1873, M699, Reel 15, Vol. K, pp. 40–41. Judge Bryan to Williams, n.d., enclosed in Porter's letter to Williams. Kershaw was the leader of South Carolina Democratic Conservatives. Joel Williamson, *After Slavery: The Negro in South Carolina During Reconstruction, 1861–1877* (Chapel Hill, 1965): 350, 355, 400, fn. 105. Some evidence fed the vain hope that Southerners would respect the rights of blacks. Ku Klux terrorism frightened even some white Democratic Conservatives and disrupted white-controlled economic operations. Although white Democratic Conservatives rarely condemned Ku Klux tactics publicly, privately they desired an end to such activity. In addition to self-serving guarantees to protect civil rights made by Democratic Conservative politicians in Congress and around the South, see Minnis to Williams, Dec. 23, 1873, S. C. F., N., and M. D. Ala.; G. Wiley Wells to Williams, Mar. 9, 1872, ibid., N. D. Miss.; Jacobson to Williams, Jan. 17, 1873, ibid., S. D. Miss.; Wharton to Williams, Mar. 23, 1872, ibid., Ky.; *The New York Times,* Sept. 10, 1871, p. 1; Louisville *Courier-Journal,* Oct. 11, 1872, pp. 1 and 2. In light of the record of civil rights violations in the South, one must conclude that the administration's desire to make peace with the South and rid itself of the expensive and onerous task of protecting civil rights prompted it to exaggerate Democratic Conservatives' distaste for Ku Klux terror and their self-serving statements of respect for civil rights into a false expectation of a genuine Southern benevolence toward the rights and safety of blacks and Republicans.

19. Minnis to Williams, Dec. 23 and 26, 1873, Apr. 4, 1874, S. C. F., N., and M. D. Ala.; Corbin to Williams, Mar. 28, 1874, ibid., S.C.; Lusk to Williams, Apr. 20, 1874, ibid., N.C.; Plato Durham to S. F. Phillips, Apr. 22, 1874, ibid.; Williams to Minnis, Dec. 8 and 29, 1873 and Apr. 8, 1874, M701, Reel 4, Instruction Book D, pp. 320, 344–345, and 485, respectively; Williams to G. Wiley Wells, July 2, 1874, ibid., p. 610; Williams to Corbin, Mar. 17, 1874, ibid., pp. 454–455; Williams to Lusk, Apr. 25, 1874, ibid., p. 514; Williams to T. J. Robertson, Mar. 17 and 31, 1874, M702, Reel 2, Vol. B, pp. 459 and 468, respectively.

20. Bristow to Williams, Oct. 19, 1873, S. C. F., Ky.; Williams to Bristow, Oct. 24, 1873, M699, Reel 15, Vol. K, p. 165.

Chapter 6: The Judicial Administration of Civil Rights Enforcement, 1870–1872

1. *K.K.K. Report,* Vol. 8, pp. 322, 562, 564–565, 567; *Charge to Grand Jury,* reported in the Huntsville *Advocate,* Nov. 12, 1871, enclosed in Judge Richard Busteed to Amos Akerman, Nov. 22, 1871, S. C. F., N. D. Ala.; *Charge to Grand Jury,* newspaper clipping, n.t., n.d., enclosed in Wm. J. Promis to Akerman, Aug. 16, 1871, ibid.; J. A. Minnis to Akerman, Nov. 18, 1871, ibid.; Akerman to Minnis, Nov. 24, 1871, M701, Reel 3, Instruction Book C, pp. 64–65.

2. The full record of the case is reprinted in *K.K.K. Report,* Vol. 12, pp. 934–987. Background to the Mississippi cases can be found in John S. McNeilly, "The Enforcement Act of 1871 and the Ku Klux Klan in Mississippi," *Publications of the Mississippi Historical Society* 9 (1906): 127–143; and James W. Garner, *Reconstruction in Mississippi* (New York, 1901): 349–353.

3. Judge R. A. Hill to Akerman, June 21, 1871, S. C. F., N. D. Miss.

4. The quotation is in *K.K.K. Report,* Vol. 12, p. 986.

5. Ibid.

6. *Charge to Grand Jury,* enclosed in Judge Hill to Benjamin H. Bristow, July 28, 1871, S. C. F., N. D. Miss.

7. Judge Hill's weakness hampered efforts of Justice Department officers in enforcing federal law despite his expansive interpretations of national civil rights enforcement authority. Deputy Marshal Huggins complained that they had to brace themselves against "the known weakness of Judge Hill." Overawed by Ku Klux terrorism, Judge Hill was even reluctant to deal firmly with parties before his court. "The council for them has gone so far as to openly say 'I defy the Court,' . . ." Huggins informed the attorney general. Huggins to Akerman, June 28, 1871, ibid. The federal marshal also complained about Judge Hill's leniency. J. H. Pierce to Akerman, June 24, 1871, ibid. During the Ku Klux cases an altercation broke out between L. Q. C. Lamar, counsel for the defendants, and a deputy marshal in which Lamar knocked the officer to the floor. Judge Hill dealt leniently with the future United States Supreme Court justice because he believed that Lamar's action was the result of an unspecified illness from which he was suffering. Professor McNeilly, however, blamed the deputy marshal for the fight. See Judge Hill to Bristow, July 28, 1871, ibid.; McNeilly, "The Enforcement Act of 1871," pp. 142–143. Judge Hill's leniency is partially explained by the need he felt to cultivate and retain the cooperation of the local bar. See p. 60.

8. E. P. Jacobson to Akerman, Aug. 4 and 7, 1871, S. C. F., S. D. Miss.

9. Akerman to Jacobson, Aug. 16, 1871, M701, Reel 2, Instruction Book B2, p. 324, R.G. 60, N.A.

10. Judge Hill to Bristow, May 13, 1872 (container 2), Bristow Papers, L.C.; Jacobson to Williams, Feb. 17, 1872, S. C. F., S. D. Miss. However, neither Jacobson's counterpart in the Northern District of Mississippi nor Williams had such doubts. See G. Wiley Wells to Williams, Mar. 5 and Apr. 2, 1872, ibid., N. D. Miss.; Williams to W. D. Porter, J. B. Kirshaw, and R. M. Sims, July 31, 1873, M699, Reel 15, Vol. K, pp. 40–41, R.G. 60, N.A. The congressional framers of civil rights legislation also had struggled with the problem of avoiding the elimination of local authority over ordinary crimes. The Ku Klux Klan Act of 1871, for example, was amended because of fears that it supplanted state criminal laws relating to crimes such as murder, manslaughter, mayhem, robbery, assault and battery, perjury, subornation of perjury, arson, and larceny, in addition to criminal obstruction of the legal process and resistance of officers in the discharge of their duty. The framers attempted to circumvent this difficulty by defining federal crimes that involved these offenses as con-

spiracies to commit murder, manslaughter, etc., with the intent or for the purpose of depriving citizens of their civil or political rights or for political purposes. See *Cong. Globe*, 42nd Cong., 1st sess., the comments of Congressmen Shellabarger, p. 477; Poland, p. 514; in the *Appendix*, Congressmen Willard, pp. 187–190; Burchard, pp. 312–316; Senator Edmunds, pp. 567–568.

11. *United States v. Avery*, 80 U.S. (13 Wall.) 251 (1871); Corbin to Akerman, Nov. 13 and 17, 1871, S. C. F., S.C.

12. Akerman to Corbin, Nov. 16, 1871, M701, Reel 3, Instruction Book C, pp. 47–48; Corbin to Akerman, Nov. 17, 1871, S. C. F., S.C.; *K.K.K. Report*, Vol. 5, pp. 78–79.

13. The proceedings of the trials were printed and published in *Proceedings in the Ku Klux Trials at Columbia, S.C. in the United States Circuit Court, November Term, 1871* (Columbia, S.C., 1872); they were also reprinted in *K.K.K. Report*, Vol. 5, pp. 1599–1990. Louis F. Post, United States Attorney Corbin's law clerk, wrote articles for several newspapers reporting the trials. Some of these reports were collected in his *Scrapbook on the South Carolina Ku Klux Trials* (container 9), Louis F. Post Papers, L.C. A brief, but good summary of the trials was written by Post and appeared in the Indianapolis *Journal*, Dec. 12, 1871 (box 2, folder 3), Halmer H. Emmons Papers, Burton Historical Society, Detroit Public Library. The Charleston *Daily Courier* presents a running account of the trials from November 1871 through early January 1872. Reynold, *Reconstruction in South Carolina* (Columbia, S.C., 1905): 202–216, is a useful, if hostile, account of the trials.

14. The indictments are in *Proceedings in the Ku Klux Trials*, pp. 825–832.

15. D. H. Starbuck to Akerman, June 28, July 9, 1871, S. C. F., N.C.; Starbuck to Bristow, Oct. 5, 1871, ibid.; Akerman to Starbuck, July 3, 6, 13, 1871, M701, Reel 2, Instruction Book B2, pp. 252, 260–261, 275–276, respectively; Bristow to Starbuck, June 10, Oct. 2, 1871, ibid., pp. 230, 388–389, respectively.

16. Stanbery's argument is in *Proceedings in the Ku Klux Trials*, pp. 16–34; the quotation is at pp. 30–31.

17. Senator Johnson's remarks are in ibid., pp. 68–88; the quotation is at p. 71.

18. For Senator Johnson's views in the 1866 civil rights debate, see *Cong. Globe*, 39th Cong., 1st sess., pp. 530, 548, 1777. For a report of his speech before Baltimore Democrats, see the Charleston *Daily Courier*, Nov. 6, 1871, p. 2.

19. Attorney General Chamberlain's arguments are in *Proceedings in the Ku Klux Trials*, pp. 34–58.

20. United States Attorney Corbin's comments are in ibid., pp. 58–69.

21. Ibid., p. 65. In fairness to Corbin, it should be recalled that he and other legal officers were overwhelmed by the magnitude of the work involved in preparing Ku Klux cases for trial. See Chapters 3 and 4. Still, overwork might help to explain a poorly constructed brief, but it fails to account for the evident hostility he expressed toward civil rights enforcement. Both are perplexing, for Attorney General Akerman visited Corbin and assisted him in preparing the prosecutions and perceived Corbin to be as committed to civil rights enforcement as he was. Akerman to Bristow, Oct. 20, 1871 (container 1), Bristow Papers, L.C. The attorney general's attitude toward Corbin is reflected in the correspondence between them.

22. *Crosby*, 25 F. Cas. 701 at 704. The editor of *The New York Times* applauded the ruling insofar as it related to congressional powers to protect voting rights. Dec. 11, 1871, p. 4. Judge Bond, sitting with District Judge William F. Giles, again upheld the constitutionality of the Enforcement Act of 1870 under the Fourteenth and Fifteenth Amendments, and ruled "that it applied to the protection of the right of suffrage of both white and colored citizens at all Elections, both State, and Federal." This ruling was made at the April 1872

term of the United States Circuit Court at Baltimore, Maryland. A. Sterling, Jr. to Attorney General, May 22, 1874, S. C. F., Md.

23. *Crosby*, 25 F. Cas. at 704.

24. *Proceedings in the Ku Klux Trials*, pp. 93–94, 139–145; Charleston *Daily Courier*, Dec. 8, 9, and 11, 1871, pp. 1, 1, and 4, respectively; New York *Tribune*, Dec. 18, 1871, in Post, ed., *Scrapbook* (container 9), Post Papers; Akerman to Corbin, Dec. 6, 1871, Letterbooks, Vol. 1, pp. 203–205, Akerman Papers; H.L.B. to Anna, Nov. 26, 1871, and n.d., Hugh L. Bond Papers, The Maryland Historical Society.

25. *United States v. Mitchell* is in *Proceedings in the Ku Klux Trials*, pp. 146–153, 451, 459; also see Charleston *Daily Courier*, Dec. 13, p. 4; 14, p. 2; 15, p. 2; 19, p. 1; 25, p. 1, and 29, 1871, p. 1; New York *Tribune*, Dec. 21, 1871, clipping in Post, ed., *Scrapbook* (container 9), Post Papers.

26. *Avery*, 80 U.S. (13 Wall.) 251; Corbin to Akerman, Dec. 22, 1871, S. C. F., S.C.; Akerman to Corbin, Jan. 2, 1872, M701, Reel 3, Instruction Book C, p. 131.

27. *Avery*, 80 U.S. (13 Wall.) 251. The precedent upon which the Court's decision was based is *United States v. Rosenburgh*, 74 U.S. (7 Wall.) 580 (1868).

28. The quotation is from Geo. H. Williams to Reverdy Johnson, Feb. 29, 1872, M699, Reel 14, Vol. 1, pp. 258–259.

29. Judge Hill to Bristow, May 13, 1872 (container 2), Bristow Papers, L.C.

30. Judge Cadwalader's ruling is not reported. Judge John Underwood made a brief reference to it in one of his charges to a grand jury. See newspaper clipping, n.t., n.d., in *Letterbook*, p. 227, John C. Underwood Papers, L.C. Judge Ballard's ruling is discussed at p. 165, fn. 71, 174. Recent civil rights struggles and federal judges are discussed in Jack W. Peltason, *58 Lonely Men* (New York, 1961); Charles V. Hamilton, *The Bench and the Ballot: Southern Federal Judges and Black Voters* (New York, 1973).

Chapter 7: The Supreme Court as Legislature: The Judicial Retreat from Civil Rights Enforcement

1. Amos Akerman to Benjamin Conley, Dec. 28, 1871, Letterbooks, Vol. 1, pp. 272–277, Amos T. Akerman Papers, Alderman Library, University of Virginia. The Supreme Court decisions here referred to are *Slaughter-House Cases*, 83 U.S. (16 Wall.) 36 (1873) and *Blyew*, 80 U.S. (13 Wall.) 581 (1872). For a political history of the period, see William Gillette, *Retreat from Reconstruction, 1869–1879* (Baton Rouge, 1979).

2. Judge R. H. Stanton to Jere. S. Black, Nov. 23, 1870 (Vol. 52, reel 26), Jeremiah S. Black Papers, Columbia University, microfilm collection; Bristow to Hoar, Apr. 22, 1869, S. C. F., Ky.; the proceedings of the lower federal court are in the *Briefs for Appellee, Blyew*, 80 U.S. (13 Wall.) 581, and in Supreme Court Case File No. 5558, R.G. 267, N.A.

3. Louisville *Courier-Journal*, Nov. 29, 1868, p. 4.

4. Ibid. See pp. 10–11 for my discussion of rulings allowing the states a voice in prescribing conditions under which civil rights were to be enjoyed.

5. Louisville *Courier-Journal*, Nov. 29, 1868, p. 4; Maysville *Bulletin*, n.d., is reprinted in Louisville *Courier-Journal*, Dec. 19, 1868, p. 1.

6. Bristow to Hoar, May 18, Apr. 22, and Nov. 9, 1869, S. C. F., Ky.; Hoar to Isaac Caldwell, Apr. 2 and 11, 1870, M699, Reel 13, Vol. H, pp. 260 and 274; Victor B. Howard, "The Black Testimony in Kentucky, 1866–1872," *The Journal of Negro History* 58 (Apr. 1973): 159; Ross A. Webb, *Benjamin Helm Bristow: Border State Politician* (Lexington, Ky., 1969): 59. United States Attorney Bristow and Caldwell had agreed to bring as a test case to the Supreme Court another case, *Commonwealth of Kentucky v. Conley*, but the agreement fell through in March 1870 for some unspecified reason. Attorney General Hoar,

therefore, advanced the *Blyew* case for argument to begin in April 1870, but defense counsel could not present their case on such short notice. The government could have moved to dismiss the appeal and could have executed sentence, or it could have proceeded ex parte, but the attorney general wanted the issues to be fully argued and settled. The case was therefore rescheduled for argument to begin on the first Tuesday of December, but, for some unknown reason, the Supreme Court delayed oral argument until 1871. J. S. Black to Mr. Chief Justice, Apr. 9, 1870, Supreme Court Case File No. 5558; Wm. M. Evarts to W. A. Meriweather, Jan. 19, 1869, M701, Reel 1, Instruction Book A1, p. 159; Hoar to Bristow, Apr. 26, 1869, ibid., pp. 214–215; Field to Bristow, May 5 and 20, 1869, ibid., pp. 224 and 242–243, respectively; Hoar to Wharton, Mar. 28, 1870, ibid., p. 468; Pleasants to Wharton, Nov. 1, 1870, ibid., p. 636; Hoar to Caldwell, Apr. 2 and 11, 1870, M699, Reel 13, Vol. H, pp. 260 and 274; Caldwell to Black, Nov. 17, 21, and 22, 1870 (Vol. 52, reel 26), Black Papers. President Johnson's attorney general, ad interim, O. H. Browning, also wanted to take a test case to the United States Supreme Court with the hope of a different outcome, presumably, than the Grant administration. The case he recommended as a test case also involved a conviction in the United States District Court for Kentucky of a white person for the murder of a black person. The Johnson administration, burdened with the impeachment of the president, never brought a test case to the Supreme Court. *United States v. Bell, The New York Times,* Mar. 9, 1868, p. 8; Cincinnati *Gazette,* June 29, 1867, p. 4; newspaper clipping, n.t., n.d., McPherson, ed., *Scrapbook on the Civil Rights Bill,* p. 154; O. H. Browning to the President, Mar. 28, 1868, M699, Reel 12, Vol. G., pp. 121–122.

7. *Briefs for Appellants, Blyew,* 80 U.S. (13 Wall.) 581. Black's brief is also reprinted in Chauncey F. Black, ed., *Essays and Speeches of Jeremiah S. Black* (New York, 1885): 539–557.

8. *Ortega,* 24 U.S. (11 Wheat.) 467; *Rhodes,* 27 F. Cas. 785 at 786–787.

9. *Briefs for Appellants at 36, Blyew,* 80 U.S. (13 Wall.) 581.

10. *Briefs for Appellee* at 19, 22–24, 30, *Blyew,* 80 U.S. (13 Wall.) 581. Bristow ignored the point raised by the *Ortega* case upon which the Supreme Court was to base its decision. Yet, he felt that he had triumphed over his opponents when the arguments had concluded. His success in the district and circuit courts probably account for his overconfidence. Bristow to Ma, Feb. 24, 1871, Mrs. James M. Gill and Mary Gill Collection of Bristow Papers, Margaret I. King Library, University of Kentucky.

11. *Briefs for Appellee* at 33–36, 39, *Blyew,* 80 U.S. (13 Wall.) 581.

12. See Chapters 1 and 6 for the lower federal court cases referred to here.

13. *Avery,* 80 U.S. (13 Wall.) 251. My discussion of this case is at pp. 98–99, 104–106.

14. *Blyew,* 80 U.S. (13 Wall.) 581.

15. *Id.* at 591, 592.

16. Wharton to Judge H. H. Emmons, Apr. 9, 1872 (box 1, folder 6), Emmons Papers. Professor Webb has concluded that the repeal of the discriminatory Kentucky statute on testimony in the state courts accounted for the Supreme Court's adverse ruling. The evidence does not support such a conclusion, nor does such a conclusion follow from the nature of the Court's opinion. The Court's interpretation of the Civil Rights Act appears to have stemmed from a conscious desire to curtail federal jurisdiction in criminal prosecutions of white defendants who had been charged with having committed crimes against black victims. Chief Justice Chase certainly believed that such cases were within the exclusive domain of the states. On the other hand, the pressure of federal prosecutions, particularly of local judges who refused to abide by the Civil Rights Act, appears to have largely accounted for the action taken by the Kentucky legislature to equalize the state's laws. Judge Stanton to Black, Nov. 23, 1870 (Vol. 52, reel 26), Black Papers; Louisville

Courier-Journal, Dec. 19, 1868, p. 1; Ross A. Webb, "Kentucky: 'Pariah Among the Elect,'" Richard O. Curry, ed., *Radicalism, Racism, and Party Realignment: The Border States During Reconstruction* (Baltimore, 1969): 128; Howard, "Black Testimony Controversy," p. 164; Victor B. Howard, "The Breckinridge Family and the Negro Testimony Controversy in Kentucky, 1866–1872," *The Filson Club History Quarterly* 49 (Jan. 1975): 56; Mary S. Donovan, "Kentucky Law Regarding the Negro, 1865–1877" (unpublished M.A. thesis, University of Louisville, 1967).

17. *Blyew,* 80 U.S. (13 Wall.) at 597–599.

18. Judge Ballard to Bristow, Apr. 3, 1872; Wharton to Bristow, Apr. 19, 1872 (container 2), Bristow Papers, L.C. *The New York Times* reacted similarly. *The New York Times,* Apr. 2, 1872, pp. 1, 4. However, the Louisville *Courier-Journal* hardly noticed the decision. Louisville *Courier-Journal,* Apr. 2, 1872, p. 1.

19. Harlan to Bristow, Apr. 15, 1872 (container 2), Bristow Papers, L.C.

20. The circuit court decision is in 15 Fed. Cases 649 (No. 8,408) C.C. La. (1870) and the Supreme Court's ruling is in 16 Wall. 36 (1873).

21. The general background of the *Slaughter-House Cases* is discussed in Mitchell Franklin, "The Foundation and Meaning of the Slaughterhouse Cases," *Tulane Law Review* 18 (Oct. and Nov. 1943): 1–88 and 218–262, especially at pp. 3–14. Also see Charles Fairman, *Reconstruction and Reunion, 1864–88,* Vol. 6, Part One of the Oliver Wendell Holmes Devise, Paul A. Freund, ed., *History of the Supreme Court of the United States* (New York, 1971): 1320–1363.

22. Franklin, "The Foundation and Meaning of the Slaughterhouse Cases," p. 23; Fairman, *Reconstruction and Reunion,* p. 1322; Harold M. Hyman, *A More Perfect Union: The Impact of the Civil War and Reconstruction on the Constitution* (New York, 1973), ch. 19; James C. Mohr, *The Radical Republicans and Reform in New York During Reconstruction* (Ithaca, 1973).

23. Fairman, *Reconstruction and Reunion,* pp. 1324–1327.

24. New Orleans *Daily Picayune,* June 4, p. 1; June 5, pp. 1, 7, 8, 9; June 7, 1870, p. 4; Fairman, *Reconstruction and Reunion,* pp. 1327–1330.

25. Oral arguments were reported in the New Orleans *Daily Picayune,* June 9, 1870, p. 2; concerning the public's interest in the case, see ibid., June 10, 1870, p. 2, and Mrs. F. J. Pratt to Judge Black, June 26, 1870 (Vol. 52, reel 26), Black papers. To avoid duplication I will not analyze Justice Bradley's views concerning national civil rights enforcement authority here. For my analysis of his views, see pp. 14–16 and 130–131 and accompanying notes.

26. The *Picayune's* editorials are in its editions for June 7, p. 4, June 8, p. 4, and June 12, 1870, p. 6; the *Times'* editorial is quoted in Fairman, *Reconstruction and Reunion,* pp. 1335–1336; and the *Bee's* editorial is reprinted in *Albany Law Journal* 1 (July 9, 1870): 11.

27. New Orleans *Daily Picayune,* June 15, 1870, p. 5; F. J. Pratt to Jeremiah S. Black, Nov. 20, 1871 (Vol. 53, reel 27), Black Papers; Fairman, *Reconstruction and Reunion,* pp. 1336–1337. The Louisiana Supreme Court again upheld the constitutionality of the corporation and injunctions against the butchers in November 1870, and the United States Supreme Court rejected a motion by the butchers to stay all actions to effectuate the monopoly. *Louisiana ex rel. Beldon v. Fagan,* 22 La. Ann. 545 (1870); *Slaughter-House Cases,* 77 U.S. (10 Wall.) 273 (1870).

28. The Radical Republican was Thomas J. Durant. Campbell viewed the case as a moral crusade against a tyrannous monopoly that was depriving the butchers of the precious right to their labor and causing them severe financial loss. He had no doubt that the federal court possessed the authority to grant relief. See J. A. Campbell to P. P. Phillips,

Apr. 12, Nov. 8, Dec. 2, 1870, and Mar. 22, 1871, Phillips-Myers Papers, Southern Historical Collection, University of North Carolina Library. For a biography of Campbell, see Henry G. Connor, *John Archibald Campbell* (Boston, 1920). Astute observers sometimes saw implications for national policy in court decisions that seemed to be unrelated. For example, the editor of the Charleston *Daily Courier* interpreted the Supreme Court's ruling declaring unconstitutional a federal tax upon the salaries of state officials as a judicial rejection of the president's and Congress's centralizing policies reflected in the Enforcement Acts of 1870 and 1871. The editor perceptively saw the implications for a civil rights policy predicated upon a broad, nationalist interpretation of national authority in Justice Samuel Nelson's opinion that posited the more narrow states' rights-oriented concept of federal powers as exclusive and as limited to constitutionally delegated authority. See Charleston *Daily Courier*, May 6, p. 2; May 8, 1871, p. 2; *Collector v. Day*, 78 U.S. (11 Wall.) 113 (1871).

29. *Briefs for Appellants* especially at 26 and 36, *Slaughter-House Cases*, 83 U.S. (16 Wall.) 36; *Supplemental Brief for Appellant, id.* especially at 26, 43. Justice Miller made references to the intent of the framers, but he did not cite the record of their debates. Professor Fairman incorrectly states that the dissenters in the *Slaughter-House Cases* failed to invoke the congressional debates leading to the adoption of the Fourteenth Amendment and sees great significance in this failure. *Reconstruction and Reunion*, p. 1372. Actually his judgment is against him. The dissenters did cite the debates in support of their broad interpretation of the amendment. Loren P. Beth similarly erred when he asserted that "all the opinions in the case evidence a deliberate refusal to go into the legislative history . . ." "The Slaughter-House Cases—Revisited," *Louisiana Law Review* 23 (Apr. 1963): 490. The error was replicated by Professor Hyman in *A More Perfect Union*, p. 535. The Source of Professors Fairman's, Beth's and Hyman's errors may have been none other than Carl Swisher, who reached the same conclusion in his *American Constitutional Development* (Boston, 1943): 338. The earliest source of this error is M. F. Taylor, "The Slaughterhouse Cases," *Southern Law Review* 3 (July 1874): 563.

30. *Briefs for Appellant* at 20, *Slaughter-House Cases*; *Supplemental Brief for Appellant, id.* at 3, 4, 8; *Briefs for Respondent, id.* at 8, 14, 15.

31. *Briefs for Respondent, id.* passim.

32. *Brief for Appellant, Bradwell v. State*, 83 U.S. (16 Wall.) 130 (1873); *Cong. Globe*, 42nd Cong., 2d sess., pp. 762, 826; *Cong. Globe*, 43rd Cong., 2d sess., pp. 1861–1864; Myra Bradwell's struggle to gain admission to the Illinois Bar is discussed in Robert M. Spector, "Woman Against the Law: Myra Bradwell's Struggle for Admission to the Illinois Bar," *Illinois State Historical Society Journal* 68 (July 1975): 229–242. For Senator Carpenter's role during the period, see Frank A. Flower, *The Life of Matthew Hale Carpenter* (Madison, Wis., 3rd. ed., 1884); E. Bruce Thompson, *Matthew Hale Carpenter: Webster of the West* (Madison, Wis., 1954).

33. *Briefs for Respondents* at 8, *Slaughter-House Cases*; Pratt to Black, Jan. 20, 1871 (Vol. 53, reel 27), Black Papers. Black withdrew from oral arguments in another case in favor of Senator Carpenter because he was overworked. It is interesting that Senator Carpenter was retained to argue the case not only because of his abilities, but also because "one of the attorneys should be a Western man on the other side of politics & one who would exert judicially, politically & sociably an influence over the Western Judges." Black believed "that Politics have influence on the —— judicial mind about these days." F. W. Pierce to Black, Feb. 2, 1871 (Vol. 53, reel 27), Black Papers. The same strategy and attitudes probably explain Senator Carpenter's replacement of Black as corporation counsel.

34. Pratt to Black, Jan. 20, 1871 (Vol. 53, reel 27), Black Papers.

35. *Slaughter-House Cases,* 83 U.S. (16 Wall.) at 61–62.

36. *Id.* at 405.

37. *Id.* at 406. The Supreme Court upheld the Civil Rights Act of 1866 in *Blyew,* 80 U.S. (13 Wall.) 581.

38. *Slaughter-House Cases,* 83 U.S. (16 Wall.) at 69.

39. *Id.* at 73–74. For the problematical nature of citizenship, see the authorities cited in n. 42 below.

40. *Slaughter-House Cases,* 83 U.S. (16 Wall.) at 74–78.

41. *Id.* at 77. Judge R. Ould criticized Miller's interpretation of the Fourteenth Amendment as "not its primary and most obvious signification." Judge R. Ould, "The Fourteenth Amendment. The Slaughterhouse Cases," *Southern Law Review* N.S. 4 (Oct. 1878): 663.

42. *Slaughter-House Cases,* 83 U.S. (16 Wall.) at 75–78. Judge Ould was critical of the majority for not having consulted the record of congressional debates for the framers' intent. He insisted that such a study would "satisfy any impartial mind, to the point of mathematical demonstration, that the framers of this amendment intended to accomplish that which the minority of the court held that the language meant." Ould, "The Fourteenth Amendment," pp. 663–664. Concerning the antebellum history of citizenship, see the more accurate assessment of Justice Field, *Slaughter-House Cases,* 83 U.S. (16 Wall.) at 94–96 and James H. Kettner, *The Development of American Citizenship, 1608–1870* (Chapel Hill, 1978). Also contrast Justice Miller's discussion of the rights of citizenship with the expressed views of lower federal court and state court judges in Chapters 1 and 6. For lower court resistance to Supreme Court civil and voting rights mandates during the Warren era, see Jack W. Peltason, *58 Lonely Men* (New York, 1961); Charles V. Hamilton, *The Bench and the Ballot: Southern Federal Judges and Black Voters* (New York, 1973).

43. *Slaughter-House Cases,* 83 U.S. (16 Wall.) at 78.

44. *Id.*

45. *Id.* at 81. Note that the equal protection clause was not the main source of the authority of the federal government to enforce civil rights in the opinion of the judges who interpreted it before *Slaughter-House* or of the legal officers who implemented it. Rather, they believed that the Constitution and laws of the United States directly secured the rights of citizens by virtue of the Thirteenth and Fourteenth Amendments. Even so, the concept of equal protection of the laws was generally thought to include state inaction as well as state action, the actions of private individuals as well as those of public officials. So, when the equal protection clause of the Fourteenth Amendment was invoked as a guarantee of the civil rights of citizens, it was applied to state inaction and the actions of private individuals.

46. *Id.* at 90, 93–98, 105. Justice Field also declared that the right to labor was "one of the most sacred and imprescriptible rights of man," and was secured to citizens as part of their inheritance from English common law.

47. *Id.* at 87–88, 105–111.

48. These conclusions are consistent with those of Charles W. McCurdy, although he emphasizes other aspects of Justice Field's opinion. See Charles W. McCurdy, "Justice Field and the Jurisprudence of Government-Business Relations: Some Parameters of Laissez-Faire Constitutionalism, 1863–1897," *Journal of American History* 61 (Mar. 1975): 970–1005. The problem, then, was not whether governmental power was exercised but the uses to which it was applied. See Yehoshua Arieli, *Individualism and Nationalism in American Ideology* (Cambridge, 1964); Joseph Blau, *Social Theories of Jacksonian Democracy* (New York, 1947); Louis Hartz, *The Liberal Tradition in America: An Interpretation of American*

Political Thought Since the Revolution (New York, 1955); James Willard Hurst, *Law and the Conditions of Freedom in the Nineteenth Century United States* (Madison, Wis., 1956).

49. *Slaughter-House Cases,* 83 U.S. (16 Wall.) at 123.

50. *Id.* at 116.

51. *Id.* at 117–119.

52. *Id.* at 123–124. See Justice Bradley's opinions in *Id.* at *Cruikshank,* 25 F. Cas. 707 and *Texas v. Gaines,* 23 F. Cas. 869 (No. 13,847) C. C. W. D. Tex. (1874), and the views he expressed in Joseph P. Bradley to Frederick T. Frelinghuysen, July 19, 1874, Joseph P. Bradley Papers, New Jersey State Historical Society.

53. *Slaughter-House Cases,* 83 U.S. (16 wall.) at 127–129. Justice Swayne's early views on federal civil rights enforcement authority are in *Rhodes,* 27 F. Cas. 785 (No. 16,151) C. C. Ky. (1867). See pp. 8–9, 10–12, 191 n. 19 for the circumstances of the opinion.

54. *Cong. Record,* 43rd Cong., 1st sess., pp. 4116, 4147–4151, 412–414; *Cong. Record,* 43rd Cong., 2d sess., p. 979, respectively; James G. Blaine, *Twenty Years in Congress: From Lincoln to Garfield,* Vol. 2 (Norwich, Conn., 1887): 419.

55. *American Law Review* 7 (July 1873): 732. The "Casey" to whom the editor referred was James F. Casey, President Grant's brother-in-law and collector of the Port of New Orleans who was associated with the Kellogg Packard wing of the Republican Party in Louisiana. The ruling seemed to have no impact upon local politics.

56. Justice Sam F. Miller to Justice David Davis, Sept. 7, 1873 (file 110), David Davis Papers, The Chicago Historical Society. For the appointment of Chief Justice Chase's successor, see *The Albany Law Journal* 8 (Aug. 30, 1873): 134; (Sept. 27, 1873): 198; (Oct. 11, 1873): 244; (Nov. 20, 1873): 339; (Dec. 6, 1873): 358; (Dec. 20, 1873): 388; (Dec. 27, 1873): 408; 9 (Jan. 10, 1874): 21; (Jan. 17, 1874): 36; *American Law Review* 7 (July 1873): 749; 8 (Oct. 1873): 159; (Jan. 1874): 354–355; Charles Warren, *The Supreme Court in United States History,* Vol. 2 (Boston, 1937): 551–561; Charles Fairman, *Mr. Justice Miller and the Supreme Court, 1862–1890* (Cambridge, 1939): ch. 2; C. Peter Magrath, *Morrison R. Waite: The Triumph of Character* (New York, 1963): 5–8.

57. Quoted in Warren, *The Supreme Court,* Vol. 2, pp. 544–545.

58. Taylor, "The Slaughterhouse Cases," p. 477. For newspaper reaction, see the Boston *Daily Advertiser,* Apr. 15, p. 1; Apr. 16, p. 1; Apr. 17, 1873, p. 2; New Orleans *Daily Picayune,* Apr. 15, 1873, p. 1; The Cincinnati *Commercial,* Apr. 15, 1873, p. 1; Chicago *Tribune,* Apr. 15, 1873, p. 1; New York *Tribune,* Apr. 15, 1873, pp. 2, 4; The Missouri *Republican,* Apr. 15, p. 1; Apr. 18, 1873, p. 2; Baltimore *Sun,* Apr. 18, 1873, p. 2; Warren, *The Supreme Court,* Vol. 2, pp. 541–546.

59. Chicago *Tribune,* Apr. 19, 1873, p. 4; *Munn v. Illinois,* 94 U.S. (4 Otto) 113 (1877).

60. Chicago *Tribune,* Apr. 19, 1873, p. 4.

61. Chicago *Tribune,* Jan. 12, p. 2; Jan. 17, p. 2; Feb. 5, p. 2; Apr. 30, p. 2; May 1, p 2; May 19, p. 2; May 31, p. 2; June 6, 1866, p. 2; Apr. 19, 1873, p. 4.

62. *The Nation* 1 (Dec. 7, 1865): 711; 2 (Mar. 1, 1866): 262–263; (Apr. 5, 1866): 122–123 (June 12, 1866): 744. The New York *Tribune* in 1866 similarly interpreted the Civil Rights Act of 1866 as securing "the common rights of human beings" to all persons and prohibiting the state and local authorities from oppressing or degrading the freedmen who were now entitled to citizenship by virtue of the act. Yet, in 1873, it applauded the *Slaughterhouse* decision because it "set up a barrier against new attempts to take to the National Government the adjustment of questions legitimately belonging to State tribunals and legislatures." New York *Tribune,* Jan. 31, p. 2; Feb. 3, 1866, p. 2; Apr. 16, 1873, p. 4.

63. *The Nation* 11 (Dec. 1, 1870): 361–362; Hampton M. Jarrell, *Wade Hampton and the Negro* (Columbia, S.C., 1949): 36–37.

64. *The Nation* 16 (Apr. 24, 1873): 280–281. See n. 1 above for Akerman's comments.

65. *Cong. Globe,* 42nd Cong., 1st sess., *Appendix,* pp. 113–117, 149–155. Congressman Bingham's rebuttal is in ibid., pp. 81–86.

66. The fallaciousness of Congressman Garfield's characterization of events leading to the change in Congressman Bingham's proposed constitutional amendment is demonstrated in *Cong. Globe,* 39th Cong., 1st sess., pp. 1088–1095, 2980.

67. Burke A. Hinsdale, ed., *The Works of James Abram Garfield,* Vol. 1 (Boston, 1882): 110–111.

68. *Cong. Globe,* 39th Cong., 1st sess., pp. 2462, 2539–2540; Robert G. Caldwell, *James A. Garfield: Party Chieftain* (Hamden, Conn., 1965): 163–165; James A. Garfield, "National Politics, Speech of Sept. 1, 1866" (Warren, Ohio, 1866); James A. Garfield to Burke Aaron Hinsdale, Mary L. Hinsdale, ed., *Garfield-Hinsdale Letters: Correspondence Between James Abram Garfield and Burke Aaron Hinsdale* (Ann Arbor, 1949): 78–79. Democratic congressman Michael Kerr of Indiana also contradicted himself in the House of Representatives in 1866 and 1871. *Cong. Globe,* 39th Cong., 1st sess., pp. 1268–1271 and *Cong. Globe,* 42nd Cong., 1st sess., *Appendix* , pp. 46–48.

69. *Cong. Globe,* 42nd Cong., 1st sess., pp. 575–576. Senator Trumbull's assertions are directly contradicted by statements he made in 1866. See *Cong. Globe,* 39th Cong., 1st sess., pp. 474–476; 497–500; 523–530; 573–574; 599–600; 1756–1759; 1775–1781.

70. See pp. 5, 8–12, 27–28, 41–42.

71. *Charge to Grand Jury,* Louisville *Courier-Journal,* Feb. 23, 1872, p. 3. United States Attorney G. C. Wharton observed that assault and murder were the usual way of resolving disputes in Kentucky, and, with the vast amount of violent crime, the federal courts would have to be tripled to provide protection to persons and property. G. C. Wharton to Geo. H. Williams, Mar. 27, 1872, S. C. F., Ky. Judge Ballard was at a loss to discover how the federal courts could assume jurisdiction over what he considered crimes against state law even when federal revenue officers were charged in the state courts for the crime of murder committed while performing their official duties. Judge Ballard to Judge Halmer H. Emmons, July 8, 1870 (box 2, folder 8), Halmer H. Emmons Papers, Burton Historical Collection, Detroit Public Library. Little wonder that he had problems over complex jurisdictional issues when he had such difficulty over a relatively simple jurisdictional question such as this. For a discussion of federal judicial jurisdiction during Reconstruction, see William M. Wiecek, "The Great Writ and Reconstruction: The Habeas Corpus Act of 1867," *Journal of Southern History* 36 (Nov. 1970): 530–548. The specific question raised by Judge Ballard was eventually decided by the United States Supreme Court in *Tennessee v. Davis,* 100 U.S. 257 (1880). There is a great body of correspondence on this case between federal legal officers in Tennessee and the attorney general in the Source Chronological File for the Middle District of Tennessee for the years 1878–1880 and in M701, Reel 8, Instruction Book H, Reel 9, Instruction Book I and Reel 10, Instruction Book K. The correspondence is too numerous to cite individually here.

72. See pp. 89–91 for a discussion of changing administration policy in 1872–1873.

Chapter 8: The Judicial Curtailment of Civil Rights Enforcement, 1874–1875

1. D. D. Shelby, "The Thirteenth and Fourteenth Amendments," *Southern Law Journal* 3 (July 1874): 524–532; M. F. Taylor, "The Slaughterhouse Cases," ibid., pp. 476–483. Reactions of legal journals to the *Slaughter-House* decision were mixed. The *Albany Law Journal* ranked it among the most important decisions ever rendered by the Supreme Court. *Albany Law Journal* 7 (May 10, 1873): 289–291. However, the *Chicago Legal News* 5 (May 24, 1873): 44 was critical of it, while the *American Law Review* 7 (July 1873): 732 called Miller's opinion "judicial legislation."

2. See, for example, the comments of the following in the *Cong. Record,* 43rd Cong., 1st sess., Senators Frelinghuysen, pp. 3451–3454; Boutwell, p. 4116; Howe, pp. 4147–4149; Morton, *Appendix,* pp. 358–361; Congressmen Purman, pp. 422–423; Butler, pp. 455–456; in the *Cong. Record,* 42nd Cong., 2d sess., Congressmen Lynch, pp. 943–945; Hale, pp. 979–980. Of course, opponents of federal civil rights enforcement authority also cited the *Slaughter-House* ruling in support of their opposition. The ambiguity of the equal protection clause was noted in the *Albany Law Journal:* "And it is by no means clear what is meant by that clause of the fourteenth amendment which prohibits any State from denying to 'any person within its jurisdiction the equal protection of its laws,'" it reported in 10 (Dec. 5, 1874): 356.

3. For example, see the opinions referred to in n. 49 below.

4. The case is cited *Meaux v. McKinney* and is reported with Judge Ballard's charge to the jury in the Louisville *Commercial,* Oct. 19, 1873, p. 5 and p. 7. Benjamin H. Bristow to Geo. H. Williams, Oct. 19, 1873, S. C. F., Ky.; Williams to Bristow, Oct. 24, 1873, M699, Reel 15, Vol. K, p. 165. Judge Ballard's earlier pronouncement on the Enforcement Act of 1871 is discussed at p. 138, and a possible explanation for his action is given at Chapter 7, n. 71.

5. *Cruikshank,* 25 F. Cas. 707. The *Cruikshank* case in the Supreme Court is cited *United States v. Cruikshank,* 92 U.S. (2 Otto) 542 (1876). For background on the case, see Mannie W. Johnson, "The Colfax Riot of April, 1873," *Louisiana Historical Quarterly* 13 (July 1930): 391–427; Horace Lestage, "The White League in Louisiana and Its Participation in Reconstruction Riots," ibid., 18 (July 1935): 615–695; Joe G. Taylor, *Louisiana Reconstructed, 1863–1877* (Baton Rouge, 1974): 267–273.

6. James R. Beckwith to Williams, Apr. 17, 1873 (telegram and letter), S. C. F., La. Reports of federal investigators are found in Beckwith to Williams, Apr. 19, 1873, ibid.; S. P. Packard to Williams, May 8 and 10, June 3, 1873, ibid.; Packard and Beckwith to Williams, May 31, 1873, ibid. Also see New Orleans *Daily Picayune,* Apr. 15–22, 1873; Johnson, "The Colfax Riot," pp. 407, 409; Ella Lonn, *Reconstruction in Louisiana after 1868* (Glouchester, Mass., 1967, reprint of 1918 edition): 240–244.

7. Williams to Beckwith, Apr. 18, 1873, M701, Reel 3, Instruction Book C, p. 699.

8. Williams to Beckwith, June 16 and 18, 1873, M701, Reel 4, Instruction Book D, pp. 84–85, 88; Beckwith to Williams, June 17, 1873, S. C. F., La.

9. The proceedings are in *Cruikshank,* 92 U.S. (2 Otto) 542, Supreme Court Case File No. 7044, R.G. 267, N.A. The indictment is summarized in Justice Bradley's circuit court opinion.

10. Beckwith to Williams, Jan. 28, May 12 and 23, 1874, S. C. F., La.; Packard to Williams, Apr. 2, 1874, ibid.; New Orleans *Daily Picayune,* Feb. 22, p. 4; 24, p. 1; Apr. 19, p. 1; 26, p. 8; and 28, 1874, p. 8; Taylor, *Louisiana Reconstructed,* pp. 142, 244–245, 495, 502; Lonn, *Reconstruction in Louisiana,* pp. 193–199, 232, 384, and ch. 21.

11. *Cruikshank,* Supreme Court Case File No. 7044; Beckwith to Williams, Apr. 29, May 23, and June 19, 1874, S. C. F., La.; New Orleans *Daily Picayune,* Feb. 26, p. 1; 27, p. 8; Mar. 12, p. 3; 13, p.1; 14, p. 4; Apr. 26, 1874, p. 8.

12. *Cruikshank,* Supreme Court Case File No. 7044; Beckwith to Williams, Apr. 18 and June 25, 1874, S. C. F., La.; New Orleans *Daily Picayune,* May 22, p. 8 and 23, 1874, p. 8. United States Attorney Beckwith immediately telegrammed a request for a copy of the *Slaughter-House* decision, since, he said, it was believed in New Orleans to abolish the criminal jurisdiction of the federal courts under the Enforcement Acts. Though an answer was apparently sent to Beckwith, it was not recorded and could not be found by this author. The evidence of a response is a notation on the wrapper of Beckwith's letter stating that the letter was answered on Apr. 19, 1873. Beckwith to Williams, Apr. 18, 1873, S. C. F., La.

13. *Cruikshank,* Supreme Court Case File No. 7044; New Orleans *Daily Picayune,* June 5, p. 8; 6, p. 1; 7, p. 2; 9, p. 2; 11, 1874, p. 1. The *Picayune* reported the case virtually daily from about mid-May to mid-June 1874.

14. The quotation is from Beckwith to Williams, June 25, 1874, S. C. F., La.; Beckwith to Williams, Apr. 29, May 23, June 11 and 19, 1874, ibid.; Packard to Williams, June 10, 1874, ibid.; New Orleans *Daily Picayune,* Apr. 26, p. 8; May 19, pp. 1 and 4; 20, p. 1; June 11, p. 1; 14, p. 4; 28, 1874, p. 4.

15. Beckwith to Williams, June 25, 1874, S. C. F., La. The source of this belief may have been Senator Matthew Carpenter, who argued the corporation's case before the Supreme Court in the *Slaughter-House Cases.* Shortly after the Court's decision, Carpenter was in New Orleans where he stated that it placed the rights secured by the Enforcement Acts of 1870 and 1871 outside the jurisdiction of the federal courts. New Orleans *Daily Picayune,* Apr. 17, p. 1 and May 21, 1873, p. 1.

16. New Orleans *Daily Picayune,* June 28, 1874, pp. 2, 4.

17. *Cruikshank,* 23 F. Cas. at 710.

18. *Id.* at 710, 714.

19. *Id.* at 710.

20. *Id.* at 711, 712.

21. *Id.* at 712, 713.

22. *Id.* at 712.

23. *Id.* at 715.

24. *Id.* at 714–716.

25. Beckwith to Williams, July 9, 1874, S. C. F., La.; Minnis to Williams, July 3, 1874, ibid., N. and M. D. Ala. Beckwith repeated his accusation after he had had a few months to reflect. Beckwith to Williams, Oct. 15, 1874, ibid., La.

26. Beckwith to Williams, Oct. 5, 1874, ibid., La.; New Orleans *Daily Picayune,* June 28, p. 4; and 30, 1874, p. 4. Bradley's diary also places him in Washington to work on his *Cruikshank* opinion and another case. See Charles Fairman, *Reconstruction and Reunion, 1864–88,* Vol. 6, Part One of the Oliver Wendell Holmes Devise, Paul A. Freund, ed., *History of the Supreme Court of the United States* (New York, 1971): 1379, fn. 280.

27. For conditions in Texas, see Andrew J. Evans to Williams, Dec. 6 and 8, 1872, Jan. 12, 1873, S. C. F., W. D. Tex.; Judge T. H. Duval to Williams, Dec. 27, 1872, ibid.; Williams to Justice Joseph P. Bradley, Jan. 27, 1873, M699, Reel 14, Vol. 1, p. 573; Charles W. Ramsdell, *Reconstruction in Texas* (New York, 1910): 190–191, 217–223. However, Lawrence D. Rice asserts that blacks were not excluded from juries. Rice, *The Negro in Texas, 1874–1900* (Baton Rouge, 1971): 255–256.

28. *Gaines,* 39 Tex. 606; *Gaines,* 23 F. Cas. 869.

29. J. Pridgen to U. S. Grant, Feb. 5 and Apr. 3, 1875, S. C. F., E. D. Tex.; Evans to Williams, Dec. 8, 1872 and Apr. 19, 1873, ibid., W. D. Tex.; Williams to Evans, Apr. 9 and 16, 1873, M701, Reel 3, Instruction book C, pp. 689 and 696, respectively; Rice, *The Negro in Texas,* pp. 57–59, 107–108; W. C. Nunn, *Texas Under the Carpetbaggers* (Austin, Tex., 1962): 104–105, 110.

30. *Gaines,* 23 F. Cas. at 870–871. *Blyew,* 80 U.S. (13 Wall.) 581 (1872); this case is discussed at pp. 108–116.

31. These points are discussed at p. 113–114.

32. See pp. 8–11, 113–114.

33. *Cruikshank,* 25 F. Cas. at 712 and 714.

34. See *Slaughter-House Cases,* 83 U.S. (16 Wall.) at 75 and pp. 124–125.

35. *Cruikshank,* 25 F. Cas. at 711–712; see my discussion in Chapter 1.

36. *Gaines,* 23 F. Cas. at 870–871.

37. *Id.* See the correspondence in nn. 27 and 29 above. Republican justices of the Texas Supreme Court were similarly removed through criminal prosecutions. See M. Priest to U. S. Grant, Feb. 25, 1874, S. C. F., W. D. Tex.; Rice, *The Negro in Texas,* p. 102.

38. Minnis to Williams, Dec. 23, 1873, July 3, 1874, S. C. F., N., and M. D. Ala; J. D. H. Duncan to Williams, Nov. 11, 1873, ibid., S. C.; G. Wiley Wells to Williams, Nov. 7, 1873, Sept. 28, 1874, ibid., N. D. Miss.; J. H. Pierce to Williams, Nov. 1, 1873, ibid.; Virgil Lusk to Williams, Apr. 20, 1874, ibid., N.C. The need for federal prosecutions was a recurring theme in the correspondence of the Justice Department. The only way to put down terrorism, in the opinion of federal legal officers, was for the national government to punish terrorists, for the fear of such punishment stopped Ku Klux crime. Clemency was expected to result in a continuation and spread of crime.

39. See, for example, Nick S. McAfee to Williams, Aug. 31, 1874, S. C. F., N., and M. D. Ala.; R. M. Wallace to Williams, Sept. 17 and 18, 1874, ibid., S. C.; and a large body of correspondence from the Western District of Tennessee around the same dates. Even during the period of relative calm, violent outbreaks in Kentucky in the fall of 1873 forced Attorney General Williams to make an exception to his policy of nonenforcement of civil rights. Williams to J. G. Hester, Sept. 4, 1873, M699, Reel 15, Vol. K, p. 89; Williams to H. C. Whitley, Sept. 4, 1873, ibid., p. 88; Williams to W. Danenhower, Nov. 15, 1873, ibid., pp. 192–193.

40. The quotations are from Gov. Kellogg to Williams, Aug. 19 and 26, 1874, S. C. F., La.; Beckwith to Williams, Oct. 5, 1874, ibid.; these letters are illustrative of many others in the file. The resurgence of violence is discussed in Taylor, *Louisiana Reconstructed,* pp. 274–304. However, United States Attorney Beckwith thought that the *Cruikshank* ruling could be distinguished from cases involving violence stemming from the fall elections, since the decision did not involve an election case and reviewed only part of the Enforcement Act. Beckwith to Williams, Oct. 7, 1874, S. C. F., La. District Judge Robert A. Hill made the same point. Judge Robert A. Hill to W. W. Dedrick, Sept. 9, 1874, enclosed in Dedrick to Williams, Sept. 10, 1874, ibid., S. D. Miss.

41. Judge Richard Busteed to Williams, Aug. 5, 1874, S. C. F., N., and M. D. Ala. Behind Judge Busteed's threatened impeachment were charges that he failed to hold court in Alabama from 1871 to 1874, that he was absent from his district most of the time, and that he spent his time in his home in New York City; that he was corrupt, tyrannical, and arbitrary as a judge in addition to being sympathetic to the Democrats. Williams to Judge Busteed, Sept. 1, 1874, M703, Reel 1, Vol. I, p. 62; Williams to Judge Busteed, Oct. 13, 1874, M699, Reel 15, Vol. K, p. 503; Walter L. Fleming, *Civil War and Reconstruction in Alabama* (New York, 1949 reprint of 1905 edition): 744.

42. McAfee to Williams, Aug. 31, 1874, S. C. F., N., and M. D. Ala.; Mayer to Williams, Sept. 1, 1874, ibid., S. D. Ala. Although Williams did not think that the political murder Judge Busteed reported to him could be brought within federal jurisdiction, the Alabama United States attorney decided to prosecute anyway. Williams to Judge Busteed, Aug. 19, 1874, M699, Reel 15, Vol. K, p. 423; Robt. W. Healy to Williams, Jan. 14, 1875, S. C. F., S. D. Ala. Only Judge Robert A. Hill suggested that the administration's policy of clemency was having beneficial results and contributed to the favorable and loyal disposition of the people of Mississippi toward the national government. Judge Hill to Williams, July 30 and Sept. 18, 1874, and newspaper clipping, n.t., n.d., ibid., N. D. Miss. But, Judge Hill's assessment is contradicted in G. Wiley Wells to Williams, Sept. 28 and Dec. 15, 1874, ibid.; Williams to G. Wiley Wells, Dec. 19, 1874, M701, Reel 5, Instruction Book E, p. 201.

43. Williams to Healy, et al., Sept. 3, 1874, found in S. C. F., S. D. Ala.; also in M701, Reel 5, Instruction Book E, pp. 13–14; and Williams to Y. E. Thomas, Sept. 30, 1874, ibid., p. 63, circular concerning the use of federal troops.

44. Williams to G. Wiley Wells, Dec. 19, 1874, M701, Reel 5, Instruction Book E, p. 201; G. Wiley Wells to Williams, Dec. 15, 1874, S. C. F., N. D. Miss.

45. The attorney general sent a circular to United States marshals announcing a sharp reduction in funds available for judicial expenses; see Williams to Peter Melandy, Nov. 30, 1874, M701, Reel 5, Instruction Book E, p. 168. He also sent letters directly to various federal legal and judicial officers admonishing them to cut expenses.

46. The quotation is from Beckwith to Williams, Dec. 11, 1874, S. C. F., La.; Beckwith to Williams, Jan. 9 and Oct. 27, 1874, ibid.; A. B. Lewis to Williams, Dec. 16, 1874, ibid.; Williams to Beckwith, Nov. 7, 1874, M701, Reel 5, Instruction Book E, p. 129.

47. Dedrick to Pierrepont, Sept. 8, 1875, S. C. F., S. D. Miss.; Judge Hill to Dedrick, Sept. 9, 1875, enclosed in Dedrick to Pierrepont, Sept. 10, 1875, ibid.; see n. 40 above.

48. Williams to Beckwith, Oct. 14, 1874, M701, Reel 4, Instruction Book D, p. 629; Williams to Murray, May 4, 1875, ibid., Reel 5, Instruction Book E, pp. 443–444.

49. *Cully v. Baltimore & O. R. Co.,* 6 Fed. Cases 946 at 948 (No. 3,466) D. N.Y. (1876); *Charge to Grand Jury—Civil Rights,* 30 Fed. Cases 1005 at 1006–1007 (No. 18,260) C. C. W. D. Tenn. (1875); *Petersburg Judges,* 27 F. Cas. 506. Judge Giles as well as Judge Bond continued to enforce civil rights legislation in criminal cases after *Slaughter-House.* A. Sterling, Jr. to Attorney General, May 22, 1874, S. C. F., Md.

50. Henry F. Farrow to Attorney General, Mar. 8, 1874, S. C. F., Ga.; Dedrick to Pierrepont, June 21, 1875, ibid., S. D. Miss.; Judge Hill to Pierrepont, Nov. 23, 1875, ibid.; Jno. G. Boyle to Pierrepont, Nov. 6, 1875, ibid., E. D. Tex.; Pierrepont to N. S. McAfee, May 4 and Sept. 11, 1875, M701, Reel 5, Instruction Book E, p. 445, and Reel 6, Instruction Book F, p. 157, respectively; Pierrepont to Gov. Edward J. Davis, July 27 and Sept. 11, 1875, M699, Reel 15, Vol. K, pp. 784–785, and Reel 6, Vol. L, p. 18, respectively; Phillips to Ned Trigg, Oct. 7, 1875, ibid., Reel 16, Vol. L, pp. 37–38.

51. Pierrepont to Gov. Ames, Sept. 14, 1875, M699, Reel 16, Vol. L, pp. 205–206.

Chapter 9: The Reinstitution of Decentralized Constitutionalism: The Supreme Court and Civil Rights, 1876

1. Geo. H. Williams to Henry Stanbery, Oct. 10, Nov. 6, 11, and 13, 1874, M699, Reel 15, Vol. K, pp. 502, 532, 543, and 548, respectively; R. H. Mart to D. W. Middleton, Oct. 23, 1874, *Cruikshank, 92* U.S. (2 Otto) 542, Supreme Court Case File No. 7044, R.G. 267, N.A.

2. The case was cited in the United States Supreme Court as *United States v. Reese, 92* U.S. (2 Otto) 214 (1876), but at the United States circuit court level it was cited as *United States v. Foushee.* The case in the circuit court was not reported in Federal Cases. For background and a discussion of the case, see William Gillette, "Anatomy of a Failure: Federal Enforcement of the Right to Vote in the Border States during Reconstruction," Richard O. Curry, ed., *Radicalism, Racism, and Party Realignment: The Border States during Reconstruction* (Baltimore, 1969): 272–277, 286–287.

3. Louisville *Courier-Journal,* Feb. 13, 1873, pp. 1, 2. A copy of the indictment is in G. C. Wharton to Williams, Nov. 10, 1873, S. C. F., Ky.; and in *Reese, 92* U.S. (2 Otto) 214 (1876), Supreme Court Case File No. 6795. The official indictment names William Garner as the victim of the discrimination, but a copy of the indictment sent by Wharton to the attorney general identified a Guy M. Smith as the victim.

4. The demurrer is in *Reese,* Supreme Court Case File No. 6795, and in *Brief for Defendants in Error, Reese,* 92 U.S. (2 Otto) 214.

5. Louisville *Courier-Journal,* Feb. 12, p. 1; 13, pp. 1 and 2; 14, pp. 3 and 4; 15, p. 4; 17, pp. 2 and 4; 21, p. 1; Nov. 7, 1873, pp. 3 and 4; Louisville *Commercial,* Nov. 7, 1873, pp. 2 and 4.

6. Williams to Wharton, Feb. 19, 1873, M701, Reel 3, Instruction Book C, p. 627; Williams to John M. Harlan, Feb. 11 and Mar. 7, 1873, M699, Reel 14, Vol. I, pp. 591, 592, 618; Williams to Wm. C. Goodloe, Feb. 19, 1873, ibid., p. 598; A. J. Falls to Col. W. A. Bullit, Feb. 11, 1873, ibid., p. 592; *United States v. Given,* 25 Fed. Cases 1324 (No. 15,210) C. C. Del. (1873). The Louisville *Courier-Journal,* Feb. 13, pp. 1, 2; 17, 1873, p. 2, erroneously reported that the Justice Department retained James Harlan to assist in the Lexington prosecutions.

7. *Given,* 25 F. Cas. at 1325–1327. This opinion is discussed at p. 19. It should be noted that shortly after rendering this opinion in the circuit court, Justice Strong joined with the majority in the Supreme Court's *Slaughter-House* decision. Evidence that might explain Strong's contradictory behavior was not discovered. Perhaps the difference in forums can shed some light. He may have felt free to rule in favor of national enforcement of civil and political rights, and possibly his personal convictions, in the circuit court where the impact of his decision was relatively limited, but was constrained to give his judicial sanction to such far-reaching powers in the Supreme Court where the implications of his judgment and his constituency were much greater.

8. Wharton to Williams, Nov. 10, 1873, S. C. F., Ky.; Judge Bland Ballard to Judge Halmer H. Emmons, Oct. 9, 1873, Halmer H. Emmons Papers, Burton Historical Collection, Detroit Public Library; Louisville *Courier-Journal,* Nov. 7, 1873, pp. 3 and 4; Louisville *Commercial,* Nov. 7, 1873, pp. 2 and 4.

9. *Brief for the United States, Reese,* 92 U.S. (2 Otto) 214, passim. Attorney General Williams also argued that suffrage was one of the privileges and immunities protected by the Fourteenth Amendment. Two months later, the Supreme Court rejected that interpretation of the amendment in *Minor v. Happersett,* 88 U.S. (21 Wall.) 162 (1875).

10. *Brief for Defendants in Error, Reese, Additional Brief for Defendants in Error, id.*

11. P. Phillips to Jno. A. Campbell, Jan. 15, 1875, and Phillips to Marr, Jan. 15, 1875, Letterbooks (container 3), Philip Phillips Family Papers, L.C. Both Phillips and Campbell were on the other side of the question in the *Slaughter-House Cases.*

12. Indictments, demurrers, and record of proceedings are in *Cruikshank,* Supreme Court Case File No. 7044, and *Brief for the United States* at 1–4, *Cruikshank,* 92 U.S. 552. Background of the case is discussed in Chapter 8.

13. 16 *U. S. Statutes at Large* 140, Secs. 16–18. Section 18 states: "That the act to protect all persons in the United States in their civil rights, …passed April nine, eighteen hundred and sixty-six, is hereby re-enacted; and sections sixteen and seventeen hereof shall be enforced according to the provisions of said act."

14. R. H. Marr, *Brief for Defendants* at 7, *Cruikshank,* 92 U.S. 552; John Archibald Campbell, *id.* at 28; David S. Bryan, *id.* at 30.

15. Bryan, *id.* at 11.

16. 7 Pet. 243 (1833); David Dudley Field, *Brief for Defendants* at 9, 11, *Cruikshank,* 92 U.S. 552; Marr, *id.* at 11–13; James H. Kettner, *The Development of American Citizenship, 1608–1870* (Chapel Hill, 1978).

17. Field, *Brief for Defendants* at 7, 8, *Cruikshank,* 92 U.S. 552.

18. *Id.* at 1–2, 22, 27.

19. Campbell, *id.* at 26; Marr, *id.* at 30–31; Field, *id.* at 27–28.

20. The quotations are in Field, *id.* at 24, 18, 13; and Campbell, *id.* at 8, respectively. Field's quotation from *Collector v. Day* is at 78 U.S. (11 Wall.) 113, 126 (1871).

21. Bryan, *Brief for Defendants* at 17, *Cruikshank*, 92 U.S. 552; Field, *id.* at 10–11.

22. Field, *id.* at 15; Marr, *id.* at 31; Bryan, *id.* at 30.

23. *Reese*, 92 U.S. (2 Otto) at 217–219; *Minor*, 88 U.S. (21 Wall.) 162.

24. *Reese*, 92 U.S. (2 Otto) at 228–238.

25. *Id.* at 238–256. Justice Hunt's dissent demonstrates that jurists could have interpreted the Fifteenth Amendment broadly enough to find authorization for the Enforcement Act of 1870 while at the same time holding that the amendment did not secure political rights generally. Justice Hunt so interpreted the Fifteenth Amendment three years earlier in the United States Circuit Court. See *United States v. Anthony*, 24 F. Cas. 829 (No. 14,459) C. C. N. D. N.Y. (1873).

26. *Cruikshank*, 92 U.S. (2 Otto) at 550.

27. *Id.* at 551–553.

28. *Id.* at 549. This was an interesting application of natural rights assumptions to reach legal positivist conclusions.

29. *Id.* at 551–552.

30. *Id.* at 554–555, 559. Justice Clifford wrote a concurring opinion that elaborated upon the inadequacy of the wording used in the indictment. The chief justice had declared sections 3 and 4 of the 1870 statute unconstitutional in the companion *Reese* case.

31. *The New York Times*, Mar. 29, 1876, p. 4; New Orleans *Daily Picayune*, Mar. 28, 1876, p. 1; *Central Law Journal 3* (May 5, 1876): 284; *University of Pennsylvania Law Review 22* (Oct. 1874): 643–644. For other accounts of public reaction see Charles Warren, *The Supreme Court in United States History*, Vol. 2 (Boston, 1937): 606–608; C. Peter Magrath, *Morrison R. Waite: The Triumph of Character* (New York, 1963): 119–134.

32. Stanley I. Kutler, *Judicial Power and Reconstruction Politics* (Chicago, 1968): 126.

33. *Veazie Bank v. Fenno*, 75 U.S. (8 Wall.) 533 (1869).

34. *Day*, 78 U.S. (11 Wall.) 113; the quotation is 78 U.S. (11 Wall.) at 124–126; *McCulloch*, 17 U.S. (4 Wheat.) 316. However, the Court distinguished federally chartered corporations from instrumentalities of the national government and upheld taxes levied by the states against them. The Court thus applied *Osborn v. The Bank of the United States*, 22 U.S. (9 Wheat.) 738 (1824) and recognized the rights of the national and state governments to tax corporations chartered by each other as essential to the exercise of their respective taxing powers. See *National Bank v. Commonwealth*, 76 U.S. (9 Wall.) 353 (1870); *Railroad Company v. Peniston*, 85 U.S. (18 Wall.) 5 (1873); *Thompson v. Pacific Railroad*, 76 U.S. (9 Wall.) 579 (1870).

35. *Case of State Freight Tax*, 82 U.S. (15 Wall.) 232 (1873); the quotation is *id.* at. 279–280; *Cooley v. Board of Port Wardens*, 53 U.S. (12 How.) 299 (1852). Also see *Case of State Tax on Foreign-Held Bonds*, 82 U.S. (15 Wall.) 179 (1873); *Railroad Company v. Maryland*, 88 U.S. (21 Wall.) 456 (1875); *Welton v. Missouri*, 91 U.S. (1 Otto) 275 (1876). Thus, the exclusive power of Congress over interstate commerce was the basis on which the Court struck down Louisiana's prohibition against segregated steamships engaged in interstate travel. See *Hall v. DeCuir*, 95 U.S. (5 Otto) 485 (1878).

36. *State Tax on Railway Gross Receipts*, 82 U.S. (15 Wall.) 284 (1873); the quotation is at *id.* at 293.

37. *License Cases*, 46 U.S. (5 How.) 504 (1847); *Woodruff v. Parkham*, 75 U.S. (8 Wall.) 123 (1869); the quotations are at *id.* at 137. In *Lane County v. Oregon*, 74 U.S. (7 Wall.) 71 (1869), the Court manifested a similar rationale in upholding the state's exclusive right to determine the manner in which state taxes should be paid. Also see *Osborne v. Mobile*, 83 U.S. (16 Wall.) 479 (1873).

38. *Munn v. Illinois*, 94 U.S. (4 Otto) 113 (1877); the quotation is taken from *Welton v. Missouri*, 91 U.S. (1 Otto) at 380. Also see *United States v. Dewitt*, 76 U.S. (9 Wall.) 41 (1870).

39. *Henderson v. Mayor of New York*, 92 U.S. (2 Otto) 259 (1876); *Chy Lung v. Freeman*, 92 U.S. (2 Otto) 275 (1876); *Welton*, 91 U.S. (1 Otto) 275. Also see *Foster v. Master & Warden*, 94 U.S. (4 Otto) 240 (1877); *Railroad Company v. Husen*, 95 U.S. (5 Otto) 465 (1878).

40. William L. Royall, "The Fourteenth Amendment. The Slaughterhouse Cases," *Southern Law Review* 4, n.s. (Oct. 1878): 576, 579; Samuel T. Spear, "State Citizenship," *Chicago Legal News* 7 (June 5, 1875): 303; also see *The Albany Law Journal* 11 (May 22, 1875): 325; Judge R. Ould, "The Last Three Amendments to the Federal Constitution," *Virginia Law Journal* 2 (July 1878): 385–400; R. McPhail Smith, "The Rebellion," *Southern Law Review* 2 (Apr. 1873): 313–355; Warren, *The Supreme Court*, Vol. 2, pp. 539–550.

41. See Solon J. Buck, *The Granger Movement: A Study of Agricultural Organization and Its Political, Economic and Social Manifestation, 1870–1880* (Lincoln, Neb., 1963); Loren P. Beth, *The Development of the American Constitution, 1877–1914* (New York, 1971); Magrath, *Morrison R. Waite.*

42. See *Munn*, 94 U.S. (4 Otto) 113.

43. *Slaughter-House Cases*, 83 U.S. (16 Wall.) 36; *Allgeyer v. Louisiana*, 165 U.S. 578 (1897); *Lochner v. New York*, 198 U.S. 45 (1905).

44. John Higham, *Strangers in the Land: Patterns of American Nativism, 1860–1925* (New York, 1968); Louis Hartz, *The Liberal Tradition in America: An Interpretation of American Political Thought Since the Revolution* (New York, 1955).

45. *United States v. Carotene Products Co.*, 304 U.S. 144 (1938).

46. James G. Randall, *Constitutional Problems Under Lincoln* (New York, 1926): 57.

47. Justice Miller's comments were reported in *The Albany Law Journal* 5 (Jan. 13, 1872): 22–24. Also see ibid., 6 (Nov. 30, 1872): 365; *American Law Review* 9 (Jan. 1875): 349–350; "The Supreme Court," ibid. (July 1875): 668–683; "The United States Courts and the New Court Bill," ibid., 10 (Apr. 1876): 398–421; "The Reorganization of the Federal Courts," ibid., pp. 558–590; Charles Fairman, *Mr. Justice Miller and the Supreme Court, 1862–1890* (Cambridge, 1939): 61.

48. See, e.g., *Strauder v. West Virginia*, 100 U.S. (10 Otto) 303 (1880); *Virginia v. Rives*, 100 U.S. (10 Otto) 313 (1880); *Ex parte Virginia*, 100 U.S. (10 Otto) 339 (1880). Although the Court rejected the narrow state action theory that equated state action to racially discriminatory statutes, it functioned almost as though it had affirmed that theory.

Index